CANADA'S CULTURAL INDUSTRIES

The Canadian Institute for Economic Policy has been established to engage in public discussion of fiscal, industrial and other related public policies designed to strengthen Canada in a rapidly changing international environment.

The Institute fulfills this mandate by sponsoring and undertaking studies pertaining to the economy of Canada and disseminating such studies. Its intention is to contribute in an innovative way to the development of public policy in Canada.

Canadian Institute for Economic Policy
Suite 409, 350 Sparks St., Ottawa K1R 7S8

PAUL AUDLEY

CANADA'S CULTURAL INDUSTRIES

Broadcasting, Publishing, Records and Film

James Lorimer & Company, Publishers
in association with the
Canadian Institute for Economic Policy
Toronto 1983

Copyright © 1983 by Canadian Institute for Economic Policy

ISBN 0-88862-458-1 cloth
ISBN 0-88862-459-X paper

6 5 4 3 2 1   83 84 85 86 87 88

Canadian Cataloguing in Publication Data
Audley, Paul.
Canada's cultural industries
1. Mass media - Economics aspects - Canada.
I. Canadian Institute for Economic Policy. II. Title.

P96.E25A92   384′.041′0971   C82-095170-6

Additional copies of this book
may be purchased from:
James Lorimer & Company, Publishers
Egerton Ryerson Memorial Building
35 Britain Street
Toronto, Ontario M5A 1R7

Cover photo, Lorimer edition: Hans Geerling

Printed and bound in Canada

Contents

Tables and Diagrams

Foreword

Canada's cultural industries are a multi-billion dollar business. However, despite this level of economic activity, no overview of the sector has been available; books, periodicals, film and television production have all been treated separately.

To rectify this situation, the institute asked consultant Paul Audley to undertake such an overview that could serve policy-makers. This he has done admirably well, and the institute is pleased to publish his base-line study which will undoubtedly be found to be of value by those concerned with the current state of Canada's cultural industries.

However, as with all our studies, the views expressed here are those of the author and do not necessarily reflect those of the institute.

Roger Voyer
Executive Director
Canadian Institute for Economic Policy

Acknowledgements

In commissioning this study, the Canadian Institute for Economic Policy provided me with an opportunity to explore the links between cultural policy and the operation of the publishing, recording, film and broadcasting industries in Canada. I appreciate the support the institute has provided and the patience of the institute and its executive director, Roger Voyer, through a number of delays in the completion of this study.

Through the period of research and drafting of this study I received skilful research and editorial assistance from Eileen Edwards. Priscilla Rojas typed several drafts of a long manuscript with many statistical tables, not only with accuracy but with corrections of any slips I might have made. I have also enjoyed working with Ted Mumford at James Lorimer & Company and with Charles Casement, who edited the manuscript quickly, tactfully and carefully. Abe Rotstein and John Hobday provided essential encouragement and support during the preparation of the manuscript.

Individual chapters were reviewed by Barry Zwicker, Harald Bohne, Earl Rosen, Allan King, Kealy Wilkinson, Alan Yates, Ray de Boer and Bob Blackwood. Their comments on the information, analysis and policy proposals in the text were extremely helpful. In addition, I received valuable additional information and advice on research sources from Ian Maclaren, director of the Cultural Industries Branch of the federal Department of Communications, and from John Watts, Gilles Lalonde and Peter Mortimer in the same branch of the federal Communications Department. I would also like to thank John Parsons for reviewing the accuracy of the information in the chapter on periodical publishing and for his assessment of my analysis of federal government initiatives affecting the periodical publishing industry. Throughout the preparation of this study I received prompt and generous assistance from many individuals at Statistics Canada, both in Ottawa and Toronto. Many other organizations, including the Audit Bureau of Circulations, the Canadian Circulations Audit Board, Magazines Canada, Elliott Research, and the Canadian Radio-television and Telecommunications Commission also provided assistance.

Acknowledgement must be made of advice on tax policy received from the late Russell Disney, then with the Toronto office of Touche Ross. The investment tax credit proposal put forward in this study was developed initially in cooperation with Russell Disney, as a means of expanding Canadian book publishing activity.

While this study has benefited from the advice of many individuals, they are, of course, not responsible for any errors that remain. The analysis and the policy recommendations that follow, while drawing extensively on published research and advice from many individuals, reflect my own assessment of the nature of Canada's problems in the cultural industries and of the course we must follow if we are to achieve our objectives.

Finally, I would ignore the most important debt incurred in preparing this study if I did not acknowledge the patience and support of my wife, Nancy, and our children David and Jessica. Although our new son Matthew, born while the text was being drafted, is too young to have offered patience or support, his delightful presence has provided both inspiration and welcome diversion.

Introduction

While this study addresses a range of issues common to any analysis of industrial strategy, it is essentially an examination of a particular aspect of cultural policy. The underlying assumptions of the sector-by-sector analysis and the proposals put forward are those that were stated by the Canadian Institute for Economic Policy in its 1981 submission to the Federal Cultural Policy Review Committee:[1]

- that Canada has no alternative but to strengthen its domestic cultural industries;
- that public policy for achieving this purpose should and must reflect a primary concern with cultural objectives; and
- that comprehensive and innovative policies for achieving these goals are urgently needed.

The definition of the cultural industries used in this study incorporates industries involved in both the manufacturing of explicitly cultural products and the electronic diffusion of cultural programming. Cultural products or programs are identified as those which directly express attitudes, opinions, ideas, values and artistic creativity; provide entertainment; and offer information and analysis concerning the past and present. Included in this definition are both popular, mass appeal products and programs, as well as cultural products that normally reach a more limited audience, such as poetry books, literary magazines or classical records.

The range of industries addressed in this report reflects a conviction that culture is expressed not just in works of art or entertainment, but in all forms of expression that reflect attitudes, opinions, values and ideas, and in information and analysis concerning the present as well as the past. Just as an awareness of our collective past is an essential component of cultural identity, so too is an awareness of what is happening now. If historians contribute to our knowledge and understanding of ourselves, so too do print and electronic journalists and reporters, as well as the critics, analysts and commentators whose work is published or broadcast in the media.

The approach reflected in this report is, therefore, one that brings together within a single framework subject matter often divided into communications policy on the one hand, and cultural policy on the other. The incorporation of the electronic media and newspapers into a broad cultural framework also recognizes the many and increasing links among the media. Sound recordings and radio, for example, are now closely interrelated, with most radio programming based on the use of recorded music and with radio air play the major factor in record promotion. In the case of traditional "theatrical" feature films, their producers depend increasingly on revenue from television and, in addition, have now begun to earn revenue from the marketing of feature films as a manufactured product in the form of a videotape or videodisc. The use of books as a basis for film and television programs, and vice versa, as well as the connections between the sound recording industry and feature films and television, have also intensified, leading to quite substantial financial flows among companies in the various sectors. In the future Canada will also follow the lead of other countries by making available on videotex some of the material that now appears in printed form in magazines and newspapers.

In addition to the varied and important links that exist among the cultural industries — some of which were noted above — the common element which justifies dealing with these industries within a single framework is the fact that in all of them the process of individual or collective creation and expression leads to the manufacturing or electronic diffusion of the resulting product. Such activities are industrially organized and characteristically have the potential to reach large and expanding audiences, with the increasing size of the audience resulting in progressively lower unit costs or costs per consumer. A natural result of the characteristics of these industries is a tendency towards increasing flows of such products and programs among nations and a tendency for those flows to be primarily from large nations to small ones.

Recent technological innovations in the distribution systems for cultural products and programs, and the evolution of large multinational conglomerates, have intensified the pressure towards unbalanced international cultural trade. The intensified pressure has, however, also created an increased awareness of the threat this trend represents for all but the largest and most powerful nations. Within UNESCO, the resulting debate has focused on the concept of a New International Information Order. In this context, information includes all aspects of what has been referred to above as cultural expression. The essential goal of the new order is to establish a pattern of more balanced two-way exchange in place of the largely one-way flows that characterize the relationships among many nations. Any move to alter the present imbalance, however, is predicated on government action in some form. The focus of a very heated debate has set those in favour of intervention against those in favour of free flow.

As Anthony Smith has noted in a recent study, the free flow doctrine has become "the prop and mainstay of a series of interconnected industries which purvey information (and entertainment) within and beyond the borders of the countries concerned." However, as Smith observes, "the free flow of one . . . merely swamps the culture of others."[2]

In his discussion of the subject of cultural dependence, Smith noted that:

> The culturally and politically debilitating effects of media dependence are perhaps most eloquently illustrated by taking an example not from the non-aligned or developing countries, but from within the developed world itself.[3]

The example, of course, is Canada. Smith describes Canada's efforts "to free itself from the gush of American exports" as "ingenious, fitful and enterprising." However, he observes acutely the dilemma that arises from being awash in the American rhetoric of "free" markets and "free" flow of information, stating that "It is extremely difficult for a society to practise free flow of media and enjoy a national culture at the same time — unless it happens to be the United States of America."[4]

The paradox, of course, is that Canada has been a world leader in developing communications technology, in large measure as a result of government initiatives designed to overcome the problem of reaching a scattered population in an enormous country. And yet, as Anthony Smith states:

> Despite the technical head starts which Canada constantly provides for herself, she has found that most of the equipment has to be imported and most of the content of her media consists of American material. Many Canadians treat the phenomenon today as a kind of running national

crisis. No country in the world probably is more completely committed to the practice of free flow in its culture and no country is more completely its victim.[5]

Throughout the 1970s, there was increasing evidence that the federal ministers responsible for developing Canadian policies related to publishing, broadcasting and the film and recording industries recognized what needed to be done if any substantial changes were to be brought about. In an important speech given in 1976, the then secretary of state, Hugh Faulkner, made the following statement:

> In all these means of communciation, which should be available to Canadians not only to learn about the world, but also to talk to one another about where they have been and where they are going, we have allowed the market forces to prevail over other considerations and the market forces have brought us very near disaster.[6]

That same speech described in realistic terms the kinds of intervention that would be necessary to create a more reasonable balance between Canadian and foreign-produced cultural products, without drawing government into any significant expanded direct role in the media.

In a speech that focused on this same theme, Faulkner's successor as secretary of state, John Roberts, argued that at the root of the drive towards separation in Quebec was a resistance to assimilation which Quebecers believed had reached a threatening stage as a result of growing integration of the economic and communications markets in North America. He went on to state that "similarly in English-speaking Canada, the integration of Canada, through the development of communications in North America into the distribution system of United States cultural industries, equally threatens to overwhelm the expression of Canadian creativity."[7]

In 1981, reflecting the increasing attention this issue was receiving in the international arena, the associate under-secretary of state for external affairs, de Montigny Marchand, addressed what he referred to as "the huge risks [that] come from being totally dependent on the creativity and the production of others and the unprecedented implications which follow for cultural and economic sovereignty — a nation's integrity." He argued that "There is . . . a growing recognition that communications and information infrastructures tailored to a country's particular needs, and the software and cultural products to fuel them, are essential for development."[8]

A few individual policy initiatives have been taken over the past decade to try to provide increased opportunities for the development of Canadian alternatives to the massive cultural imports which flood into the Canadian market. Where distinctive Canadian alternatives have been developed and their production is adequately funded — whether in the case of magazines, books, records, films or television programs — they have consistently proved to be far more attractive to the Canadian public than competing imported products. *Maclean's* magazine, for example, with a far lower editorial budget than is invested in the United States in *Time* or *Newsweek*, outsells *Time* in Canada by two to one and *Newsweek* by six to one. Similarly, *Saturday Night* outsells the comparable U.S. publications, *Atlantic Monthly* and *Harper's*, by five to one and ten to one respectively. Canadian records for children are another example of domestic products that have been astonishingly successful. [However, there are still many important areas in which the production of distinctive high quality Canadian cultural products is very limited and where the range of choices available to the public includes little or nothing that is Canadian.]

There is widespread public support for government measures of assistance to Canadian cultural activities. A study of public attitudes carried out in 1979 for the federal Department of the Secretary of State found that 83 per cent of Canadians were in favour of government support for cultural activities.[9] With respect to the cultural industries specifically, 83.8 per cent thought support to broadcasting was important or very important, while in the case of book publishing, the movie industry, the recording industry and magazine publishing, 73.2, 64.2, 60.7 and 50.3 per cent thought government support was important or very important. The percentage that did not think it important was remarkably low: less than 20 per cent for broadcasting and book publishing, less than 30 per cent for the record and movie industries, and 38.3 per cent for magazine publishing.

On more specific policy issues, comparable results have been obtained. A 1980 Gallup Poll showed that 67.4 per cent of Canadians supported the policy of the Canadian Radio-television and Telecommunications Commission (CRTC) requiring that television broadcasters exhibit 50 per cent Canadian programming.[10] An earlier Gallup Poll of 1975 showed that 59 per cent of Canadians thought Canada's culture and way of life were influenced too much by American television, with 65 per cent of Canadians under thirty years of age agreeing that this was the case. Only 35 per cent of Canadians disagreed. The percentage that agreed that the influence of American television was excessive had risen from 49 per cent in 1970.[11]

Similarly, a September 1980 survey carried out by CROP Inc. showed that 60 per cent of Canadians felt that movie theatres in Canada should be required to show Canadian films at least 10 per cent of the time. Only 23 per cent disagreed. Support for such a requirement had risen 5 percentage points since November 1977, while disagreement had declined by 10 percentage points. The same survey showed that 65 per cent favoured a similar requirement for films shown on television, while only 20 per cent disagreed. A November 1980 survey by the same firm found that 63 per cent of Canadians agreed that some of the revenue from pay-television services in Canada should be used to subsidize the production of Canadian programs, while 27 per cent disagreed.

In summary, both the actual purchasing habits of Canadians and their responses to various surveys of opinion indicate strong support for Canadian cultural products. There is, in fact, a great deal of evidence that the public is well ahead of the government and would support stronger and more effective measures than have yet been taken.

This study provides for the first time a comprehensive examination of trends through the 1970s in each of the major cultural industries in Canada and an examination of the current situation. While it is outside the scope of this book to provide detailed policy proposals to the government of Canada, the study identifies major issues and problems, and suggests a number of major policy changes designed to strengthen cultural expression and the cultural industries in Canada.

As will be evident from the analysis that follows, the cultural industries merit careful attention from an economic as well as a cultural perspective. If the industries covered in this study are the major instruments of cultural expression in Canada, they are also the major vehicles for the advertising of goods and services to the public. Canadian newspapers, periodicals and radio and television account for three-quarters of all media advertising expenditure in Canada.

In the case of periodicals and television, however, Canada has had a long-standing and serious problem as a result of the extensive "spillover" of American magazines and television signals into Canada. The result has been not just to limit the revenues of Canadian magazines and television, but to provide ready access to Canadian consumers for advertisers of U.S. goods and services, while providing Canadian producers of goods and services with less efficient advertising vehicles than they require.

As a broad generalization, those Canadian media which depend on local advertising — mainly radio and newspapers — earn per capita advertising revenues close to those of their U.S. counterparts, while magazines and television, which depend primarily on national advertising, earn revenues at less than half the U.S. per capita rate. While cause and effect are not easy to disentangle, it is clear that the ability to develop Canadian industries with a strong domestic market base is affected very directly by the effectiveness with which Canadian goods and services can be advertised.

At both federal and provincial levels, a concern to encourage Canadians to purchase Canadian rather than imported products has been expressed in generic advertising campaigns urging Canadians to "buy Canadian." One of the assumptions made in this study is that it is even more important that Canadian companies have access to effective advertising vehicles to promote their goods within Canada. To the extent that advertiser-supported U.S. television services and U.S. magazines penetrate the Canadian market, they act as powerful vehicles for the advertising of U.S. goods and services.

In an interesting opinion survey carried out in 1977, Canadians were asked how they felt about commercials for Canadian and American products on television. Over three-quarters of the respondents preferred Canadian product advertising, while only 6.5 per cent did not. (The remainder expressed no opinion.)[12] The results suggest that the vast majority of Canadians are aware that border spillover advertising can and does cost Canadians jobs. In the same survey, three-quarters of Canadians also favoured Canadian rather than American-made commercials, provided the quality was acceptable. Only 6.6 per cent disagreed.

A second important economic issue is the direct economic effects of the relative strength or weakness of the cultural industries in Canada. In the area of direct employment, for example, the advertiser-supported cultural industries (excluding the book publishing, sound recording and film industries) provided 75,836 jobs in 1980, 30 per cent more than in 1970. In addition, in the broadcasting and cable television industries alone, extensive hardware expenditures are being made that can have an important impact on the growth of related supplier industries. There is also an extensive network of freelance workers, including writers, performers and technical workers, who provide the creative and specialized skills that are essential to the operation of these industries. While these direct economic benefits and potential benefits cannot be delineated as precisely or as comprehensively as would be desirable, information has been drawn together in this study from a variety of sources which provides clear evidence of the extensive scope of their importance. From the perspective of Canada's balance of payments, it should also be noted that in 1980 Canada had a deficit in commodity trade and royalty and licence payments in the cultural industries sector in excess of three-quarters of a billion dollars.

In large measure because of the substantial economic importance of the cultural industries, a sharp conflict has developed over the objectives that ought to be pursued through public policy initiatives. This study, as already indicated, is predicated on the view that cultural goals ought to be primary and that what is required is an approach to the cultural industries that effectively integrates a concern for the achieving of well-defined cultural goals with an understanding of the structure and operation of the industries themselves. Included within the scope of such cultural goals would be concerns with quality, diversity, local, regional and national cultural expression, an acceptable proportion of production in French as well as English, exchanges between the language groups and among the regions of Canada, and so on. Cultural industries development policies and plans ought to be shaped primarily to ensure that the end result will be a strengthening of those private- or public-sector production and distribution companies, structures and activities that are contributing to achieving Canada's cultural objectives. Communications Minister Francis Fox expressed support for this position in a 1981 speech to the Canadian Conference of the Arts, arguing that the development of these industries was essential if Canadian cultural expression was to be served, but that if the industry development that occurred was of a kind that did not serve cultural purposes, then it did not help him to fulfil his department's mandate. In summing up that view, he stated that "the emphasis of my interest is on the *culture*, not the industry."[13]

Others, however, have rejected this position vehemently, arguing essentially that while nations like Canada have been concerning themselves with "national" cultural expression, consumers want something they usually refer to as "world class products." Those who adopt this view usually argue that priority, or even exclusive attention, should be given to attempting to develop "economically viable" private-sector corporations which can compete in the global cultural marketplace rather than to providing opportunities for cultural expression to Canadians.

In an extreme form, this position has been stated by Robert Russell in a 1980 paper, "Corporate Opportunities in the Cultural Marketplace." Russell's interest is in the role of the multinational corporation in pushing culture beyond the confines of the state. His thesis is that a "global marketplace" is emerging, dominated by a few major multinational corporations, and that something he calls a "global class culture" is being established. Russell draws a distinction between national and global culture, the former embodied in or fostered by the state, the latter embodied in the multinational corporation. While Russell acknowledges that "culture breeds strong feelings among nationalists, traditionalists, and the cultivated," he believes that their opposition to the emerging global culture of the multinationals can and will be overcome.

Russell views his theoretical efforts as an attempt to provide a basis for "a business theory of culture." His vision of the future is suggested in the following passage:

> The role of expanding empires has fallen to the creature of the electric and electronic age, the trans-national corporation. The state, unable to create wealth, nor to further distribute it, is sinking in a sea of paper (from which it was only recently born). And a new "civilization" of corporations rises like an electronic storm, and unhampered by national barriers or state controls, moves about the globe with freedom and verve, gathering wealth, building new empires, new rules, a new way of life.[14]

One of the difficulties with the concept of the emerging global culture of the multinational corporations is that it has been presented both by Russell and its other advocates in unusually vague terms. As Desmond Smith has asked recently:

> What on earth is "world class" supposed to mean? Is the unreleased Canadian movie *Bear Island* "world class?" Would Margaret Atwood, whose works are found in bookstores from Venice, California to Venice, Italy qualify? Did the poet Dennis Lee think "world class" when he wrote *Alligator Pie?*[15]

Implicit in much of the analysis that some proponents of a "world class" strategy have put forward is the assumption that cultural products produced in Canada which express Canada's culture cannot be world class. The related assumption is that no one else in the world would be interested in any Canadian cultural products that were distinctive or recognizable as Canadian.

Because the nature of "world class" products is never made clear, it is by no means certain how either business or government should proceed if they decided to focus on developing a "world class" production capacity in Canada. However, where this strategy seems to be leading is simply towards acceptance of an increasingly marginal position for French-language production in Canada, while leaving English-language producers in a position in which they must attempt to respond primarily to the interests and demands of the American market. This approach appears also to have led its supporters to the conclusion that the future domination of the Canadian cultural marketplace by multinational companies is inevitable and that the largest Canadian communications companies ought to pursue aggressive programs of expansion outside Canada and especially in the United States. Insofar as such views come to be held by government planners and their consultants, they, of course, take on the nature of self-fulfilling prophecies.

This study is predicated on the view that the world is somewhat more complicated than the "world class versus Canadian" dichotomy suggests. As Desmond Smith's examples indicate, the simple fact that a film or a book can be identified as Canadian does not mean that it will not, therefore, satisfy the standards of people in other countries; nor does the fact that it is not identifiably Canadian mean that it is, therefore, going to be acceptable either in Canada or abroad. Once one gets past the rhetoric, it is by no means certain that there is always, or even most of the time, a conflict between realistic policies that give primacy to cultural objectives and policies that produce the greatest economic benefit. The option of producing cultural goods in Canada primarily for export markets is no more than a naive fantasy. Even the U.S. television production industry, for example, earns only 10 per cent of its total revenues from foreign markets.

The reason for drawing attention to this debate about the objectives of cultural industries policy is that the design of any specific public policy measures to strengthen these industries will be affected substantially by the objectives on which such proposals are based. Any assessment of the success or failure of existing policy measures will also reflect the standard by which one chooses to judge success or failure.

Before proceeding to analyze the print, sound and video sectors of the cultural industries, it must be noted that it was necessary to exclude from this study any comprehensive discussion of copyright, despite the fact that copyright law provides the fundamental basis for the operation of the cultural industries. While attention has been drawn to some specific copyright issues, a full-scale study at least as extensive as this one would be required to deal properly with the copyright issue. However, the following analysis rests on the assumption that, if the interests of Canadians as creators of copyright materials and of Canadian companies as producers of such materials are not accorded protection at least as effective as that provided in other countries, particularly those with which Canada has extensive trade relationships, then development strategies cannot be successful. A revision of the copyright law is now in progress and the resulting changes in the law will, for better or worse, have a decisive effect on cultural industries development.

Part I

Print

Print

As is evident from Table P-1, the print media demonstrated a remarkable consistency in their appeal to the public over the period 1929 to 1976. These figures, while based on U.S. data, would almost certainly be parallelled in Canada, although comparable domestic data are not readily available.

The same table indicates a striking consistency in the percentage of personal consumption expenditure allocated to the print and audio-visual industries combined. Over a forty-eight-year period, there was little change in the 3 per cent of consumer spending which went to these industries. What this pattern suggests, of course, is that new media can only become established by attracting revenue away from existing media. In addition, as the individual chapters that follow indicate, newspapers and magazines still were receiving 40 per cent more advertising revenue in 1980 than the electronic media (see Table P-2).

The fact that the print media continued to flourish in the face of the rise of the movie industry, radio and, more recently, television is credited by many observers to the fact that their function cannot be effectively duplicated by any other industry. The real test, of course, will be the effect of videotex on the print media, since videotex is simply a means of putting words and still pictures on a TV screen rather than a printed page.

Donald Campbell, chairman and chief executive of Maclean Hunter Ltd., remains convinced that "the shape of things to come for print and electronic communications will be basically similar to the patterns that prevail today."[1] Comparable views on the future strength of the print media have been expressed by Roy Megarry, publisher of the *Globe and Mail*. Other observers note that costs are rising in the print media and that some categories of advertising might, in the future, be well served by videotex. However, there seems at least to be an agreement

3

TABLE P-1
PERCENTAGE OF U.S. CONSUMER SPENDING ON PRINT AND AUDIOVISUAL MEDIA, SELECTED YEARS, 1929-76

Year	Media Expen. as % of Per. Consump. Exp.	Newspapers, Magazines, Sheet Music	Books & Maps	Total Print	Radio, TV Recv'rs, Records, Instruments	Radio & TV Repairs	Movie Admis.	Total AV Media[1]
1929	3.37%	20.65%	11.86%	32.51%	38.85%	1.00%	27.64%	67.49%
1933	2.76	33.20	12.04	45.24	15.45	1.11	38.19	54.75
1940	2.94	28.26	11.23	39.43	23.70	1.53	35.27	60.50
1945	2.82	28.66	15.44	44.10	10.22	2.61	43.07	55.90
1950	3.25	23.92	10.78	34.70	38.74	4.53	22.02	65.29
1955	2.94	25.10	11.64	36.74	38.53	6.97	17.81	63.31
1960	2.67	25.32	15.06	40.38	39.39	9.25	10.98	59.62
1965	3.00	22.23	15.98	38.21	46.61	8.00	7.19	61.80
1970	2.97	22.33	18.75	41.08	45.38	7.20	6.33	58.91
1974	3.04	26.01	11.20	37.21	48.99	4.58	9.21	62.78
1975	3.00	25.49	11.54	37.03	49.53	4.80	8.62	62.95
1976	2.94	25.12	11.15	36.27	49.88	4.58	9.27	63.73

Note: [1] Totals for print and audiovisual media may not add up to 100% due to rounding.

Source: U.S. Bureau of Economic Analysis.

4

TABLE P-2
NET ADVERTISING REVENUES BY MEDIA, 1966-81
($000's)

Year	Broadcast		Newspapers			Periodicals					Other Print	Outdoor	Total All Media
	Radio	TV	Dailies	Weekend Supplement	Weeklies, Semi-Tri	General Magazines	Business Papers	Farm Papers	Directories— Phone, City	Relig., School & Other	Catalogues, Direct Mail	Billboards, Car Cards, Signs, Etc.	
1966	80,048	100,392	234,915	17,457	34,457	21,872	29,650	5,714	37,155	3,650	172,340	73,975	811,559
1967	88,457	111,253	239,810	15,918	44,752	22,940	32,429	6,036	40,150	3,700	183,037	84,494	872,976
1968	95,018	114,872	260,072	17,227	49,903	23,765	28,067	5,893	43,330	3,454	186,961	86,000	914,562
1969	107,483	131,176	296,159	19,395	50,387	26,448	30,683	6,255	48,331	3,395	201,671	93,000	1,014,383
1970	113,667	139,295	301,392	19,842	52,076	26,168	30,809	5,845	53,341	3,850	217,299	96,500	1,060,084
1971	124,688	147,671	327,887	23,131	55,565	26,307	29,732	5,441	62,378	4,839	238,555	98,033	1,144,227
1972	144,703	166,025	374,465	25,938	63,848	31,431	31,899	7,216	71,390	5,714	270,999	109,271	1,302,905
1973	160,300	198,517	428,134	23,348	75,328	35,808	36,136	6,975	86,502	7,188	304,327	116,858	1,479,421
1974	182,854	225,190	496,965	23,656	84,100	47,823	44,353	7,750	99,812	7,214	368,439	132,509	1,720,665
1975	207,679	265,631	564,638	23,134	90,713	70,932	55,557	8,141	117,127	10,692	386,604	137,635	1,938,483
1976	241,800	322,598	661,422	25,790	109,267	67,938	71,003	9,280	135,947	10,009	435,702	153,000	2,243,756
1977	269,080	375,564	703,605	21,475	123,477	71,338	78,120	10,440	158,586	12,165	471,574	162,600	2,458,024
1978	305,475	441,755	762,571	21,000	146,925	105,168	82,269	10,703	176,670	12,679	543,501	182,100	2,790,815
1979	352,010	526,828	827,984	19,574	181,724	138,288	88,117	13,397	203,054	11,274	656,919	211,000	3,220,169
1980	391,985	610,334	892,000	17,100	210,000	152,000	97,800	15,000	236,000	11,500	744,679	236,000	3,614,398
1981	440,000	695,000	967,000	20,500	236,000	182,000	113,000	16,000	275,000	12,000	840,000	265,000	4,061,500

Source: Maclean Hunter Research Bureau, *A Report on Advertising Revenues in Canada, 1981* (figures for 1966-79 are Statistics Canada actuals; for 1980-81, Maclean Hunter Research Bureau estimates, except "Broadcast" data which are actuals for 1980).

that no major changes will occur until the 1990s at the earliest. Many respected industry analysts are convinced that major shifts will not occur, at least in the household as opposed to the business market, until it is possible for ''hard copy'' to be produced at a reasonable cost in the customer's house. For the present, and at least for the next decade as well, there appears to be little doubt that the print media will maintain their current important position. The following three chapters describe in greater detail the daily newspaper, magazine and book publishing industries in Canada.

Daily Newspaper Publishing 1

Introduction

Viewed from a purely economic perspective, the newspaper industry in Canada is a remarkable success story. In the Preface to the 1970 (Davey) *Report of the Special Senate Committee on Mass Media*, the committee noted that "Newspaper publishers, in particular, repeatedly told the Committee that they sought no special favours from the Government." On the basis of its own research, the committee commented, "Certainly none are required."[1] The economic strength of Canadian newspaper publishing contrasts sharply with the problems that exist in magazine and book publishing, as well as in the recording and film industries. If one could be satisfied with economic success alone, then there would be no justification for public concern about Canadian newspapers.

And yet, a purely economic perspective is not acceptable as a basis for assessing this and other cultural industries. The special nature of publishing and other communications industries was argued forcefully in the 1961 (O'Leary) *Report of the Royal Commission on Publications*. Responding to arguments that magazines should be looked at exclusively from an economic perspective, the *Report* stated that:

> The nature of modern communication is such that its effects carry enormous social and political, as well as economic implications. Like the two sides of a coin, the "cultural" and "economic" are virtually inseparable and neither can provide a complete perspective in itself.[2]

The newspaper is an extremely influential medium. The 1981 (Kent) Royal Commission on Newspapers noted that almost 90 per cent of Canadians read a daily newspaper in the course of an average week. Newspapers appeal to the public as voters, consumers and sports fans;

theatre, concert and movie goers; television watchers, book readers and radio listeners; as members of local, provincial, regional and national communities; as investors, homeowners, renters and so on.

For many commentators, the prime importance of the newspaper is its role in a free society as an instrument of democracy. While the press is not the only vehicle for the reporting of news and expression of opinion, it provides by far the greatest variety and depth of reporting and opinion on a day-to-day basis. As a result, the effective functioning of the press is a concern that affects the most central values and institutions in our culture. The Royal Commission on Newspapers reflects a broad awareness that the newspaper industry is now in a period of transition. Whatever precise actions one considers appropriate in response to the changes that are occurring, there is little disagreement on the need to ensure that the functions now carried out by the press, with respect to freedom of expression and the right of citizens to the information they require to act intelligently and responsibly, are protected.

Newspapers are also essential to the arts and to other cultural industries — book publishing, film and television, in particular — both as an advertising vehicle and a review medium. They also provide the most regular reporting and discussion of issues that are of concern to the arts and to the cultural industries. For example, the newspapers themselves have been almost the only source of extensive coverage and comment on the Kent Commission, a fact that in itself led to serious concerns about the objectivity of the information being provided to the public on the findings and recommendations of the commission. Newspapers play a special role in the development of a sense of community and, in an effectively functioning democratic society, perform the essential role of providing ongoing detailed information, analysis and opinion on public issues. The 1970 Special Senate Committee on Mass Media commissioned research on the effects of the shutdown of the Vancouver newspapers during a prolonged strike. More than half of the respondents said they felt deprived of news and information during the strike. Most of those who missed the papers during the shutdown cited the coverage of major front-page news stories and the editorial page as the sections of the papers they missed most. Over two-thirds of the respondents indicated they were not adequately served by radio and television as alternative sources for news and information. The *Report* of the committee concluded that "The experience in Vancouver and in other cities where lengthy strikes have occurred, suggests that no other medium can be an adequate substitute."[3]

More recently, the 1981 Royal Commission on Newspapers commissioned a national readership study which explored public attitudes towards newspapers. This study found that 60 per cent of Canadians believed that newspapers had specific responsibilities different from those of television or radio news.[4] The most frequently mentioned reason for this perception of the special responsibilities of newspapers was their function in providing more detailed, in-depth, comprehensive coverage. The second reason cited was their provision of more local and community news than radio or television.

A 1978 Statistics Canada survey of reading habits provides evidence of the relative importance that readers attach to the various sections of the newspaper. As Table 1-1 indicates, newspapers are read primarily for local, national and world news, although very substantial percentages of total readers also reported that they regularly looked at features, the arts and entertainment section, editorials, sports and other sections of the paper.

TABLE 1-1
PERCENTAGE OF THE POPULATION WHO READ VARIOUS SECTIONS OF THE NEWSPAPER

	Read Usually	Read Sometimes	Total
Local/regional news	62%	18%	80%
National news	49	23	72
World news	44	24	69
Feature stories	31	28	59
Art, entertainment	28	28	56
Classified ads	24	30	54
Other ads	16	33	49
Editorial page	24	24	48
Comics	26	21	47
Sports	28	19	47
Homemaking	22	18	40
Business, finance	13	18	31

Source: Table published in *Leisure Reading Habits* (Infoscan Inc., 1980) (based on 1978 "Survey of Selected Leisure Activities: Reading Habits" carried out by Statistics Canada as a supplement to the monthly Labour Force Survey).

The national readership study prepared for the Kent Commission also examined the level of public interest in various categories of newspaper content. Respondents were asked to indicate the kinds of news coverage in which they were very interested. While the highest number of respondents, 68 per cent, said they were very interested in local and regional news, almost as many, 66 per cent, replied that they were very interested in world and international news. The other news categories in which 50 per cent or more of the respondents said they were very interested were health and medicine, how to be a better consumer, and what's happening in Canadian politics.[5]

Because of this reliance by the public on newspapers, it is a matter of legitimate and serious public concern that they provide reliable and adequately comprehensive news and information and that they accurately reflect the range of opinion, ideas and attitudes that exist within Canada on issues that are of importance or concern to the public.

In writing about the general role of communications in Canada, the 1961 O'Leary *Report* noted that " . . . often our communications are more swift than sure . . . Facts are often dramatized into distortions and false dimensions given to reality, this when the need for more truthful communications has never been so vital."[6] The *Report* went on to add, "It is in the sphere of criticism, of informed debate and discussion, in the search for truth, that the character of communication becomes important." The printed word is not merely a medium of information, but one "of disputation, of criticism."[7]

Finally, the reliance Canadians place on newspapers as a source of information, and of varying perspectives on public issues, gives the industry a special role among the cultural industries in developing and maintaining a sovereign Canada. Again, the point was made with clarity and force in the 1961 O'Leary *Report*:

> . . .communications are the thread which binds together the fibres of a nation. They can protect a nation's values and encourage their practice. They can make democratic government possible and better government probable. They can soften regional asperities and bring honourable compromises. They can inform and educate in the arts, the sciences, and commerce. They can help market a nation's products and promote its material wealth. In these functions, it may be claimed — claimed without much challenge — that the communications of a nation are as vital to its life as its defences, and should receive at least as great a measure of national protection.[8]

Recognition of the important roles of the newspaper industry as a vehicle for gathering and disseminating a wide range of information, as an essential instrument in any genuinely democratic society, and as a major means for developing a sense of mutual understanding and self-knowledge at the local, regional and national levels, has led to concern over the way in which the industry is controlled in Canada and the quality, quantity and sources of the news, information and opinion produced by the newspapers in Canada. The federal government's awareness of problems related to the newspaper industry first became evident in the establishing of the Special Senate Committee on Mass Media in 1969. Then, in September 1980, the federal government established the Royal Commission on Newspapers which reported to the government in July 1981. The Kent Commission was established with the strong support of all political parties in the federal House of Commons and reflected a widespread concern over the way in which the press is controlled and operated in Canada.

This growing interest in the press is by no means unique to Canada. A 1977 study produced in association with the International Press Institute noted that "virtually all of the developed countries have discovered that they require a system of newspapers which their economic circumstances will no longer sustain," and that each country during the decade of the 1970s initiated discussions of its newspaper industry in circumstances of "extreme alarm."[9]

The concern underlying these initiatives is that an objective press must be a diverse press. In Canada, this view has been forcefully presented in a speech by the chief commissioner of the Canadian Human Rights Commission, Gordon Fairweather. Drawing attention to the fact that "Freedom of speech cannot take place in the abstract, but must occur through the use of various instruments," Fairweather argued that "The constitutional guarantee of freedom of the press is an empty exhortation, if at the same time Parliament does not enact a Competition Act that has as one of its major goals a healthy, lively rivalry between newspapers in the major cities in Canada."[10] Leaving aside the fact that revised legislation would not on its own achieve the objectives Fairweather describes, his comments express one of the principal reasons for examining the newspaper industry and for exploring measures which might encourage the diversity of sources and the quality of information that are a prerequisite of an informed public.

Trends in Daily Newspaper Publishing

Background

While newspaper publishing, at least in Europe, dates back to the early seventeenth century, the newspaper in its present form is a much more recent development. The potential scale of a newspaper publisher's activity remained quite limited for two centuries. As late as 1800, the maximum potential circulation of a newspaper was 1,000 copies; by 1830, the maximum circulation had risen to 4,000 copies — hardly what we would consider a mass medium. However, by the early twentieth century, the newspaper had developed into a large and powerful industry — transformed by the forces of technological development and its increasingly important roles as an instrument of democracy, a purveyor of an increasing range of information and entertainment, and the major vehicle for advertising mass-produced goods. By 1901, there were 114 daily newspapers in Canada, with a total circulation of 600,000.

Circulation Trends

As Table 1-2 indicates, daily newspaper circulation has continued to grow quite steadily throughout this century, maintaining its per capita circulation levels despite the arrival of radio and television. It is really only in 1980, after the closing of the *Montreal Star* in late 1979 and the *Ottawa Journal* and *Winnipeg Tribune* in 1980, that the circulation per capita figure drops slightly. The three papers together had a total circulation of about 300,000 on closing. Despite the resulting decline in per capita circulation, there will be a significant rebound as the circulation for the remaining English-language paper in Ottawa expands, and with a second Winnipeg daily now replacing the *Tribune* as a competitor to the *Free Press*.

The circulation figures in Table 1-2 are based on average *daily* circulation levels, the traditional basis for analyzing and comparing newspaper circulation trends. However, there have been significant changes in the circulation patterns of daily newspapers, with weekend circulation becoming increasingly important and Sunday newspapers a quite recent development in Canada. In order more accurately to measure circulation trends, the Kent Commission used the concept of aggregate weekly circulation. Using this basis for measurement, the commission compared 1970 and 1980 circulation.

Aggregate weekly circulation of daily newspapers actually increased by 16.5 per cent between 1970 and 1980. As Table 1-3 indicates, there were some significant shifts in the patterns of circulation, with

TABLE 1-2
SIZE AND GROWTH TRENDS FOR DAILY NEWSPAPERS IN
CANADA, 1901-80, BASED ON AVERAGE DAILY CIRCULATION

Year	Number of Papers	Total Circulation	Average Circulation per Paper	Per Capita Circulation
1901	114	600,000	5,300	0.105
1950	95	3,310,000	35,600	0.236
1955	95	3,780,000	37,800	0.237
1960	113	3,850,000	34,100	0.216
1965	104	4,250,000	39,700	0.216
1970	112	4,757,000	42,500	0.224
1975	114	4,886,000	42,900	0.212
1979	120	5,413,000	45,100	0.229
1980[1]	117	5,174,955	44,230	0.216

Note: [1] 1980 figures are based on September circulation levels and reflect the closing of the *Montreal Star* in 1979 and the *Ottawa Journal* and *Winnipeg Tribune* in 1980.

Sources: Report of the Special Senate Committee on Mass Media, 1970, and Canadian Daily Newspaper Publishers Association.

TABLE 1-3
DAILY NEWSPAPER CIRCULATION BY CATEGORY, 1970 AND
1980, BASED ON AGGREGATE WEEKLY CIRCULATION
(000's)

	1970	% of Total	1980	% of Total	% Change
Total weekday circulation	23,063	82.8	25,905	79.8	+11.4
Total Saturday circulation	4,739	17.0	5,163	15.9	+ 8.9
Total Sunday circulation	48	0.2	1,377	4.2	+2,768.8
Aggregate weekly circulation	27,851	100.0	32,445	100.0	+16.5
English-language	23,090	82.9	26,504	81.7	+14.8
French-language	4,761	17.1	5,942	18.3	+24.8
Morning papers	6,900	24.8	11,450	35.3	+65.9
Evening papers	20,951	75.2	20,537	63.3	−2.0
All day papers	n/a	n/a	458	1.4	—
Total competitive	16,826	60.4	17,001	52.4	+ 1.0
Total non-competitive	11,024	39.6	15,445	47.6	+40.1
Total independent	11,567	41.5	7,412	22.8	−35.9
Total chain	16,284	58.5	25,033	77.2	+53.7

Sources: ABC Fas Fax and publisher's statements; *Canadian Advertising Rates and Data*; and publishing records as compiled for the Royal Commission on Newspapers, 1981.

French-language circulation increasing more rapidly than English, and morning papers showing greatly increased circulation while evening circulation declined slightly. In addition, the circulation of chain-owned papers grew by 53.7 per cent, while that of the independents declined 35.9 per cent; and the circulation of papers in cities without competing papers increased by 40.1 per cent, while that of papers in competitive situations increased by just 1 per cent.

While French-language circulation increased more rapidly than English-language between 1970 and 1980, it remained considerably lower in relation to the size of the French-language population than the circulation of English-language papers, accounting for 18.3 per cent of circulation in 1980. By comparison, the percentage of the population whose mother tongue was French was 25.7 per cent. The growth in French-language circulation was accounted for largely by the tabloids, *Le Journal de Montréal* and *Le Journal de Québec*. The circulation of *La Presse* and *Le Soleil* declined, while that of *Le Devoir* increased by 8 per cent.

The Quebec government's 1978 White Paper on cultural development expressed concern over the relative weakness of the daily press in Quebec, noting that ''Although Quebec has almost 27 per cent of the total population of Canada, it is home to only 10 per cent of the dailies circulating in the ten provinces.''[11] Outside Quebec as well, the Moncton-based daily, *L'Evangeline*, has been experiencing difficulties in continuing to publish for its Acadian audience. With the exception of Ottawa's *Le Droit*, which has many of its readers in Quebec, *L'Evangeline* is the only French-language daily newspaper published outside Quebec. The particular concern expressed in the Quebec White Paper was that ''Whole regions are deprived of daily papers which could give coverage of events in community life (political, cultural, or economic) that are of concern to them.''[12]

If one uses the standard of aggregate weekly circulation to measure circulation trends in relation to population growth, then per capita circulation levels increased from 1.29 in 1970 to 1.33 in 1980. However, while circulation growth outstripped the growth in total population, it did not keep pace with either the growth in adult population (18 years and over) or in the number of households in Canada. While the adult population in Canada increased by 20.3 per cent between 1970 and 1980 and the number of Canadian households by 30.5 per cent, aggregate weekly circulation increased by 16.5 per cent.[13]

14

Advertising and Circulation Revenue

Advertising represents the major source of the daily newspaper industry's revenue. In 1981, the daily newspaper industry received 23.8 per cent of all media advertising revenue — substantially more than was received by any other sector of the print or broadcast media. Television, which ranked second, received 17.1 per cent of total advertising.

As Table 1-4 indicates, the daily newspapers' share of total media advertising was quite steady at between 29 and 30 per cent between 1961 and 1976, but has been slipping steadily since that time. Between 1976 and 1981, the daily newspapers' share of total media advertising declined from 29.4 to 23.8 per cent.

In an effort to maintain their lion's share of total media advertising revenue, the daily papers established the Newspaper Marketing Bureau in 1979. The purpose of the bureau is to make the daily papers a more attractive vehicle for national advertisers and, as a result, to recapture a larger share of national advertising. While 27 per cent of the daily newspapers' revenue had come from national advertising in 1965, the comparable figure for 1979 was 8.5 percentage points lower (see Table

TABLE 1-4
DAILY NEWSPAPER ADVERTISING REVENUE AS A PERCENTAGE OF TOTAL MEDIA ADVERTISING, SELECTED YEARS, 1961-81

Year	Net Newspaper Advertising Revenue	All Media Advertising Revenue	Newspaper Advertising as % of All Media
	($000's)		
1961	174,159	565,306	30.8
1965	220,822	741,743	29.8
1970	301,392	1,060,084	28.4
1975	564,638	1,938,483	29.1
1976	661,422	2,243,756	29.4
1977	703,605	2,458,024	28.6
1978	762,571	2,790,815	27.3
1979	827,984	3,220,167	25.7
1980	892,000	3,614,398	24.7
1981	967,000	4,061,500	23.8

Source: Maclean Hunter Research Bureau, *A Report on Advertising Revenues in Canada, 1981* (figures for 1961-79 are Statistics Canada actuals; for 1980-81, Maclean Hunter Research Bureau estimates).

TABLE 1-5
DAILY NEWSPAPERS:
COMPONENTS AND TRENDS IN NET ADVERTISING REVENUE
($000's)

	1965		*1979*	
National	58,500	(27.3%)	155,507	(18.8%)
Local	109,000	(50.8%)	449,917	(54.3%)
Classified	47,000	(21.9%)	222,560	(26.9%)
Total	214,500		827,984	

Source: Maclean Hunter Research Bureau, *A Report on Advertising Revenues in Canada, 1981* (based on Statistics Canada data).

1-5). This change reflected a loss of national advertising to television. Research conducted for the Kent Commission indicated that the daily newspaper industry's share of national advertising revenue dropped from 31.6 per cent in 1975 to 25.5 per cent in 1978. Television's share showed a corresponding increase, rising to 55.6 per cent in 1978 from 48.8 per cent three years earlier.

There is some evidence to suggest that the daily newspaper industry has begun to reverse the decline in revenues from national advertising. In a speech to the 1980 Annual Newspaper Awards dinner, the late Martin Goodman, then president of the *Toronto Star*, noted that the newspaper industry's share of national advertising increased in 1980 for the first time in five years and that the industry's increased share of national advertising added $24 million to industry revenue. Estimates by the Maclean Hunter Research Bureau suggest that revenue from national advertising accounted for 19.9 per cent of daily newspaper revenue in 1981, up from 18.8 per cent in 1979.

An additional factor in any recovery of the newspapers as a national advertising medium must also be the increasing fragmentation of the television market, which is making it more difficult to reach a large percentage of the Canadian public through ads placed on Canadian television stations or networks. Increased television audience fragmentation may well represent a real opportunity for newspapers to improve significantly their position as a major national advertising medium in the future.

Table 1-5 also indicates that classified advertising has become increasingly important to the success of daily newspapers over the past twenty years. While newspaper publishers are generally confident of their ability to retain their hold on local or retail advertising, and relatively optimistic that they can expand their share of national advertising, most acknowledge that the development of videotex services in Canada may create a shift in certain categories of classified advertising away from newspapers. Recent cable television industry applications to the CRTC to use a television channel for real estate advertisements provide an excellent example of the potential for erosion of newspapers' classified advertising revenue.

A further positive factor affecting daily newspaper advertising revenue is the fact that the cost of advertising on television has been increasing at a rate significantly faster than the rate for newspapers, or indeed for most other media. These increases in television rates appear to reflect a shortage of available advertising spots in peak viewing time in major markets and may help to account for the extraordinarily high profits of the television industry. Table 1-6 indicates the percentage change that has occurred in the cost of a variety of media in the period 1971-80. As will be seen later in this chapter, newspapers have been able to hold their rate of increase in advertising rates without sacrificing profitability. Because of their availability and relatively low cost, newspapers are likely to benefit most from rising costs for television time.

While advertising revenue represents, by a substantial margin, the most important source of daily newspaper revenue, the industry also receives a significant share of its total revenue through the sale of copies to the public. Canada's daily papers in fact sell their product in two markets: the public marketplace and the advertising market.

TABLE 1-6
MEDIA ADVERTISING COST TRENDS,
1971-80[1]

	1971	1975	1980
Television	100.0	138.0	230.5
Radio	100.0	138.0	191.2
Daily newspapers	100.0	131.0	176.9
Consumer magazines	100.0	117.0	160.3

Note: [1] Basis for comparison 1971 to 1980 is the cost of reaching 1,000 readers/viewers with an advertising message.

Source: The Canadian Media Directors' Council, *Media Digest, 1976* and *1980*.

Success in one market is linked to success in the other. The advertisers judge whether or not to place their ads in the daily newspapers to a significant degree on the basis of how many people are willing to buy copies. The specific concern of advertisers is usually to reach a high proportion of the population in a particular geographic area. As a result, scattered sales outside a newspaper's basic market area do not necessarily add to the paper's attractiveness to advertisers. Moreover, if any category of the newspaper industry's current advertising customers could reach their market through some more efficient means, then that portion of the industry's revenue would disappear. As research for the Kent Commission noted, "Any technological innovation which enabled the advertiser routinely to contact the consumer directly and vice-versa, would unhinge the economic foundation on which journalism and the newspaper are at present based."[14]

Newspapers are able to sell to a wide audience primarily because their revenue from advertising allows them to charge their customers only a fraction of the real cost of production. (Indirectly, however, the public pays anyway, as advertising is an expense included in the cost of the goods the advertisers are selling.) As Table 1-7 indicates, the

TABLE 1-7
DAILY NEWSPAPER ADVERTISING AND CIRCULATION
REVENUE
($000's)

Year	Advertising Revenue	% of Total Revenue	Circulation Revenue	% of Total Revenue
1961	174,159	73.6	62,550	26.4
1965	220,823	73.5	79,652	26.5
1970	301,392	73.3	109,978	26.7
1975	564,638	77.0	168,030	22.9
1977	703,605	78.4	193,348	21.6
1978	762,571	81.9	200,449	18.1
1979	827,984	79.1	218,357	20.9
1980	987,305	78.8	266,091	21.2

Sources: The Special Senate Committee on Mass Media, *Report,* vol. 2, *Words, Music and Dollars* (Ottawa: Queen's Printer, 1970), p. 172; Statistics Canada, *Culture Statistics: Newspapers and Periodicals, 1976-77* (Cat. No. 87-625); Statistics Canada, *Printing, Publishing & Allied Industries* (Cat. No. 36-203).

proportion of total revenue derived from subscribers and purchasers of newspapers declined quite substantially between 1970 and 1978. Whether or not this was based on a generally shared conviction among newspaper publishers that they could best compete with the major "free" media — particularly radio and television — if they kept their prices at a minimum, is not at all certain. Regardless of motivation, the industry as a whole kept prices to subscribers at a level which reduced the percentage of total revenue derived from sales from 26.7 per cent in 1970 to 18.1 per cent in 1978. But that trend seems to have been reversed in 1979 and 1980, with circulation accounting for 21.2 per cent of revenue in 1980.

Local Monopoly and Ownership Concentration
The total number of daily newspapers in Canada has hardly changed at all throughout this century. There were 114 dailies in 1901 and there are 117 in 1981. However, what has changed in a fundamental way is the number of dailies located in individual cities and the ownership and control of the industry.

At the turn of the century, according to W.H. Kesterton, sixty-six dailies were published in the eighteen communities in Canada which had more than two daily papers.[15] A further seventeen communities had two daily papers. Moreover, at that time, the pattern was one newspaper, one owner. In fact, just prior to the First World War, there were 138 daily papers in Canada and 138 publishers.[16] All that has changed.

According to the Kent Commission, there were only sixteen cities in Canada in 1981 which had more than one daily newspaper. Eighty-three Canadian cities have only one daily paper, while a further three have one daily paper in French and one in English, and an additional six have two papers in the same language, but produced by the same publisher. Currently, only seven cities in Canada have two or more daily papers in the same language and under different ownership — Edmonton, Calgary, Winnipeg, Toronto, French-speaking Montreal, Quebec City and St. John's.[17]

Competition in the daily newspaper industry has also been greatly reduced in the sense that there has been a steady expansion in chain ownership of the daily newspapers. In 1981, 75 per cent of the 117 daily newspapers were under group or chain ownership, and these group-owned dailies accounted for 77 per cent of total daily newspaper circulation, up from 56 per cent in 1970. While the three major groups in 1958 — Southam, Sifton and Thomson — accounted for 25 per cent of total circulation, the three largest by 1970 (Southam, Thomson and FP Publications) accounted for 44.5 per cent. By 1980, the two largest chains alone — Thomson and Southam — accounted for 48 per cent of national circulation, while the three largest accounted for 56.5 per cent (see Table 1-8). A single independent paper, the *Toronto Star*, accounts for a larger share of national circulation than the third largest chain, with 10.9 per cent.

Concentration levels are also extremely high if one looks separately at the English- and French-language components of the industry. Southam, the largest English-language chain, accounts for almost a third of national English-language circulation, while the three largest English-language chains account for 67 per cent. The largest single English-language paper, the *Toronto Star*, accounts for a further 13.3 per cent of English-language circulation. Quebecor, the largest French-language daily newspaper chain, accounts for 46.5 per cent of French-language circulation. The three French-language chains account for 90 per cent of French-language daily newspaper circulation.

In most developed countries, a transaction such as the takeover of the FP chain by Thomson newspapers in 1980 would have been subject to government review. So, too, would the more recent takeover by Torstar Corporation of the weekly newspaper chain, Inland Publishing Ltd. The Inland group of weekly newspapers operates in the same area as both Torstar's daily paper, the *Toronto Star*, and its existing chain of weekly papers, Metrospan publications. Either of the above transactions would, for example, have been subject to review in Britain, where the Monopolies and Mergers Act requires review and approval of any transaction which would bring total circulation of any newspaper owner to more than 500,000 copies a day. By comparison, at the time the Kent Commission was established, there was little legal basis under Canadian competition law for restricting the expansion of newspaper chain control. Commenting on a unanimous Supreme Court decision of November 1976, which ruled that the K.C. Irving interests had not violated the law in acquiring all five English-language daily newspapers in New Brunswick, William Stanbury noted that "If one were to adopt the logic of the Supreme Court, a single firm could acquire all the dailies in Canada."[18]

The May 1981 decision by the federal government to lay charges in connection with an alleged conspiracy in the closing of the *Montreal Star*, the *Ottawa Journal*, and the *Winnipeg Tribune*, does not provide any basis for revising Stanbury's opinion that Parliament in Canada has provided no effective basis for preventing further increases in

TABLE 1-8

NUMBER OF DAILY NEWSPAPERS AND CIRCULATION BY OWNERSHIP, 1970 AND 1980

	Number of Dailies		Aggregate Weekly Circulation (000's)		% of National Newspaper Circulation	
	1970	1980	1970	1980	1970	1980
Independent	45	29	11,567	7,412	41.5	22.8
Thomson	30	40	2,398	6,865	8.6	21.2
Southam	11	14	4,965	8,693	17.8	26.8
Quebecor	2	2	526	2,762	1.9	8.5
Sun Group	—	3	0	2,197	—	6.8
Desmarais	4	4	1,820	1,711	6.5	5.3
Unimedia	—	2	0	871	—	2.7
Irving	5	5	623	793	2.2	2.4
Armadale	2	2	633	715	2.3	2.2
Sterling	—	11	0	292	—	0.9
Bowes	3	3	64	93	0.2	0.3
James Johnston	—	2	0	41	—	0.1
FP Publications	8	—	5,039	0	18.1	—
Dingman	2	—	126	0	0.5	—
Green	2	—	91	0	0.3	—
Total	114	117	27,851	32,445	99.9	100.0

Source: Royal Commission on Newspapers, Research Studies, vol. 1, *Newspapers and Their Readers* (Ottawa: Supply and Services Canada, 1981).

concentration of control over the press in Canada. In initiating this legislation, the government did not challenge the takeover of FP by Thomson, but acted instead on the subsequent alleged conspiracy between Thomson and Southam to close the *Journal* and the *Tribune*, as well as on the earlier alleged conspiracy between FP and Southam to close the *Montreal Star*.

The newspaper chains themselves see little future for competition between or among rival daily papers in the vast majority of Canadian cities. In an interview in August 1980, Ken Thomson is reported to have said, "The economics in North America are very tough. There are very few markets that could support two newspapers."[19] The significance of the interview became clear when, two weeks later,

Thomson and Southam announced the closing of the *Ottawa Journal* and the *Winnipeg Tribune*, and the sale of Thomson's interest in the *Montreal Gazette* and Pacific Press to Southam, leaving Southam as publisher of both the *Vancouver Province* and the *Vancouver Sun*. In a single day, as a result of the decisions of just two companies, competition between English-language daily papers in four major cities disappeared.

While Thomson's pessimism with regard to the possibility of daily newspaper competition certainly was self-serving, it is nonetheless quite clear that for the newpaper *owners* at least monopoly is best. Most advertisers also recognize that they get a lower cost per thousand rate for advertising in monopoly markets and, perhaps surprisingly, the cost of advertising in newspapers which suddenly find themselves in a monopoly position does not appear to increase. Thomson, in particular, has always had a strong corporate preference for avoiding competitive markets. An analysis of FP, Southam and Thomson operations prior to the Thomson takeover of FP showed that, in 1979, 87.4 per cent of FP's circulation was in competitive markets, as was 55.5 per cent of Southam's; by contrast, only 10.7 per cent of total Thomson circulation was in competitive markets.[20]

The tendency towards local monopoly papers is inherent in newspaper publishing. The costs associated with creating the editorial content of competing newspapers, and of setting up the press to produce the first copy, are similar regardless of the circulation of the paper. As a result, the higher the circulation, the lower the unit costs. Distribution costs also decline proportionately with increased sales. The results of this tendency towards monopoly were well described in the following passage in the *Report* of the Davey Committee:

> . . .in natural monopoly industries where two or more firms are competing, their separate shares of the available market are always unstable. They can't sit still. If one competing unit is larger than the other or even if they are of roughly equal size, they battle for supremacy. One firm may cut advertising rates and buy circulation, thus boosting production and lowering its per unit costs — and in the process forcing the rival firms' costs upward.
>
> The larger one newspaper becomes, the easier it becomes to grow larger still. The bigger one newspaper grows, the slimmer are its smaller rival's chances of survival. Its only hope is to cut production costs—which usually means skimping on editorial quality—and to find advertisers willing to pay two or three times more to reach the kind of readers the smaller newspaper attracts.[21]

However absolute this trend towards monopoly local dailies may be, it must also be recognized that the enormous financial resources of a chain such as Thomson affect the potential for continuing competition at the local level. As William Stanbury noted in the article mentioned above, a huge conglomerate such as the Thomson organization has the ability "to discipline a paper's less affluent competitors,"[22] whether through reduced advertising rates or aggressive circulation expansion programs operated at a loss. An article in the November 1978 edition of *Content* magazine, describing the attempt to build a strong local paper, *Kelowna Today*, in a market already served by the Thomson-owned *Kelowna Daily Courier*, indicates the potential that the chains have to outlast any would-be competitor. It will be interesting to watch what happens to the fledgling *Winnipeg Sun*, set up after the closing of the *Tribune*, once the spotlight is no longer on the newspaper chains.

In the absence of any public policies designed to offset this trend towards one-newspaper cities, Canada has reached the position described above, with just seven Canadian cities having competing daily papers. In most European countries, governments have intervened to try to preclude the results of this trend. As a matter of public policy, in many other countries, competition among local papers is fostered through a variety of measures, including direct subsidies, loans for modernization, tax incentives, etc., as well as competition legislation.[23]

Any analysis of the degree of competition and diversity of control in the newspaper industry must recognize two additional factors. The first is what some analysts call the "umbrella" model of newspaper competition.[24] The "umbrella" concept describes the competition that exists among national papers, major metropolitan dailies, newspapers in "satellite" cities or suburbs, local dailies in smaller cities, and the weekly newspaper industry itself, a degree of competition that is somewhat greater than the term "local monopoly" suggests.

Recognizing that a great many Canadian dailies have some circulation outside their major market, the Kent Commission assessed the number of daily papers that were actually available to readers in Canadian cities. A newspaper was considered to be available in a city if its ratio of aggregate weekly circulation to households exceeded 2 per cent. On this basis, there were 113 English-language cities reached by daily papers in 1980 and twenty-two French-language cities—almost unchanged from 1971 (see Table 1-9). However, there were only eight English-language cities in which just one daily paper was available in 1980—down from twenty-one in 1971. Similarly, there

TABLE 1-9
NUMBER OF CITIES REACHED[1] BY DAILY NEWSPAPERS,
1971 AND 1980

Number of Newspapers Reaching Cities (Resident plus Non-Resident Papers)	Number of Cities			
	English		French	
	1971	1980	1971	1980
1	21	8	5	2
2	37	47	2	—
3	22	26	—	15
4	16	16	14	5
5	10	7	1	—
6	4	6	—	—
7	2	3	—	—
Total cities reached by a resident or non-resident daily	112	113	22	22
Total cities with a resident daily	86	94	7	8

Note: [1]A newspaper is considered to reach a city when its ratio of aggregate weekly circulation to households exceeds 2 per cent. For example, a newspaper would be assumed to reach a city with 50,000 households if 1,000 copies per week were sold in that city.

Source: Royal Commission on Newspapers, Research Studies, vol. 4, *The Newspaper as a Business* (Ottawa: Supply and Services Canada, 1981).

were just two French-language cities in which just one paper was available in 1980, by comparison with five in 1971. Other changes in the availability of alternative papers (using this minimum definition of availability) were relatively slight, with two exceptions. The number of English-language cities in which two or three English papers were available increased from fifty-nine to seventy-three, reflecting the decline in the number of English cities in which it was not possible to acquire an alternative daily. In addition, the number of French-language cities with access to three papers increased from zero to fifteen, reflecting a decline, on the one hand, in the number of cities with just one or two available papers, and, on the other hand, a marked decline in the number of cities with access to four or more dailies.

There are, of course, also weekly newspapers published in many of the markets served by daily newspapers. The existence of both a degree of overlap of daily newspaper circulation and of weekly papers operating in the same areas as the daily papers must be recognized in assessing the overall trend towards monopoly daily papers in Canadian cities. However, the extent of circulation overlap for daily papers is usually limited, and only rarely is home delivery of a non-resident daily paper available. In addition, while the circulation of daily and weekly papers overlaps substantially, the editorial content of the weeklies is usually different in its emphasis from that of daily papers. In fact, there are substantial differences in editorial content among the various categories of newspapers, with the weeklies focused mainly on community news, the smaller dailies, in suburbs or smaller local cities, on local city or suburban regional news, and the major dailies on international, national, provincial and regional news. There is, as a result, probably more complementariness than competition in editorial content. Each kind of paper tends to be regarded as the primary vehicle for a certain category of information. Consequently, while there is overlap and, therefore, some diversity of information, the "umbrella" environment is unlikely to be fully competitive with respect to editorial content.

Further, there is the question of the ownership or control of the different kinds of newspapers in any "umbrella." Even to the extent that there is competition within any "umbrella" area, a significant degree of common ownership exists in many areas. In the case of the Winnipeg market, for example, the Thomson-owned national paper, the *Globe and Mail*, competes with the Thomson-owned *Winnipeg Free Press*; in the case of the Metropolitan Toronto area, the Torstar-owned *Toronto Star* competes with Torstar's Metroland community newspapers.

In the United States, the major newspaper chains, uneasy about possible Justice Department intervention, have been careful to avoid buying papers that have overlapping distribution. Aware that U.S. competition policy sometimes leads to strong Justice Department action, the major publishing groups have tried to avoid the accusation that they control all of the papers under any particular "umbrella." In the absence of an effective competition policy and legislation in Canada, however, the newspaper chains have never had any cause to be concerned about possible government objections to similar transactions in the Canadian industry.

The second additional factor affecting competition is the degree to which the need for diverse sources of information is met by competition between newspapers and other media which also provide news, information and analysis. Newspaper owners and publishers themselves tend to offer different views on this matter, depending upon whether they are arguing the case that newspapers are a unique and, therefore, especially important medium of information, or defending themselves against the accusation that they have too much control over the critically important instruments for communicating information to the public.

The views expressed to the Kent Commission by the Thomson newspaper chain are instructive on this point. The Thomson brief to the commission states that:

> The daily press has always had the ability to cover a wide range of current and topical events in some depth and to reach large audiences with this information. This ability has imparted to the press a unique role in our society. That role has been, not only to enlighten and to inform large numbers of people, but to give the public the opportunity to be heard.[25]

However, although the Thomson submission argues that the daily newspapers play a unique role, the brief also takes the view that "The public has access to a rich variety of information services" and that "it uses all of them in shaping its views."[26] The Thomson brief goes on to contend that, despite the increasing predominance of local daily newspaper monopolies and the high level of concentration of control over the industry as a whole, "no one medium and no one operator has a monopoly on the news and information received by the public."[27] Similarly, Southam Inc., in referring to its daily newspapers, sometimes speaks of "their unique role as the major medium of information and news,"[28] and at other times shifts the emphasis and argues that "daily newspapers are of significant importance, but not absolutely essential to the workings of the modern community."[29]

No one can disagree with the notion that other media—magazines, books and, particularly, radio and television—provide alternative sources of news, information or opinion to those found in newspapers. However, it is also generally true that magazines and books lack the immediacy, while radio and television characteristically lack the depth, provided by newspaper coverage. Anyone who doubts the relative lack of depth and diversity in other news media should try to select and edit from any daily newspaper, a three-, five- or ten-minute radio newscast, or to organize a 15- or even a 30-minute television newscast, taking account, in the case of television news, of the time that goes into providing the visual coverage which television alone can offer. The result of this exercise is a very strong confirmation of the

26

view that the other media are, at present, a very effective additional source of information, but a thoroughly inadequate substitute.

When considering the problems of competition between different levels of newspapers under a single "umbrella," a related issue emerges: the case in which the newspapers and other information media are under the common ownership of a single individual or corporation. Attention has focused particularly, both in Canada and abroad, on instances in which the different media in a single community or region are under the control of a single individual or corporation. If newspaper monopoly markets are a legitimate cause for concern, then it is even more alarming if the newspaper owner also owns a local radio or television station. This situation is often as much a problem to local advertisers, wary of the influence on advertising rates in a non-competitive media environment, as it is to the public, concerned over the concentration of control of local sources of information and opinion.

In the United States, the Federal Communications Commission acted to limit media cross-ownership, prohibiting newspapers from constructing or purchasing any broadcast facilities that would overlap the markets served by their newspapers. A 1977 Court of Appeals decision in the United States went further, requiring that existing enterprises be split up. In Canada, the (Bryce) Royal Commission on Corporate Concentration recommended in its 1978 *Report* that the CRTC "be empowered to prevent the owners of broadcasting stations from also owning newspapers and other print media that circulate in the same market."[30]

A final and more general issue related to the patterns of present and future control in the newspaper industry arises from the observations offered elsewhere in the Bryce Commission's *Report*. The *Report* notes that "Many Canadians are profoundly concerned with what they think is the considerable power that large corporations have to influence official decisions and public opinion."[31] While the *Report* concludes that the commission found little explicit evidence to justify this fear, the perception is rooted firmly enough in reality to merit more careful examination. Since newspaper publishing is itself a large, profit-oriented enterprise, the newspapers might well be seen to have a basic commitment to the business community's views on public issues rather than to a wider range of interests. This concern has special force in those cases in which the newspaper is owned by a company with a wide range of investments in other industries outside newspaper publishing. Moreover, this apprehension is particularly acute in

27

situations in which there is monopoly control of the press locally or a high degree of corporate concentration within a region or a country—as there already is in Canada.

The following section from a brief by W.F.W. Neville, Professor of Political Studies at the University of Manitoba, presented to the Kent Commission during its public hearings in Winnipeg, raises issues in relation specifically to the Thomson newspaper chain:

A second specific issue that arises out of these developments is conflict of interest. In the last few years, we have had a Royal Commission on Corporate Concentration; we have had ongoing debates on combines legislation, foreign ownership, the pharmaceutical industry, energy policy, telecommunications policy, the role of the state in the insurance industry, transportation, land development, and as we have seen in the most recent budget, the related questions of publicly and Canadian-owned oil companies. All of these involve serious questions of public interest and public policy; and one would expect in the process of debate on them, newspapers would be a source of information, analysis and opinion. The Thomson newspapers, however, which include the *Winnipeg Free Press*, are part of an international conglomerate (with what views on questions of "foreign" ownership?) and are part of a stable of operations which include insurance companies, television companies, drugstore chains, oil companies, trucking companies, property development companies, real estate holdings, import companies, and a host of others behind whose innocuous names any number of activities may be taking place.

A politician, however saintly, with the range of interests identified here, would be morally, if not legally, disqualified from expressing an opinion, still less from voting, on a large number of issues confronting all three levels of government at the present time; and the newspapers in this conglomerate would appropriately be amongst the first to make the point. However, the question that begs to be asked is, who protects the newspapers' virtue? Its owners, its publishers and editors may be as saintly as our saintly politicians, but is their role and that of their newspapers really compatible with the other interests of the Thomson empire? I submit to the Commission that it is not. Just as government has deemed that ownership of the chartered banks is not compatible with certain other kinds of activity, such a determination is required here.[32]

It is not, of course, merely in relation to the Thomson group that such issues arise. The diverse interests of the Irving family in New Brunswick and of Power Corporation in Quebec represent similar conflicts of interest which compromise the credibility of the press.[33] By comparison, other newspaper groups, Southam and Torstar for

28

example, have confined their investments either to publishing alone or to the communications sector of the economy.

Southam, particularly, has consistently stated that "The company will have no financial interest in enterprises outside the communications field"; that "Officers of the company and senior publishing executives may not act as directors of other unrelated firms operated for profit"; and finally, that "Officers, editorial personnel, and other key publishing executives are expected to remain free from political and other outside activities, if such activities might influence or appear to influence free expression in any of the company's newspapers."[34] However, it is worth noting that while officers, editorial personnel and other key publishing executives are, as a matter of policy, precluded from any political involvement, Southam itself makes political contributions to "the federal party in power and to the party forming the official opposition."[35] It is interesting to note that questions concerning this practice were raised at the 1976 Southam Annual Meeting. The editor of *Content* magazine asked whether, if the New Democratic Party formed the government or the official opposition, the payments would continue. Southam's president, Gordon Fisher, is reported to have replied that "The NDP would not get money from Southam Press Limited." Asked to explain that policy, *Content* reported that he replied, "Because we believe in the Canadian two party system." Such incidents, of course, help to corroborate the view that while Southam may not have conflicts of interest related to *other* business holdings, its own position as a major communications corporation does not make it easy for the company to function as an impartial instrument of democracy.

The response to the conflict of interest problem during the Kent Commission hearings sometimes took the form of praise for the model of non-profit publishing companies such as the one which publishes the French-language daily *Le Devoir*; at other times resulted in expressions of support for the quality and fairness of CBC journalism; and sometimes expressed itself in proposals for a national public-sector newspaper. In all cases, the underlying concern was to achieve a better balance and greater objectivity in news coverage, and to ensure that there really were genuinely competing and diverse sources of information and analysis available to the public.

Throughout the Kent Commission hearings, the Southam chain took great pains to distinguish itself from the Thomson chain in particular, stating in its submission that Southam "has avoided the conflicts of interest that inevitably flow from commercial activity outside the industry."[36] But Southam also made it clear to the commission that there was no way the company could guarantee that conflicts would not develop in the future:

> There is no action that our company can take that would prevent a takeover by commercial enterprises with conflicting interests. This is in contrast to specific provisions of the Bank Act and legislation that has been proposed for other financial institutions that are designed to prevent the formation of control groups in individual companies in those industries.[37]

At present, as Southam's brief states, "No shareholder holds more than 5 per cent of equity," and "There is no Southam family holding company or voting trust."[38] Given this situation, a takeover of Southam would indeed be possible, although members of the founding family still retain 40 per cent of equity.

On the basis of the federal government's current policies, it appears that past and present governments have been far more interested in seeing that money is dispensed fairly and impartially by the banks than in seeing that information and analysis of public issues is dispensed fairly and impartially by newspapers and other media. It seems ironic that, while firm laws are in place for the purpose of avoiding conflicts of interest in decisions related to the supply of financing, very little has been done to avoid conflicts related to the supply of information. The Banks and Banking Law Revision Act, 1980 prohibits any single interest from holding more than 10 per cent of equity in a bank, while also prohibiting the banks from owning more than 10 per cent of any corporation outside the banking industry. Comparable laws related to publishing and broadcasting, although they would require substantial changes in ownership structure, would go a long way towards avoiding direct conflicts of interest and improving public confidence in the media. Such laws would need to address the issue of conflicts of interest affecting directors and officers of such companies, as well as companies and their shareholders. The fact that such measures appear Utopian is a measure both of the values of Canadians and the concentration of power that rests with those who already control the media in Canada.

It is extremely difficult to determine how aware the public is of the present degree of concentration of media control, or how objective it believes the coverage provided by the media is. However, public attitudes on both issues were explored in research conducted for the

Kent Commission in January 1981.[39] Asked to identify which medium was most fair and unbiased, 29 per cent of adult Canadians surveyed chose newspapers, by comparison with 32 per cent for radio and 53 per cent for television. Just over half (53 per cent) of adult Canadians believed that newspapers tended to represent one group's interests more than others. Asked which group's interests newspapers represented most, 45 per cent said that of government, while 39 per cent said that of business and advertisers. Only 6 per cent thought newspapers represented most the interests of their readers. Seventy-two per cent of respondents agreed that newspapers often play down stories that could offend advertisers.

Respondents were also asked to indicate how concerned they were about different ownership situations. The highest percentage of respondents (79 per cent) expressed concern over one company owning the television, radio and newspaper outlets in a single area, closely followed by the 78 per cent who expressed concern if one company owned all of the papers in a province. A substantial majority also expressed concern over one company owning all local papers (72 per cent) or many papers in Canada (68 per cent), or if one company was involved in more than one form of mass communication. However, there was not majority public support for federal financial support for papers going out of business (55 per cent expressed concern), while 61 per cent expressed concern at the federal government's financing a national newspaper in the way it finances the CBC.

Those surveyed not only expressed concern over various aspects of media concentration; they also indicated their belief that there were problems inherent in the increasing existence of monopoly local newspapers. Seventy-two per cent believed that it was necessary to read more than one newspaper to make sure they got all sides of a story, with 68 per cent of those who lived in a city without local competing papers expressing a desire to have someone set up competition for the local daily paper. Of those newspaper readers who read only one newspaper on weekdays, 50 per cent expressed interest in reading more than one daily paper if different types were readily available. This interest in having alternative papers available is reflected in the actual reading habits reported by Canadians. While 42 per cent of Canadians read just one daily, 33 per cent read two and an additional 14 per cent read three or more. Only 11 per cent reported that they did not read daily newspapers at all.

Profitability

The most obvious indications of the financial health of daily newspapers are the rapid rate at which they are being purchased at increasingly high multiples of dollars per reader and the tremendous speed with which the newspaper groups have grown over the past decade. The heated bidding in the 1979 war for control of the FP Publications newspaper chain provided the most visible example, with major bids coming from a group headed by Conrad Black, in partnership with John Bassett, George Gardiner and Fredrik Eaton, from R. Howard Webster, as well as from the Thomson group. The bidding, which began at just over $100 million, soared to $165 million before Thomson succeeded in acquiring the chain.

High daily newspaper industry profits are nothing new. As part of its research program in 1970, the Davey Committee carried out a systematic analysis of industry profits for the ten years 1958 to 1967. The committee found that the overall pre-tax profits, as a percentage of total equity capital for all newspapers over the ten-year period, ranged from 23 to 30 per cent. Moreover, its research showed that corporations which comprised newspaper groups and were publishing newspapers with a circulation of over 100,000, had been earning even higher profits. The committee's *Report* noted that the pre-tax rate of return on equity for such groups in 1967 was 57.2 per cent.[40]

In 1981, the Kent Commission reported that "The newspaper industry is, by a considerable margin, more profitable than the steel industry, or the manufacturing sector as a whole, or the retailing and service industries. Despite recent setbacks, which are common throughout the economy, it is more profitable than it was a decade ago."[41] On the basis of return on net assets, the Kent Commission noted that the average for the period 1958 to 1967 was 26 per cent. This figure had increased to 33.4 per cent for the period 1974 to 1980.

Towards the end of the period 1974 to 1980, there was a downturn in industry profits. The industry's return on net assets employed fell below 30 per cent in both 1978-79 and 1979-80, reaching 21.6 per cent in 1979-80. However, even at this lower level, the newspaper industry's return remained high by comparison with that of other industries. Only the broadcasting industry was able to earn consistently a return comparable to that of the daily newspaper industry. Research conducted for the Kent Commission cautioned that this downturn should not necessarily be interpreted as constituting a continuing trend, since it reflected both major work stoppages and a significant increase in capital expenditures on labour-saving production technologies that would not show results in decreased costs for several years.

32

The profit decline in 1978-79 and 1979-80 also reflected a weakening economy generally, a trend that has continued. While share profit for the Thomson, Southam and Toronto Sun chains improved in 1981 over 1980, profit fell for Torstar and Quebecor, in both cases reflecting rapidly increasing interest charges on loans made to finance expansion. In the first half of 1982, the advertising revenues of the newspaper industry began to be affected by the rapid deterioration in the Canadian economy. This advertising revenue decline marks the unusual severity of the current economic recession, since the communications sector has usually been untouched by the periodic recessions in the economy. Barring a further decline in the economy, the prospects are good for a return to extremely high profits for daily newspapers as the economic benefits to the chains of mergers and new technologies begin to be felt.

Table 1-10 indicates the rapid growth that has occurred in the major newspaper corporations. While the Sun group was only established in 1971, its growth has also been remarkably rapid, with revenues increasing almost tenfold, from $8.3 million in 1974 to $81.9 million in 1981. The growth of the principal chains has been based on daily newspaper earnings. Lord Thomson, for example, noted in his

TABLE 1-10
SELECTED FINANCIAL DATA: MAJOR NEWSPAPER GROUPS
($000's)

	1969	1974	1979
Southam Inc.			
Revenue from operations	104,765	221,920	484,235
Pre-tax operating income	12,261	28,484	55,507
Pre-tax return on equity	34.1%	48.6%	34.8%
Thomson Newspapers Ltd.[1]			
Total revenue	92,860	170,113	319,650
Pre-tax income	28,673	63,179	125,511
Pre-tax return on equity	47.9%	37.1%	39.3%
Torstar Corporation			
Total revenue	52,275	114,836	371,100
Pre-tax income	5,826	16,735	51,996
Pre-tax return on equity	28.9%	43.6%	49.3%

Note: [1]For Thomson Newspapers, the first column of figures is for 1968 rather than 1969. Data for 1969 were not available.

Source: Annual reports for each company.

33

presentation to the Kent Commission that "Everything that my family has today, and in terms of opportunities for the future, goes back to our newspaper organization."[42] The Kent Commission *Report* stated that "Of the $140 million in dividends paid by Thomson Newspapers between 1973 and 1980, $100 million has flowed into other Thomson interests."[43]

Economic Impact

The Kent Commission estimated total employment in the daily newspaper industry in Canada at 22,000. Despite the high profits of the industry, average wages over the period 1974 to 1980 have not kept pace with inflation, increasing from $9,300 in 1974 to $16,000 in 1980.[44]

The daily newspapers, in almost all cases, do their own printing and, therefore, are surveyed as a manufacturing industry. Table 1-11 provides a breakdown of the major categories of employment in the daily press for 1974 and 1980. The reduction in production staff levels reflects major capital investments in new computerized typesetting and photocomposition equipment, virtually all of which is acquired outside Canada. Canadian dailies reported capital expenditures of $55 million in 1980, up from $33 million in 1978. Table 1-12 provides a breakdown of expenditures for daily papers in 1974 and 1980. While newsprint costs have increased slightly as a percentage of total expenditure, the increase has been more than offset by reductions in printing costs.

The value added by the newspaper industry in 1979, including both daily and weekly papers, was $935.1 million. Value added is the difference between the total revenues an industry earns and its

TABLE 1-11
PERCENTAGES OF EMPLOYMENT BY DEPARTMENT
IN CANADIAN DAILY NEWSPAPERS

	1974	1980
Editorial	20.3	22.3
Production	35.7	30.6
Marketing, sales, circulation and distribution	31.2	33.8
Administration	9.7	9.8
Other	3.1	3.5

Source: Report of the Royal Commission on Newspapers, 1981.

expenditures on materials, parts and purchased services. The daily papers account for more than 85 per cent of the value added by the newspaper industry as a whole.

TABLE 1-12
PERCENTAGES OF DAILY NEWSPAPER EXPENDITURE BY CATEGORY

	1974	1980
Production expenses—newsprint	19.9	23.1
printing	26.8	22.7
Circulation and distribution	13.4	15.0
Advertising and marketing	9.3	9.5
Administration and other	14.5	12.3
Editorial expense	16.1	17.4

Source: Report of the Royal Commission on Newspapers, 1981.

TABLE 1-13
IMPORTS AND EXPORTS BY COMMODITY FOR PUBLICATIONS ($000's)

Commodity	1965		1970		1975	
	Import	Export	Import	Export	Import	Export
Newspapers	2,775	3,429	4,728	10,153	4,095	6,267
Periodicals	47,225		66,388		114,352	21,368
Books	68,597	2,503	126,078	7,055	205,254	17,278
Total	118,597	5,932	197,194	17,208	323,701	44,913

Commodity	1979		1980		1981	
	Import	Export	Import	Export	Import	Export
Newspapers	6,770	18,598	8,140	29,380	10,925	51,907
Periodicals	257,520	38,663	277,243	53,283	310,931	39,686
Books	354,130	39,680	394,445	55,293	447,559	55,889
Total	618,420	96,941	679,828	137,956	769,421	147,482

Source: Statistics Canada, *Exports: Merchandise Trade* and *Imports: Merchandise Trade* (Cat. Nos. 65-202 and 65-203).

The printing, publishing and allied industry sector, of which newspaper publishing constitutes a major part, was one of the few sectors of Canadian manufacturing which generated a significant increase in employment over the decade 1971 to 1981. Employment in the sector increased by 53 per cent during this period by comparison with an increase of just 31 per cent in the manufacturing sector as a whole.

Although Canada has, at present, a rapidly escalating deficit with other countries in the international flow of publications (over $600 million in 1981), Canadian newspapers are an exception. As indicated in Table 1-13 (on the previous page), trade in newspapers is both relatively limited and shows a balance in Canada's favour.

Editorial Content

The relationship between the editorial and advertising content of newspapers is nicely suggested by the industry term "news-hole," which describes the space not filled by advertising. The October 28, 1980 federal budget raised the issue of advertising and editorial content by proposing to end the sales tax exemption which applied to newspaper and magazine publishers in cases in which more than 90 per cent of a single issue, or more than 70 per cent of the content in more than 50 per cent of all issues over the preceding three months, was devoted to advertising. This apparently modest attempt to distinguish a newspaper from an advertising circular met with an extremely hostile response from the Canadian Daily Newspaper Publishers Association whose members evidently thought that this standard was too high. The publishers did not say what the appropriate level should be—it has been declining for years—but they certainly were not advocating the same tax exemption for advertising circulars. They wish to be free, it appears, to provide any mix that includes both advertising and editorial content, however little of the latter there may be.

There is, of course, an economic motivation to expand advertising content and reduce editorial content or reduce expenditure on editorial content. Newspaper publishers get paid to carry advertising content, whereas they have to buy editorial material. While Canadian data are not readily available, the ratio of advertising to editorial content in daily papers in the United States dropped from 50/50 in 1945 to 65/35 in 1973.[45] This largely reflected a more rapid growth in advertising content than in editorial content, rather than a shrinking of editorial content. However, there is clearly a point beyond which declining investment in editorial content will lead to such a significant decline in

36

readership that the resulting advertising revenue losses will affect a paper's profitability or competitive position. In the case of monopoly markets, of course, with no directly competing daily, the motivation to improve a paper editorially is much weaker.

The willingness of newspapers to invest in producing high quality Canadian content varies substantially. The Kent Commission, for example, noted that the average level of expenditure on news and editorial content by papers owned by the Thomson chain was 24 per cent below the industry average.[46] Lower levels of investment in editorial content are reflected in Thomson's profits, which are also far higher than the industry average. Virtue is not rewarded.

If there is a more direct and powerful economic motivation to concentrate on expanding advertising content rather than improving and expanding editorial content, there is also an economic motivation for individual papers to buy editorial content rather than to produce it themselves. It is more costly to hire a reporter or columnist than it is to buy national or international news, features or syndicated columns. Most newspapers provide coverage themselves of those primarily local events and stories they cannot buy from anyone else, while relying mainly, regardless of their financial resources, on national or international wire services and syndicated material to cover national and international stories.

This is not to suggest, however, that the results of this practice are necessarily bad. In fact, the advantage of a cooperative approach to national or international reporting can certainly be to provide a quality and range of reporting that would never be possible if each paper tried to do the job itself. Within Canada, of course, the major common source of reporting is Canadian Press (CP), a cooperative news service owned by the daily newspapers, which acts both as a distributor of material provided to the service by the individual member publishers and as an initiator of material through its own staff. Canadian Press provides a news service to broadcasters as well as newspaper publishers through its subsidiaries, Broadcast News, which serves commercial broadcasters, and Press News Ltd., which has been supplying a news service to the Canadian Broadcasting Corporation since 1941. The CP wire service operates both French- and English-language services.

The importance of CP in national development is not widely understood. In fact, CP's function is so little recognized that the Davey Committee, in its 1970 *Report*, was able to write, "Magazines constitute the only national press we possess in Canada."[47] If that statement is true at all, it is only in the very technical sense that individual magazines, unlike newspapers, actually make their way across the country. In the case of the newspaper industry, what travels across Canada is CP's daily wire service report, which, on the average, includes about 300 columns sent to each member newspaper for the full English-language service and 55-60 columns for the French-language service. Through this common service, the daily newspaper industry in Canada functions collectively as a "national press."

The late Martin Goodman, when he was president of Canadian Press, argued that "CP's ability to transmit quickly across the country so all Canadians can share information at the same time is not only a vital resource for member papers, but a precious cultural resource."[48] There can, in fact, be little doubt that CP's function is extremely important in establishing among the regions and communities within Canada a shared pool of information and an increased level of knowledge of local, regional and national problems, perceptions and identity.

How well Canadian Press performs its functions is another question. The 1970 Davey Committee *Report* found that CP did "supremely well" its job of exchanging stories prepared by its member papers. However, the *Report* also expressed some criticism of the CP's Canadian news coverage at that time, noting that coverage of the arts and cultural matters and of currents of social change was weak, and that the French-language papers in CP were poorly served by comparison with the English papers. In both cases, however, the Davey *Report* was quite sympathetic to CP's problems in these areas; CP felt that its own focus, by contrast with that of member papers, should be on what it called "hard news" rather than analysis of social and cultural trends, and noted that the French-language service was subsidized significantly and that French-language members themselves felt CP was doing its best to serve their needs.

Since 1970, there have been significant changes in CP's domestic operations. The non-management editorial staff has increased from 216 in 1971 to 299 in 1981. Less than half of CP's domestic news report now originates with member papers, the bulk of the report now being based on CP staff reporting. Additional attention is given to the arts and cultural activity, and some improvements have been made in the French-language service.[49] And yet, there remain real reasons for dissatisfaction. CP can only do as well as the financial support of the cooperative's member papers permits; and it is impossible to avoid the fact that, while the CP service has grown over the decade, the contribution of member papers has not kept pace with the phenomenal growth in revenue and profit that has occurred in the daily newspaper industry. While there was real growth in CP's budget between 1971 and 1980, with expenditure by CP and its subsidiaries increasing from $7 million to $20 million, growth in CP's assessment to member papers was relatively limited in relation to increased industry revenue, increasing by 152 per cent. For purposes of comparison, industry advertising revenue increased 201 per cent, from $327.9 million to $987.3 million, and combined advertising and circulation revenue by 180 per cent. In 1980, CP's assessment to members had increased just 8 per cent over the previous year, substantially less than the rate of inflation, and the anticipated increase prior to the closing of the Winnipeg and Ottawa papers had been only 6.5 per cent.

There is a great deal that CP could do if the industry provided additional support. At the beginning of 1981, CP itself had a list of an additional twenty-one priority editorial positions it wanted to fill in order to improve its service.[50] The list included a sportswriter in Edmonton, a television writer in Toronto, a legal affairs writer to cover the Supreme Court and other major legal institutions and issues, a reporter to cover the North, a general assignment writer for Alberta, and consumer affairs and/or business reporters and editors in Toronto, Ottawa, Montreal, Vancouver and Edmonton.

CP's French-language service remains particularly weak and is likely to remain limited as long as the French-language service is run simply as a regional CP office rather than a separate branch of the CP service. According to the Kent Commission, just one-tenth of CP's editorial staff works in CP's French service, providing copy for French-language papers which account for 18 per cent of national circulation and serve the 26 per cent of the population whose mother tongue is French. Just two of the nineteen seats on the CP Board of Directors are reserved for French-language publishers.[51]

Too much of CP's coverage still focuses on Parliament and the legislatures across Canada. Too little exchange of information occurs concerning the lifestyles, attitudes, hopes and expectations of people in the various regions and the two official language groups within Canada. The result of this narrow approach was expressed eloquently in an article by David Ablett, in which he noted that the press "covers national political life as if it were a series of traffic accidents, one event to be recorded and put aside for the next event, ever focused on Parliament while carefully remarking that real power is somewhere else."[52]

Where CP's service is weakest is in the coverage of foreign news

39

from a Canadian perspective. CP's failure to offer foreign news from a Canadian perspective drew the strongest criticism CP received from the Davey Committee. The *Report* argued that "CP could be, and should be doing a better job for the people of Canada. . .it should have more staffers abroad, reporting the world scene as Canadians speaking to Canadians."[53] Instead of covering foreign affairs itself, CP relies on copy from its foreign affiliates—the American service, Associated Press; the British service, Reuters; and the French service, Agence France-Presse. This reliance alarmed the Davey Committee:

> We do not suggest that the Associated Press, for example, is not a fine news service. It is. But it is an American news service and no amount of tinkering with AP copy in CP's New York office will give it a Canadian character. An American reporter, writing for an American audience, writes in the American idiom, which is not the Canadian idiom. He writes from a background of American experience and the American national interest, which are not the Canadian experience and the Canadian interest. He uses American illustrations which are not Canadian illustrations, and he draws on a literature, a history, and a political tradition which are his and not ours.[54]

The daily newspaper industry chose to ignore the views of the Davey Committee. Instead of providing the resources to expand CP's limited full-time foreign staff, they cut it back from twelve in 1971 to five in 1981. CP now has two full-time editorial staff employees in Washington, two in London, and one in New York. There is not one Canadian Press employee in Moscow, Peking, Brussels, or anywhere in the Middle East, West Germany, or the whole of Africa and Latin America. Whatever job CP may do of watching and reporting Canadian affairs, it chooses systematically not to look at the vast majority of the world.

The problem, in a nutshell, is a financial one. CP can buy the whole of the Associated Press wire service, for example, for just $500,000, so why spend many times that amount to cover world news for itself? Just as most local papers tend to rely on CP for other than local domestic news, so collectively the industry tends to rely almost exclusively on foreign wire service copy to cover foreign news. In both cases, the result is that different points of view, written from the region's or the nation's perspective, are characteristically lacking in the daily press in Canada. Indeed, there is a direct and powerful financial disincentive to provide that perspective, especially in situations where there are monopoly daily papers.

What is certain is that the Canadian situation is complicated substantially by the fact that the industry here can, to a significant extent, choose between producing Canadian editorial content and importing foreign content. The Davey Committee made two critically important observations. First, "the industry as a whole can readily afford to supply its audience with the Canadian content it has long needed." Second, "they don't try hard enough to improve their product because there is no economic incentive to do so—quite the reverse."[55] With the diminishing of competition, the challenge is to devise public policies that stimulate and reward expenditure on Canadian editorial content. The alternative is almost certainly a deterioration in the quality and variety of newspaper content and a weakening of those very papers that now stand out because they are making a responsible effort to serve the public interest as well as to make a profit.

Current Public Policy

As noted in the Introduction, this study is focused primarily on cultural policy issues, with the cultural concern broadly defined to include every aspect of cultural identity, including the expression of attitudes, opinions, ideas and values, and the transmitting of information to the general public. Within this broad cultural policy framework, newspapers are of obvious importance.

In the past, the newspaper industry has not been considered by the federal government to fall within the broad framework of cultural policy concerns. There is no department or agency of the federal government at present which has responsibility on a continuing basis for assessing policy issues related to the industry from the perspective of cultural policy. This deficiency, in retrospect, probably had a great deal to do with the government's failure to act on the 1970 recommendations of the Davey Committee.

There has been a strong tendency to accept the view that governments do not now and should not in the future have anything to do with the newspaper industry. It is sometimes argued by those who advance this view that the industry must accept no assistance—direct or indirect—from the government and that there should be no intervention of any kind. However, the reality is that public policy has had a major effect on the newspaper industry, which has received and is receiving a great deal of public assistance. At the federal level, two aspects of policy are of substantial importance—taxation and postal rates.

The major public support now provided to newspapers is that which results from their exemption from the 9 per cent federal sales tax. The estimated value to the newspaper industry of this federal government tax expenditure in 1980 was $70 million.[56] The purpose of such tax expenditure is to grant a subsidy or provide an incentive for those engaging in a specific activity.

In the case of both newspapers and periodicals, section 19 of the federal Income Tax Act also makes provision that advertisers may only deduct from their taxable income expenditures for advertisements in the Canadian market that are placed in Canadian newspapers or magazines. Canadian newspapers and magazines are defined to include both a requirement of 75 per cent Canadian ownership and a provision that they be edited, typeset and printed in Canada and that they not be produced under licence from a foreign publisher or include more than 20 per cent of the editorial content of a foreign publication. This provision, implemented in two stages—most recently in the provisions of Bill C-58 in 1976—has the effect of both encouraging advertisers to use Canadian rather than foreign publications to reach their Canadian audiences, and discouraging takeovers of Canadian publications by foreign interests. Its effect has been to make possible the development of the powerful Canadian-controlled newspaper publishing companies that now exist in Canada.

The newspapers also benefit from concessionary postal rates provided by the federal government. The Kent Commission noted that the postal rate concession to newspapers in 1980 was valued at more than $27.5 million.

Combining the value of the sales tax and postal rate measures, both of which are indirect rather than direct support measures, federal assistance to the newspaper industry is worth close to $100 million annually. While the value of the section 19 provisions cannot be estimated, the legislative provisions involved establish the basic framework within which the newspaper industry functions, affecting both its ownership and control and its advertising revenue base. Quite clearly, this is not an industry that accepts nothing from the government.

Policy Issues and Proposals
The newspaper industry is owned and controlled in Canada and its operations provide substantial economic benefits. Because newspapers are primarily a local medium, newspaper publishing, unlike magazine

and book publishing, is a sector in which there has been, up to the present time, limited trade with other countries.

Profits from the newspaper industry have allowed the chains to diversify both into non-communications investments and into other communications areas, including videotex, magazine publishing, book publishing, retail book distribution, and film production. Their potential for expansion in the magazine, book, recording and film industries—which could be quite beneficial—is substantial, although up to 1982 that involvement has been relatively limited.

The CRTC has in the past made decisions on the newspaper industry's investment in radio and television broadcasting on the basis of an assessment of each individual case, without reference to any firm policy on cross-media ownership issues. Apart from broadcasting, the major area of investment by the newspaper industry has been the magazine production industry, a reflection in large measure of substantial public policy initiatives (see chapter 2). Many of the most attractive companies from an investment perspective in the magazine, book, record and film industries are foreign-controlled, and equity participation in such firms is not usually available. A more detailed analysis of the factors affecting the attractiveness of investment in these other industries is contained in the following chapters. As long as excessive concentration of control was avoided, however, such expansion would appear desirable.

The major issues affecting the newspaper industry at present are corporate concentration, the editorial quality of daily papers, especially in situations where they have a local monopoly, and the establishing of a framework for the development of electronic publishing that will protect Canada's sovereignty and its economic and cultural interests. The last of these issues is largely outside the scope of this study.

Incentives for Editorial Improvement

The (Kent) Royal Commission on Newspapers recommended that federal tax policy be used to provide a system of incentives to encourage higher levels of investment by newspapers in their editorial content. What specifically the commission proposed is that the taxation of any newspaper-owning company should be reduced by 25 per cent of the amount by which its editorial expenditures exceeded the average proportion for all daily papers in the previous year. Conversely, the newspapers would be liable to a surtax of 25 per cent of the amount by which their editorial expenditure fell short of the industry average for the previous year.

Just how significant such a measure might be is evident in the research findings of the Kent Commission. While the commission found that, on the average, editorial expenditure accounted for 15 per cent of revenue, the ratio varied from over 20 per cent to under 10 per cent. Moreover, the proportion of revenue invested in editorial content varied markedly within the categories of small, medium and large newspapers. There appeared to be little or no correlation between the proportion of investment in editorial expense and either circulation, revenue or other economic factors. The Kent Commission, in fact, concluded that "the ratio of output to input"—what is spent editorially for what is acquired in revenue—varied mainly according to the policy of the proprietor. The current tax policy of the federal government provides no reward to those responsible newspaper proprietors who commit a higher than average share of their revenues to improving the quality and scope of their editorial content.

This proposal by the Kent Commission has substantial merit. It appears both reasonable and necessary, as already argued, to begin to reward responsible newspapers and to make skimping on editorial expenditure less tempting. Responsibility to shareholders should be made to conflict less with the responsibility to produce a good newspaper. The pattern of local monopoly control renders such an initiative essential.

It is worth noting, however, that there are other measures that might be adopted to achieve the same purpose. It might be preferable, for example, simply to eliminate the exemption newspapers now enjoy from the federal sales tax and make provision for the same level of tax expenditure support to be provided through a refundable tax credit based on a designated percentage of the amount each newspaper-owning company spends on editorial content. This approach would be of no less benefit than the sales tax exemption to the industry as a whole, but the benefits would be directly related to each publisher's editorial expenditures. If one adopted such an approach without making the tax credit refundable, the elimination of the sales tax might harm the interests of financially weaker papers. However, if the tax credit were offered on a refundable basis, this problem would not arise.

A particularly strong additional reason for this fundamental change in tax policy would be to provide an incentive for the development of electronic publishing. The Kent Commission noted that "A way will have to be found, as videotex develops and perhaps threatens the existence of newspapers, to invigorate the journalistic base."[57] The shift in tax expenditure policy from a sales tax exemption on the production of printed newspapers to a refundable tax credit based on editorial expenditure would facilitate the necessary expansion of the industry into videotex production.

Because foreign editorial content can be acquired for far less than it costs to produce Canadian editorial content, whether for newspaper or videotex publishing, it would probably be desirable to make the tax credit applicable only to editorial content originated by Canadian publishers and to exclude expenditure on editorial content acquired from foreign publishers. Such an approach would reflect and reinforce the provisions of section 19 of the Income Tax Act, which links the deductibility of advertiser expenditures to publications originating most of their own content.

The sales tax exemption policy now in place tends to help the strongest newspapers because it applies to manufacturing costs for both editorial and advertising content. Its retention does not seem desirable. As will be noted in the magazine and book publishing chapters that follow, the effects of the sales tax exemption in those industries is even less desirable, since in both industries it primarily benefits foreign publications.

Competition and Concentration

As noted already, there are really three issues that arise in relation to ownership concentration in newspaper publishing. First, there is the issue of the degree of concentration of ownership that should be permitted within the newspaper industry itself. Second, there is the issue of cross-media ownership, particularly as it affects local newspaper, radio and television holdings. Third, there is the concern over the conflicts of interest that may arise when newspaper owners have substantial holdings outside the media.

The Kent Commission focused much of its attention on the development of cross-media ownership and the control of newspapers by companies with extensive non-media holdings. In adopting this focus, the commission reflected the conclusions of the Bryce Commission on Corporate Concentration, which it quoted as follows:

> It is the trend of one medium expanding into other media areas and of ownership of media interests by industrial or commercial interests that seem to us the most significant to the public interest at this time and the areas where greatest concern should be focused.[58]

The Kent Commission itself stated that "the worst feature of concentration is not the ownership of several newspapers by one company; it is their ownership by a 'conglomerate,' a company having, or associated with, extensive other interests."[59]

The effects of concentrated ownership of the newspaper industry were stressed in testimony before the Kent Commission by Beland Honderich, chairman of Torstar. He stated that such concentration:

> . . . .place[s] in the hands of relatively few people power to control what their newspapers publish. Even if this control is not exercised directly, it is exercised indirectly through budget controls and the selection of publishers and editors. For the same reason that individual newspaper publishers tend to hire people that reflect their opinions, the owners of group newspapers select people whose opinions do not vary too greatly from their own.[60]

Having examined the existing patterns of ownership and control of the newspaper industry, the Kent Commission concluded that "The structure of the newspaper industry that has now been created, that existing law and public policy have permitted, is clearly and directly contrary to the public interest."[61] As a result, the commission agreed that "The only acceptable direction is to reinvigorate the national influence of independent editorial voices."[62] In the absence of major changes in public policy, the commission recognized that "the process of concentration will continue to a bitterer end: company will take over company, agglomeration will proceed until all newspapers are divisions of one or two great conglomerates."[63]

The ideal solution would clearly be to pass legislation that in many respects would parallel the Bank Act—specifically through limiting the extent of individual shareholdings in newspaper or, preferably, in media companies and at the same time limiting the shares newspaper or media companies could hold in any individual business outside the media. Such a policy would require substantial divestment, but would restore to the media industries, and especially the newspaper industry, a legitimacy they do not now have and cannot have in present circumstances. Some companies in the newspaper industry already follow such a policy, but since these companies are, in fact, vulnerable to takeover by large conglomerates, there is no possibility, in the absence of new legislative measures, for companies such as Southam to protect themselves from such takeovers.

Judging, presumably, that the implementation of such legislation would be politically unacceptable, the Kent Commission sought to implement measures that were more modest in their scope, but which addressed what the commission had concluded were the major problems arising from the present ownership of the industry. The approach proposed had two components.

First, the commission proposed that a Canada Newspaper Act be passed which would "contain provisions to prevent any further increase in concentration and to reduce the worst features of the concentration that has hitherto been allowed to develop."[64] Specifically, the proposed act would prohibit the purchase of a newspaper by any company(ies) or individual(s) if their total net assets outside the newspaper industry exceeded their newspaper assets. In addition, the act would allow companies already owning newspapers to acquire new ones only if they owned fewer than five, had less than 5 per cent of total newspaper circulation, and owned no newspaper within 500 kilometres of the paper being acquired.

The commission proposed that divestment be required in cases of cross-media ownership of newspapers and broadcasting outlets in a single location. In addition, the commission recommended that divestment be required where two or more papers which were the sole or predominant newspapers in one language in a province or region were under common ownership. All of these provisions would be contained in the proposed legislation. Finally, with respect to control of papers within a single "umbrella," the commission recommended that common ownership of national and local dailies not be permitted and that divestment be required. In the case of common ownership of local daily papers and weekly papers within the same region, common ownership would not be permitted in the future, but no divestment in existing situations would be required.

Still unsatisfied with the enormous conflicts of interest that would exist even if all of the above measures related to ownership were adopted, the commission went further, advocating that to deal with these conflicts, distance should be created between the owners of newspapers who had substantial conflicting proprietorial interests and the editorial departments of the newspapers affected. These measures would include the requirement of clear contractual agreements between the owner and the editor-in-chief of such papers and the establishing of an advisory committee, including representatives of the proprietor, the journalistic staff, and the community. The commission noted that comparable measures had been required by the Thomson interests when they sold the *Times* of London.

The Kent Commission also proposed that a Press Rights Panel be established within the Canadian Human Rights Commission. The panel would receive the reports of the proceedings of the advisory committees referred to above, as well as copies of the contracts and reports of the editors-in-chief. In addition, the panel would oversee compliance with the provisions of the proposed Canada Newspaper Act, would have the authority to permit reasonable exceptions to the proposed arithmetical guidelines, and would rule on some acquisitions of newspapers.

The Kent Commission's recommendations met with heavy opposition precisely on the basis of the proposed advisory committees and contractual requirements and the Press Rights Panel. In the resulting fuss, the urgency of the need for new legislative measures dealing expressly with ownership concentration in the newspaper industry, and cross-media and conglomerate ownership, received less attention than it deserved. Measures that were proposed as an alternative to legislating a reduction in conglomerate ownership therefore became the Achilles heel of the Kent Commission, largely through misrepresentation of the commission's recommendations.

In May 1982, nine months after the submission of the Kent Commission's recommendations, the federal government announced its response. As a basis for that response, the government acknowledged the special importance of the newspaper industry as a source of in-depth daily news coverage. Diversity of information sources was acknowledged to be a cornerstone of democracy, and concentration of power over the press was accepted as an issue of great concern. The government announced that it would ask Parliament to pass a newspaper act and would amend other legislation to prevent any newspaper owner from gaining control of more than 20 per cent of national daily newspaper circulation. The rule would not be retroactive, thereby leaving the Thomson and Southam chains with all of their current papers and, in both cases, more than 20 per cent of circulation.

The Kent Commission's proposals for divestiture in what it considered the worst cases of existing concentration of control over daily papers were rejected. All or almost all of the papers in individual provinces or regions will be permitted under the proposed legislation to remain under a single owner, despite the public concern over this issue that was noted earlier, and the Thomson chain will retain control of both the national paper, the *Globe and Mail*, as well as thirty-nine of the remaining 104 English-language daily papers. The Kent Commission's recommendation that new or smaller existing chains not be allowed to acquire papers if they already had more than 5 per cent of circulation was also rejected in favour of a 20 per cent limit. In the absence of any measures that address concentration in a region or linguistic category, the 20 per cent limit will permit a single owner to acquire all of Canada's French-language papers and will allow three chains to control up to 83 per cent of English-language circulation. There is clearly some disagreement over what constitutes diversity of newspaper ownership.

Justifying this approach to concentration of chain control in the newspaper industry, the government expressed its view that business decisions made under the rules of an earlier day should not generally be subject to rollbacks. In adopting this approach, the government not only disagreed with the Kent Commission, but also with Senator Keith Davey, who had chaired the Special Senate Committee on Mass Media a decade earlier. Because "press concentration in Canada has become almost total," Davey had expressed his support for a reasonable measure of divestment. He went on to note that:

> There seems some feeling that divestment is unconstitutional, or unfair, or retroactive legislation, or something. It is none of those things. It is the standard method of dealing with restrictions of competition, used more frequently in the free enterprise United States than here.[65]

The Kent Commission's recommendations with respect to cross-media ownership met with a more mixed and uncertain response. The commission's proposal that local daily papers not be allowed to own or control non-daily papers which are dominant in the daily's own market area was put aside for further study. In addition, the recommendation that the owner of a daily paper not be allowed to own or control a television or radio station or a cable system in the same location was rejected. Instead of dealing with such local cross-media ownership through the newspaper act, the cabinet issued a directive to the Canadian Radio-television and Telecommunications Commission (CRTC) asking it to deny new broadcasting licences and licence renewals to applicants who owned a daily newspaper in the same market area as the broadcasting station or cable system for which a licence or licence renewal was sought. However, the CRTC will be free to make exceptions if it believes there is sufficient competition to protect the public interest or if it thinks that forced divestiture will create exceptional hardship for the owner.

The cabinet directive will necessitate a particularly careful review by

49

the CRTC when it considers the renewal of specific broadcasting licences held by the K.C. Irving Group in New Brunswick, Maclean Hunter, the London Free Press Holdings Ltd., Armadale Co. Ltd. in Saskatchewan, Power Corporation's newspaper subsidiary, Gesca Ltée, Southam, and the Burgoyne family holdings in St. Catharines, Ontario. However, the CRTC will be free to exercise its discretion on a case-by-case basis and the real effects of this aspect of the government's response to the Kent Commission will not be clear until a pattern of CRTC decision-making is established. Some of the businesses affected, however, are pleased that the CRTC will retain discretionary power over cross-media ownership and confident that their local cross-media interests will be allowed to continue. Others believe the cabinet directive will lead to a much tougher approach by the CRTC.

The final aspect of ownership concentration addressed by the Kent Commission was that of non-media conglomerate ownership of newspapers and broadcasting outlets. The commission argued that this was the single most serious problem impeding the free and effective operation of the daily press in Canada and reducing public confidence in the objectivity of the press. The government rejected the commission's recommendation that companies primarily involved in industries other than newspaper publishing not be permitted to purchase newspapers. Instead, any non-media conglomerate, i.e., any company whose non-media assets exceed the value of its media assets, will have to demonstrate to the Restrictive Trade Practices Commission that any paper it wants to buy will be run independently of and free from the influence of its other interests. Given that control over budget and senior management constitutes effective control of a newspaper and that no newspaper owner, conglomerate or otherwise, will ever give up either of these basic proprietorial rights, this apparent compromise approach is of little or no value in addressing the problem of conglomerate ownership.

The government also rejected the recommendation that in cases where existing owners of daily papers have substantial interests in addition to the daily paper involved, advisory committees be established and written contracts be drafted with the editors-in-chief. The idea of a Press Panel was also rejected. Instead, a Canadian Advisory Council on Newspapers will be set up to receive complaints about press reporting in daily papers that are not members of effective press councils. The Advisory Council will also help promote debate on the press and will report biennially on the state of the industry.

One welcome positive element in the federal government's response to the Kent Commission is its acknowledgement that Canadian papers provide too little coverage of both Canadian and foreign news. In the case of Canadian news, few papers maintain their own reporters in other parts of Canada, while in the case of foreign news, the vast majority of the papers rely on foreign news agencies rather than paying the cost of having Canadians report to Canadians on important world events and issues. However, the Kent Commission's proposed tax measures to encourage and reward editorial expenditure were rejected. Instead, a five-year program of direct grants will be provided to offer cost-sharing assistance to individual newspapers for the establishing of new out-of-province or foreign news bureaus. The maximum per bureau grant will be $50,000 on a dollar for dollar matching basis, up to a maximum of $1 million annually. The criteria for such grants are simply economic, with federal support provided automatically in relation to industry initiatives.

While the proposed system of matching grants may have some significant effect if it is accepted and used by the industry, it represents a very small-scale attempt to offset the lack of existing incentives for improvements in editorial quality. Total editorial expenditure in 1979-80 was $184.5 million, which represented 15.9 per cent of total industry revenues of $1,163.2 million.

In announcing its response to the Kent Commission's recommendations, the federal government has made no effort to justify the continuation of its existing $70 million tax expenditure provided through the industry's exemption from the federal sales tax. The government's statements also make no mention of whether the $30 million postal rate subsidy should be continued or revised. Since what is involved is $100 million in public expenditure, it is imperative that such spending be subjected to a careful analysis to ensure that it reflects the purposes for which these funds are being committed, while giving the government no discretionary powers related to such expenditure through which it could influence editorial policies. As already argued, there are in the case of the tax expenditure policy alternative measures available which would serve the purpose of improving the quality of Canada's newspapers. The refundable tax credit described above is an example of such a tax measure.

In the case of the postal rate subsidy, current policy can probably be justified as a means of ensuring that all Canadians, including those in rural areas, have access to Canadian newspapers without prohibitive cost. However, the precise impact of the $30 million postal rate subsidy was not examined by the Kent Commission, nor has it yet been examined by the Department of Communications, which has since 1979 had responsibility for the subsidized postal rates provided to newspapers, magazines, books and other categories of "cultural" mail. An expenditure of this magnitude requires, particularly in a time of economic constraint, very careful analysis and justification.

The government's response to the problems of the newspaper industry constitutes essentially a holding action. With the exception of the possible move to reduce local cross-media concentration, the government has opted simply to try to preserve the status quo. Tax policy will remain the same; concentration of control over daily papers will not be allowed to increase; the conglomerates will be left in control of the many Canadian papers they already own, while some probably ineffective efforts will be made to head off conglomerate takeovers of additional papers.

While even a holding action is better than no action, the government's response is simply inadequate. It does not deal effectively with the two primary problems of the industry. While it acknowledges the need for incentives to invest in editorial content, it offers at this stage only a very limited incentive. While it recognizes the conflicts of interest that arise from conglomerate ownership of the press, it does nothing effective either to reduce such conflicts or to mitigate their effects.

A modest minimum response to the conflicts of interest of owners of daily newspapers would be to require that they declare those conflicts regularly. It would be a valuable addition to the information provided by daily papers if once or twice a year their readers could find in each newspaper a list of the domestic and foreign corporations controlled by the newspaper's owner. Surely the same newspapers that press for freedom of information laws affecting governments have an obligation to make available information on the business interests of their owners. An informed public must have such information.

The urgency of action on the problem of conglomerate ownership is expressed forcefully in the statement of principles adopted by the Canadian Daily Newspaper Publishers Association in 1977:

> the operation of a newspaper is in effect a public trust . . . its overriding
> responsibility is to the society which protects it and provides its freedom
> . . . The newspaper keeps faith with its readers by presenting the news
> comprehensively, accurately and fairly . . . The newspaper should hold
> itself free of any obligation save that of fidelity to the public good . . .
> Conflicts of interest, and the appearance of conflicts of interest, must be

avoided. Outside interests that could affect, or appear to affect the newspaper's freedom to report the news impartially should be avoided.

No one has made the case for further action more effectively than the industry itself in its statement of principles. The action now announced by the government should be seen as just the beginning of an attempt to increase the freedom of newspaper publishers from outside pressures and conflicts of interest and to create an objective incentive system that rewards responsible newspaper publishers.

Periodical Publishing

2

Introduction

Magazines, unlike newspapers, are primarily a national rather than a local medium. The national character of magazines led the Davey Committee in 1970 to focus attention on the role of the magazine industry as a genuinely national press with the potential to play an important role in the development of Canada. Existing Canadian magazines cover an extremely wide variety of topics—news, politics, sports, the arts, geography, history, crafts and so on.

Largely because the magazine industry is not primarily a local medium, it is far more exposed to foreign competition than are newspapers. In addition, while daily newspapers provide their readers with both foreign and Canadian-originated content (the former coming mainly from foreign wire services and syndicated feature services), Canadian magazines are, in almost all cases, dependent on editorial content they themselves originate. The principal exceptions are *TV Guide* and *Reader's Digest* which, because they make extensive use of foreign-originated content, have a considerable competitive advantage over other Canadian magazines. Further, while there is a substantial degree of common content in daily papers across Canada, primarily as a result of the cooperative news service, Canadian Press, each Canadian magazine has a unique content which is usually initiated exclusively for its own use. All of these factors and many more have made the development of the magazine industry much more difficult than that of the newspaper industry. However, largely as a result of measures taken by the federal government over the past five years, there has been substantial growth in the industry.

Prior to presenting any data on the magazine industry, it should be noted that no regular national statistical survey of the industry is conducted and all of the information available is to some degree incomplete. There is not even a generally agreed upon definition either of a periodical or of the periodical industry, nor has there been any recent major examination of the industry, although in 1982 the Department of Communications initiated new research which should prove valuable.

Under the broad category of magazines or periodicals, a considerable variety of types of publications are included. The most recent Statistics Canada publication dealing with the industry provides separate data for consumer magazines (general interest publications), roto magazines (weekend newspaper supplements), religious magazines, ethnic magazines, farm magazines, trade magazines, TV guides, and directories. However, the terms used for various categories of periodicals vary and the distinctions are not always clear-cut. Within the consumer category are included magazines on a great variety of subjects, ranging from limited circulation literary and scholarly publications to mass circulation news or sports magazines.

The Canadian Market

Magazine Readership
A survey carried out for the Kent Commission indicated that 78 per cent of all Canadians read magazines. While 30 per cent of magazine readers reported that they read one or two issues a month, 27 per cent reported that they read three or four, and 21 per cent read five or more. Magazine readership was much higher in the 18-24 and 25-34 age groups (at 87 and 86 per cent respectively) than in the 35-54 or 55+ categories (75 and 67 per cent). Magazine reading also varied significantly on the basis of educational level: 66 per cent of those with less than high school graduation read magazines by comparison with 88 per cent for those with at least high school graduation.[1]

Magazine Circulation
Circulation data for magazines can be calculated on either a per issue basis or an annual basis. The latter provides a more reliable picture of the size and strength of various components of the magazine industry.

Table 2-1 indicates the general trends in national per issue circulation. While these statistics need to be approached with caution, they suggest that in the Canadian consumer magazine industry, circulation has risen from just under 23 million copies in 1976 to about 33 million in 1980, an increase of 43 per cent. Circulation of trade or business magazines appears to have risen by over 50 per cent.

TABLE 2-1
TOTAL CIRCULATION OF CANADIAN
PERIODICALS PER ISSUE, 1976-80[1]
(000's)

	1976	1977	1978	1979	1980
Consumer magazines	22,691	26,412	32,412	27,115[2]	26,699[2]
TV guides	—	—	—	6,165[2]	5,873[2]
Religious magazines	895	968	976	877	796
Scholarly journals	13	13	—	—	—
Ethnic magazines	—	—	—	176	112
Farm magazines	2,252	2,512	2,315	2,297	2,378
Roto magazines	9,279	9,703	9,700	8,552	4,024
Trade or business magazines	5,726	6,468	7,634	7,359	8,622
Directories	—	—	—	2,922[3]	4,311[3]

Notes: [1]Reporting in some years is incomplete to a significant degree and definitions of categories vary. For example, only 278 of 426 consumer magazines reported in 1980. All 1980 reportings were unusually incomplete. Data for all years for scholarly and ethnic magazines are fragmentary; for scholarly journals 1980 circulation is estimated at 150,000 per issue, rather than the 13,000 indicated in this table.

[2]Circulation figures for TV guides and consumer magazines were separated in 1979 and 1980.

[3]Circulation figures for directories are included only for 1979 and 1980.

Source: Statistics Canada, *Culture Statistics: Newspapers and Periodicals, 1976-77, 1978* and *1980* (Cat. No. 87-625).

Annual circulation, however, provides a more accurate measure of the relative strength of the Canadian magazine industry, since the industry includes magazines published with varied frequency. To provide a better basis for estimating the annual size of the market and the Canadian magazine publishers' market share, a special analysis of national circulation for consumer magazines was carried out with the assistance of the Audit Bureau of Circulations (ABC). The year for which circulation was analyzed was 1979 and consumer magazines were defined to include TV guides. In 1979, an estimated 500 million copies of paid-circulation consumer magazines were sold. An additional 42 million copies of controlled-circulation or completely advertiser-supported consumer magazines were also circulated. For paid-circulation mazagines, ABC was able to provide precise data for individual magazines, both Canadian and foreign, that accounted for

TABLE 2-2
ABC-AUDITED CONSUMER MAGAZINE CIRCULATION,[1] 1979

Canadian-Originated Magazines		"Canadian" Editions and "Adaptations"[2]		Foreign Magazines	
Copies (millions)	% of Total	Copies (millions)	% of Total	Copies (millions)	% of Total
101	29	88	25	165	46

Notes: [1]Includes both subscription and newsstand sales.
[2]Includes *Reader's Digest, Time, TV Guide*.

Source: Audit Bureau of Circulations.

70 per cent of total circulation, or 350 million copies. Table 2-2 indicates the breakdown of these 350 million copies.

Of the total ABC-audited circulation of consumer magazines, 46 per cent was accounted for by imported foreign magazines and 54 per cent by magazines produced in Canada. However, of that 54 per cent of circulation, almost half of the circulation of Canadian-produced consumer magazines was accounted for by three publications, *Time*, *Reader's Digest*, and *TV Guide*, all of which make extensive use of foreign-originated content and therefore have a major competitive advantage over other Canadian-produced magazines. If one combines foreign consumer magazines and those Canadian magazines which draw on content produced originally for a foreign magazine, then such publications account for 71 per cent of the total Canadian circulation of ABC-audited consumer magazines.

A study prepared for the federal Department of the Secretary of State by the Bureau of Management Consulting (BMC) in 1981 found that 81.7 per cent of the circulation of all Canadian-produced consumer magazines (i.e., Canadian-originated plus Canadian editions or adaptations) was accounted for by English-language publications in 1979, while 17.4 per cent consisted of French-language publications produced in Canada.[2] Bilingual periodicals accounted for 0.8 per cent of circulation of consumer periodicals produced in Canada in 1979.

For business periodicals, comparable audited circulation data for Canadian and U.S. publications are not readily available. However, for Canadian-produced business periodicals, the BMC study referred to above reported total annual circulation of 79.8 million copies in

1979, up from 72.6 million in 1978. Of that total circulation, 12 per cent was accounted for by French-language periodicals, 13.2 per cent by bilingual periodicals, and 74.8 per cent by English-language periodicals.[3] Comprehensive data on the importing of foreign business magazines are not available, but such imports are substantial.

No accurate and comprehensive data are available on the quantity of foreign periodicals of all categories entering Canada or on Canada's exports. However, as Table 2-2 indicates, foreign consumer magazines audited by ABC alone accounted for imports of 165 million copies in 1979. In 1979, Canada accounted for 68.7 per cent of the U.S. periodical industry's total revenue from export sales.[4] Imports from the United States accounted for 93.2 per cent of all Canadian imports of periodicals in terms of their value in Canadian dollars.[5] By comparison, Canada's exports of periodicals have been estimated at 2 million copies annually for business magazines and 1.7 million for consumer magazines.[6] While Statistics Canada's commodity export data suggest that periodical exports from Canada in 1981 were valued at $39.1 million, it is not possible to identify any Canadian publishers who might have accounted for such exports; nor is the figure compatible with the BMC estimate of total exports of 3.7 million copies annually. The Statistics Canada export figure probably reflects the value of periodical printing done for foreign publishers by Canadian printers rather than the export of Canadian magazines.

The Magazine Industry in Canada

Advertising Revenue

Table 2-3 provides evidence of the rapid growth in advertising revenue, especially for Canadian consumer magazines, that has occurred over the decade. In the case of consumer magazines, advertising revenue increased by 156 per cent between 1977 and 1981. This rapid rate of increase is almost certainly linked to the changes in the federal Income Tax Act (Bill C-58) which were passed in 1976 and came into effect on January 1, 1977. Between 1977 and 1979 alone, consumer magazines increased their share of total media advertising from 2.9 per cent to 4.3 per cent, or from $71.3 million to $138.3 million, an extremely sudden and rapid increase.

These advertising revenue data represent the most reliable and comprehensive data now available on the magazine industry and, as already noted, they show a rapid rate of increase between 1977 and 1981. Magazines are primarily dependent on national rather than local

TABLE 2-3
NET NATIONAL ADVERTISING REVENUE FOR PERIODICALS, 1966-81
($000's)

Year	General or Consumer Magazines	Business or Trade Magazines	Farm Papers
1966	21,872	29,650	5,714
1970	26,168	30,809	5,845
1975	70,932	55,557	8,141
1976	67,938	71,003	9,280
1977	71,338	78,120	10,440
1978	105,168	82,269	10,703
1979	138,288	88,117	13,397
1980	152,000	97,800	15,000
1981	182,000	113,000	16,000

Source: Maclean Hunter Research Bureau, *A Report on Advertising Revenues in Canada, 1981* (1966-79 data are Statistics Canada actuals, 1980 and 1981 are Maclean Hunter Research Bureau estimates).

advertising and recent data confirm the relatively low level of national advertising revenue available to the Canadian magazine industry by comparison with its U.S. counterpart. While U.S. consumer magazines had revenues of US$2,932 million from national advertising in 1979, Canadian consumer magazines had revenues of just C$154 million (see Table 2-4). Similarly, while U.S. business magazines had revenues of US$1,575 million from national advertising, Canadian

TABLE 2-4
REVENUE FROM NATIONAL ADVERTISING, SELECTED MEDIA: CANADA AND UNITED STATES, 1979
($ millions)

	Canada	United States
Television	395	7,472
Consumer magazines	154	2,932
Business magazines	88	1,575
Radio	96	828

Sources: Maclean Hunter Research Bureau; McCann-Erickson (domestic currencies).

business magazines had revenues of just C$88 million. If the Canadian consumer and business magazines had earned national advertising revenues at a per capita rate the same as that in the United States, they would have earned an additional $160.8 million and $81 million respectively in 1979 (see Table 2-5).

A major factor limiting the advertising revenue of Canadian magazines, of course, is the spillover of U.S. magazines into Canada. Most U.S. magazines carry a great deal of advertising for multinational companies whose products are being marketed in Canada as well as in the United States. To the extent that such companies can rely on U.S. magazines to reach Canadian audiences, they are less inclined to advertise separately through their Canadian subsidiaries. On this issue, an excellent study prepared for the federal Department of the Secretary of State noted that "One of the major obstacles to expanding the advertising revenue base for Canadian periodicals has been the high level of U.S ownership and control, coupled with the commercial effectiveness of U.S. spillover advertising."[7] In the case of the automobile industry in Canada, for example, Litvak and Maule, the authors of this study, note that while the four U.S. automobile companies spent $91.6 million on magazine advertising in the U.S. in 1977, their Canadian subsidiaries spent less than 2 per cent of that amount, or $1.7 million, on magazine advertising in Canada.[8]

These patterns of reliance on U.S. media are aggravated by the high percentage of the Canadian advertising market accounted for by U.S.-owned and -controlled advertising agencies in Canada. Such agencies, working with their parent firms, are much more likely to see their activities in Canada on behalf of their major multinational clients with subsidiaries in Canada as part of an integrated North American

TABLE 2-5
**ADDITIONAL NATIONAL ADVERTISING REVENUE IN CANADA
TO MATCH U.S. TOTALS, 1979**
($ millions)

Television	406.7
Consumer magazines	160.8
Business publications	81.0
Total, 1979	648.5
Estimated total, 1982	860.0

Source: Maclean Hunter Research Bureau.

advertising plan, based as far as possible on the use of U.S. media to reach the Canadian market. This is not to suggest that all multinational advertisers based in the U.S. and all the subsidiaries of foreign agencies behave in this way, but simply that available studies suggest that this is generally the pattern.[9] The findings of the Davey Committee on this issue led its members to state in their *Report*: "We wonder about the adequacy of laws compelling Canadian ownership of the mass media if the mass media's greatest source of revenue is controlled from a foreign country."[10]

The production of Canadian editions of U.S. magazines along the lines of *Time* or *Reader's Digest* complicate the already difficult problem of Canadian magazines in securing access to advertising revenue. As far back as 1961, the *Report* of the O'Leary Royal Commission on Publications noted that "Canadian editions are the ultimate refinement in the reuse of secondhand editorial material to provide a vehicle for a new set of advertising messages."[11] The O'Leary Commission estimated that *Time* magazine's Canadian edition at that time paid less than 2 per cent of the actual cost of the editorial material used in its Canadian edition. Seventeen years later, *Time's* 1978 financial statement for its Canadian edition showed total editorial expenses of $15,275.

Had this pattern of Canadian editions produced for the Canadian market not been considerably curtailed by federal tax and customs legislation passed in 1964 and 1976, a substantial number of additional Canadian editions would almost certainly have been established.[12] Because of the low price they pay for foreign editorial content, any magazines produced in Canada which can acquire a substantial share of their content from an existing foreign source of editorial copy have a major advantage over publications which must originate most or all of their own content.

The O'Leary *Report* in 1961 noted that at that time Canadian "editions," i.e., magazines with largely foreign content but Canadian advertising, were getting over 40 per cent of the total amount spent on consumer magazine advertising in Canada. When legislation was passed in 1964 which provided a tax deduction to advertisers in Canada only when they advertised in Canadian magazines, it provided an exemption for the Canadian editions of both *Time* and *Reader's Digest*, the very publications that had been identified as having an unfair advantage over Canadian publications. When the issue was examined again by the Davey Committee ten years later, it found that *Time* and *Reader's Digest* had increased their share of consumer magazine advertising in Canada from 43 per cent to 56 per cent, a result which O'Leary had predicted.[13] The issue was addressed again in 1976 in legislation which effectively removed the exemption for *Time* magazine. However, an accommodation was reached with *Reader's Digest*, which left the U.S. company in control of its Canadian subsidiary and able to benefit from continued treatment as a Canadian magazine.[14]

The *Reader's Digest* situation was made possible by careless drafting of the provisions of the federal Income Tax Act, which require that eligible publications must be Canadian-owned, but not that they must be effectively controlled in Canada by Canadians. The *Reader's Digest* set up a charitable foundation with Canadian directors to hold 75 per cent of the shares of its magazine. The *Digest*'s continued ability to operate as though it were a Canadian magazine was also made possible by a decision to permit the company to treat material drawn from the editorial pool of the parent company as material produced for the Canadian edition as long as the material was condensed or edited separately in Canada. As a concession to the government, *Reader's Digest* agreed to expand its use of Canadian articles.

While *Time* magazine lost its status as a Canadian magazine for income tax purposes, it has continued to benefit from postal rates that differ very little from the concessionary rates provided to Canadian magazines. The effect is a public subsidy of *Time*'s advertising rates. This issue will be looked at in more detail later.

Both *Time* and *Reader's Digest* continue to account for a substantial but significantly reduced percentage of all Canadian advertising in consumer magazines. In 1979, the two magazines accounted for 22.2 per cent of the revenues of major English-language consumer magazines. *Reader's Digest*'s French-language edition also earned 16.9 per cent of the revenues of major French-language consumer magazines in 1979.[15]

There is a circular character to the arguments that have been made about advertising in Canadian magazines. The big advertisers and the advertising agencies have tended to argue that there was not a wide enough range of effective, high quality Canadian magazines available to them, while the magazine publishers point out that without advertising support the variety and quality of Canadian magazines cannot be improved. While the existence of a Canadian magazine industry may be a matter of relative indifference to multinational companies which can rely on spillover advertising in U.S. publications, it is not a matter of indifference to Canadian companies producing Canadian goods and services. For such companies, the existence of a strong domestic magazine industry and other media are important as a means of reaching the Canadian market in a cost-effective way.

Circulation Revenue

While newspapers receive only 20 per cent of their total revenue from their subscribers, the corresponding figure for magazines is typically considerably higher. While Table 2-6 is a composite of information from difference sources, it is useful at least as a general basis for industry assessment. For all periodicals, these data suggest that circulation accounts for 29 per cent of total revenue, with the remaining 71 per cent coming from advertising. However, Statistics Canada data for 1975 through 1978 indicate that for consumer magazines, circulation revenue accounts for between 40 and 45 per cent of total revenue.

If one assumes that for the periodical industry revenue from circulation has continued to account for about 30 per cent of total revenue, then total industry revenue in 1981 would have been over

TABLE 2-6
CANADIAN ADVERTISING AND CIRCULATION REVENUE FOR PERIODICALS, 1978 AND 1979
($000's)

	Canadian Periodicals			U.S. Periodicals		
Year	Advertising	Circulation[1]	Total	Advertising	Circulation[2]	Total
1978	210,819	86,900	297,719	-	240,700	240,700
1979	251,075	101,000	352,075	-	295,200	295,200

Notes: [1] The circulation revenue data are based on the Statistics Canada Printing, Publishing and Allied Industries survey and understate actual circulation revenue significantly, according to an April 1981 *Interim Profile of the Periodical Publishing Industry in Canada* prepared for the Department of the Secretary of State.
[2] The same *Interim Profile* indicates that these figures may be inaccurate because they exclude all direct mailings from U.S. publishers to individual subscribers in Canada and do not take account of the fact that a substantial percentage of the copies imported in bulk for newsstand distribution may not actually be sold.

Sources: Maclean Hunter Research Bureau, *A Report on Advertising Revenues in Canada, 1981*, for advertising revenue, and Statistics Canada, *Culture Statistics: Newspapers and Periodicals, 1980*, for circulation revenue.

$400 million. However, given the more rapid growth of consumer periodicals with their higher proportion of circulation revenue, a more accurate estimate would probably be in excess of $450 million, or a little less than half the size of the Canadian daily newspaper industry. Over 60 per cent of that revenue is probably earned by consumer magazines.

· While Table 2-6 suggests that 74.5 per cent of the circulation revenue of magazines in Canada is earned by foreign magazines, with the remainder divided between Canadian-originated magazines and adaptations or Canadian editions, the actual level of circulation revenue for Canadian magazines is probably significantly higher than the table indicates, while the precise value of all foreign imports is difficult to estimate accurately.

Profitability

Until 1981, no acceptable data on the profitability of Canadian magazine publishing had been available. Even the Davey Committee, in its major mass media study in 1970, did not carry out any research that would suggest a basis for estimating profitability.

The traditional difficulty of earning profits in consumer magazine publishing, however, received special attention in the Davey Committee *Report*.[16] That report drew attention to the difficulties of *Saturday Night* magazine and noted that while Maclean Hunter's consumer magazines had revenues of $130 million between 1905 and 1960, they produced a total profit over that period of just $410,600. The tax policy changes made in 1964 and 1976 represent an effort to greatly improve the profit potential of Canadian magazine publishing, thereby stimulating substantial new investment.

As the circulation and advertising revenue figures noted already would suggest, the industry has responded to a significant extent, although expansion of the Canadian industry still does not seem to have kept pace with the expansion of the Canadian market for magazines. It should be stressed that there are other factors that account for the increased strength of magazine publishing in North America. However, what the 1976 tax changes appear to have done is to provide the necessary push to ensure that a substantial share of that growth occurred in the Canadian industry.

In 1981, an analysis of the profitability of ninety-three companies which were primarily in the periodical publishing industry was conducted as part of the *Interim Profile of the Periodical Publishing Industry* prepared for the Department of the Secretary of State. What makes the study particularly useful is the fact that it excluded *Time, Reader's Digest* and *TV Guide*, all of which have, as noted earlier, a marked advantage over other Canadian publishers. The years 1975 and 1977 were chosen, since they might indicate whether the 1976 changes to the federal Income Tax Act affecting the deductibility of advertising expenditures had shown any immediate effects on Canadian periodical publishers.

For the ninety-three companies included, profitability increased from 9.4 per cent in 1975 to 16.6 per cent in 1977 (see Table 2-7). In both 1975 and 1977, companies with sales of between $100,000 and $1,000,000 showed a higher return on equity than the larger companies. However, that comparison is somewhat misleading, since it reflects primarily the limited equity capital invested in these firms by comparison with the larger companies. In both 1975 and 1977, companies with sales of over $1 million accounted for approximately 80 per cent of total revenue for the ninety-three companies and for 82.3 and 88.7 per cent of pre-tax profits in 1975 and 1977 respectively. Just

TABLE 2-7
FINANCIAL ANALYSIS FOR 1975 AND 1977 FOR CANADIAN PERIODICAL PUBLISHING FIRMS
($000's)

Sales Range	Year	Number of Firms	Profits[1]	Sales	Assets	Equity	Profit-ability[2]
0-100	1975	23	−100	1,029	681	− 78	—
	1977	20	− 53	1,227	930	−142	—
100-500	1975	53	464	11,044	5,874	1,575	29.5%
	1977	45	341	10,750	4,007	795	43.0%
500-1,000	1975	11	273	6,901	2,594	823	33.2%
	1977	18	516	12,972	5,601	1,300	39.5%
1,000+	1975	6	2,973	74,863	78,175	36,094	8.2%
	1977	10	6,326	103,060	99,972	40,944	15.5%
All firms	1975	93	3,610	93,837	87,324	38,414	9.4%
	1977	93	7,130	128,009	110,510	42,897	16.6%

Notes: [1] Profit is net profit before income taxes.

[2] Profitability is pre-tax profit as a percentage of equity investment.

Source: *Interim Profile of the Periodical Publishing Industry in Canada,* vol. 1 (Department of the Secretary of State, 1981).

six of the companies had sales of over $1 million in 1975 and ten in 1977.

For the purposes of comparison of profitability, the periodical publishers' results were compared with those of all companies classified in SIC 288 (Publishing) and SIC 289 (Printing and Publishing). The average profitability of all reporting firms in 1975 was 30.4 per cent, which dropped to 25.2 per cent in 1977. While these figures may suggest that the profitability of Canadian periodical publishing is improving by comparison with that of other kinds of publishing, it is, of course, not possible to assume that this is occurring on the basis of results for just two selected years. Further, because these figures combine the results of business magazine publishing and consumer magazine publishing, it is also not valid to conclude that there was a marked improvement in the profitability of consumer periodical publishing, although the figures suggest that such improvement occurred.

Concentration

The periodical publishing industry in Canada is highly concentrated, even by comparison with the newspaper publishing industry. While no comprehensive and precise data are available, the figures in Table 2-8 and Table 2-9 (page 68) provide a generally accurate impression of the degree of concentration.

Maclean Hunter is, by a wide margin, the major publisher of both consumer and business magazines in both French and English. In 1979, the consumer magazines published by Maclean Hunter accounted for 36.1 per cent of the total revenues of English-language magazines which were members of the industry association, Magazines Canada, and for 44.3 per cent of the revenues of the French-language consumer magazines in the association. The *Interim Profile* of the industry prepared for the Department of the Secretary of State in 1981 also suggests that Maclean Hunter's business magazines accounted for 55.9 per cent of the gross advertising revenues of English-language magazines for which advertising data were available, and 61.2 per cent for such French-language magazines.

While Maclean Hunter's consumer magazines are paid-circulation publications, dependent on revenues from both subscribers and advertisers, the second largest consumer magazine publisher, Comac, produces controlled-circulation magazines which depend entirely on revenue from advertisers. Comac accounted for 17.9 per cent of the advertising revenues of major English-language consumer magazines and 10.7 per cent of the revenues of French-language magazines.

66

TABLE 2-8
SHARE OF GROSS ADVERTISING REVENUE FOR FIVE MAJOR CONSUMER MAGAZINE PUBLISHERS, ENGLISH- AND FRENCH-LANGUAGE, 1978 AND 1979
(Magazines Canada Members)[1]

	1978		1979	
	$000's	% of Total	$000's	% of Total
English-Language				
Maclean Hunter	25,512	34.4	31,553	36.1
Comac Communications[2]	14,376	12.3	15,656	17.9
Reader's Digest	9,090	12.3	10,631	12.2
TV Guide Ltd.	8,582	11.6	9,949	11.4
Time Canada Ltd.	6,884	9.3	8,764	10.0
Total	64,444	87.0	76,553	87.6
French-Language				
Maclean Hunter	5,557	40.1	6,807	44.3
TV Guide Ltd.	3,874	27.9	4,316	28.1
Reader's Digest	2,182	15.7	2,593	16.9
Comac Communications	1,622	11.7	1,639	10.7
Nous Magazine Ltd.[3]	633	4.6	Not available	
Total	13,235	100.0	15,355	100.0

Note: [1] Magazines Canada estimates that its members account for 90 per cent of Canadian consumer magazine advertising revenue.

[2] Comac, a subsidiary of Torstar, is involved exclusively in the publishing of controlled-circulation magazines.

[3] Includes *Nous* only.

Source: *Interim Profile of the Periodical Industry in Canada*, vol. 1.

In consumer magazine publishing, the position of publishers of "adapted" magazines remains very strong. The three publishers of such magazines — Reader's Digest, Time and TV Guide — accounted for 33.6 per cent of the total advertising revenues of major English-language consumer magazines, and 45 per cent of French-language consumer magazine revenues. All three publications have a very substantial competitive advantage over other magazines produced in Canada because of their use of existing foreign editorial content.

67

TABLE 2-9
SHARE OF GROSS ADVERTISING REVENUE FOR MAJOR
BUSINESS PERIODICAL PUBLISHERS, ENGLISH- AND
FRENCH-LANGUAGE, 1978[1]

	$000's	% of Total
English-Language		
Maclean Hunter	19,009	55.9
Southam	10,043	29.5
CB Media	1,375	4.0
Whitsed Publishing	1,230	3.6
Pacific Rim	568	1.7
Total	32,225	94.7
French-Language		
Maclean Hunter	1,051	61.2
Southam	463	27.0
La Cie des Editions Horlogères	131	7.6
Publications Plein Air	71	4.1
Total	1,716	99.9

Note: [1] Shares in this table are of gross advertising revenue for the 64 English- and 11 French-language periodicals for which this study found data available.

Source: *Interim Profile of the Periodical Industry in Canada*, vol. 1.

Both Time and Reader's Digest are controlled by their U.S. parent firms, while control of TV Guide is now held by Canadians as a result of acquisition of the firm by Canadians following the 1976 income tax legislation. Until recently, 33 per cent of the shares of Reader's Digest were held in Canada. However, the parent firm made an offer to the Canadian shareholders late in 1982 and now owns all of the shares in the Canadian subsidiary.

While Reader's Digest earns a very substantial share of French-language consumer magazine advertising revenue, the French-language edition of the Digest, *Selection du Reader's Digest*, uses few articles which originate in Quebec. Most of the copy of the French-language edition is drawn from the English-Canadian edition and the "international" pool of editorial material.[17]

In business magazine publishing, the only major company involved other than the dominant firm, Maclean Hunter, is Southam. Southam's business magazines accounted for 29.5 and 27 per cent respectively of English- and French-language advertising revenues.

Economic Impact

The available data on which economic impact estimates for the periodical publishing industry can be based are somewhat limited. The information available on direct employment in the printing and publishing of periodicals is based on a survey which excludes some important companies in the industry.[18] In addition, there is no comprehensive information available on the number of freelance writers employed by Canadian magazines or the total amount of payment to periodical writers. However, the normal pattern in the industry is to purchase articles from freelance writers rather than to rely on staff writers.

While the above qualifications must be kept in mind, a generally reliable assessment of economic impact can be made from the information that is available. While Statistics Canada's survey of printing, publishing and allied industries excludes some periodical publishing firms, it provides a useful basis for assessing the economic benefits derived from the industry's operations. It must be noted that this survey includes in periodical publishing the publication of directories, although they are excluded from most other industry data in this chapter. Directories accounted for just over 8 per cent of total circulation per issue for Canadian-produced periodicals, but for 46 per cent of periodical advertising revenue.

The printing, publishing and allied industries survey indicates that the gross revenues of the periodical publishing firms included in the survey was $450 million in 1979. Just over $208 million of this revenue was accounted for by directories. The value added by both the printing and publishing of periodicals in 1979 was $375.9 million for companies included in the survey. Periodical printing and publishing accounted for 11,132 man-years of employment, paying a total of $170.5 million in wages and benefits.

Canada runs a major deficit in trade in the magazine industry. The deficit in 1979 was $219 million and rose by 24 per cent to $271 million in 1981. However, it should be noted that the commodity trade data on which these figures are based include imports and exports by printers as well as publishers. As a result, the trade figures require a more careful look to assess the flow of editorial content between Canada and the rest of the world.

The Statistics Canada data indicate imports of $310.9 million in

1981 and exports of $39.7 million. In the case of the import data, it is unlikely that the imports include any copies of Canadian magazines that are printed outside Canada, because the provisions of the federal Income Tax Act related to the deduction of Canadian advertising expenditures require that eligible publications be typeset and printed, as well as edited and published, in Canada. As a result, the imports are probably almost entirely imports of foreign magazines. In the case of magazine exports, however, the estimate of exports provided in the BMC's *Interim Profile* of the industry, combined with information provided by the External Trade Division of Statistics Canada, suggests that most of the $39.7 million in magazine exports are accounted for by the printing of foreign magazines by Canadian printers. The export of Canadian magazines appears to be very limited.

Distribution

In the case of controlled-circulation magazines, copies are distributed free to selected households. The particular households chosen are normally above-average in education and income. In Canada, the Post Office has been used for the delivery of most controlled-circulation magazines.

Paid-circulation magazines may either be distributed to paid subscribers through the Post Office or sold on a single-copy basis on the newsstands. To the extent that paid-circulation Canadian magazines have been successful in the Canadian market, they have largely been successful in achieving high circulation through post office delivered subscriptions rather than through single-copy newsstand sales. An examination of ABC-audited foreign and Canadian magazines for 1979 revealed that, while foreign magazines achieved 70.9 per cent of their total sales through single-copy newsstand distribution, the corresponding figure for Canadian magazines was just 16.8 per cent (see Table 2-10). The actual percentage of single-copy sales for most major paid-circulation Canadian magazines is much lower — in the case of many major Canadian magazines below 10 per cent (see Table 2-10).

The problem of newsstand distribution was addressed as long ago as 1961 by the O'Leary Royal Commission on Publications, which noted that:

> The major Canadian magazines derive only 10 per cent to 25 per cent of their sales through newsstands, while the corresponding figure for major U.S. magazines is 49 per cent of those sold in Canada. There is a good

TABLE 2-10
BREAKDOWN OF SINGLE-COPY AND SUBSCRIPTION SALES
FOR ABC-AUDITED CANADIAN AND AMERICAN MAGAZINES,
1979

	Single Copy		Subscription		Total	
	Copies	%	Copies	%	Copies	%
Canadian Magazines[1]	1,012,610	16.8	5,003,890	83.2	6,016,500	100.0
Foreign Magazines[2]	4,854,372	70.9	1,990,513	29.1	6,844,885	100.0

Sample Circulation for Individual Magazines

Chatelaine (English)	64,534	6.5	935,614	93.5	1,000,148	100.0
Chatelaine (French)	14,800	5.3	262,744	94.7	277,524	100.0
Ladies Home Journal	70,766	70.2	30,040	29.8	100,806	100.0
McCall's	89,446	86.1	14,440	13.9	103,886	100.0
Maclean's	30,470	4.8	608,998	95.2	639,468	100.0
Newsweek	27,022	42.2	37,011	57.8	64,033	100.0
Time	45,037	13.9	279,796	86.1	324,833	100.0
L'Actualité	10,790	4.6	224,981	95.4	235,771	100.0
Alberta Report	1,829	5.2	33,509	94.8	35,338	100.0

Notes: [1] Canadian magazines exclude *Time* and exclude television guides, which would, of course, not be represented in the mix of foreign magazines.

[2] For foreign magazines, circulation breakdown is only for magazines with circulation of 40,000 copies or more in Canada.

Source: Audit Bureau of Circulations.

reason for this — Canadian magazines do not receive comparable exposure on newsstands.[19]

In fact, the O'Leary Commission found that, on the average, Canadian magazines as early as 1950 had depended for 82.8 per cent of their revenue on subscriptions, almost the same percentage as in 1979.[20] The same observation concerning the lack of success of Canadian magazines on the newsstands was made by Ontario's Royal Commission on Book Publishing in 1973 which observed that, while Canadian magazines accounted for only 2.5 per cent of newsstand sales in Ontario in 1971, they accounted for 14.4 per cent of subscription sales.[21] The 1981 *Interim Profile* of the industry suggests that "One of the reasons for the higher subscription levels of Canadian-produced magazines may be the dominance of the retail newsstand outlets in Canada by imported consumer magazines."[22]

71

The chain of distribution to the newsstands in simplified form is as follows:

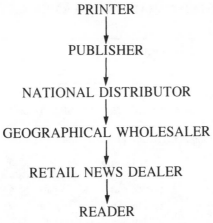

PRINTER

↓

PUBLISHER

↓

NATIONAL DISTRIBUTOR

↓

GEOGRAPHICAL WHOLESALER

↓

RETAIL NEWS DEALER

↓

READER

For foreign magazines, which account for the bulk of newsstand sales, the national distributor in this chain is usually located outside Canada. Ninety-three per cent of Canada's $310.9 million in imports in 1981 came from the United States. United States publishers tend to use the same national distributors to cover both the U.S. and Canadian market. Some of the major U.S. publishers control their own national distributors. The only major Canadian-controlled magazine distributor is Coast to Coast Distributing, a subsidiary of Maclean Hunter.

The major national distributors tend to be large companies which are often part of major publishing/communications conglomerates. The national distributors supply a network of about forty geographical wholesalers, each of which operates with a substantial monopoly in the area served. Two large wholesalers account for an estimated 40 per cent of total sales. While almost all of the national distributors are foreign-controlled, almost all of the geographical wholesalers are Canadian-owned. The Ontario Royal Commission, which conducted a special inquiry into the periodical distribution system, concluded that "geographical wholesalers of periodicals . . . are completely dominated by the national distributors who supply them," observing that "with few exceptions these national distributors are located outside Canada."[23]

In many respects, the magazine industry's newsstand distribution system parallels the system for film distribution, which is examined in chapter 6. Specifically, the magazine distribution companies, like the film distributors, are in most cases American companies which deal with Canada as a part of their domestic market. There are relatively few of them, with the largest eight or nine companies accounting for 90 per cent of newsstand sales, and in most cases the distribution companies are owned by American publishing firms. They, like the film distributors, are not much interested in dealing with Canadian material, since Canada represents considerably less than 10 per cent of their total market.

It is interesting to note that the only major publisher of paid-circulation Canadian magazines, Maclean Hunter, has its own distribution company which was set up after years of frustration in having its magazines distributed by foreign-controlled companies. In the mass paperback book industry, it is also true that the only Canadian publishers that have been successful are those that acquired either control of or a substantial direct interest in the Canadian operations of the major American publisher/distributors.

The growing importance of newsstand sales cannot be avoided. For the U.S. industry, newsstand sales of magazines exceeded subscription sales for the first time in 1977, accounting for 52.1 per cent of total revenue.[24] There are more than 12,000 retail outlets in Canada which are served by the national distributor/wholesaler system, and a study published by the Department of the Secretary of State in 1980 estimated that net sales in the news outlets in 1978 were over $200 million.[25] The same study states that magazine sales at newsstands are increasing at a more rapid rate than subscription sales and quotes industry sources as saying that "the growing increase in single copy magazine sales at the expense of subscriptions is due largely to increased subscription costs and the decline in postal services." The study concludes that "the success of Canadian periodical . . . publishers hinges on their ability to gain access to the wholesalers' serviced retail accounts."[26]

Access to the newsstand market, of course, is of greatest interest and importance for Canadian magazines which have the potential to attract a large audience. Other magazines may require a quite selective penetration of retail outlets in locations where they can be expected to sell. The Canadian Periodical Publishers Association functions as a distributor for many of the smaller magazines which are members, providing an alternative to the commercial distribution companies. For smaller magazines, postal distribution remains the most realistic channel of access to readers. In practice, however, it should be stressed that most magazines require and benefit from some degree of retail outlet exposure. Such exposure is a significant element in most magazine promotion strategies.

In Quebec, the situation in distribution is somewhat different. The de Grandpré Committee in 1972 found that certain foreign interests were making strong efforts to establish control over the Quebec market; that Quebec's own distributors were relatively weak; and that periodical publishing was developing very slowly in Quebec. The committee also found that French-language publications were under-represented in retail outlets.[27] A second study prepared six years later did not find the same reasons for concern. The study found that between 10 and 20 per cent of the periodicals sold in Quebec were French-language Quebec publications, but that these publications accounted for between 65 and 70 per cent of the total number of copies sold each month.[28] While this study did not provide detailed and comprehensive information, it suggests that periodical publishing in Quebec developed quickly through the 1970s. The picture presented by this 1978 study suggests a very different situation from that found by the Davey Committee in 1970. The Davey Committee had found that "apart from a few small publications that specialize in such topics as golf or snowmobiling, there is no successful consumer magazine that is independently owned in Quebec."[29] The same serious problems are at least suggested in the figures comparing circulation and advertising revenues in 1978 and 1979 for French- and English-language magazine publishers which appeared in this chapter. It has not been possible to reconcile the differing pictures of French-language publishing presented in the 1978 Quebec study and other analyses.

One major difference in Quebec, however, is that there is a strong alternative to the U.S.-dominated national distributor/geographical wholesaler system which serves the rest of Canada and, to a more limited extent, Quebec as well. There are two province-wide distributors, Dynamic Circulation and Distribution Eclair, while, in addition to the regional wholesalers, there is a network of regional distributors who cover specific regions and may do business with the provincial distributors, wholesalers or publishers.[30] However, the 1978 Quebec study recognized the influence that distributors can have over publishers, noting that "the distributor and the publisher often have a very different conception of the market, and it is usually the distributor who has the last word."[31] The study concluded that there were still difficulties involved in the distribution of new magazines, or magazines for more limited audiences, and reported that the French company, Hachette, still held a powerful position in the Quebec industry, through its involvement with Mr. Benjamin (of the very large Montreal-based geographical wholesaling firm, Benjamin News) in Les Messagerie de Presse Internationale, the largest distributor-importer in Quebec. Hachette refused to cooperate with the 1978 Quebec study.

Current Public Policy

Periodicals, like books and newspapers, now benefit from major federal tax expenditures. Specifically, the industry is exempt from the provisions of the federal Excise Tax Act. This 9 per cent tax is not levied on the $310.9 million in imported magazines which entered Canada in 1981, nor is it levied on the manufacturing costs of *Time*, of *Reader's Digest*, or of Canadian-originated magazines such as *Maclean's, L'Actualité, Owl* and so on. While no precise estimate is available of the value of this exemption, a reasonable estimate would be that its cost to the federal government in 1981 was $35-45 million.[32] Because this exemption applies to both Canadian and foreign publications and because imports of magazines, unlike imports of newspapers, are very substantial, at least two-thirds of the benefits probably flow to foreign publications. If the sales tax exemption is viewed as a measure designed to encourage Canadian magazine publishing, it is therefore, extremely inefficient. In addition to providing the same benefits to foreign- as to Canadian-published magazines, it also provides precisely the same benefits to Canadian editions of foreign magazines as to Canadian publications. Further, as was noted in relation to newspapers, this incentive is worth most to magazines that carry most advertising and, therefore, tends to help most those magazines that least need such help.

The total value of the postal rate subsidies provided for periodical publishers by the federal government was estimated to be $90 million in 1981-82. This amount represents the difference between the revenue the Post Office collects from publishers and the actual cost of delivery and is included in the amount carried in the Blue Book as a charge against the budget of the Department of Communications.

Historically, periodicals handled by the Canadian postal service fall into four broad categories:

1. foreign periodicals received from foreign postal services under international agreements on the carriage of mail (foreign mail);
2. foreign periodicals trucked into Canada and mailed through the Canadian postal service (mailed in Canada);

3. foreign periodicals printed in Canada and mailed through the Canadian postal service (printed and mailed in Canada);
4. Canadian periodicals (statutory rate).

Until relatively recently, Canada Post received no revenue for handling foreign periodicals received from foreign post offices. International agreements simply assumed that there would be a balance between incoming and outgoing mail. In fact, Canada ran and still runs a large deficit. In the case of all second class mail (newspapers and magazines), for example, Canada Post received 85,933,000 pieces from the U.S. postal service in 1974-75, while shipping only 12,750,000 to the U.S. The huge imbalance of over 73 million publications added substantially to Canada Post's costs.

In an effort to reduce this financial cost, the 1961 O'Leary *Report* noted that

> As far back as 1908, the Post Office Department has encouraged foreign publishers to mail their periodicals in this country by offering advantageous rates. Without legislative foundation, this ''Mailing in Canada'' privilege permits foreign publishers, when authorized by the Department, to forward bulk shipments of their publications to representatives at some of the larger centres in Canada for mailing to their Canadian subscribers.[33]

The rates for these foreign publications mailed in Canada have usually been set just far enough below the cost foreign publishers would have to pay in their home country for mailing to Canada to cover the cost of bulk shipping into Canada plus some financial advantage. What this meant was that the rate Canada Post could charge was dictated by the international rates the U.S. charged its own publishers. Canada had little leverage in this situation because the alternative was to collect no revenue for the handling of foreign magazines.

This situation has now changed. The 1979 Universal Postal Union Agreement, which came into effect in January 1981, makes provision for the first time for countries which are party to the agreement to be fairly compensated for any imbalance in the flow of mail. Canada will now receive fair compensation even if U.S. magazines are mailed through the U.S. postal service. As a result, while the ''mailed-in-Canada'' rate may still be continued as a special non-statutory category, there is no longer any reason to set that rate unrealistically low, or even to continue the rate category. One result of the 1979 agreement was a 55 per cent increase in 1981 in the international rate for magazines charged by the U.S. postal service. In effect, the 1979 agreement prevents the U.S. government from continuing to subsidize the export of U.S. magazines through unrealistically low international rates, and as a result, at the same time frees Canada from the obligation to provide heavily subsidized rates to foreign magazines.

While historically there have been sound reasons for the establishing of the mailed-in-Canada rate, it is more difficult to understand or justify the "printed and mailed in Canada" rate. Until 1979, this rate gave, without legislative authority, foreign magazines such as *Time* and *Reader's Digest* the same level of postal subsidy as that prescribed by statute for Canadian magazines. This practice is particularly astonishing in the light of the analysis contained in the O'Leary and Davey Committee *Reports* which described the inherently unfair competition these magazines constituted for Canadian publishers. For two decades, however, while we have lamented the unfair advantage *Time* and *Reader's Digest* have had over Canadian magazines, we have continued to provide major postal subsidies, thereby subsidizing the advertising rates they were able to offer Canadian advertisers. While slight adjustments were made to *Time*'s postal rates in 1979 and in 1982, the rates remain very close to the statutory rates paid by Canadian magazines. In the case of *Reader's Digest*, the magazine, while still foreign-controlled, is now being given the same rates as Canadian magazines.

While the rate classifications are complex, the basic rate levels in Table 2-11 indicate the difference in the rates charged to each category of paid-circulation magazine before and after April 1, 1982. Three things are obvious from this table. First, the government has continued to provide vitally important support to Canadian magazines through the

TABLE 2-11
COMPARISON OF BASIC POSTAL RATE LEVELS FOR CANADIAN AND FOREIGN MAGAZINES BEFORE AND AFTER APRIL 1, 1982 RATE INCREASES

	Canadian Magazines	Foreign Magazines		
		Printed and Mailed in Canada	Mailed in Canada	Mailed from U.S.
Up to April 1, 1982	3.4¢	3.8¢	15.2¢	46.0¢(U.S.)[1]
After April 1, 1982	4.0¢	5.0¢	30.4¢	46.0¢(U.S.)

Note: [1]Roughly 56¢ Canadian at 1982 currency levels.

provisions of the reduced rates provided for by statute. Given the Canadian magazine industry's dependence on postal delivery, this policy is extremely important. Second, the government has made a substantial adjustment to the mailed-in-Canada rate, thereby reducing the extent of public subsidy to foreign magazines. Taking into account the difference in value of the Canadian and U.S. currencies, the government could raise the rates substantially higher before it would become tempting for U.S. publishers to mail with the U.S. postal service; and even if they did, Canada Post would be fairly compensated. There is nothing now to prevent the phasing-out of the "mailed-in-Canada" rate; the rationale for heavy subsidy to foreign magazines no longer exists.

The post office handled a reported 44 million pieces of mail under the mailed-in-Canada rate in 1977-78. Assuming that the same volume was handled in fiscal 1981-82, the U.S. publishers benefiting from that rate paid $13.6 million less to mail with the Canadian post office in that year than they would have paid to mail through the U.S. postal service, without taking account of the difference in value of the two currencies. Adjusting the subsidy level to reflect the currency differences, the benefit to U.S. publishers was over $18 million. The actual subsidy — calculated as in the Blue Book on the basis of the difference between the amount of revenue received and the full cost of delivering these 44 million magazines — might be significantly higher. In 1982-83, the doubling of the mailed-in-Canada rate will reduce the difference between the cost to these U.S. publishers of mailing from the U.S. and mailing in Canada to about $11.5 million.

The U.S. government has now asked for formal discussions of the 1982 increases in the mailed-in-Canada rate under the General Agreement on Tariffs and Trade (GATT), arguing that any provisions that give Canadian magazines better rates than foreign publications are discriminatory. This move by the current U.S. administration is surprising, given that differences in the rates charged by Canada Post to foreign and Canadian magazines have existed for decades. The key problem now is that the 1979 Postal Union Agreement has deprived the U.S. of its ability to indirectly control the rates charged by Canada to American periodicals. Deprived of the ability to subsidize the export of American magazines, the U.S. government appears to want instead to force the Canadian government to subsidize the distribution of U.S. magazines to the same extent as it subsidizes Canadian magazines. The U.S. case has little merit, since it is legitimate under GATT to subsidize cultural goods. However, the real point may be to try to discourage Canada from taking further action to try to curtail the massive spillover of U.S. cultural products into Canada.

The one area in which current postal rate policy remains a major problem is that of the rates charged to foreign magazines printed and mailed in Canada, the most prominent of which is *Time* magazine. As the figures above indicate, *Time* is paying 25.4¢ a copy less than other U.S. magazines (e.g., *Newsweek*) to mail its publication in Canada and an astonishing 51¢ a copy (Canadian currency) less than it would cost *Time* to mail its publication from the United States. Since *Time* mails approximately 15 million copies a year in Canada, in 1982-83 it will pay $3.8 million less than the mailed-in-Canada rate charged to *Newsweek*, and $7.7 million less than it would cost *Time* to use the U.S. postal service to reach its Canadian readers. In a time of tight financial constraint and with many culturally important Canadian companies and institutions in severe difficulty, such expenditures of public funds are impossible to justify.

The *Reader's Digest* also benefits from major postal subsidies through the federal Department of Communications, although the magazine cannot qualify as Canadian according to the definition of "a Canadian magazine" which was approved by senior officials of the department for use in the development of its *Interim Profile* of the industry. That definition includes a provision that Canadian periodicals be both owned and *controlled* in Canada, a definition that *Reader's Digest* cannot meet. *Reader's Digest* will pay $4.3 million less than the mailed-in-Canada rate now charged to other foreign magazines (a rate that is still heavily subsidized) and $8.7 million less than the mailing costs charged to other U.S. magazines which are mailed from the United States. *Reader's Digest* receives a comparable subsidy from the Canadian public for the mailing of its books in Canada.

With respect to newsstand distribution, the Ontario Royal Commission on Book Publishing carried out an analysis of the problems that confront both Canadian mass paperback book and periodical publishers in achieving newsstand distribution. As a result of a recommendation by the Royal Commission, Ontario enacted Bill 64, *An Act to Provide for the Registration of Businesses Engaged in the Distribution of Paperback and Periodical Publications*.

Bill 64 represented an effort to curb foreign control over magazine and paperback distribution in Ontario. It reflected the Royal Commission's conclusion that such control was the major factor in hindering effective newsstand distribution for Canadian publications and the growth of the industry. The act provides that no corporation shall carry on business in Ontario as a distributor of paperback books or periodicals, if more than 25 per cent of its beneficially-held shares are in the hands of non-residents or under the control of non-residents. An exemption was provided for corporations already carrying on business prior to June 14, 1971, as long as they continued to be under the ownership and control of the same non-resident interests. No comparable legislation yet exists elsewhere in Canada.

Distribution on the newsstands continues to be a major problem for most publishers of Canadian magazines. The provisions of Bill 64 were an important factor in preventing foreign ownership of most of the geographical wholesalers in the province of Ontario.

The legislation has also been an important factor in establishing a somewhat increased level of Canadian control in mass market paperback distribution and, as a result, some improvement in access to paperback racks for Canadian-authored books. However, the act has not yet had the same impact on the control of periodical distribution companies. The relatively limited general impact of Ontario's Bill 64 on the distribution of Canadian periodicals and paperbacks appears to reflect primarily the fact that the recommendations of the 1973 Ontario Royal Commission with respect specifically to improved market access for Canadian publications were not acted upon.

Finally, it should be noted that the provisions of the federal Income Tax Act with respect to the deduction of the cost of Canadian magazine advertising are complemented by a related provision that the entry into Canada of foreign periodicals which contain more than 5 per cent Canadian advertising is prohibited under the provisions of schedule C of the Customs Tariff. Without this measure, the intent of that provision of section 19 of the federal Income Tax Act could be relatively easily circumvented. The basis for both measures is the belief that a nation's domestic advertising expenditures should support its own media.

Unfortunately, while these provisions concerning the import of periodicals containing domestic advertising were passed into law, the regulations that have been developed, as a 1978 study for the Department of the Secretary of State observed, "provide substantial escape clauses for advertisers and publishers to structure their advertisements so that spillover advertising can occur."[34] As an example, the regulations exempt advertisements which make broad references to products being "available in Canada," "prices slightly higher in Canada," "available at leading jewellers in Canada," etc. If such ads are not directed specifically to Canadian consumers, it is

80

difficult to see why such information would be included. There is also little or no provision in Revenue Canada for the administration of these provisions of the act, although they are of basic importance to the development of the Canadian magazine industry.

Policy Issues and Proposals

There are a number of areas in which public policy affecting magazines can and should be changed. The overall effect of these changes would be to reduce the combined level of direct and indirect expenditure of public funds. That effect would be achieved by reducing or eliminating the now substantial support provided to foreign magazine publishers. Support to Canadian magazine publishers could then remain at least as high as at present through the concessionary postal rates and tax expenditure, with additional funds available to provide increased direct support for culturally important periodicals and expanded financial assistance for the business-like development of Canadian magazines, where such support can be justified on a business-like basis.

The revenues of the Canadian magazine industry have been growing at a substantial rate over the past five years. However, the value of magazine imports has also been increasing. The challenge now is to adopt measures that will consolidate the gains that have already been made, while encouraging additional growth in the industry. In developing more precise policies for this purpose, special attention will have to be given to the non-commercial and smaller magazines which serve culturally important functions in the arts, scholarship and so on.

Taxation

The existing federal sales tax exemption for magazines should be eliminated — the resulting savings in federal tax expenditure would be in the order of $35-45 million. In its place, the federal government should implement a refundable tax credit based on the editorial expenditures of Canadian magazines. Canadian magazines should be defined as they are for the purposes of section 19 of the Income Tax Act, with the additional requirement that they be controlled in Canada. The tax credit should be set at a level that would ensure that it more than adequately compensated the Canadian magazine industry for the loss of the sales tax exemption.

Because the proposed tax measure would affect only Canadian magazines, it would result in a significant reduction in federal tax expenditures affecting the magazine industry. Further, since it would be based on editorial expenditure, it would benefit magazine publishers in proportion to their investment in editorial content. The impact would be to encourage high quality editorial content, in part at least by encouraging higher levels of remuneration to magazine writers.

It should be stressed that this proposal would by no means obviate the need to continue to provide direct support to literary, scholarly or other culturally important and obviously non-commercial periodicals. That need exists in all countries and will continue to exist in Canada. However, because the above change in tax policy would result in an overall reduction in tax expenditure, it would be possible to provide expanded direct support to such publications.

There is a second tax issue that also requires attention. There is widespread concern in the magazine industry that the federal government is not enforcing the magazine advertising deductibility provisions of section 19 of the Income Tax Act and the related customs regulations. To the extent that these provisions are seen to be open to abuse, potential investors in the Canadian magazine industry will be discouraged. There must be a regular sampling to ensure that ineligible advertising expenditures are not being deducted. An initial study should be done to determine whether there is any basis at all for claims that violations of the law are occurring. With respect to the related customs regulations, these should be revised in consultation with Canadian publishers and effective enforcement should be provided for through Revenue Canada.

Postal Rates
A substantial immediate reduction in the subsidy to foreign magazines printed and mailed in Canada is a matter of great urgency. If the current 25.4¢ a copy gap is not narrowed, there will almost certainly be a number of additional U.S. magazines opting to print in Canada and, like *Time* magazine, sell advertising in competition with Canadian publishers at rates subsidized by the Canadian government. Since the cost of the editorial content of such publications is close to zero, the development of this model of Canadian editions of U.S. publications, in direct disregard of the findings of both the O'Leary and Davey inquiries, has the potential to set Canadian magazine publishing back twenty years and to do so at major expense to the Canadian public.

On the issue of the establishing of Canadian editions, the conclusions of the O'Leary *Report* remain inescapable:

> The right of Canadians to their own media of communications implies that they should not be served with merely a rehash of editorial matter

cheaply obtained from abroad for reuse in the re-publication in Canada of periodicals which are not much more than facsimiles of those abroad. Here is something which, whatever may be said of its ethics, does not benefit the public.[35]

The rates for foreign magazines printed and mailed in Canada should not be subsidized at all through the cultural budget of the Department of Communications. Such rates should rise quickly to the mailed-in-Canada rate and subsequently should reflect the rate the U.S. postal service would charge *Time* if it were mailed from the United States, rather than, as at present, the statutory rates which were intended by Parliament to benefit Canadian magazines.

In the case of *Reader's Digest*, that publication should be reclassified immediately for purposes of subsidy by the Canadian public as a foreign magazine "printed and mailed in Canada." In the near future, subsidies to *Reader's Digest* through the cultural budget of the Department of Communications should be ended. As in the case of *Time* magazine, the rates should be set at a level that reflects the rates charged by the U.S. postal service for U.S. magazines mailed into Canada.

On the issue of defining a Canadian periodical, the O'Leary Commission made the following observations:

> The final determination of a periodical's character is made by its owner, and the simplest and most effective test of a periodical's responsibility is the citizenship duties of its proprietor.

As a result, the commission concluded that a Canadian periodical is one that is "owned either by Canadian citizens or, if a corporation, by a company incorporated under the laws of Canada or of one of its provinces, and which is controlled and directed by Canadian citizens."[36] *Reader's Digest*, as presently constituted, does not meet this requirement, and its continued support from the cultural budget of the Department of Communications cannot be justified.

The provision of tens of millions of dollars in subsidy to foreign magazines, in a period when many Canadian companies in the cultural industries are experiencing severe financial difficulties, is unacceptable. The cultural support program of the Department of Communications should be adjusted to redirect such support to Canadian companies and Canadian production activities. If this is done, far greater economic as well as cultural benefits will result. In the case of foreign magazines mailed in Canada, such publications are neither written, edited, designed, typeset nor printed by Canadians. In the case of foreign magazines printed and mailed in Canada, only the running off of copies is done on Canadian presses, with almost all of the writing and all of the editing, design and typesetting — which provides most of the jobs and all the cultural impact — done outside Canada. Communications Minister Francis Fox has already recognized the need to re-examine the rates for foreign magazines printed and mailed in Canada, acknowledging that "These periodicals have been able to benefit from lower Canadian postal rates *and from increased access to Canadian advertising dollars as a result of current policies*" (emphasis added). On the more general issue of the focus of postal rate subsidy, the minister has also stated, "I do favour [the] general view that postal rate privileges should be considered within the context of an overall support strategy for books, magazines, and newspapers."[37]

It is also, at present, a serious problem for Canadian magazines — especially for smaller or new magazines — that it often takes three or four weeks for magazines mailed in Vancouver to reach Toronto or for magazines mailed in Winnipeg to reach Fredericton. Many Canadian magazine publishers would be willing to pay a little more, if in return they could be guaranteed delivery anywhere in Canada within a specified period. This problem is not a frivolous or minor one and merits careful attention from the federal government.

Action should also be taken to strengthen the Canadian-controlled sector of the magazine distribution industry. Ideally, this would involve close cooperation between the federal and provincial governments and between governments and the magazine publishers. Increased Canadian control over magazine and mass market paperback distribution companies in Canada should become the explicit policy of the federal government as part of a strategy for further strengthening the Canadian magazine industry. Such a policy should be reflected in the decisions of the Foreign Investment Review Agency with respect to any new foreign ownership of the periodical distribution system. In the periodical industry, as in both the recording and film industries, little progress will be made unless efforts to strengthen publishing and production activity are combined with the creation of a stronger domestic distribution capacity.

Book Publishing 3

Introduction

Over the past decade, book publishing has received far greater attention from governments in Canada than either newspaper or magazine publishing. This greater attention reflects the basic unresolved policy issues that have made Canadian book publishing a sector characterized by missed opportunities and escalating problems which have adversely affected the development of Canada's domestic book publishing industry and inhibited cultural expression through books by Canadian writers. While the importance of the industry in achieving cultural and educational development objectives has been recognized and substantial direct financial assistance has been provided, no coherent and comprehensive approach has yet been developed which would create an industry able effectively to achieve those objectives. The development of such an approach is particularly difficult because it requires the cooperation of the federal and provincial governments.

In announcing a major program of support to the Canadian book publishing industry in 1979, the then secretary of state, John Roberts, outlined the varied functions that Canadian books perform:

> Books by Canadians — books that articulate the ideas, attitudes and values of Canadians and that provide information concerning every aspect of our individual, regional, and collective identity — are essential to the development of a greater knowledge of ourselves. As a basic educational tool, as an important vehicle of scientific knowledge, as a storehouse and distribution system for culture and information, and more recently, as a flexible instrument of mass communication, books are in many ways at the core in any country of an effective system for transmitting information and ideas and for facilitating the development of a shared creative vision. Books have an important effect on other cultural activities — providing the basis for critical debate in magazines

85

and newspapers, and stimulating the development of theatre, radio, or television adaptations.[1]

The most recent information on the extent of book readership in Canada indicates that 72 per cent of Canadians had read at least one book in the last three months (before the survey date of January 1, 1981). In addition, the average number of books read in the three-month period was 5.4 per capita.[2]

The Canadian Market

Market Growth

In the newspaper and magazine fields, "circulation" data are kept — largely to meet the demands of advertisers — and these figures provide a basis for estimating the number of copies of both newspapers and magazines that are sold annually. On this basis, it is possible for both newspapers and magazines to determine trends from year to year in the number of copies sold. For the book publishing industry, however, such data are not made available on a regular and systematic basis. Instead, what is usually available are simply sales revenue statistics.

Despite the inadequacy of the available information concerning the number of copies of books sold, it does seem clear that book markets in Canada, as in all West European countries and the United States, expanded steadily in terms of the number of copies sold through the 1960s and 1970s. In West Germany, France and the United Kingdom, the number of copies of books sold increased by 80, 12 and 133 per cent respectively between 1967 and 1977.[3] While the quantities of books sold in Canada can only be guessed at, what is certain is the fact that the revenues of the book publishing industry have been growing more rapidly than the Gross National Product (GNP). U.S. data also indicate that the revenues of the book publishing industry in that country increased by 324.4 per cent between 1958 and 1976 — more rapidly than the rate of growth of the American GNP, which increased by 278.2 per cent during the same period.[4]

For Canada, virtually no information either on the book market or the book industry is available prior to 1969. In 1969, a major study carried out for the federal Department of Industry, Trade and Commerce by the consulting firm, Ernst and Ernst, estimated the total value of the Canadian market at that time at $222 million in publishers' sales. The Ernst and Ernst study was able to collect historical sales data for 1964 to 1969 from thirty-six publishers. The data for these firms, which accounted for 81 per cent of total 1969 sales, indicated that sales had grown steadily at an average rate of 13 per cent annually during the period 1964 to 1969, a growth rate slightly greater than that of the GNP.[5]

No systematic attempt to estimate the size of the Canadian market was made again until 1975 when Statistics Canada began to produce estimates on the basis of a statistical survey of the industry. The survey was initiated in an incomplete form in 1972 and expanded to cover the entire industry in 1975. Table 3-1 indicates the estimated size of the domestic market for selected years between 1969 and 1980. In the period 1975 to 1980, for which the most reliable data are available, revenue from book sales in Canada increased by 95.4 per cent, while the GNP grew by 75.3 per cent.

Sales of Imported and Canadian-published Books
While the performance of Canadian magazines is not impressive by comparison with Canadian newspapers, Canadian-published books have a slightly smaller share of the domestic market than Canadian magazines. As Table 3-2 demonstrates, Canadian-published books accounted for only 27.6 per cent of total revenue from book sales in the Canadian market in 1980. Included in this 27.6 per cent are the sales of foreign books reprinted in Canada, sales of adaptations of foreign books, and sales of books originated by Canadian publishers, the majority of which are written by Canadians. Books in this Canadian-published category may be printed either in Canada or abroad.

As Table 3-2 also indicates, books handled on an exclusive agency

TABLE 3-1
ESTIMATES OF THE CANADIAN DOMESTIC BOOK MARKET, 1969-80[1]
($ millions/% increase)

	1969	1975		1978		1979		1980	
Book sales	222	476.7	114.7%	685	43.7%	816.5	19.2%	931.7	14.1%
GNP	79,815	165,343	107.2	230,353	39.3	261,961	13.2	289,859	10.6

Note: [1] Estimates are for sales revenue at the point of first delivery rather than retail value.

Sources: 1969 data are based on a study prepared for the Department of Industry, Trade and Commerce by the consulting firm, Ernst and Ernst (*The Canadian Book Industry*, October 1970). All other data are from Statistics Canada (Cat. No. 87-601). Caution should be used in comparing the 1969 market estimate and later Statistics Canada data.

TABLE 3-2
ESTIMATES OF DOMESTIC MARKET SHARE FOR CANADIAN-PUBLISHED AND AGENCY BOOKS, SELECTED YEARS, 1969-80
($ millions/%)

	1969[2]		1975		1978		1979		1980	
Supplied by Canadian Publishers/Agents										
Canadian-published	77.2	34.8%	122.9	25.8%	188.5	27.5%	208.2	25.5%	256.7	27.6%
Agency sales[1]	83.7	37.7	162.6	34.1	246.0	35.9	300.2	36.8	307.5	33.0
All book sales	160.9	72.5	285.5	59.9	434.5	63.4	508.4	62.3	564.2	60.6
Direct Imports	61.1	27.5	191.2	40.1	250.5	36.6	308.1	37.7	367.5	39.4
Total Sales										
Canadian-published	77.2	34.8	122.9	25.8	188.5	27.5	208.2	25.5	256.7	27.6
Imported	144.8	65.2	353.8	74.2	496.5	72.5	608.3	74.5	675.0	72.4
	222.0	100.0	476.7	100.0	685.0	100.0	816.5	100.0	931.7	100.0

Notes: [1] All agency sales included in this table are of imported books. The agent holds exclusive rights to market these books in Canada, but does not necessarily or usually hold copyright, which is the right to print copies of these books.
[2] As noted in Table 3-1, the 1969 data are from a different source than those for other years and should be used with some caution.

Sources: 1969 data are based on *The Canadian Book Industry* (Department of Industry, Trade and Commerce, 1970). 1975-80 data are based on Statistics Canada's survey of book publishers and agents (Cat. No. 87-601).

basis accounted for $307.5 million or 55 per cent of the total domestic revenues of Canadian-based publishers in 1980. All of the agency sales reported in this table are of imported books. The remainder of imports, valued at $367.5 million in 1980, are purchased directly from abroad by individuals, institutions, retailers and wholesalers.

Of Canada's total imports, 83.3 per cent came from the United States, 7.1 per cent from France, and 5.2 per cent from the United Kingdom in 1981. Canada accounts for about half of all exports by the U.S. book publishing industry and U.S. book publishers tend to see the Canadian market simply as an extension of their own.

Between 1978 and 1981, there was a very substantial shift in the pattern of Canada's book imports. The percentage of imported books coming from the United States increased from 76.2 to 83.3 per cent, while the percentage coming from France declined from 10.7 to 7.1 per cent and the percentage from the United Kingdom declined from 7.8 to 5.2 per cent. The increased share of imports for U.S. publishers and the corresponding decline in French-language imports and imports from the United Kingdom may well reflect the decision made by the federal government to reduce the tariff on imported U.S. books to zero on January 30, 1979. Previously, a tariff of 10 per cent had been levied on U.S. imports for sale to the general public. The tariff had not applied to books from the United Kingdom or France. It is difficult to avoid the conclusion that the tariff decision was the major factor in this shift in import patterns, which had previously been relatively stable for most of the 1970s. The U.S. share of total imports increased from 76.2 per cent in 1978 to 78.8 per cent in 1979, 80 per cent in 1980, and 83.3 per cent in 1981.

Sales by Language and Authorship
French-language books, according to Statistics Canada estimates, accounted for $115.5 million or 14.1 per cent of total book sales of $816.6 million in Canada in 1979. This represented no change from 1975 in the share of the market accounted for by French-language book sales.

On the basis of Statistics Canada data, it is possible to estimate the division of sales of Canadian-published books in the Canadian market on the basis of authorship as well as language (see Table 3-3). In addition, it appears reasonable to assume that virtually all of the $608.3 million in sales of direct imports and imports by agents in 1979 was accounted for by foreign-authored books.

Of total French-language sales of $115.5 million, approximately

89

TABLE 3-3

DOMESTIC SALES OF CANADIAN-PUBLISHED BOOKS BY AUTHORSHIP CATEGORY FOR FRENCH- AND ENGLISH-LANGUAGE BOOKS, 1979 ($000's/% of total)

Language of Publisher	Original Canadian-Authored Books		Original Foreign-Authored Books		Adaptations		Authorship not Reported		Total Sales for Titles Reported On	
English	40,291	48.2%	14,569	20.1%	16.581	22.9%	1,042	1.3%	72,482	100.0%
French	6,105	84.1	576	7.9	570	7.8	—		7,262	99.8
Total	46,395	58.2	15,145	19.0	17,151	21.5	1,042	1.3	79,744	100.0

Source: Statistics Canada, unpublished data based on reports to Statistics Canada on the sales of newly-published titles. These reports accounted for 46 per cent of total domestic sales for Canadian-published English-language books, but just 15 per cent for French-language books.

TABLE 3-4

ESTIMATED COMPOSITION OF DOMESTIC BOOK SALES BY LANGUAGE OF BOOK AND AUTHORSHIP CATEGORY, 1979 ($ millions/% of total)

	Canadian-Published Books[1]						Agency Imported Books[1]		Total Domestic Sales[1]	
	Original Canadian-Authored[2]		Original Foreign-Authored[2]		Adaptations[2]					
English-language	89.0	13.3%	36.6	5.5%	32.2	4.8%	511.9	76.4%	669.8	100.0%
French-language	42.0	36.3	3.9	3.4	3.9	3.4	65.7	56.9	115.5	100.0
Other language	0.6	1.9	—		—		30.7	98.1	31.3	100.0
Total	131.6	16.1	40.5	5.0	36.1	4.4	608.3	74.5	816.6	100.0

Notes: [1] The estimated totals for Canadian-published and agency books and direct imports in French, English and other languages are Statistics Canada figures.

[2] The estimates of sales of Canadian-published books within each language category are based on actual Statistics Canada data shown in Table 3-3. The English-language estimates appear to be accurate to within two or three percentage points; the division of French-language sales among Canadian-authored, foreign-authored and adapted titles is based on limited data, but appears reasonably consistent with industry estimates.

$42 million in revenue or 36 per cent was accounted for by original Canadian-authored books. The remaining $73.5 million in French-language sales was accounted for primarily by imports, which accounted for sales of $65.7 million or 57 per cent, and by foreign-authored books published in Canada and adaptations, which accounted for roughly 8 per cent of French-language sales (see Table 3-4). Since 26 per cent of Canadians report that French is their first language, whereas French-language books account for just 14.1 per cent of total sales, it can be assumed that to a significant degree francophone Canadians read English-language books. However, it should also be noted that Canadians whose mother tongue is French on the average report that they read fewer books than those whose mother tongue is English. A 1981 study for the Kent Commission on Newspapers indicated that while 76 per cent of English-speaking Canadians had read a book in the previous three months, the figure for French-speaking Canadians was 66 per cent. Further, while the number of books read per capita by English-language Canadians over a three-month period was 6.0, the number for French-language Canadians was 4.4.[6]

By far the largest percentage of English-language book sales were accounted for by imported books — $511.9 million or 76.4 per cent of a total of $669.8 million in 1979. An additional 10.3 per cent of English-language sales, producing revenue of $68.8 million, were accounted for by foreign-authored books published in Canada and by adaptations. Just 13.3 per cent of English-language book sales were accounted for by original Canadian-authored books.

Of the $31.3 million in sales of books in languages other than English, 98.1 per cent was accounted for by imports. Just $600,000 in sales were accounted for by sales of Canadian-published books.

Sales by Book Category

The market for books is actually a variety of relatively separate markets. No comprehensive figures are available on the composition of the domestic book market. Specifically, no information is available for the $336.7 million in direct imports made by retailers, wholesalers, individuals or institutions in Canada as to either the kind of book being imported or the identity of the importer. However, for the sales made by book publishers and exclusive agents in Canada, which account for 61.1 per cent of domestic sales as well as reported exports of $97 million, such information is available (see Table 3-5).

The largest volume of book sales made by publisher/agents in Canada in 1979 was accounted for by what the book industry refers to as "trade books" (not to be confused with trade magazines, which

TABLE 3-5
NET BOOK SALES[1] BY COMMERCIAL CATEGORY OF BOOK
AND LANGUAGE OF PUBLISHER, 1979
($ millions/% of total)

	English-Language		French-Language		Total	
Textbooks	129.0	25.9%	20.5	26.2%	149.4	25.9%
Trade books	238.0	47.7	42.3	54.0	280.3	48.3
Professional & technical	34.8	7.0	2.2	2.8	37.0	6.4
Scholarly	12.6	2.5	4.3	5.5	16.8	2.9
Reference	72.2	14.5	0.9	1.1	73.1	12.7
Not specified	12.2	2.4	8.1	10.3	20.3	3.5
Total	498.8	100.0	78.3	99.9[2]	576.9	100.0
% of total	(86.5)		(13.6)		(100.1)[2]	

Notes: [1] Unlike Table 3-4, this table includes export sales of $98.1 million, as well as domestic sales. Of the total exports of $98.1 million, $97.1 million are exports of English-language books and at least 91 per cent of English-language exports are of trade books. As a result, this table tends to overstate the degree of importance of the English-language trade book market.

[2] Percentages may not add to 100 due to rounding.

Source: Statistics Canada, *Book Publishing: An Industry Analysis, 1979.*

have a very different meaning). Trade books are books produced for sale to the general public and include fiction, children's books, and non-fiction books in a wide variety of categories. Such books accounted for 48.3 per cent of the industry's total sales in 1979. By comparison, textbooks accounted for 25.9 per cent of sales, while professional and technical books, reference works and scholarly books combined accounted for 22 per cent of sales. Since almost all exports are of trade books, the percentage of sales in the Canadian market accounted for by trade books was significantly lower, accounting for just under 40 per cent of total domestic sales. Textbooks accounted for an estimated 30 per cent of domestic sales, while professional and technical books, scholarly books and reference works accounted for just under 25 per cent of domestic sales.

Foreign Markets

While Canadian-published books accounted for sales of $208.2 million in domestic sales in 1979, Statistics Canada data also indicate that they

TABLE 3-6
FOREIGN OR EXPORT[1] SALES BY CANADIAN BOOK
PUBLISHERS ($000's)

	Original Canadian- Authored Books	Original Foreign- Authored Books	Adaptations	Total[1]
ENGLISH-LANGUAGE				
Textbooks	69	141	1	212
Professional & technical	64	33	81	177
Scholarly	115	45	—	160
General reference	51	114	77	597
Trade books	1,696	81,694	4,369	87,759
Total	2,053	82,026	4,528	88,962
FRENCH-LANGUAGE				
Textbooks	21	4	3	28
Professional & technical	11	—	—	11
Scholarly	69	2	—	71
General reference	84	3	—	87
Trade books	123	434	33	590
Total	307	444	36	786
TOTAL				
Textbooks	90	145	4	239
Professional & technical	74	33	81	188
Scholarly	184	47	—	230
General reference	135	117	77	684
Trade books	1,819	82,128	4,402	88,349
Total	2,360	82,470	4,563	89,749

Note: [1] It remains unclear whether this $90 million in sales is accounted for by the actual export of books produced in Canada or whether it represents primarily the sales in foreign markets of books which are simply published by Canadian-controlled companies, but may be produced outside Canada.

Source: Statistics Canada, unpublished data.

accounted for an additional $97.3 million in export sales. The U.S. market accounted for 72.7 per cent of reported exports in 1979, France for 13.5 per cent, and the United Kingdom for 6 per cent.

However, it is important to note the nature of Canada's reported book exports. Detailed information is available for the export of individual titles which accounted for $89.7 million in 1979 or 92 per cent of total exports (see Table 3-6 on the previous page). Those data indicate that 91.9 per cent of all reported exports were of books by foreign authors which were published by Canadian book publishing companies, while an additional 5.1 per cent of export sales were accounted for by adaptations. Original books by Canadian writers accounted for just 2.6 per cent of reported exports. Less than 1 per cent of total export sales were accounted for by French-language books.

From the perspective of cultural exchange with other countries, these figures suggest that very little of the work of Canadian authors is read outside Canada. However, this would be an inaccurate conclusion. In fact, it is common practice in the international book publishing community that, instead of selling copies of domestic books in foreign markets, the publishing rights are divided among publishers in different countries on a territorial basis. The work of many Canadian writers is published separately by American, British, French and other publishers, as well as being published in Canada.

It must be noted that there are serious problems with these reported "export" sales. First of all, the $97.3 million in exports reported in Statistics Canada's book publishing industry survey for 1979 differs very markedly from the $39.7 million reported in Statistics Canada's merchandise trade figures for 1979 (see Table 1-13), despite the fact that the latter figure includes the exports reported by Canadian printers as well as Canadian book publishers. A preliminary investigation by Statistics Canada suggests that there have been major errors in the volume of export sales reported in the book publishing survey. Sales of foreign-produced books have been incorrectly reported as exports.[7] Actual book exports by publishers in Canada are probably close to $10 million rather than $100 million.

The Book Publisher/Agent Industry in Canada

Location and Language

Publishers based in Ontario accounted for sales of $422.6 million or 82.9 per cent of the total sales of the book publishing industry in 1980, while publishers in Quebec accounted for $78.7 million or 15.4 per cent of sales (see Table 3-7). Although book publishing activity outside Quebec and Ontario remains relatively limited, the sales of companies in other provinces increased 71.2 per cent between 1978 and 1980, from $4.8 million to $8.2 million. By comparison, total

TABLE 3-7
NET BOOK SALES BY PROVINCE FOR THE CANADIAN BOOK PUBLISHER/AGENT INDUSTRY,[1] 1978 AND 1980

	1978		1980	
Province	$000's	% of Total	$000's	% of Total
Ontario	328,916	82.5	422,586	82.9
Quebec	64,751	16.3	78,688	15.4
British Columbia	2,669	0.7	4,688	0.9
Other	2,095	0.5	3,497	0.7
Total	398,431	100.0	509,457	99.9

Note: [1] The table includes only the sales accounted for by companies selling either just their own publications or both their own and imported books. It excludes the sales of companies which act only as exclusive agents for foreign publishers.

Source: Statistics Canada, *Book Publishing: An Industry Analysis, 1978* (Cat. No. 87-601) and unpublished data for 1980.

sales for the industry as a whole increased by 27.9 per cent in the same period, reaching $509.5 million in 1980.

An additional $106 million in sales were accounted for in 1980 by companies in the book publisher/agent industry which act only as exclusive agents for foreign publishers. Most of the sales of companies in this category (73 per cent) were accounted for by the sale by subsidiaries of foreign book publishers of books imported from their parent companies. Companies located in Quebec and Ontario accounted for all of this $106 million in sales.

While most companies in the Canadian book publisher/agent industry are involved exclusively in publishing and marketing either English- or French-language books, there are exceptions. In particular, a number of companies which are classified as English-language firms because most of their revenue is derived from English-language sales, are also involved to a substantial degree in publishing and marketing French-language books. As Table 3-8 indicates, English-language companies accounted for $20.9 million in revenue from the sale of French-language books in 1979. While these French-language book sales represented only 4.2 per cent of the total revenues of English-language publishers, they represented 21.6 per cent of total French-language book sales reported in 1979 by both French- and English-language publisher/agents in Canada.

TABLE 3-8
NET BOOK SALES BY LANGUAGE OF PUBLISHER/AGENT[1] AND LANGUAGE OF BOOKS SOLD, 1979
($000's)

Language of Book	English and Other	French	Total
English	477,313.8	2,127.7	479,441.5
French	20,869.2	75,748.0	96,617.2
Other	430.4	419.3	849.7
Total	498,613.4	78,295.0	576,908.4

Note: [1] Publisher/agents are classified as English, French or other on the basis of the language of the books which account for most of their sales.

Source: Statistics Canada, *Book Publishing: An Industry Analysis, 1979.*

Domestic Market Share

The domestic market for books is dominated by foreign book publishers and distributors. The basis for their dominance is both the fact that roughly 75 per cent of all the books sold in Canada are imported and the absence of effective public policies related to the control of book publishing and distribution in Canada. Because over 83 per cent of all imports come from the United States, the dominant foreign book publishers are American.

To a substantial and increasing extent, U.S. publishers are supplying Canada directly from the United States, usually through the medium of U.S.-based book distributors of various kinds. As Table 3-9 indicates, the percentage of total sales of imported English-language books accounted for by direct imports from English-language publishers increased from 51.7 per cent in 1975 to 56.8 per cent in 1979. English-language direct imports jumped from $158.3 million in 1975 to $309.5 million in 1979. The major increase occurred between 1978 and 1979, when direct imports jumped from $235.2 million or 53.4 per cent of total imports to $309.5 million or 56.8 per cent.

Although French-language imports are relatively limited by comparison with English-language imports, the pattern in the French-language sector has been the reverse. While direct imports accounted for 69.3 per cent of total sales in 1975, they represented only 42.8 per cent of the total in 1979. However, the volume of French-language sales involved is small enough that it does not affect the basic pattern, which is that Canadian book buyers are, to a steadily increasing extent,

96

TABLE 3-9
DOMESTIC MARKET SHARE FOR FOREIGN AND CANADIAN-CONTROLLED PUBLISHER/AGENTS BY LANGUAGE OF PUBLISHER/AGENT, 1975 AND 1979
($ millions/% of total)

Category of Book	English-Language Market							French-Language Market	
	Estimated Domestic Market	Domestic Sales for Canadian Book Publisher/Agents by Country of Control						Estimated Domestic Market	Domestic Sales for Canadian Book Publisher/Agents[1]
		Canada		Foreign		Total			
1975									
Canadian-published	103.0	35.7	34.6%	67.3	65.4%	103.0	100.0%	19.9	19.9	100.0%
Imported	306.3	31.9	10.4	116.1	37.9	148.0	48.3	47.5	14.6	30.7
Total	409.3	67.6	16.5	183.4	44.8	251.0	61.3	67.4	34.5	51.2
1979									
Canadian-published	174.8	78.0	44.6	96.8	55.3	174.8	100.0	33.5	33.5	100.0
Imported	545.0	48.9	9.0	186.6	34.2	235.5	43.2	63.3	36.2	57.2
Total	719.8	126.9	17.6	283.4	39.4	410.3	57.0	96.8	69.7	72.0

Note: [1] Separate figures for foreign and Canadian-controlled companies in the French-language sector of the industry cannot be provided because of Statistics Canada's requirements concerning the confidentiality of individual respondents' survey data.

Source: Statistics Canada, *Book Publishing: An Industry Analysis, 1975 and 1979* (Cat. No. 87-601).

bypassing the structure of the book publisher/agent industry in Canada in acquiring books. While only preliminary data are available for 1980, they indicate that this trend is accelerating. These 1980 Statistics Canada data indicate that direct imports for 1980 increased by 19 per cent, which would bring total direct imports to over $400 million, while imports distributed by book publishers in Canada dropped 2 per cent and imports by firms which act only as exclusive agents increased by just 11 per cent.

In 1979, as already indicated, the tariff on imported trade books from the United States was reduced to zero. Earlier in this chapter it was noted that there is strong evidence that, as a result, there was a shift to a significantly higher proportion of Canada's total book imports coming from the United States. The data for 1979 and 1980 suggest very strongly that a trend has also been established towards the direct supply of the Canadian market from abroad. What this implies is a substantial undermining of the English-language Canadian book publisher/agent industry because that industry depends on the marketing of imported books for between 55 and 60 per cent of its total domestic sales revenue. To the extent that the domestic book publisher/agent industry becomes a less important supplier of the Canadian market, its reduced revenue makes it more difficult to develop a competitive Canadian book publishing industry and book distribution structure. This problem will be looked at in greater detail later.

In 1979, English-language Canadian book publisher/agents accounted for total domestic sales of $410.3 million, which represented 57 per cent of a domestic English-language market estimated at $719.8 million. Of their total revenue of $410.3 million, 57.4 per cent or $235.5 million came from the sale of imported books. By far the largest portion of those imports, 79.2 per cent, was handled by the Canadian subsidiaries of foreign book publishing companies. Canadian-published books accounted for an additional $174.8 million in revenue.

Canadian-controlled companies in the English-language publisher/agent industry accounted for only 17.6 per cent of total English-language book sales in Canada in 1979. The federal government has stated as its objective that the Canadian-controlled sector of the book publisher/agent industry should play a dominant role in both the English- and French-language markets in Canada. The federal government's objective cannot be achieved in the English-language market if direct imports continue to increase and if the vast majority of those imports which are handled by the Canadian book publisher/agent industry continue to be imported by foreign-controlled subsidiaries.

The level of foreign control in the French-language industry is quite significant, but much lower than for the English-language industry. While figures showing the extent of foreign control in the French-language industry in 1979 are not available, preliminary data for 1980 indicate that foreign-controlled book publisher/agent companies accounted for sales of $16.3 million or 26.7 per cent of reported industry sales of $61.1 million. If one assumed that, in 1979, 25 per cent of the industry's sales of $69.7 million (see Table 3-9) were accounted for by foreign-controlled firms, then Canadian-controlled companies in the French-language industry had total revenues of $52.3 million in 1979, which represented 54 per cent of the estimated total domestic market for French-language publishers.

The present high level of foreign control in the English-language industry developed steadily through the 1950s and 1960s. At the beginning of that period, most successful Canadian-controlled companies depended on two major activities for their revenue and profitability. First, without exception the major successful Canadian-controlled book publishers all acted as exclusive agents in the Canadian market for books published by the leading American and British publishers. Second, they were virtually all actively involved in producing Canadian textbooks for use in the schools.

Beginning in the 1950s, and at an accelerating pace throughout the 1960s, the leading American publishers in particular, watching the success their agents were having in Canada, decided they should terminate their agency contracts and instead establish directly-controlled subsidiaries in Canada. Because many of those foreign book publishers were major educational publishers, the withdrawal of their business both weakened the position in the educational market of the Canadian companies which had acted as agents and created powerful foreign competition for domestic publishers. Combined with changes in the curriculum policies of the provincial education authorities which were described in detail in the government of Ontario's Royal Commission on Book Publishing, this process of change eroded the financial base of the Canadian-controlled book publisher/agent industry. With no foreign ownership review procedure then in place, foreign book publishers were able to establish a position of very substantial dominance in the Canadian industry, reducing the Canadian-controlled sector to a relatively minor role in its domestic marketplace. As a by-product of this process, the development of strengthened domestic book distribution systems became dependent on the approval and support of foreign-controlled companies.

In order to understand the Canadian book publishing industry, it is essential to recognize that it is an industry which is engaged in two quite distinct major activities: the importing of books on the basis of an assignment of *marketing* rights for Canada, and the publishing of books on the basis of the acquisition of publishing rights or the right to reproduce copies of particular titles for sale in Canada. In the case of the importing of books, the Canadian firm typically pays none of the very substantial editorial, design, typesetting and artwork costs and is able to import only as many copies as are necessary to meet Canadian demand. As a result, the risks involved are relatively low and, because most of Canada's imports come from larger countries with typically larger print runs, the cost per copy of such imports is much lower on the average than the cost of producing Canadian books.

By comparison, both the investment and risk involved in originating new Canadian publications are far higher. All of the editorial and design costs must be paid for and a full print run of each book must be financed. While original Canadian publications can, and usually do, achieve higher sales in the Canadian market than comparable imports, their greater appeal to Canadian readers does not necessarily mean that they are profitable. One can compare the competitive advantage of imported books over Canadian books with the advantage that foreign magazines have over Canadian magazines. In both cases, the Canadian market can be satisfied by imported publications at relatively limited incremental costs.

Profitability

The fact that foreign-controlled firms handle most of the industry's import sales translates itself into an enormous competitive advantage over the Canadian-controlled sector. Statistics Canada noted in its financial analysis of the industry that Canadian-owned firms spent twice as large a percentage of net sales on design and production, general editorial costs and royalties as did the foreign-owned firms.[8] A study carried out for the federal government by its Bureau of Management Consulting indicates the extent of additional investment required to finance publishing activity as opposed to agency or import sales. That study found that while $140,000 is sufficient to finance $1 million in sales of imported books, it costs $465,000 to finance $1 million in sales of original Canadian general interest or trade books, and $878,000 to finance the same level of sales of Canadian textbooks.[9]

For foreign-owned firms, profits from the sale of imported books provide the major source of equity capital. By contrast, Canadian firms tend to rely heavily on debt capital. Statistics Canada data indicate that in 1977 the Canadian-controlled firms were spending three times as great a percentage of net sales on bank charges and interest as were the foreign-owned firms. These higher operating costs incurred by Canadian-controlled publishers are reflected in their profitability by comparison with their foreign-controlled competitors. For 1977, the typical foreign-controlled firm earned a profit of 7 per cent of net sales by comparison with an average loss of 0.4 per cent of sales for Canadian-controlled firms. These comparisons probably understate the actual profitability of the foreign-controlled firms since there is some evidence to suggest that, with complete control over transfer pricing, many of the parent firms choose to take their profit outside Canada, running their Canadian operations on a nominally break-even basis.

Export Sales
With the exception of a single firm, Harlequin, export sales by Canadian book publishers have been relatively limited. Total reported export sales increased substantially between 1975 and 1979, rising from $29.6 million to $97.3 million. Roughly 90 per cent of those exports are accounted for by Harlequin books. As indicated in Table 3-6, over 97 per cent of exports are of books by foreign rather than Canadian authors or of adaptations.

While export sales reported by Canadian-controlled companies increased from $26.7 million in 1975 to $93.6 million in 1979, exports by foreign-controlled firms were $2.9 million in both 1975 and 1979. However, as already noted, these export figures do not appear to be reliable.

The Production of Canadian Books
While Canadian-controlled book publishing companies account for less than one-third of the industry's total sales, they produce most of the new titles that are published in Canada each year. In 1975, Canadian-controlled firms published 2,193 titles, which represented 70 per cent of the 3,127 titles the industry published that year. Canadian-controlled companies produced 3,556 titles in 1979, which represented 78 per cent of the new titles published that year (see Table 3-10). While foreign-controlled companies accounted for roughly 70 per cent of total industry revenue in 1979 and were operating very profitably, they produced only 21.6 per cent of all new Canadian titles published.

TABLE 3-10
BOOKS PUBLISHED, REPRINTED AND IN PRINT FOR FOREIGN AND CANADIAN-CONTROLLED PUBLISHERS, 1975 AND 1979

Country of Control	1975			1979		
	Titles Published	Titles Reprinted	Titles in Print	Titles Published	Titles Reprinted	Titles in Print
Canada	2,193	1,892	16,563	3,556	2,525	27,264
U.S.	786	868	4,903	751	758	5,036
U.K.	148	250	1,037	227	347	2,259
Total	3,127	2,010	22,503	4,534	3,630	34,559

Source: Statistics Canada, *Book Publishing: An Industry Analysis, 1975* and *1979*.

The publishing activity of the foreign-controlled firms is focused on those particular markets which are most likely to be profitable. They produce a substantial majority of the English-language Canadian textbooks and professional and technical books being produced and account for a very substantial majority of sales in these categories. Foreign-controlled firms dominate both the English-language textbook market and the market for professional and technical books because of the powerful sales base provided by the handling of imports from their parent companies. As noted earlier, these import sales used to provide the basis for the operations of Canadian-controlled companies.

In higher risk areas of publishing, the foreign-controlled companies are not involved to a substantial degree. As the Association of Canadian Publishers stated in its brief to the Federal Cultural Policy Review Committee, ''87 per cent of the books in the areas of literature, poetry, drama, social science, and economics are published by the Canadian-owned sector.''[10] While expanded direct support has permitted the Canadian-owned sector to continue to carry out this culturally essential function, there is widespread recognition that substantial structural initiatives are required if the present policies are to represent more than a temporary holding action.

It should, however, be recognized that individual Canadian books can, and usually do, outsell comparable competing foreign titles in the Canadian market. Not surprisingly, given a choice, Canadians are usually more interested in Canadian books than foreign books. However, Canadians do not in all sectors of the market have access to Canadian books and, even where they do, the preference for Canadian books does not mean that their production is usually profitable. Price expectations are set by foreign publications. While certain Canadian books can be published profitably, the publishing of Canadian books is far more risky, requires more capital, and tends in present circumstances to be less profitable than simply importing books as an agent.

Economic Impact

Since most Canadian book publishing firms do not have their own printing facilities, the economic impact of book manufacturing and book publishing can be estimated only by combining information from the Statistics Canada survey of printing, publishing and allied industries with information from the survey of book publishers and agents.[11] In virtually all major book publishing firms, as noted already, the publishing of Canadian books is integrated with the marketing of imported books.

The printing, publishing and allied industries survey indicates that the book publishing industry's sales of *Canadian-manufactured* books in 1978 were $224.3 million, up from $77.2 million in 1969, an increase of 190.5 per cent. By comparison, if the Ernst and Ernst estimates for 1969 were accurate, total book sales in the Canadian market over that same period increased by 208.6 per cent, from $222 million to $685 million.

As Table 3-11 indicates, the value added by book manufacturing and

TABLE 3-11
CONTRIBUTION OF PUBLISHING OF
CANADIAN-MANUFACTURED BOOKS TO THE ECONOMY, 1978

Canadian GNP 1978	$ millions	% of GNP	% of Value Added by Printing, Publishing and Allied Industry Group
Total estimated value added of Canadian printing, publishing and allied industry group	2,592.5	1.13	
Value added:			
book publishing	197.3	0.09	7.6
periodical publishing	375.9	0.16	14.5
newspaper publishing	935.1	0.41	36.1
	1,508.3	0.66	58.2

Source: Statistics Canada, *Printing, Publishing and Allied Industries, 1978* (Cat. No. 36-203).

the publishing of Canadian-manufactured books accounted for just 7.6 per cent of the value added by the printing, publishing and allied industry group and for just 0.09 per cent of GNP in 1978. By comparison, newspaper and magazine publishing accounted for 36.1 and 14.5 per cent respectively of the total value added by the printing, publishing and allied industry group.

However, it must be remembered that the book publishing industry earns most of its revenue from the sale of imported books. This fact is reflected in the employment figures for the industry. While the manufacturing sector survey indicates that there were 5,536 man-years of employment in book manufacturing and publishing, the book publishing survey indicates that there were an additional 2,200 jobs in companies engaged in both publishing and exclusive agency sales and a further 1,341 in companies which functioned only as exclusive agents. Total employment, then, in the book manufacturing and publisher/agent industry in 1978 was 9,077. At least 3,500 of these jobs are threatened by the present trend towards importing foreign books directly from foreign suppliers rather than through the subsidiaries or exclusive agents of those companies in the Canadian market.

While there are a significant number of jobs linked to the exclusive agency aspect of the operations of the book publisher/agent industry, it is the publishing of books in Canada that generates by far the greatest economic benefit. First, the majority of Canadian-published books are also Canadian-manufactured and, therefore, produce printing employment. Second, it is only publishing activity that generates editorial, design and production jobs within publishing companies. Even with the industry's present heavy reliance on imports, these activities account for 18.5 per cent of all full-time employment in Canadian book publishing companies. These employment figures exclude the Canadian writers who now make their living from royalties earned on the sale of their books. They also exclude the many freelance editors and designers who work for the book publishing industry, but are not employees.

Imports of books, largely from the United States, represent a significant element in Canada's balance of payments deficit. Statistics Canada's commodity trade data indicate that the value of imported books in 1981 was $447.6 million, while exports in the same year were $55.9 million (see Table 1-13). While the major concern in relation to this heavy dependence on imported books must be cultural, the trade imbalance of almost $400 million is also very significant from an economic perspective.

104

Distribution

It is widely recognized that a substantial share of the industry's difficulties arise from failure to develop wholesale and retail distribution structures that would permit the industry effectively to supply a substantially higher percentage of the total domestic market, as well as to increase export sales. The most obvious measure of this failure to develop Canada's own domestic distribution is the degree to which individuals, retailers, wholesalers and institutions in Canada simply buy books directly from outside Canada, bypassing completely the Canadian publisher/agent industry.

Diagram 3-1 (page 106) illustrates the basic channels through which trade or general interest books reach their market. Most of the sales of mail order distributors are accounted for by publications they produce themselves and do not distribute through other channels. By comparison, book clubs sell the same titles that are available in retail bookstores, sometimes printing their own copies, sometimes purchasing copies from the publisher.

In the United States, book clubs, mail order "houses" and mass paperback publishers account for a very substantial percentage of the total revenue of the book publishing industry. As Table 3-12 (page 107) indicates, the U.S. industry earns 8.2 per cent of its total revenue from book club sales, 8.3 per cent from mail order, and 9.9 per cent from the sale of mass paperback books. By comparison, the publishers' sales of trade books through wholesaler and retail bookstore channels represent 13.7 per cent of total sales.

As Table 3-13 (page 108) shows quite clearly, the percentages of revenue earned by the book publisher/agent industry in Canada from these various segments of the market are quite different. Book club sales in Canada accounted only for 1.1 per cent of total sales and mail order sales for just 0.5 per cent of total net sales in 1979. Mass market paperback sales were considerably stronger, but still represented just 5.9 per cent of total net sales, a much smaller percentage than mass market paperback sales in the United States (9.9 per cent).

More importantly, if one looks specifically at sales of indigenous Canadian-published books rather than at combined sales of Canadian books and imported titles, the situation is really much more serious. Book club sales for Canadian works accounted for just 0.2 per cent of total sales, by contrast with the U.S. figure of 8.2 per cent. Mail order sales accounted for 0.8 per cent by comparison with 8.3 per cent in the United States, and mass market sales for 5.4 per cent compared with 9.9 per cent. In the case of mass market paperbacks, it is also

DIAGRAM 3-1
CHANNELS OF DISTRIBUTION FOR GENERAL INTEREST BOOKS

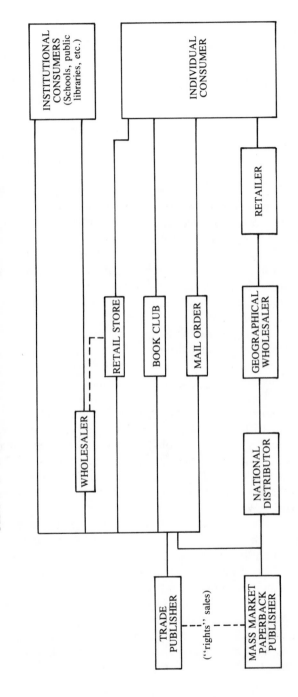

Note: In Canada, some of these channels are either non-existent or so underdeveloped that individual and institutional customers buy directly from foreign distributors.

106

TABLE 3-12

BOOKS SOLD BY CATEGORY AS A PERCENTAGE OF TOTAL U.S. PUBLISHERS' RECEIPTS, SELECTED YEARS, 1963-76

	1963	1967	1971	1972	1973	1974	1975	1976
Trade hardcover	6.4	6.6	8.3	8.4	8.3	8.7	8.2	7.9
Trade paperback	1.0	1.3	2.4	2.6	2.7	2.8	2.9	2.8
Juvenile	6.2	6.9	3.8	3.7	3.4	3.3	3.3	3.0
Total trade	13.6	14.8	14.5	14.7	14.4	14.8	14.4	13.7
Book clubs	8.5	7.8	7.8	8.0	8.2	8.0	8.0	8.2
Professional	9.8	10.2	12.1	12.7	12.7	13.2	13.2	13.4
Mail order	—	—	6.7	6.6	6.9	7.0	7.3	8.3
University press	1.1	1.3	1.3	1.4	1.3	1.3	1.3	1.3
Mass market paperback	5.2	5.4	7.8	8.4	8.9	8.3	8.9	9.9
Religious	4.8	4.6	3.7	3.9	3.9	3.7	4.1	4.1
General books % of total sales	43.0	44.1	53.9	55.9	56.3	56.3	57.2	58.7
College text	9.5	12.0	13.0	12.5	12.3	12.8	13.9	13.5
Elementary and high school text	18.1	17.7	17.1	16.5	17.1	16.9	16.9	15.1

Source: Reproduced from Benjamin M. Compaine, *The Book Industry in Transition: An Economic Study of Book Distribution and Marketing* (White Plains, N.Y.: Knowledge Industry Publications, 1978), p. 27.

important to bear in mind the fact that sales of foreign-authored books published in Canada accounted for most of the 5.4 per cent of sales. The sales of Harlequin mass market titles would account for considerably more than half of domestic sales of mass market titles published in Canada.

From a cultural perspective, it is a matter of serious concern that Canadian-authored books have so little exposure to the public through book clubs, mail order publishers, and the mass paperback distribution system. From an economic perspective also, it is unsatisfying to see that a relatively limited volume of the books sold through these channels are supplied by Canadian book publisher/agents.

The Canadian book publishers are also substantially affected by the size and structure of the retail bookstore system itself. With respect to the number and quality of retail bookstores in Canada, there has always been concern here, as in the United States, that there were not enough

TABLE 3-13

DOMESTIC BOOK SALES BY LANGUAGE AND CUSTOMER CATEGORY FOR THE BOOK PUBLISHER/AGENT INDUSTRY, 1979 ($000's)

Customer Category	English and Other		French		Total		% of Sales[1]	
	Own Books	Total Sales	Own Books	Total Sales	Own Books	Total Sales	Own Books	Total Sales
Exclusive distributor agent	3,032.9	3,645.8	4,955.4	8,263.1	7,988.3	11,908.9	3.8	2.4
Mass paperback wholesaler or distributor	11,068.8	19,279.7	49.5	9,023.3	11,118.3	28,303.0	5.4	5.9
Other wholesalers or distributors	5,719.7	16,329.9	665.5	2,855.0	6,385.2	19,184.9	3.1	4.0
Book clubs	452.9	5,371.8	—	—	452.9	5,371.8	0.2	1.1
Retail stores	25,768.6	93,713.9	9,101.4	28,062.9	34,870.0	121,776.8	16.9	25.5
Mail order houses	1,607.2	2,468.2	—	—	1,607.2	2,468.2	0.8	0.5
Government and special libraries	5,057.7	9,038.5	37.3	204.0	5,095.0	9,242.5	2.5	1.9
Public libraries	7,512.0	12,474.1	61.7	243.0	7,573.7	12,717.1	3.7	2.7
Elementary & secondary schools	44,562.6	72,372.7	3,039.6	4,121.5	47,602.2	76,494.2	23.0	16.0
Post-secondary institutions	14,064.6	36,244.2	68.0	337.3	14,132.6	36,581.5	6.8	7.6
Direct to general public (door-to-door)	40,533.9	87,721.9	730.9	3,620.0	41,264.8	91,341.9	20.0	19.1
Other sales — specified	1,896.4	22,369.7	418.9	691.3	2,315.3	23,061.0	1.1	4.8
Other sales — not specified	12,228.9	20,282.7	14,141.5	19,564.3	26,370.4	39,847.0	12.8	8.3
Total	173,506.2	401,313.1	33,269.7	77,015.7	206,775.9	478,298.8	100.1	99.8

[1] Percentages may not add up precisely to 100 due to rounding.

Source: Statistics Canada, Book Publishing: An Industry Analysis, 1979.

retail bookstores that provided a good selection of books to the public, particularly outside the larger urban communities. A U.S. study published in 1978 stated that "The major problem has been the inaccessibility of much of the population to books because bookstores have been concentrated in high population density areas."[12] However, the expansion of the chain stores has made at least the most popular titles more readily accessible.

While the weakness of the retail bookstore system in the United States is, to a significant degree, compensated for by the book clubs and mail order publishers and mass market distribution, the same cannot be said of the marketing channels open to Canadian publishers. Only in Quebec has action been taken to try to resolve this distribution problem, through a policy which will be described below.

The second aspect of the retail bookstore system that is now causing concern is the growing strength of the major retail bookstore chains, outlets which are organized for the purpose of mass marketing books through extensive chains of specialized outlets. As Table 3-14 indicates, the chain stores have been increasing their share of total sales quite rapidly, from 32 per cent in 1973 to 44 per cent in 1978. When more recent figures become available, they will almost certainly indicate that this trend has continued and that by 1982 considerably more than half of all retail bookstore sales were accounted for by the chains.

In a 1981 brief to the Federal Cultural Policy Review Committee, the Canadian Booksellers Association (CBA) expressed its concern, on behalf of the independent bookstores, that the expanding power of the three major bookstore chains would limit the variety of Canadian books that could be published. The same concern has been stated both by the Association of Canadian Publishers, which represents the Canadian-controlled English-language publishers, and by the Writers' Union of Canada. The focus of their concern is that the chain stores are

TABLE 3-14
RETAIL BOOKSTORE SALES, 1973 AND 1978
($ millions)

	1973		1978	
Chain stores	48	(32%)	142	(44%)
Independent stores	102	(68%)	183	(56%)
All stores	150	(100%)	325	(100%)

Source: *Canada Handbook, 1981*, p. 214.

weakening the independent stores and that the existence of the independent stores is necessary if the public is to be offered a wide variety of titles, particularly of Canadian titles. As the CBA's brief states, while any two independent book stores will carry different titles, two outlets of any chain will be stocked with a more limited and uniform supply of books.

This is obviously an area in which cultural and industrial concerns conflict. Variety and innovation are culturally to be valued, while a purely economic approach would discard such concerns as leading to inefficiency and waste. It is the balancing of the two concerns that presents the greatest challenge in defining policies for the cultural industries. If one accepts the need to protect diversity and variety in the book industry, then there is good reason to try to develop measures that will provide some protection for the independent bookstores. Measures that help to achieve this purpose have been pursued in most European countries, as well as in the province of Quebec. Similarly, one may wish to provide a takeover review mechanism which would prevent a single bookstore chain from achieving a position of overwhelming dominance in the industry. There are, in 1982, no public policies in place that would prevent the existing chains from merging. It is not impossible that within the next ten years a single chain could develop which controlled a third, or even half, of all retail bookstore sales in Canada. In addition, while the Foreign Investment Review Agency would review any foreign takeover of the retail chains, there is no government policy at present which would provide a basis for rejecting the takeover of the Canadian chains by the major retail chains in the United States, although the Ontario Royal Commission on Book Publishing concluded in 1973 that the integration of Canadian and American bookstore chains would prejudice the survival of a separate Canadian book publishing industry.

The comparison of book sales made through the various channels of distribution, including book clubs, mail order publishers, and mass market distributors, reflects the degree to which foreign rather than Canadian distributors in each of these sectors supply the Canadian market with books acquired from foreign rather than Canadian publishers. The result of the weakness of the book distribution system in Canada is to reduce both the industry's sales of imported books and also its sales of Canadian-published works. As a result, Canadian books are far less readily available to potential buyers in Canada, and the total sales and potential profitability of Canadian book publishing is adversely affected, as is book manufacturing activity in Canada.

It is extremely difficult to see how any substantial progress can be made towards the strengthening of the Canadian book publishing industry until real progress is made towards resolving these distribution problems. Moreover, it is hard to imagine that the Canadian book publisher/agent industry, on its own, could resolve the weaknesses of the distribution system. Before examining possible policy initiatives, however, it is important to recognize the degree to which public-sector institutions constitute the market for books in Canada.

The Public-Sector Market

As Table 3-13 indicates, book publishing differs from both newspaper and magazine publishing in that public-sector institutions — including government departments and agencies, public libraries, and elementary, high school and college textbook and library markets — account for such a substantial percentage of the total market. An estimated 30 per cent of all book sales are made to public-sector purchasers. As a result, the purchasing policies of governments and government agencies are a key factor in determining the success or failure of Canadian books, Canadian publishers and the Canadian book distribution system.

Statistics Canada data on expenditure by university, college, school and public libraries indicate that total expenditure on books by libraries in Canada in 1979 was approximately $115 million. Some of these purchases are made directly from the publisher/agent, others from Canadian or foreign wholesaling companies which specialize in supplying libraries. There has been a long-standing dispute over the degree to which libraries in Canada fulfil their responsibility to develop and maintain collections of Canadian books. The *Summary of Briefs and Hearings*, prepared by the Federal Cultural Policy Review Committee, noted that "Brief and brief . . . argued that Canadian libraries (both public and school) do not allocate sufficient resources to building and maintaining their Canadian collections, or are not able to allocate such resources because of funding restrictions."[13] The only systematic examination of the soundness of these claims dealt with books of Canadian fiction for young people. The author of that study concluded that "Canadian libraries are not buying even award winning Canadian books."[14]

This failure to purchase Canadian publications has been linked directly to the practice of publicly-funded libraries buying from foreign and primarily U.S. book wholesalers. Foreign suppliers do not market many Canadian publications. The Book and Periodical Development

Council, an organization which represents Canadian writers, publishers and retailers, has argued that the purchasing power of the libraries could form the basis for a greatly strengthened domestic book distribution system and that such a system is necessary if Canadian publications are to be marketed successfully to libraries in Canada. While the needs of the university libraries are more complex and require special attention, there seems to be no reason whatever why the needs of public libraries, elementary and high school libraries and community college libraries, as well as a substantial percentage of the requirements of university libraries, could not be met entirely within Canada at acceptable levels of service and price. The result would be to strengthen the book wholesaling industry in Canada, but more importantly, to strengthen the book publishing industry itself and ensure that Canadian publications are marketed effectively to libraries in Canada. From both an economic and cultural perspective, this is a desirable objective.

The book industry itself, with assistance from the federal government, has already taken steps to improve book ordering in Canada, taking advantage of electronic data processing and transmission technologies. On the basis of a major research study, the industry established the Canadian Telebook Agency in November 1981 to create a common computerized data base for the industry as a whole. The agency will also have responsibility for coordinating the development of an automated industry system for rapid processing of orders from terminals in bookstores or institutions anywhere in Canada.

However, this problem of efficient supply of books to library and other markets has a circular character. It is difficult for the industry to justify the investments necessary to modernize its service structure unless the government-funded institutions have made a commitment to make more systematic use of Canadian suppliers. On the other hand, it is difficult for the governments and the institutions they fund to make this commitment until they are convinced they will be well served. The problem will only be resolved if both industry and the government-funded institutions are able to work closely together. It is not at all encouraging to note that, despite the initiatives the industry has taken, the Canadian Library Association continues to insist "that libraries must remain free to buy foreign books and periodicals wherever it is most advantageous to them."[15]

The position the Canadian Library Association has taken ignores completely the fact that almost all libraries are government-funded institutions and that the governments which fund them are also, at the provincial as well as the federal level, spending tens of millions of dollars to try to strengthen Canadian writing and the Canadian book publishing industry. At present, there is no doubt that, to a significant degree, the efforts governments are making to develop writing and publishing in Canada are undercut by the purchasing policies of Canadian libraries which are funded by the very same governments.

The second major part of the public sector is, of course, the textbook market at the elementary, high school and post-secondary levels. In 1979, the Canadian book publisher/agent industry reported revenues of $149.4 million from the sale of textbooks. This represented 26 per cent of the industry's total revenues of $576.9 million from domestic and export sales, and a higher percentage (31 per cent) of domestic sales. As Table 3-15 indicates, 59 per cent of total revenue from textbook sales was accounted for by sales of Canadian-published texts, 41 per cent by the sale of imported texts. Of the total sales of Canadian-published textbooks, original Canadian-authored textbooks accounted for an estimated $50 million in revenue, adaptations for $31 million, and Canadian-produced copies of foreign-authored texts for $7 million in sales.[16] Net sales of imported texts accounted for $61.7 million in revenue. Seventy-nine per cent of the industry's sales of Canadian-published texts were made in the elementary and high school market, the remaining 21 per cent at the post-secondary level.

The development of Canadian-authored and -manufactured textbooks for use in classrooms in elementary and high schools has occurred as a result of government policy. In Ontario and Quebec in particular, it has traditionally been an important matter of public policy that the textbooks used in the schools should be developed specifically by Canadian educators for Canadian use, and that the editing, typesetting and printing of such texts should be done in Canada.

In the English-language sector, the policy of the Ontario government was particularly firm on this matter, at least until the 1960s. Because per pupil expenditure was high and because the Ontario market represented a major portion of the national market, the province's policies provided the basis for the development of a strong educational publishing industry and a significant volume of book manufacturing. However, changes in Ontario's curriculum and textbook approval systems, combined with a decentralization of authority to the local school boards and a decision in 1969 not to allocate specific funds for textbooks and learning materials, created a crisis in the industry. The Ontario Royal Commission on Book Publishing, established to

TABLE 3-15
NET BOOK SALES BY COMMERCIAL CATEGORY OF BOOK AND LANGUAGE OF CANADIAN BOOK PUBLISHER/AGENT, 1979
($000's)

	English and Other		French		Total		
	Own Books[1]	Imported Books	Own Books	Imported Books	Own Books	Imported Books	Total
Textbooks							
elementary, high school	56,443.1	19,206.6	12,953.3	2,230.4	69,396.4	21,491.0	90,887.4
post-secondary	13,988.9	26,530.7	3,962.1	771.1	17,951.0	27,301.8	45,252.8
level not specified	86.6	12,641.5	263.5	294.9	350.1	12,936.4	13,286.5
	70,518.6	58,432.8	17,178.9	3,296.4	87,697.4	61,729.2	149,426.7
Trade books	156,113.2	81,868.3	10,135.8	32,172.1	166,249.0	114,040.4	280,289.4
Professional & technical	19,127.3	15,627.7	524.7	1,172.1	19,652.0	17,325.1	36,977.1
Scholarly	3,173.6	9,393.3	237.6	4,016.5	3,411.2	13,409.8	16,821.0
Reference	10,302.0	61,858.8	723.6	224.8	11,025.6	62,083.6	73,109.2
Not specified	9,848.7	2,349.1	5,462.9	2,624.3	15,311.6	4,973.4	20,285.0
Total	269,083.4	229,530.0	34,263.5	44,031.5	303,346.9	273,561.5	576,908.4

Note: [1] "Own Books" includes foreign books reprinted in Canada, adaptations of foreign books, and original Canadian publications. This table includes export as well as domestic sales, which is reflected almost entirely in the high figure for English-language sales of Canadian-published or "own" trade books.

Source: Statistics Canada, *Book Publishing: An Industry Analysis, 1979.*

investigate the problem, reported to the Ontario government in 1973 that

> While our educational system has been developing its present admirable flexibility, the de facto displacement of Canadian textbooks in our schools by foreign learning materials of every kind has been proceeding apace.[17]

Ontario did not act on the major recommendations of its Royal Commission and is now, like the other provinces, in a position in which it has difficulty in getting the Canadian texts it needs to implement its curriculum. Because per pupil expenditure in Ontario has fallen to the lowest level in Canada, the province no longer represents the major market for publishers that it once was (see Table 3-16). Ontario now accounts for approximately 30 per cent of the English-language Canadian textbook market. While the province still gives preference to Canadian-authored and -manufactured texts, it has had to implement subsidy programs to permit the development and publication of Canadian texts and learning materials. In implementing these programs, worth approximately $4 million annually, the Ontario

TABLE 3-16
EXPENDITURES ON TEXTBOOKS FOR NINE PROVINCES,[1]
1978-79

Province	Enrolment	Total Expenditure on Texts	Per Pupil Expenditure on Texts
Prince Edward Island	27,212	$ 931,500	$34.23
Newfoundland	153,473	3,800,000	24.76
Alberta	447,989	9,889,093	22.07
British Columbia	544,901	9,775,876	17.94
Manitoba	232,308	3,716,928	16.00
Nova Scotia	196,227	2,943,405	16.00
Saskatchewan	220,858	3,017,860	13.65
New Brunswick	160,673	2,040,424	12.70
Ontario	1,833,047	19,998,665	10.91

Note: [1] Data for Quebec are not available.

Sources: Canadian Book Publishers Council, based on reports from Provincial Book Bureaus, and Ontario Ministry of Education, "Provincial Summary: Expenditures for Textbooks and Reference Books, and Library Books 20/9/79."

Ministry of Education rejected the Royal Commission's recommendation that such assistance be restricted to Canadian-controlled book publishing firms. As a result, a substantial majority of the development, production and promotion subsidy provided has been given to foreign-controlled companies. By contrast, the Ontario Arts Council, the Ontario Development Corporation, and the Ontario Ministry of Citizenship and Culture, all of which provide substantial loan and direct grant support to the industry, restrict their support to Canadian-owned and -controlled firms, as recommended by the Royal Commission.

In other provinces, there appears to be growing concern to have available textbooks written by Canadians that meet the curriculum requirements established by Canadian educational authorities. In a general sense, the findings of the report of the Organization for Economic Cooperation and Development on Canada's educational system seem to have provided a focus for the concern over the absence of objectives for Canada's national educational system. A survey carried out by the president of the Canadian Educational Association in 1980 revealed that among a wide range of individuals in the educational system throughout Canada, there was a recognition of the need for a national office of education which could deal with interprovincial, federal-provincial and international issues related to education. One suggestion made was that an important function of that office might be to support the publication of Canadian textbooks so that Canada would not be so dependent on American classroom material.[18] In fact, a national office could provide a focus for research, policy development and programs that might permit the coordination required to ensure that national, regional and provincial needs for Canadian textbooks are better served.

At the post-secondary level, the textbook market is, of course, not subject to the same centralized curriculum and textbook approval system. Instead, within each university or college's broad framework of educational programs and courses offered, individual instructors or professors establish lists of required or recommended texts. In the 1975 report of the Commission on Canadian Studies, the commissioner, T.H.B. Symons, noted that the absence of an adequate range of suitable Canadian textbooks and other academic publications was a major obstacle to the development of Canadian studies in post-secondary educational institutions.[19] The problem is especially serious in French-language educational institutions. A recent seminar on Scholarly Communication and Canadian Studies, funded by the Social

Science and Humanities Research Council, reflected this concern. There is a growing recognition of the need to provide significant government subsidy if an acceptable range of Canadian post-secondary textbooks is to be available.

What should be clear from this examination of the public-sector book market is the potential — through a more cooperative approach by governments to curriculum, textbook selection, library procurement policy and, where necessary, direct assistance programs — to create greater publishing opportunities for Canadian writers, to strengthen the book publishing and distribution system, and to provide the educational system and the public with a broader selection of high quality Canadian publications. Almost all of the public-sector market is within the jurisdiction of the provincial governments. As a result, before any serious actions were taken, it would have to be clear to the provinces that writers and publishers located everywhere in Canada, as well as the public in every province, would benefit.

It should be noted that there is also the potential for the provincial governments to use their purchasing power in a way that strengthens the retail bookstore system. The Quebec government has used its purchasing power since passage of the 1971 Booksellers Act to direct government purchases through accredited bookstores rather than buying directly from publishers or from wholesalers. Revised legislation, Bill 51, which was passed in 1979, excludes textbooks from this requirement, but still directs school and public library purchases through the accredited bookstores. The system is used to reward bookstores which volunteer to meet established standards, including standards related to the range of Canadian books carried in stock. Other booksellers are free to operate in Quebec, but do not benefit from government purchases.

The results of this Quebec policy are suggested in Table 3-17. While just 23.6 per cent of the English-language industry's sales are channelled through retail bookstores, the comparable figure for the French-language industry is at least 40.8 per cent. Given the relatively high level of French-language industry sales not allocated to a specific customer category (28.5 per cent), the actual level of sales through retail bookstores may well be even higher than 40.8 per cent. It is worth considering the possibility that, if comparable policies had been in effect in other provinces, retail bookstores would have accounted for English-language industry sales of over $160 million in 1979 rather than $94 million. If this change occurred, the greatly strengthened retail bookstore system would, as it has in Quebec, greatly improve public access to trade books, and particularly to Canadian trade books.

TABLE 3-17

**PERCENTAGE OF DOMESTIC SALES BY CUSTOMER CATEGORY
AND LANGUAGE OF PUBLISHER/AGENT, 1979**

	English and Other Language Publishers	French-Language Publishers
Retail stores	23.6	40.8
Public libraries	3.1	0.4
Government & special libraries	2.3	0.3
Elementary & secondary schools	18.2	6.0
Post-secondary institutions	9.1	0.5
Library wholesalers or distributors	4.1	4.2
Mass paperback wholesalers or distributors	4.8	13.1
Book clubs	1.4	—
Mail order houses	0.6	—
Direct to the general public	22.1	5.3
Other sales — specified	5.6	1.0
Other sales — not specified	5.1	28.5

Source: Statistics Canada, *Book Publishing: An Industry Analysis, 1979.*

Current Public Policy

Development of a Canadian-controlled Book Publishing Industry

In both magazine and newspaper publishing, the federal government has pursued a policy that demonstrates its conviction that Canadian newspapers and magazines ought to be owned by and under the editorial and managerial control of Canadians. That policy has been reflected in the Income Tax Act since 1965 and is now evident in the postal rate policy which the government has been pursuing since 1979. However, as of 1982, legislative measures based on a parallel concern regarding book publishing are not yet in place, reflecting the relatively more recent recognition of the difficulties that will have to be addressed if a strong Canadian-controlled book publishing industry is to be developed and maintained.

Both at the federal and provincial levels, studies have been conducted that provide clear evidence of the cultural dangers and economic disadvantages inherent in a high level of foreign ownership and control of the book publishing industry. The strong financial advantages of the foreign-controlled book publishing firms are well understood and the need for intervention to assist the Canadian-controlled sector of the industry, and to support directly or improve the environment for the publication of books written by Canadians, has been recognized.

Because the level of foreign control over book publishing in Canada is extremely high, the conclusions of the various studies that have been published over the past decade deserve closer attention. Three general approaches to this problem can be identified. The first focuses attention on the issue of editorial sovereignty: Should foreign individuals and companies have ultimate decision-making control in an industry responsible for choosing which intellectual and imaginative works by Canadians ought to appear in book form? The second approach involves an examination of the degree to which foreign and Canadian-owned firms are involved in the publishing of original books by Canadian writers. The third approach looks at the question of whether the foreign-controlled firms have an effect on the environment within which Canadian books are published.

Whether in principle it is important for Canadians to have ultimate control over publishing decisions is an issue that was addressed at length by the 1961 Royal Commission on Publications. The commission concluded that

> Canada's particular responsibilities, her government, her constitutional structure, her ideals and aspirations, her memories and milestones, even her discords, are facts in her existence which cannot be approached understandingly or usefully by communications media owned and controlled in another country, even though that country be friendly.[20]

In connection with the book publishing industry and the whole of the book trade, this issue was also addressed in the recent Quebec White Paper on cultural development. The White Paper states that "The book industries (publishing, distribution, sales) are a powerful force for the cultural expression of a community" and "It is intolerable for any country, for any people or national group, that these should be in foreign hands."[21]

A similar concern with this aspect of foreign control was expressed by the Ontario Royal Commission on Book Publishing. The commission argued that "The dangers of foreign domination can be seen most easily in educational publishing, although they could be pointed to in other areas as well" and pointed out that "It hardly seems necessary to argue that the history of our own country in relation to North America and the world should be presented from a Canadian perspective."[22] The final report of the commission noted that certain kinds of books would be unlikely to be published by firms whose ultimate responsibility was to foreign owners. As an example, a long list of books on issues related to Canadian economic and cultural sovereignty was cited, not one of which was published by a foreign-controlled firm. The commissioners concluded that such works were extremely unlikely to be produced by foreign-controlled firms and that "It is not necessary to be an ultra-nationalist to say that this country must always possess a publishing facility which is prepared to present, and promote if necessary, every point of view on such basic issues."[23] However, the commission report tempered these comments by observing that there was much more competition in book publishing than in the other media and that, at least in the production of books for the general public, a cross-section of points of view on every subject was likely to become available in the situation which prevailed at that time. The commissioners then turned their attention to the importance of maintaining a balance between foreign- and Canadian-controlled firms if a wide range of Canadian books and the full spectrum of Canadian opinion were to continue to be available.

While most analysis of the industry has given attention to the importance of the location of ultimate editorial control, it should not be surprising that representatives of the foreign-controlled subsidiaries all claim that their parent firms have no direct involvement in editorial decision-making in Canada. However, even if these assurances were accepted, there are other indirect but equally powerful means through which editorial decision-making can be affected by the parent firm. The principal means of control is through the parent firm's selection of the senior staff of the subsidiary. Through this control the parent firms decide who will be in control of the publishing activity of the subsidiary. Further, the senior staff of the subsidiary cannot help being conscious of who their employer is and of what his interests are.

Information has already been provided indicating the degree to which foreign- and Canadian-controlled firms are involved in publishing Canadian books. As Table 3-9 indicates, there is no doubt that the foreign-controlled sector of the industry accounts for substantial sales of Canadian books. However, it is the Canadian-controlled sector of the industry that accounts for a very substantial majority of the original Canadian books being published. Most of the publishing of original Canadian-authored books that the foreign-owned firms have done has been for the textbook market. These titles are produced to meet the requirements established by the various educational authorities in the provincial governments. However, despite these provincial government requirements the sale of foreign textbooks and adaptations of foreign textbooks to Canadian schools has increased substantially since the early 1960s. The Ontario Royal Commission devoted much of its attention to this problem and, as noted already, reached the conclusion that even in Ontario, which had maintained a formal requirement that, wherever possible, texts be written by Canadians and printed in Canada, "the de facto displacement of Canadian textbooks in our schools by foreign learning materials of every kind has been proceeding apace." Therefore, while in the past this was a market sector for which publishers were obliged to produce original Canadian books, the effective compulsion to do so appears to have diminished.

Outside the textbook area, the involvement of foreign-controlled publishers in producing books by Canadian writers has been slight. In 1979, although foreign-owned firms accounted for 70 per cent of English-language publishers' sales, they produced only 15 per cent of all new books about Canada and just 3 per cent of all books of Canadian literature. Commenting on this disproportion in the publishing of culturally important Canadian books by Canadian and foreign-owned publishers, the Ontario Royal Commission stated that "For the latter, apparently, Canadian literature suffers all the commercial drawbacks of a regional literature."[24] By contrast, as the Association of Canadian Publishers stated in an August 27, 1982 letter to the Honourable Herb Gray, at that time the federal minister of industry, "This commitment to Canadian authors and their work is natural for publishers who see Canada as their primary market, who understand this nation and its cultural needs and who have a commitment to serving those needs."

The third aspect of the impact of foreign-controlled subsidiaries that requires attention is their potential to change the environment in which Canadian publishing occurs. The Ontario Royal Commission report noted that "there is likely to be a period following the immigration of a foreign publishing firm during which it will accommodate itself, often remarkably well, to the regional interests of the Canadian market." During this period, the commissioners noted, the subsidiary was "likely to count aloud its Canadian publishing projects and to profess. . .a desire to publish still more." However, the commission continued:

At the same time, it is likely to be boosting at every opportunity the editorial bargains that could be available if there were only a wider use made of foreign copyrights, particularly in Ontario, where Canadian preference is strongest. It will constantly allude to the publications of its home office which embody research that 'cost millions.' And it is likely to decry any regulations designed to create a still more congenial market for the Canadian-manufactured book, even though it publishes Canadian books itself.[25]

In fact, the commission noted that the foreign-controlled firms had made efforts to have existing regulations, whose purpose is to encourage the production of original Canadian books, changed. Specifically, the commission noted that "Another pressure resulting from the operation of the subsidiaries at the elementary and high school levels has been for the modification or elimination of the Canadian preference policy—in the Ontario Department of Education's listings on Circular 14."[26] (Circular 14 is Ontario's list of learning materials approved for use in elementary and high school courses.) As the foreign-controlled sector of the English-language industry has expanded, this pressure has increased.

The general and growing dominance by foreign-controlled firms also affects the environment within which Canadian trade books are published. The foreign-owned firms, as noted elsewhere in this study, are in an extremely awkward position from which to mount a sustained, concerted effort to develop expanded markets for trade books in Canada. It continues to be the case that only a small percentage of the direct mail and, in particular, the book club market is served by publishers in Canada (see Table 3-17). There is still not one major Canadian book club, and yet the subsidiary firms have never become involved in any way in the efforts of the Canadian sector of the industry to capture a substantial share of this market. To become involved in such an effort would involve competing with the parent firms which now handle this aspect of their exports through foreign, principally American-based, book clubs. And yet, the weakness of this and other subsidiary markets has a major effect on the profitability of publishing Canadian books for the general public.

While the argument has been made that any foreign control in book publishing is undesirable, the more commonly held view has been that expressed in the general industry study prepared by the Bureau of Management Consulting. The authors of that report concluded that "a relatively strong foreign presence in the market may not necessarily have an adverse cultural impact."[27] The problem has been to establish at what point the foreign presence should be considered more than "relatively strong" and at what point the risks of an undesirable effect on Canadian cultural development become unacceptably high.

The Ontario Royal Commission report shared this view that what was important was the balance between Canadian- and foreign-controlled firms. While the report expressed the opinion that the publishing of original Canadian titles would flourish "if existing Canadian houses can continue to flourish," it also warned in the following passage of the consequences of the failure of the remaining firms under Canadian ownership and control.

> If they should vanish, many of the Canadian alternatives to trade and educational books would disappear with them, and there would be little compulsion on the subsidiaries to continue to be as active in fostering domestic writing as they have been in the past. The pressures on the Ontario Department of Education to set aside its traditional Canadian preference policy would become almost irresistible. . .[28]

The authors of the Royal Commission report did not have available comprehensive statistical information on the industry. However, it is now obvious that domestic firms in the English-language industry have not flourished. Moreover, the comparative financial data on the Canadian- and foreign-controlled sectors of the industry suggest that, without steadily expanding direct assistance to Canadian-controlled firms, the imbalance will increase.

The federal government stated in 1979 that its objective was that "the Canadian-controlled sector of the book publisher/agent industry should play a dominant role in both the English and French-language markets in Canada." In 1982 that objective is, of course, far from being achieved. In the English-language sector, Canadian-controlled firms account for just 17.6 per cent of domestic sales. The comparable figure for French-language publishing was much higher, at over 50 per cent. However, even in the French-language sector, the level of foreign control is increasing. While foreign-controlled book publisher/agents accounted for just over 11 per cent of the sales of the French-language sector in 1975, their share of sales had increased to over 25 per cent in 1980.

The current policy objective of the federal government has been reflected in the decisions of the Foreign Investment Review Agency (FIRA) on cases involving new foreign ownership in book publishing. The legislation under which FIRA operates, of course, requires the agency to take into account the industrial policies of the government. As a result, most transactions which involve new foreign ownership and control of companies in the book publisher/agent industry in Canada have been rejected.

While no change of policy has been announced, there is some recent evidence to suggest that this policy may be changing. After rejecting in July 1982 an application from the American book publishing company, Harper & Row, to take over control of Lippincott, a company which acted as exclusive agent in Canada for foreign medical textbooks, the federal government, just two months later, allowed an American firm, the Herald Company of Syracuse, New York, to take over control of Random House Canada, one of the largest firms in the book publisher/agent industry in Canada. Random House is primarily involved with general interest and mass paperback publishing and one would have expected that control of the firm would have been considered much more important than in the case of Lippincott. The decision quite clearly runs counter to the federal government's stated objective of greatly increasing the degree of Canadian control over the book publisher/agent industry in Canada.

In addition to using the instrument of the Foreign Investment Review Agency, the federal government and the provinces have also provided an increasing amount of direct financial assistance to the industry, in almost all cases restricting such support to Canadian-controlled companies. The major component of federal support is the Book Publishing Development Program. Assistance through this program, which was initiated in 1979-80 with an initial two-year commitment, began at $5.7 million in 1979-80 and rose to $6.8 million in 1980-81. In addition, the Canada Council provides substantial assistance to the industry, with $3.8 million allocated in 1979-80 for such purposes as translation grants, promotion assistance, publication subsidy, and the purchase and distribution of Canadian-authored books to non-profit institutions in Canada and abroad.

At the provincial level, a number of provinces, including Newfoundland, Quebec, Ontario, Alberta and British Columbia also provide support in the form of loans, loan guarantees and interest subsidies, as well as direct subsidies towards the publishing of certain kinds of titles. With the exception of the Ontario Ministry of Education, all provincial government departments and agencies have restricted their support to Canadian-controlled companies.

Because 83 per cent of the industry is located in Ontario, the financial assistance provided by the Ontario government is particularly important. Ontario has loan guarantees outstanding to Canadian-controlled firms valued at more than $5 million and provides interest subsidy to such firms at half the prime rate. This Ontario program was revised in 1978 and loan guarantees to any single firm under the revised program may not exceed $250,000, while interest subsidies are restricted to $50,000. The interest subsidy program has been particularly valuable to this debt-dependent industry in a period of high interest rates.

The Ontario Arts Council provided publishing grants totalling $470,000 in 1979-80 to Canadian-controlled firms and made available a further $470,000 which the same firms may channel to writers preparing manuscripts for them. The Ontario Ministry of Education also provided approximately $4 million in book publishing support in 1979-80. Of this total, $0.5 million was provided for English-language and French as a second language projects; $2.4 million for the development or translation and publication of French-language texts and learning materials; and $1.5 million in promotion subsidy which takes the form of free distribution of sample copies of Canadian textbooks to Ontario schools. Approximately 10 per cent of these funds were provided by the federal government. However, the Ministry of Education, unlike the Ontario Development Corporation, the Ministry of Citizenship & Culture, the Ontario Arts Council, other provinces and the federal government, has not restricted its support to Canadian-controlled firms or given such firms preference. A quite substantial majority of this subsidy, which began in 1974, has benefited foreign-controlled firms, and as a result the ministry's direct assistance has tended further to weaken the position of the Canadian-controlled firms, including those firms for whom the Ontario government has guaranteed loans and provided interest subsidy support and Arts Council assistance.

Despite this anomaly in its policy, the Ministry of Education continues its traditional practice of requiring, wherever possible, that textbooks approved for use in Ontario schools be original texts written by Canadian authors and manufactured in Canada. Over 90 per cent of the titles listed for use in elementary and high schools in Ontario meet this criterion. While the low level of per pupil expenditure in Ontario makes this a less significant policy that it once was, it remains for the English-language industry the essential basis for production of Canadian-authored textbooks.

Ontario has also extended the terms of its Small Business Development Corporation Act to include book publishing, in order to try to stimulate the flow of badly needed equity capital into Canadian-controlled book publishing firms. The terms on which the province has done so reflect a recognition of the need to formulate policies with an integrated focus on cultural and industrial objectives. Companies benefiting from such investment must be primarily engaged in the publishing of books by Canadian writers. This measure is, however, restricted to small businesses.

In summary, the objective of developing a greatly strengthened Canadian-controlled book publishing industry is being pursued through the provision of the Foreign Investment Review Act, as well as through direct financial subsidy, loan guarantees and, in the case of Ontario, a tax incentive for investment. Clear objectives have been established by the federal government, but they are far from being achieved. In particular, it should be noted that most of the major foreign book publishing firms already have subsidiaries in Canada and, therefore, the Foreign Investment Review Agency is a factor mainly in cases in which the ownership of the foreign parent firm changes hands, bringing the takeover of the subsidiary under review.

Sales Tax Exemption

Books, like magazines and newspapers, are now exempt from the 9 per cent federal sales tax. This exemption affects the $448 million in imported books which entered Canada in 1981, as well as the manufacturing costs incurred by Canadian publishers for those books they produced in Canada. In 1980, Canadian book publishers spent a total of $60.7 million on book manufacturing.

The value of this federal tax expenditure in relation to imported books alone was over $40 million in 1981. An additional cost of approximately $6.3 million in 1981 was related to the exemption as it applied to books manufactured for Canadian publishers (assuming an increase of 15 per cent in manufacturing expenditure over 1980). The exemption, of course, affects equally the manufacture of foreign and Canadian-authored books. Since only 29 per cent of all sales of Canadian-published books are of original works by Canadian authors, it can be estimated reliably that out of the total tax expenditure of over $46 million less than $2 million, or 4 per cent of the total cost of the tax exemption, benefits the publishing of books written by Canadians.

Most European countries do not provide an exemption for books from the value added tax, which is the equivalent of the federal sales tax in Canada. West Germany, France, Sweden, Italy and Finland, for example, all levy value added taxes on books at rates varying from 6 per cent to over 20 per cent.

Tariff Elimination

The basic difficulties that have to be addressed in developing Canadian book publishing all arise from the fact that foreign books can be imported into Canada at relatively little cost and with relatively little risk by comparison with the publishing of Canadian books. The importer normally bears none of the cost of developing such books and is free to import only as many copies of each title as are needed, without ever running the risk of producing a full print run.

Precisely parallel problems confronted the United States in developing its own book publishing industry in competition with British publishers. In response, the United States pursued a policy of restricting to 1,500 the number of copies of any foreign-produced book in English which could be imported without loss of copyright protection. The United States applied this policy between 1891 and 1954 and, in a modified form—in which it applies only to books by American nationals—the policy remains in effect with respect to all countries except Canada. Canada became exempt from this provision on January 1, 1978.

By comparison, the Canadian approach to addressing the competitive advantage of foreign and primarily U.S. books, had been to permit them entry but to levy a 10 per cent tariff on books from countries with Most Favoured Nation status. Books imported for use by educational institutions and certain other minor categories of imports were exempt. In 1977, the tariff was applied on imports from the United States valued at $92.2 million or 47.7 per cent of total imports from that country, producing tariff revenue of $9.2 million.

The 10 per cent tariff was reduced to zero on January 30, 1979. While it was generally recognized that elimination of the tariff would increase significantly the competitive advantage of U.S. general interest or trade publications over Canadian books, the decision was taken both because the United States was insisting on it as the price of exempting Canada from the provisions of its own import controls in 1978 rather than 1982, and because it was anticipated that Canadian printers would gain additional orders from U.S. publishers as a result of the early exemption.

As indicated earlier in this chapter, the zero-rating of the tariff appears to have resulted in a shift in the pattern of Canada's book imports, with a substantially higher percentage of imports, over 83 per cent in 1981, coming from the United States than had previously been the case. In addition, there is some evidence that the percentage of imported books being purchased directly from foreign-based suppliers rather than through domestic book publisher/agents increased significantly after the zero-rating decision was taken. However, the federal government has already decided to continue indefinitely the zero-rating of the tariff. The decision to do so was supported by almost all organizations in the writing, publishing and printing industries, reflecting a firm commitment to the principle of tariff-free entry for all foreign books, so long as the United States does not reinstate its traditional protectionist policy in relation to Canadian-manufactured books.

Postal Rate Subsidy

The second largest single expenditure benefiting book publishing and distribution in Canada is the subsidized "book rate" for postal distribution. Its value is just slightly lower than that of the tax expenditure that results from the sales tax exemption. The cost of this subsidy, now borne by the Department of Communications as part of the federal cultural budget, was approximately $40 million in 1981-82.

The decision to transfer responsibility for postal rates affecting publications from the Post Office to the Department of Communications in 1978 reflected two factors. The first was a general commitment to increase postal rates quite substantially, in order to recover a much higher percentage of the Post Office's costs through rate revenue. The second factor, however, was a recognition that if there were major categories of mail for which subsidized rates should be continued, then such subsidies should, in the future, be justified on the basis of national policies with respect to cultural development, education, the arts and Canadian publishing.

With respect to newspapers and magazines, the result was a number of changes in rate levels in 1979 and in 1982, designed to ensure that postal rate subsidies were primarily of benefit to Canadian newspapers and magazines. However, no action has so far been taken which would bring postal rate structures and subsidies for books into line with the government's policy towards the publishing of Canadian-authored books, the development of a Canadian-controlled book publishing industry, or the development of a strengthened Canadian book distribution industry. At present, the $40 million expenditure is made on the basis of a single subsidized rate category which is available to any publisher, wholesaler, book club, direct mail publisher or retailer, regardless of whether any Canadian books are being sold or whether any or all of the books sold are acquired from the Canadian book publisher/agent industry or from abroad. Foreign distributors who simply truck their shipments across the border to Canadian postal stations benefit from the same rates as Canadian distributors. In the case of U.S. companies, it would cost them far more to mail to Canada through the U.S. Post Office.

The volume of mail order sales of books has been increasing rapidly in Canada. Revenue from mail order sales increased from $61.5 million in 1975 to $123.7 million in 1980.[29] The 86.5 per cent increase over that period was significantly more rapid than the 71.3 per cent increase in total sales of books in the Canadian market. Almost all of these sales were of foreign books and, as Table 3-13 demonstrates, few were purchased from the Canadian publisher/agent industry. Similarly, foreign wholesalers who buy mainly or exclusively from foreign-based publishers also make substantial sales in Canada and can benefit from subsidized postal rates in the same way as Canadian wholesalers.

Retail Bookstores

As has been noted earlier, the Quebec government is unique in Canada in using its purchasing power to strengthen the retail bookstore system in that province. While the result is that the Quebec government pays somewhat more for the library books it purchases, there are also significant economic as well as cultural benefits that result. The most obvious benefit is a very much larger retail bookstore system than would otherwise exist. For Quebec trade publishers, who fare badly in the mass paperback and book club markets and have an exceptionally weak public library system, the retail bookstore system is their essential, primary channel of distribution. The effectiveness of measures that have comparable effects on the character and size of retail bookstore systems has been recognized in recent studies carried out for the Council of Europe.[30]

Mass Paperback Distribution

In the preceding chapter on magazine publishing, the difficulty for Canadian magazines in achieving effective newsstand distribution was documented. In that chapter also, the Ontario government's legislative response to that problem was described. The Paperback and Periodical Distributors Act, which affects both magazine and mass paperback book distribution, has been a key factor in achieving some improvements in the distribution of Canadian-authored and -published mass paperback books and provides Ontario with the potential to further assist in the strengthening of Canadian mass market book publishing. This legislation, with some expansion along the general lines recommended by Ontario's Royal Commission on Book Publishing, could serve as a useful model for action in other provinces.

Policy Issues and Proposals

At the centre of concern in the development of policy alternatives for the development of book publishing and the book trade in Canada has been a desire to minimize direct long-term government involvement in the industry, while ensuring that Canada's educational, cultural and informational needs are satisfied. On the basis of all of the studies that have been carried out and the data that are available, it seems clear that the current weakness and the continuing decline of the Canadian-controlled sector of the industry have consequences that seriously affect the development of a well-articulated, diverse and balanced awareness of Canadian realities and interests.

To counteract these trends in the industry, action is required which will either encourage or require the divestiture by foreign publishers of their controlling interest in their Canadian subsidiaries, or provide the existing Canadian-controlled companies with very substantial long-term assistance, whether direct or through tax incentives. The latter approach, given the already established dominance of the industry and, in particular, of the educational market by the subsidiaries of foreign book publishing companies and their established financial strength and competitive advantage, presents substantial difficulties and cannot be undertaken with any assurance of success. However, a combination of measures of both kinds, along with action to improve the distribution of Canadian books might, if pursued vigorously and with the cooperation of both federal and provincial governments, prove successful.

The essential need now is to formulate new initiatives that will substantially strengthen the present approach. From the preceding material, it should be evident that through forgone sales tax and postal revenues alone, the government now is investing over $85 million annually in assistance related to book publishing and distribution. However, these measures treat both Canadian and foreign publishers and distributors equally and also benefit equally both Canadian and foreign-authored books. As a result, given the preponderance of foreign publishers and distributors and of foreign-authored and -produced books in the Canadian market, these measures primarily benefit foreign publishers and have no positive effect on the expansion of Canadian book manufacturing, the reduction of Canada's large trade imbalance, the development of a Canadian-controlled book publishing and distribution industry, or the creation of greater opportunities for the publication and effective distribution of works by Canadian writers.

The major recent measure taken by the government with respect to book publishing was the 1979 decision to zero-rate for a three-year trial period the tariff on imported fiction and general interest books from the United States. In 1982, if that tariff were still in place, the federal government would have collected in excess of $20 million.

In the light of the continued serious weakness of the Canadian book publishing industry, the following combination of measures should receive serious consideration.

Sales Tax
The federal government should eliminate the sales tax exemption for books. However, as an essential precondition for such a change, alternative measures should be provided to support the publishing of Canadian-authored books and the development of the Canadian-controlled book publishing and distribution industry.

Postal Rate Policy
The present subsidized book rate should be eliminated. That rate now applies to any books shipped in Canada by any publisher, book club, wholesaler or retailer. Unlike the rates provided for Canadian newspaper or magazine publishers, no criteria focus or restrict that support so that it reflects national objectives.

In place of the present policy, a new two-tiered rate structure should be established. Just as Canadian newspaper and magazine publishers now require a second-class mailing number to qualify for special rates, so Canadian book publishers, book clubs, mail order publishers, wholesalers and retailers would be required to meet specific criteria and to register with the Post Office in order to qualify for special rates.

The following categories should be established:

- *Category A - Canadian Book Rate*
  The lowest rates, perhaps somewhat lower than the current book rate, would be provided to book publishers, book clubs, mail order publishers, wholesalers and retailers that are primarily engaged in the sale of Canadian-authored and -manufactured books, i.e., those for whom the sale of Canadian-authored books accounted for more than 50 per cent of total revenue.

131

- *Category B - Canadian Book Distribution Rate*
  Rates at approximately the current book rate would be provided to all Canadian-based book publisher/agents and also to any book club, mail order distributor, wholesaler or retailer that acquired at least 75 per cent of the books it sold from the Canadian-based book publisher/agent industry.

The above structure would provide greatest benefit to publishers and distributors whose major focus is on Canadian-authored and -manufactured books. It would also continue the present level of support for those publishers, distributors and retailers who constitute the book industry *in Canada*. Subsidy to foreign distributors using the Canadian Post Office would be discontinued, as would subsidy to any Canadian-based company (whether book club, wholesaler or retailer) which did not purchase primarily from Canadian publisher/agent suppliers.

The special lower rate for category A should have the effect of stimulating and strengthening publishers, book clubs and other distributors whose main involvement is in producing or marketing books by Canadian writers. At the same time, this policy would not restrict support to Canadian-owned companies. Instead, its focus would be on building a stronger, more integrated book publishing and distribution system which might realistically hope to capture a larger share of the total domestic market. One obvious impact of such a policy is that public institutions would find that purchasing from a supplier who was part of the Canadian system would become economically more attractive by comparison with purchasing from foreign suppliers.

Tariff Policy
The position of the federal government on the zero-rating of the existing tariff on imported books is settled, at least for the foreseeable future. The government's decision to continue zero-rating indefinitely now has widespread industry support and, unless there is a change in U.S. policy, no reconsideration is likely. While there are legitimate reasons for concern about the decision, the government has kept open the possibility of a reversal should there be compelling reasons in the future.

Strengthening the Canadian-controlled Sector of the Industry
The federal government's policy on the strengthening of the Canadian-controlled industry should continue to be reflected in the

decisions of the Foreign Investment Review Agency in all cases involving new foreign ownership of book publishing companies. With the exception of the recent Random House decision, FIRA decisions have quite consistently reflected the policy of expanding Canadian control of the book publisher/agent industry.

Subject to a reasonable expectation with respect to equity investment, the federal government, perhaps through the Federal Business Development Bank, ought to provide loan capital or loan guarantees to assist in the acquisition by Canadians of foreign-controlled book publishing companies whose ownership and control are under review by FIRA. Such action would be consistent with promises made by the government during the last federal election campaign.

The decision by the federal government to continue the Book Publishing Development Program until 1984-85 is an important indication of the serious commitment that has been made to the strengthening of the Canadian-controlled sector of the book publishing industry. Twenty-five million dollars has been committed to this program over the three years ending in 1984-85. However, some changes should be made in the existing guidelines. Under the existing guidelines, funds are provided on the same basis regardless of whether the recipient publisher is simply reprinting foreign books in Canada, producing adaptations of foreign books, or publishing books by Canadian writers. Subsidy related to foreign-authored works in 1979-80 absorbed 19 per cent of the total funds in the major component of the program. Because the printing of foreign-authored and -published books and the production of adaptations already have a major competitive advantage over Canadian-originated books, this policy is particularly undesirable. While these activities are important to the development of the industry, they should be undertaken only if they are commercially sound ventures. The last thing needed in Canada is a program that subsidizes the publishing of foreign-authored books and adapted foreign textbooks, which is what the program does under the existing guidelines. The parallel would be to offer subsidies to *Time* magazine and *Reader's Digest* on condition that they sold their shares to Canadians.

The need for changes to the current guidelines has been recognized already both by the book publishing industry associations and the minister of communications. Subsidy to adaptations of foreign books, mainly textbooks, should be discontinued completely. In the case of foreign-authored books, subsidy should be discontinued unless the

133

editing, design, typesetting and printing of the books are carried out in Canada. Even if this requirement is met, not more than a designated percentage, perhaps 25 per cent of the support any single publisher receives, should be related to foreign titles.

An Investment Incentive Program

At the present time, book publishers are taxed on precisely the same basis whether they import all the books they sell or rely exclusively on the sale of Canadian books which they themselves develop and produce. In this respect, those book publishers primarily committed to initiating and publishing new books by Canadian writers are not accorded treatment parallel to that accorded to companies classified as manufacturing sector businesses, which now benefit from tax incentives related to the research and development expenditures involved in developing new products. The Income Tax Act now provides manufacturing sector firms with an investment tax credit on the basis of their expenditures "for the purpose of creating new, or improving existing materials, devices, products or processes." The purpose of the investment tax credit is to stimulate expenditure in the development of new products.

Given the comparably high level of investment and risk involved in the development of new Canadian-authored books, the substantial time lag between investment and return (varying from eighteen months to five years), and the cultural and educational importance of books by Canadian writers, an investment tax credit should be provided to Canadian-controlled book publishing companies based on all non-recurring costs involved in the development of new books by Canadian writers. The categories of expenditure included would be editorial and design costs, typesetting, artwork, negatives, plates, etc. Excluded, of course, would be paper, printing and binding costs. The proposed incentive should be available only to companies 75 per cent of whose beneficially-held shares are owned by Canadians and which are effectively controlled in Canada. While careful research would be required to judge the precise level at which the investment tax credit should be set, 25 per cent of eligible expenditures would probably provide an effective incentive. The level of the investment tax credit might vary for companies in different regions of Canada, as is now the case with the existing credits contained in the Income Tax Act.

The result of such a measure would be to increase the attractiveness of investment in firms benefiting from the incentive by improving the after-tax yield on such investments and, at the same time, to make it more attractive for Canadian book publishing companies to invest in initiating new books by Canadian writers. This proposed measure should be provided as a refundable tax credit, which would result in Canadian-controlled book publishing firms benefiting from its effect even in years in which they did not earn a profit.

The tax expenditure involved in this proposal would be substantially lower than the $46 million now incurred in relation to the sales tax exemption. This tax incentive should be seen as part of an overall strategy for the development of the domestic book publishing and distribution industry. Because it is an indirect support measure, the tax initiative would be an important component of a transitional strategy that would permit the re-establishing of greater distance between government and the book publishing industry. It will, however, continue to be necessary to take other measures such as those proposed in this chapter to develop the industry's distribution capacities. In addition, direct subsidy, such as the Canada Council and the Social Science and Humanities Research Council provide to support the publishing of non-commercial books, will continue to be necessary.

Provincial Procurement Policy

A more cooperative policy among governments is an essential ingredient of any effective strategy for developing a stronger Canadian book publishing industry. If such policies and practices are to be developed, then they must be seen to benefit all of the provinces.

In textbook publishing, a national policy with respect to curriculum planning, textbook selection criteria, and the establishing of standards for classroom and library expenditures, as well as special textbook development assistance, would be extremely valuable. Few educators are attracted by the prospect of simply using more foreign textbooks and learning materials. The same cooperation is desirable to strengthen the quality of distribution services to libraries across Canada.

What can make such a cooperative effort attractive is the kind of recognition evident in the federal Book Publishing Development Program of the need to encourage the development of book publishing outside Ontario and Quebec. The federal program provides for three levels of assistance: Southern Ontario is treated as the base level, with a higher level of assistance given to French-language publishers in Quebec and English-language firms in Alberta and British Columbia, and the highest level of assistance to firms outside these categories. As noted already, the refundable investment tax credit could contain comparable provisions.

Retail Bookstores

In the absence of effective competition legislation in Canada, there is nothing whatever to prevent an extremely high level of concentration of control developing in the retail bookstore business. This issue requires consideration before, rather than after, one firm ends up with control of 30 or 40 per cent of retail book sales.

As a basis for guidance in FIRA cases, the federal government ought also to establish policy objectives related to the need for Canadian ownership and control of retail bookstores and book wholesaling companies. Foreign takeovers and new foreign participation in the wholesale and retail sectors should not be permitted. The practical arguments for such a policy have been made effectively in many industry studies.

At the provincial level, provinces other than Quebec should give careful consideration to the policy of making provincial book purchases through retail bookstores wherever possible rather than buying directly from the book publishers or from book wholesalers. Both the positive and negative economic implications of such a policy require evaluation, as well as the important cultural benefits that would result from additional bookstores being established in smaller communities which are either not well served now or not served at all.

Book Clubs

Whatever action is taken to strengthen the retail bookstore business will still leave many parts of Canada beyond the reach of the bookstore system. Moreover, for many book buyers, regardless of where they live, the convenience of direct mail purchasing will continue to lead many individuals to rely on book clubs.

The postal rate policy proposed above will have important implications for book clubs, although there will need to be some careful research done prior to substantial expansion occurring. This area is one in which, on a cooperative basis, a group of companies, or the French- or English-language sectors of the industry as a whole, might take action to expand direct mail sales. Alternatively, a single major firm might decide to expand into this field. The possibility of such an initiative has received careful evaluation in the past by major Canadian firms. With the conditions governing postal subsidy to foreign book clubs substantially altered, the potential for the success of such an initiative would be much greater. Foreign-controlled book clubs might also change the way they operate in Canada, increasing their purchases from the publisher/agent industry in Canada.

Part II

Sound

Sound

The sound recording industry and radio are vehicles for the recording and distribution of sound. A wide variety of types of materials are either recorded or broadcast on the radio, including dramatic, educational and documentary materials, with radio also serving as an important source of news and current affairs programming. However, at least since the arrival of television, both the sound recording industry and radio have primarily been used to provide access to music. In the case of sound recordings, the vast majority of all records and tapes sold are of recorded music, while for radio broadcasting, music accounts for a substantial majority of all broadcast time.

The recording industry and radio are, as a result, both major components of the music industry, although they are involved in non-musical recording and broadcasting as well. While the recording industry and radio are part of the music industry, they by no means constitute all of it. As a result, the analysis contained in the following two chapters is not an analysis of the music industry, in that it does not deal in any detail, for example, with either live or telecast concerts, which are an important part of the music industry, or with music publishing, the vehicle through which songs and musical compositions of all kinds are made available by copyright holders for recording and broadcast use.

The following chapters also do not focus attention or analysis on songwriters or musical composers in Canada or on Canadian performers of popular or classical music. However, they begin with the premise that Canadians who are involved in the creation and performance of music ought to have a fair chance to have their music recorded and played on radio stations in Canada. Or to put the same point from the perspective of a record buyer or radio listener, it ought to be possible to buy the recorded work of Canadian creators and performers of music in Canadian record stores or from record clubs, and to hear their work, either live or recorded, on radio stations in Canada.

To a very significant extent, the activities of the sound recording and radio broadcasting industries are closely interrelated. The use of sound recordings provides radio broadcasters with an inexpensive, varied and high quality source of programming, accounting on the average for 50 per cent of air-time for private-sector AM stations and a higher percentage for FM stations. From the perspective of the recording industry, decisions by the public on whether to buy a particular recording are influenced primarily by having heard the recording on the radio. Because of the Canadian-content requirements established by the Canadian Radio-television and Telecommunications Commission (CRTC) to provide the public with an opportunity to hear Canadian musical performances and Canadian compositions, the link between radio and the record industry has special significance in this country.

The following chapters give particular attention to how well the recording industry and radio broadcasting in Canada now work to achieve the purpose of providing opportunities for balanced Canadian participation in the recording and radio broadcasting industries.

The Recording Industry

Introduction

The development of sound recording technology in the 1870s brought about a major improvement in access to music. Subsequent improvements in the quality of both sound recording and playback equipment make it possible to enjoy the best performances of an extremely wide range of music in one's own home. A wide variety of both "serious" and "popular" music is available on records and tapes, as well as a variety of non-musical recordings, including dramatic, poetic and other literary works. Sound recordings are also used as teaching aids in the educational system.

By comparison with the attention which governments in Canada have accorded the magazine, book, film or broadcasting industries, the recording industry has, until very recently, been ignored. From an economic perspective, the industry is relatively small and categorized as part of the "miscellaneous" manufacturing industry group, while as a cultural activity its significance has been largely overlooked by government. That indifference now appears to be disappearing, with a major study of the industry expected to be released by the federal Department of Communications in 1983 and significant policy initiatives anticipated by the industry.

The attention given to the industry at the present time reflects a concern that talented composers, songwriters and performers who are Canadian ought to have a reasonable opportunity to have their work recorded and promoted, at least in Canada and, ideally, abroad as well. In particular, there is now greater recognition given to the fact that, in the case of classical music, it makes little sense to support live performances of Canadian music and by Canadian performers without also giving attention to ensuring that there are opportunities for the recording of such performances.

The Canadian Market

Ownership of Record Players and Tape Recorders

The most significant factor affecting record and tape sales is, of course, the number of households that have record players and tape recorders. As Table 4-1 indicates, there was a 49 per cent increase between 1970 and 1979 in the number of Canadian households owning record players. The percentage of all households in Canada with record players increased from 69.6 per cent in 1970 to 77.3 per cent in 1979. Table 4-1 also indicates that there has been a quite significant increase in recent years in the percentage of Canadian households owning tape recorders. While in 1973, just 31.6 per cent of Canadian households owned tape recorders, the percentage had increased to approximately 50 per cent by 1979.

For the recording industry, the shift to rapid growth in sales of tape recorders rather than record players has important implications. Unlike the record player, the tape recorder can be used to make recordings as well as to play purchased pre-recorded material. While there are no

TABLE 4-1
HOUSEHOLDS OWNING RECORD AND TAPE PLAYBACK EQUIPMENT, 1970-79

Year	Total Households in Canada	Households Owning Record Players		Households Owning Tape Recorders	
1970	5,464,000	3,932,000	69.6%	—	—
1971	5,779,000	4,049,000	70.1	—	—
1972	6,108,000	4,332,000	70.9	—	—
1973	6,266,000	4,532,000	72.3	1,981,000	31.6%
1974	6,493,000	4,834,000	74.4	—	—
1975	6,703,000	5,073,000	75.7	2,325,000	34.7
1976	6,918,000	5,294,000	76.5	—	—
1977	7,022,000	5,434,000	77.4	2,621,000	37.3
1978	7,320,000	5,768,000	78.8	—	—
1979	7,558,000	5,840,000	77.3	[1]	[2]

Notes: [1] Households with open-reel recorders, 748,000; casettes and other types, 3,405,000.

[2] The percentage owning open-reel recorders is 9.9%; the percentage owning cassette and other types is 45.1%. The percentage owning either open-reel or cassette recorders is between 45.1% and 55%.

Source: Statistics Canada, *Culture Statistics: Recording Industry, 1978* (Cat. No. 87-615).

blank records for sale, blank tapes are sold in increasingly large quantities and can be used to record live concerts, radio broadcasts, or material on records or pre-recorded tapes. While precise data for Canada are not available, in most countries sales of blank tapes exceed sales of pre-recorded tapes by a margin of 2 to 1.[1]

Throughout the period 1970 to 1978, there was also an increase in the number of records and tapes sold annually to each household which owned playback equipment. While the average household with a record player purchased 10.3 records in 1970, the figure increased to 12.3 in 1978. Similarly, while each household with a tape recorder purchased 4.1 pre-recorded tapes in 1973, the figure rose to 7.4 in 1977.

Over 60 per cent of Canadians 15 years of age and over report that they play records or tapes every week. Those who listen to records and tapes report that they spend an average of six hours listening each week.[2] In addition, the majority of the 19.4 hours listeners devote to radio broadcasting each week is spent listening to the broadcast of recorded music.

Trends in Record and Tape Sales in Canada

It was only in 1977 that a Statistics Canada survey of the recording industry was initiated. As a result, there are no precise historical data available on the recording industry's sales. However, for the period prior to 1977, there are both data concerning the volume and the value of record imports and exports, and the value of Canadian record manufacturing activity. It is therefore possible to determine with considerable accuracy the trend in record and tape sales in Canada prior to initiation of the recording industry survey.

Table 4-2 indicates the steady and rapid growth in net shipments of records and tapes by manufacturing companies in Canada from 1970 to 1978. In terms of units sold, there was an increase in combined disc and tape sales from 44.1 million in 1970 to 94.1 million in 1978. While the number of units sold increased 113 per cent over this nine-year period, revenue from shipments of recordings increased 293.5 per cent during the same period, reaching a level of $258.5 million in 1978.

The import and export of records and tapes is relatively limited. The major reason for this limited international trade in recordings is that the manufacture of recordings is relatively inexpensive and, if there is a reasonable level of demand anticipated for a particular recording, it is cheaper to manufacture it locally than it is to import copies. However,

TABLE 4-2

NET SHIPMENTS OF RECORDS AND TAPES MANUFACTURED IN CANADA BY RECORD PRESSING AND TAPE DUPLICATING COMPANIES, 1970-81

	1970	1972	1974	1976	1978	1979	1980	1981
Millions of units								
Record discs — 7"	15.5	16.8	14.8	18.1	17.3	20.7	16.8	14.1
Record discs — 12"	25.0	29.4	32.0	38.9	53.9	53.9	52.4	54.4
	40.5	46.2	46.8	57.0	71.1	74.6	69.1	68.5
Recorded tapes								
8-track	2.9	5.9	9.7	15.6	15.7	11.0	5.2	2.6
Cassettes	0.7	1.0	1.1	2.8	7.2	9.0	10.2	14.8
	3.6	6.9	10.8	18.4	23.0	20.0	15.4	17.4
Total	44.1	53.1	57.6	75.4	94.1	94.6	84.5	85.9
Millions of dollars[1]								
Discs, all sizes	49.9	63.7	92.7	112.9	188.5	229.2	209.8	219.7
Tapes, all formats	15.8	24.9	39.0	47.2	70.0	74.3	60.3	71.4
Total	65.7	88.6	131.7	160.1	258.5	303.5	270.1	291.1

Note: [1] Sales revenue is at distributor's net selling price.

Source: Statistics Canada, *Production and Sale of Phonograph Records and Pre-Recorded Tapes in Canada* (Cat. No. 47-004).

the tariff which Canada imposes on imported records and pre-recorded tapes is also a significant factor.

As Table 4-3 indicates, although imports have usually exceeded exports, the total volume of trade is very limited by comparison with either the total sales of recordings or the level of imports and exports in the magazine or book industries. The 4.7 million records exported in 1978 was equal to just 7 per cent of all records produced in Canada that year; while the 7.5 million records imported equalled just over 10 per cent of the number of records produced in Canada.

On the basis of Tables 4-2 and 4-3, it appears reasonable to conclude that just over 97 million records or tapes were sold in the Canadian market in 1978, up from about 46 million in 1970. The extent of growth in that period can be seen by comparing the 293.5 per cent growth in the revenue of record pressing and tape duplicating companies between 1970 and 1978 with the increase of 168.8 per cent

TABLE 4-3
IMPORTS AND EXPORTS OF RECORDS,[1] 1970-81
(millions)

Year	Imports Units	Imports Dollars	Exports Units	Exports Dollars	Balance Units	Balance Dollars
1970	3.0	3.1	1.4	0.5	−1.6	− 2.6
1971	3.6	3.9	1.8	0.5	−1.8	− 3.4
1972	5.7	5.5	1.2	0.7	−4.5	− 4.8
1973	6.0	7.0	2.9	1.6	−3.1	− 5.4
1974	9.1	10.4	2.1	1.5	−7.0	− 8.9
1975	9.8	13.0	1.6	1.5	−8.2	−11.5
1976	7.4	12.0	1.5	1.9	−5.9	−10.1
1977	7.7	14.7	2.5	2.9	−5.2	−11.8
1978	7.5	16.2	4.7	9.4	−2.8	− 6.8
1979	9.3	20.6	5.4	15.3	−3.9	− 5.3
1980	7.6	19.4	8.1	25.0	+0.5	+ 5.6
1981	6.8	24.0	7.3	24.8	+0.5	+ 0.8

Note: [1] Import and export figures for pre-recorded tapes are not available, but are believed to be very limited.

Source: Statistics Canada, *Exports: Merchandise Trade* and *Imports: Merchandise Trade* (Cat. Nos. 65-202 and 65-203).

in the Gross National Product in the same period.

Beginning in 1977, as noted above, Statistics Canada initiated a survey of recording companies, as opposed to record manufacturers, in order to obtain information not available from the manufacturing sector survey. As Table 4-4 indicates, the survey of the recording industry

TABLE 4-4
RECORDING INDUSTRY REVENUE FROM RECORD AND TAPE SALES, 1977-80

Year	Record & Tape Sales ($000's)	% Increase	Consumer Price Index
1977	182,030.9		
1978	224,114.5	+23.1	+ 9.0
1979	238,829.0	+ 6.6	+ 9.1
1980	235,063.2	− 0.2	+10.1

Source: Statistics Canada, *Recording Industry, 1978*, and unpublished data.

shows a sharp increase in sales between 1977 and 1978, followed by real declines in revenue in both 1979 and 1980. Revenue from disc and tape sales increased just 4.9 per cent, from $224.1 million in 1978 at wholesale value to $235.1 million in 1980, far less rapidly than the rate of inflation. The reversal of the rapid rate of record industry growth after 1978 also occurred outside Canada. According to the Recording Industry Association of America, for example, retail sales of records in the United States declined 11 per cent from 1978 to 1979, without taking account of inflation, and stayed at the same level in 1980.[3]

Sales by Category of Music
Two-thirds of all reported recording industry revenue comes from the sale of rock and related kinds of popular music (see Table 4-5). Such records are primarily promoted on radio stations which devote their broadcast time to a limited range of records, usually the "top forty." Much of the volatility of the record industry is linked to its dependence on producing the relatively few hit records that account for the bulk of the industry's revenue. Adult-oriented popular music of various kinds accounts for the second largest percentage of sales, 15.5 per cent in

TABLE 4-5
DISC AND TAPE SALES OF CANADIAN RECORDING INDUSTRY BY MUSICAL CATEGORY, 1980[1]

Musical Category	Sales	
	Dollars	% of Total
Adult-oriented popular music	36,517,007	15.5
Top 40 or rock-oriented music	157,092,316	66.8
Classical and related music	8,429,646	3.6
Jazz	1,329,264	0.6
Country and folk	15,621,768	6.6
Children's	4,384,167	1.9
Other	1,295,502	0.6
Unallocated	10,453,845	4.4
Total	235,123,515	100.0

Note: [1] This table excludes sales by reporting companies of imported finished discs and tapes and almost certainly understates the total sales in categories in which imports are substantial (e.g., classical, jazz and children's records).

Source: Statistics Canada, unpublished data from recording industry survey.

1980. Country and folk music accounted for 6.6 per cent of sales.

Classical recordings accounted for 3.6 per cent of reported disc and tape sales in 1980, up from a reported 2.7 per cent in 1979. By comparison, sales of classical recordings tend to account for a substantially larger percentage of sales in most European countries. In France, for example, classical recordings accounted for 10.5 per cent of industry sales in 1978.[4] The proportion of classical record sales in the United States was 4.1 per cent in 1979, considerably closer to the level reported in Canada.

According to the information reported to Statistics Canada by the recording industry in 1980, other categories of recorded music accounted for only very limited percentages of total record sales — e.g., children's records 1.9 per cent and jazz 0.6 per cent.

It must be recognized, however, that the above figures almost certainly understate the proportion of total record sales in Canada that are accounted for by classical, jazz and children's records. As noted above, the general pattern in the industry is that most classical discs and tapes and most jazz recordings, as well as recordings in any category in which demand is not high for each individual recording in the category, are imported as finished discs and tapes rather than manufactured in Canada from imported masters. While Statistics Canada's book industry survey covers both imports and domestically produced books, the recording industry survey does not provide information at present on sales of imported discs and tapes. The industry's estimated revenue at wholesale value from imported discs and tapes was approximately $30 million. Assuming that these imports were primarily in the less popular categories of music, the proportion of total record sales for these categories is significantly understated.

Sales of Canadian-Content Recordings

The recording industry survey also provides information concerning the volume of record and disc sales for recordings which contain Canadian content. Under criteria established originally by the CRTC, a particular musical selection is deemed to be Canadian if it meets at least two of the following criteria:

- the instrumentation or lyrics were principally performed by a Canadian;
- the music was composed by a Canadian;
- the lyrics were written by a Canadian;
- the live performance was wholly recorded in Canada.

In the recording industry survey, a Canadian disc or pre-recorded tape is defined as one which contains at least one musical selection that meets the CRTC criteria. While the situation arises relatively rarely, this definition would categorize as Canadian a long-playing record on which only one of twelve selections was classified as Canadian.

In 1979, the sale of Canadian-content recordings produced net revenue of $20.3 million, which represented 8.5 per cent of the industry's total wholesale revenue from disc and tape sales of $238.8 million. In 1980, sales of Canadian-content recordings declined to $18 million or 7.6 per cent of total industry wholesale revenues of $235.1 million from the sale of recordings.

Sales by Language of Recording
The Statistics Canada survey does not provide information on the relative level of sales for records with French- and English-language vocal content. However, a study prepared for the CRTC in September 1981 estimated that French-language recordings accounted for 15 per cent of total sales in Quebec.[5] On the basis of the CRTC estimate for the Quebec market, it can be estimated that recordings with French vocal content account for approximately 4 per cent of total sales in the Canadian market. By comparison, recordings with French-language vocal content accounted for 41 per cent of total sales in France, while English-language vocal recordings accounted for 30 per cent of total sales. The remainder of record sales in France were of classical, jazz, orchestral background music and other non-vocal categories of recording.

Sales According to Origin of Master Tape
The production of master tapes is at the core of the recording industry. Producing a master tape brings together musical compositions, musical performers, and the special skills and technical equipment required to produce a prototype recording from which copies can subsequently be manufactured.

As Table 4-6 indicates, most of the discs and tapes sold by the recording industry in Canada are made from imported master tapes. In 1977, the industry provided a sales breakdown according to the origin of the master tape for 87 per cent of its total sales. Of these sales, 85.8 per cent were accounted for by recordings made from imported master tapes; 14.2 per cent from tapes produced by the reporting organization or leased from a production company in Canada. For 1980,

TABLE 4-6
REVENUE OF RECORDING INDUSTRY FROM DISC/TAPE SALES
BY ORIGIN OF MASTER RECORDING, 1977-80
($000's)

Origin of Master	1977	1978	1979	1980
Produced by reporting organizations	5,510	10,170	10,969	11,483
Leased from production company in Canada	16,945	12,611	14,567	12,665
Leased from production company outside Canada	135,226	158,203	190,373	187,508
Unspecified	24,349	43,131	21,439	23,468
Total	182,030	224,113	237,348	235,124

Source: Statistics Canada, *Recording Industry, 1978* and *1979* (Cat. No. 87-615) and unpublished data.

comparable information is available covering 90 per cent of the industry's total revenue from disc and tape sales. A somewhat higher percentage of sales in 1980 (88.6 per cent) was accounted for by the sales of recordings made from imported master tapes, compared with 11.4 per cent for recordings made from master tapes produced by the reporting organization or leased from a production company in Canada.

Estimated Composition of Total Domestic Sales
On the basis of the import data on finished discs and tapes combined with the domestic sales of Canadian-manufactured discs and tapes, it is possible to estimate reliably the composition of sales of recordings in the Canadian market in 1980. Imported discs and tapes account for just over 11 per cent of total sales, while records and discs manufactured in Canada from imported masters account for a further 79 per cent of sales. Combining the two figures, it is evident that about 90 per cent of all discs and tapes sold in Canada are manufactured from masters produced outside Canada. Discs and tapes made from Canadian-produced masters account for an estimated 10 per cent of total sales in

TABLE 4-7
ESTIMATE OF COMPOSITION OF SALES OF RECORDINGS IN THE CANADIAN MARKET, 1980
($ millions)

Canadian-Manufactured Recordings				
Produced from Canadian Master Tapes		Produced from Imported Master Tapes[2]	Imported Recordings	Total[4]
Canadian Content[1]	Other[2]			
18.0 (6.8%)	8.8 (3.3%)	208.3 (78.6%)	30.0[3] (11.3%)	265.1

Notes: [1] As reported in unpublished Statistics Canada data based on 1980 survey of the recording industry.

[2] Based on the assumption that the 10 per cent of total sales of Canadian-manufactured discs and tapes not allocated on the basis of origin of master tape can be divided on the same basis as the 90 per cent of sales for which such information is available (see Table 4-5).

[3] This estimate is based on the fact that imports are valued at customs at $2.55 per unit, whereas the recording industry reports that, valued at the record companies' income level, the average revenue per unit is $4.00. This adjustment of the import value reported in Table 4-4 provides an estimate of the value of imports that is comparable to the value for sales of Canadian-manufactured records.

Source: Statistics Canada, Cat. No. 65-203 and unpublished data from recording industry survey.

Canada. Of this total, 7 per cent is accounted for by Canadian-content recordings (see Table 4-7).

The Recording Industry in Canada

The annual survey of the recording industry covers both those companies that produce masters and those that lease masters. In the case of master production, the company credited with production must both incur the financial risk of producing the master and have proprietary and copyright claim on it. In lease arrangements, this right is assigned to another company which, through the lease arrangement, acquires the right, subject to financial compensation, to exploit the copyright that exists in the work through the manufacture and sale of discs and tapes made from it.

As Diagram 4-1 indicates, the company that produces a master may not be the same firm that arranges and finances the manufacture and

DIAGRAM 4-1
STRUCTURE OF THE RECORD INDUSTRY

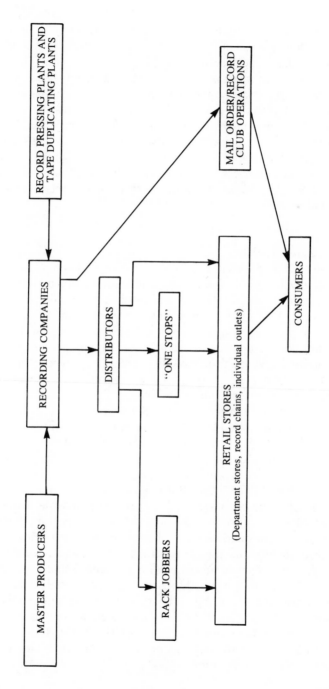

RECORD PRESSING PLANTS AND TAPE DUPLICATING PLANTS

MAIL ORDER/RECORD CLUB OPERATIONS

MASTER PRODUCERS

RECORDING COMPANIES

DISTRIBUTORS

"ONE STOPS"

RACK JOBBERS

RETAIL STORES
(Department stores, record chains, individual outlets)

CONSUMERS

sale of records and tapes from it. However, many companies function as both master producers and recording companies. A record company is one that generates sales of discs and tapes either from masters it owns or from masters it leases from other companies.

Some of the largest record companies own their own record pressing or tape duplicating plants, while others buy pressing and duplicating services from unaffiliated manufacturers. Only the largest record companies own their own distribution subsidiaries and some are further integrated into the rack jobbing, "one stop," mail order or record retail chain business as well. Rack jobbers and "one stops" are record wholesalers who act as intermediaries between record distributors and retailers.

Foreign Ownership

The recording industry in Canada is characterized by an exceptionally high level of foreign ownership and control and a high level of vertical integration. As Table 4-8 indicates, foreign-controlled companies accounted for 85 per cent of total revenue from the sale and lease of recordings and related record industry activities in 1980. Foreign-controlled companies accounted for 84 per cent of the industry's wholesale revenue from the sale of records and tapes, for 75 per cent of revenue from the lease of master tapes, and for 88 per cent of revenues from related record industry activities. These related activities include the manufacture of records, tape duplication, music publishing and the wholesale and retail distribution of tapes and records.

A high level of foreign ownership and control is, however, not unique to the Canadian industry. In France, for example, the six largest distributing firms, which accounted for between 66 and 72 per cent of total sales in 1979, were all foreign-controlled. This high market share represents the total sales of the distribution firms owned by these companies and would have been 5 to 10 per cent lower for their revenue from distribution of their own recordings alone. The majors act as distributors for many smaller independent record labels. The largest French firm accounted for between 5 and 6 per cent of total sales.[6] On a world-wide basis, the same half-dozen companies dominate the recording industry outside the communist countries, although the degree of dominance is rarely as high as in Canada. Four of the largest firms are American — CBS, WEA, RCA and MCA; one is British — Thorn-EMI; and one a joint venture of German and Dutch companies — Polygram.

152

TABLE 4-8

TABLE 4-8
REVENUE OF RECORDING INDUSTRY BY SOURCE AND
COUNTRY OF CONTROLLING INTEREST, 1977-80
($000's/% of total)

	Sale of Discs/Tapes		Revenue from Lease of Master Tapes		Revenue from Related Activity		Total Revenue from Recording Industry Activity	
CANADIAN-CONTROLLED								
1977	20,092	16.5%	1,818	48.4%	14,548	13.4%	46,458	15.8%
1978	48,859	21.8	2,471	43.6	15,146	10.7	66,476	17.9
1979	29,079	12.2	1,682	27.8	18,471	16.3	49,232	13.7
1980	36,731	15.6	1,221	24.7	12,243	12.2	50,195	14.8
FOREIGN-CONTROLLED								
1977	151,938	83.5	1,936	51.6	94,111	86.6	247,985	84.2
1978	175,256	78.2	3,194	56.4	126,588	89.3	305,039	82.1
1979	209,749	87.8	4,375	72.2	94,942	83.7	309,066	86.3
1980	198,332	84.4	3,720	75.3	87,753	87.8	289,807	85.2
TOTAL								
1977	182,031		3,754		108,659		294,443	
1978	224,114		5,665		141,734		371,515	
1979	238,829		6,057		113,413		358,299	
1980	235,063		4,942		99,996		340,001	

Source: Statistics Canada, *Recording Industry, 1978* and *1979* and unpublished 1980 data.

The dominant position of foreign-controlled companies in Canada is based primarily on their access to imported foreign master tapes from which they manufacture records or tapes for sale in the Canadian market. Sales of records produced from imported foreign masters accounted for 92 per cent of the revenue the foreign-controlled record companies earned from the sale of discs and tapes manufactured in Canada in 1979 (see Table 4-9). While the Statistics Canada survey does not at present provide such information, it also appears likely that the vast majority of sales of imported finished discs and tapes are accounted for by foreign-controlled firms marketing recordings imported from their parent firms. Only 2 per cent of the reported revenues of the foreign-controlled firms from disc and tape sales came from the sale of recordings made from masters the foreign-controlled

TABLE 4-9
REVENUE FROM DISC/TAPE SALES BY ORIGIN OF MASTER TAPE AND COUNTRY OF FINANCIAL CONTROL, 1977-79

Origin of Master	Canadian Financial Control			Foreign Financial Control			Total		
	1977	1978	1979	1977	1978	1979	1977	1978	1979
Produced by reporting organization	3,115	4,537	6,895	2,395	5,633	4,074	5,510	10,170	10,969
Leased from production company in Canada	4,087	9,321	2,781	12,858	3,290	11,786	16,945	12,611	14,567
Leased from production company outside Canada	12,890	6,358	5,791	122,336	151,845	184,582	135,226	158,203	190,373
Unspecified	10,000	28,644	12,131	14,349	14,487	9,308	24,349	43,131	21,439
Total	30,092	48,858	27,598	151,938	175,255	209,750	182,030	224,113	237,348

Source: Statistics Canada, *Recording Industry, 1978 and 1979.*

154

firms had produced in Canada. A further 6 per cent of their disc and tape sales, however, came from the sale of discs and tapes produced from masters which the foreign-controlled firms leased from other production companies in Canada.

As Table 4-9 indicates, the data on the breakdown of disc and tape sales by Canadian-controlled companies on the basis of the origin of the master are quite incomplete, accounting for only 56 per cent of total disc and tape sales. Of the sales for which a breakdown is provided, 44.6 per cent of revenue came from recordings based on masters these companies produced themselves, a further 18 per cent from recordings based on masters leased from production companies in Canada, and the remaining 37.4 per cent from the sale of discs and tapes produced from imported masters. While incomplete, these figures at least make it clear that a far higher percentage of the revenues of Canadian-controlled firms comes from recordings based on Canadian masters than is the case for foreign-controlled companies.

Concentration
The twenty largest companies in the 1980 Statistics Canada survey — of which ten were foreign-controlled — accounted for 99 per cent of total industry revenue. The ten foreign-controlled firms had average revenues of $29 million, while the ten largest Canadian firms had average revenues of $4.6 million.

While there are quite a substantial number of smaller record companies in Canada, the financial significance of smaller companies is slight. The twenty-five companies with revenues of less than $1 million each which reported to Statistics Canada in 1980 accounted for just 1 per cent of the total revenue of the recording industry. However, these smaller firms were of much greater creative significance. Their role in initiating new Canadian recordings is reflected in the fact that they earned 19.6 per cent of total industry revenue from the sale of discs and tapes based on masters produced by the reporting company, as well as earning 7.8 per cent of all industry revenue from the lease of master tapes.[7]

As Table 4-10 indicates, the few largest firms in the industry also have a major and expanding share of total industry revenues. The six largest companies in the industry accounted for 77.3 per cent of record and tape sales in 1980, an increase from 59.2 per cent in 1977. The six largest firms also accounted for 79.9 per cent of total revenues in 1980, by comparison with 75 per cent in 1977. All of these companies are foreign-controlled.

TABLE 4-10
REVENUE OF SIX LARGEST RECORD INDUSTRY COMPANIES
1977 AND 1980
($ millions)

	Record & Tape Sales	Total Revenue from Record/ Tape Sales and Related Industry Activities
1977		
Revenue of six largest firms	110.0	202.6
Total industry revenue	185.8	270.0
1980		
Revenue of six largest firms	181.7	271.0
Total industry revenue	235.1	339.0

Source: Statistics Canada, unpublished data based on survey of the recording industry for 1977 and 1980.

Profitability

Canadian-controlled companies not only account for a relatively small share of total industry revenues, they also earn substantially lower profits than the foreign-controlled companies. In 1980, the aggregate pre-tax profit of the Canadian-controlled sector of the industry was 1.2 per cent of sales. By comparison, the foreign-controlled sector reported aggregate pre-tax profits equal to 5.3 per cent of sales.

On a per company basis, as Table 4-11 indicates, Canadian-controlled companies had an average pre-tax loss of 5.5 per cent of sales, by comparison with an average profit of 5.2 per cent of revenue for foreign-controlled companies. The average profit for all companies was 3.8 per cent. In assessing these figures, it should be kept in mind that the average profit of companies in the survey declined by approximately 40 per cent from the previous year and that 1979 and 1980 were extremely difficult years for the industry, after a decade of rapid growth. In all such comparisons, of course, it is essential to bear in mind the use that foreign companies can, and frequently do, make of transfer pricing techniques to reduce the profits taken in the subsidiary firms in Canada. The real financial strength and advantage of the foreign-controlled firms is always difficult to assess because of this factor.

In the absence of historical data, the summary balance sheet

156

TABLE 4-11
AVERAGE RECORDING COMPANY PROFIT BEFORE TAXES
BY COUNTRY OF CONTROL AND REVENUE GROUP, 1980

Size and Country of Origin	Number of Companies	Average Before Tax Profit per Company ($000's)	Average Before Tax Profit as % of Revenue
Less than $100,000	15	−26.2	−87.6
$100,000-$999,000	9	14.1	3.8
$1 million and over	19	683.4	3.9
Foreign-controlled	10	1,530.0	5.2
Canadian-controlled	33	−76.6	−5.5
All companies	43	295.8	3.8

Source: Statistics Canada, *Recording Industry, 1980,* Service Bulletin vol. 5, no. 2, Cat. No. 87-001 (February 1982).

information shown in Table 4-12 provides a more accurate comparison of the relative financial strength of the Canadian- and foreign-controlled sectors of the recording industry. As that table reveals, at

TABLE 4-12
BALANCE SHEET DATA FOR CANADIAN- AND
FOREIGN-CONTROLLED RECORDING COMPANIES, 1980

	Canadian-controlled Companies	Foreign-controlled Companies
Current assets	$ 19,459,704	$ 192,119,907
Non-current assets	6,072,782	24,165,870
Total assets	25,432,491	217,409,360
Current liabilities	24,273,612	129,467,513
Long-term liabilities	3,076,140	(541,040)
Shareholders/owners equity	344,415	15,334,714
Retained earnings	(2,261,676)	73,148,173
Total equity	(1,917,261)	88,482,887
Total liabilities	25,432,491	217,409,360
Number of companies	28	10

Source: Statistics Canada, unpublished data from the 1980 survey of the recording industry.

the end of a decade of rapid industry expansion, the Canadian-controlled recording sector is in an extremely vulnerable position, lacking the financial resources to compete effectively. The Canadian-controlled sector of the industry reported a negative equity position at the end of 1980.

Import and Production of Master Tapes
At the root of the unequal competition between the smaller Canadian-controlled companies and the major multinational firms is the very unequal level of risk and investment associated with manufacturing from imported master tapes by comparison with production based on master tapes originated in Canada. Parallels can be drawn with the inherent financial advantages which foreign magazines have over Canadian magazines or foreign books over their Canadian counterparts. In all these cases — as well as those that will be looked at in the following chapters — foreign-produced content can be imported at relatively little cost and relatively little risk. The foreign master has already been paid for and there will be effective spillover promotion supporting its marketing in Canada.

As already demonstrated, the recording industry in Canada is essentially organized around the sale of discs and tapes produced from foreign masters. The companies that perform that function in Canada will naturally dominate the domestic marketplace. Since that function is performed primarily by the subsidiaries of the major foreign multinationals, they have a powerful dominant position in the Canadian marketplace.

It has been the practice of Revenue Canada to calculate the 15 per cent Most Favoured Nation tariff on the basis of the physical value of the imported master tape in almost all cases. In what might fairly be considered a form of dumping, almost all foreign master tapes come into Canada valued as though they were blank tapes. The value of the creative performance which is on the tape is ignored, although it incorporates the potential for the importer, as well as the exporter, to earn very substantial revenue because of its value as a copyright protected property. However, at the equivalent cost of blank tape, such masters enter Canada valued at roughly $25, paying a duty of less than $4.00. This Revenue Canada policy reflects the practice of the foreign recording companies of charging none of the cost of producing master recordings to the subsidiary and requiring no advance against future royalty earnings. Only a nominal fee is charged for duplicating the master tape.

By comparison, the cost of producing an original master tape for an album in Canada may vary from $10,000 to over $100,000. The following total amounts were reported to have been spent on producing masters in the period 1977 to 1980. Comparable figures for earlier years are not available.

1977	1978	1979	1980
$4.6 million	$3.7 million	$4.6 million	$5.6 million

Not only are these expenditure levels extremely low, they obviously fluctuate substantially and the increase over the past three years is not keeping pace with inflation. However, it should be kept in mind in evaluating these figures that they do not, according to industry sources, represent the full value of total recording costs because of the practice in the independent production sector of relying to some extent on contributed services from artists and musicians, as well as in some cases giving the recording studios in which a master tape is produced a percentage of future earnings rather than paying cash.

The risks involved in initiating a new recording are very substantial. While the returns can be large, it has been estimated that even in the United States only one recording in five is successful. In Canada, the ratio is significantly higher. What justifies the risk in both countries is the enormous potential earnings that can come from developing a successful artist or group, or producing a "hit" record.

In the case of smaller independent companies, once they have developed a master recording, they may either license its release by another — usually a major — record company or sell manufactured records/tapes to such a company for distribution. Under a licence agreement, the major record company/distributor bears the risk of financing the manufacturing, distribution and promotion costs. Under the second arrangement, the manufacturing and promotion costs are paid by the independent. In both cases, most or all of the cost of producing the master tape is paid by the independent producer.

If the independent can afford the cost of manufacturing discs and tapes, then this arrangement rather than a licensing arrangement, provides a higher margin and, therefore, a much greater opportunity for the independent record producer to earn a significant return. However, many independents have no alternative but to rely on the major firms to finance production, thereby restricting their own potential to profit from the master tapes they develop.

The break-even point on a new recording varies in relation to the initial cost of producing the master. While costs may sometimes be recovered on sales of as few as 15,000 to 20,000 copies, on the average, 50,000 copies must be sold to break even. Although this level of sales can be achieved in the Canadian market alone, revenue from foreign markets is important to companies originating recordings in Canada. In particular, for French-language Canadian recordings, sales in France are of great importance.

Record Releases in Canada

Table 4-13 indicates the content of the new releases issued by both foreign- and Canadian-controlled companies in 1977 and 1979. It should be noted that these figures on the number of new releases include only those recordings which were manufactured in Canada. Imported discs and tapes are not included. In 1979, a total of 1,698 singles were released, of which 393 or 23.1 per cent qualified as Canadian content. The same year, 2,496 albums were released, of which 13.1 per cent or 326 qualified as Canadian content.

In a brief to the Federal Cultural Policy Review Committee, the Canadian Independent Record Production Association (CIRPA), which represents Canadian-controlled record production companies, stated that

> the large multinational companies exist primarily as manufacturers and distributors of proven hit music from outside Canada. Most of the creative work of discovering, recording and promoting Canadian musical talent is in the hands of the small, Canadian-owned companies — the independents.[8]

This claim is supported by the figures in Table 4-13, which indicate that in 1979 Canadian-controlled companies, which accounted for less than 15 per cent of total industry revenue, released 154 Canadian-content singles and 169 albums based on masters they themselves produced, while the foreign-controlled record companies released 103 Canadian-content singles and 53 albums based on masters they had produced themselves. The foreign-controlled companies were relatively more active in releasing Canadian-content recordings based on leased masters and, if Canadian-content releases based on leased masters are included, the foreign-controlled firms accounted for just under 50 per cent of Canadian-content singles released in 1979 and 36 per cent of Canadian-content albums. As CIRPA noted, "much of the Canadian talent the majors release on their own labels comes from independent producers or self-produced albums by musicians."[9]

TABLE 4-13
NUMBER OF NEW RECORDINGS BY CONTENT, ORIGIN OF MASTER TAPE AND COUNTRY OF FINANCIAL CONTROL, 1977 AND 1979

Country of Control and Origin of Master Tape	With Canadian Content				Without Canadian Content			
	7" Singles		12" Albums/Tapes		7" Singles		12" Albums/Tapes	
	1977	1979	1977	1979	1977	1979	1977	1979
Canadian financial control								
Master tape								
• produced by reporting company	187	154	217	169	3	4	5	54
• leased from other companies in Canada	69	41	61	29	1	7	35	17
• leased from companies in other countries	12	3	16	11	175	126	207	378
	268	198	294	209	179	157	247	449
Foreign financial control								
Master tape								
• produced by reporting company	114	103	78	53	—	1	—	37
• leased from other companies in Canada	88	46	68	36	6	4	16	17
• leased from companies in other countries	56	46	59	28	1,599	1,143	2,387	1,667
	258	195	205	117	1,605	1,148	2,403	1,721
Total: All companies	526	393	499	326	1,784	1,305	2,650	2,170

Source: Statistics Canada, *Recording Industry, 1978 and 1979.*

Language of Lyrics of New Releases

As Table 4-14 indicates, 86 per cent of all new singles released in Canada in 1979 contained English-language lyrics, 12.5 per cent were French, while 1.5 per cent were either instrumental or unclassified. Of the albums released the same year, 72.7 per cent had English lyrics and 7.6 per cent French, while 19.8 per cent were instrumental or unclassified. Of the Canadian-content recordings released in 1979, 26 per cent of singles and 26.4 per cent of albums were French; 72.3 per cent of singles and 60.7 per cent of albums were English; while 1.8 per cent of singles and 12.9 per cent of albums were instrumental or unclassified.

Some radio broadcasters operating French-language stations have complained that they have difficulty meeting the CRTC requirement that 65 per cent of their vocal content should be in French because of a lack of French-language recordings. In response to these complaints, the CRTC carried out an analysis of the number and variety of French-language recordings available in Canada, using other sources in addition to Statistics Canada. The study indicates that the Statistics Canada survey does not include all of the French-language recordings available in Quebec. In the case of new Canadian-content recordings, for example, the study found that there were 170 singles and 168 albums produced in 1979 rather than the 102 and 86 respectively reported to Statistics Canada. The study also found that, if imported as well as Canadian-manufactured discs and tapes were included, the number of new French-language LP's available in Quebec annually was much higher than the 103 indicated in the Statistics Canada survey, which includes only those manufactured in Canada.[10]

Musical Category of New Releases

Table 4-15 indicates the number of new releases produced in six basic categories. While there are significant difficulties involved in categorizing certain individual recordings, these figures provide a general picture of the kinds of recordings being manufactured and released in Canada. They do not, of course, include imported records and, therefore, probably understate significantly the total number of newly-released records which became available in Canada in 1977 and 1979. Most record imports are of titles for which there is a relatively limited demand in Canada.

As Table 4-15 indicates, the number of new releases in the jazz and classical music field which contain Canadian content was relatively limited. There were also very few Canadian children's recordings

NEW RECORD RELEASES BY LANGUAGE AND CONTENT, 1977 AND 1979

	With Canadian Content				Without Canadian Content			
	7″ Singles		12″ Albums/Tapes		7″ Singles		12″ Albums/Tapes	
	1977	1979	1977	1979	1977	1979	1977	1979
English lyrics	370	284	264	198	1,317	1,186	1,649	1,616
French lyrics	105	102	126	86	144	111	116	103
Other, including instrumental music	51	7	109	42	323	19	885	451
Total	526	393	499	326	1,784	1,316	2,650	2,170

Source: Statistics Canada, *Recording Industry, 1978 and 1979.*

TABLE 4-15

NEW RELEASES BY MUSICAL CATEGORY, 1977 AND 1979

	With Canadian Content				Without Canadian Content			
	7″ Singles		12″ Albums/Tapes		7″ Singles		12″ Albums/Tapes	
	1977	1979	1977	1979	1977	1979	1977	1979
Adult-oriented popular music	94	69	94	63	402	193	430	413
Top 40 or rock-oriented music	239	206	110	125	638	915	681	1,140
Classical	—	—	36	22	—	—	293	217
Jazz	—	3	12	4	14	13	226	163
Country and folk	131	99	150	81	248	174	230	169
Children's	1	1	28	6	53	2	12	32
Other	10	5	42	10	65	19	91	36
Unspecified	41	10	27	15	364	—	687	—
Total	516	393	499	326	1,784	1,316	2,650	2,170

Source: Statistics Canada, *Recording Industry, 1978 and 1979.*

released, although more recently, with some Canadian records for children achieving phenomenal success, the production of such records is increasing. Top forty or rock music releases accounted for 66 per cent of all singles released in 1979, while adult-oriented popular music accounted for an additional 15 per cent and country and folk music for 16 per cent of new releases. Only 3 per cent of singles released were in the classical, jazz or children's category, with the remainder of released recordings not categorized.

Most of the classical, jazz and children's recordings released were albums, classical recordings accounting for 10 per cent of all releases, jazz for 7 per cent, and children's for 2 per cent. However, as in the cases of singles, top forty or rock accounted for the largest number of new albums released, 51 per cent, while adult-oriented popular music accounted for a further 19 per cent and country and folk music for 10 per cent.

Economic Impact

As already indicated in Table 4-3, Canada has a relatively small surplus ($800,000 in 1981) in trade in records and pre-recorded tapes. Most recordings sold in Canada are also manufactured here. However, in the recording industry, commodity import and export data do not provide an accurate reflection of international transactions. The international flow of payments related to the use of leased master tapes represents the major element in international exchange.

The recording industry in Canada reported in 1980 that it spent $71.9 million for the payment of mechanical royalties, licence fees and advances, almost as much as the $77.7 million the industry reported that it spent on record manufacturing that year. Given that only 8 per cent of industry sales were of recordings containing any Canadian content, it can be estimated that at least $66 million or 92 per cent of such payments were for the use of foreign masters. By comparison, according to the Statistics Canada survey, the recording industry in Canada received revenues of just $1.9 million in mechanical royalties, licence fees and advances from foreign sources. This figure appears to industry sources to be understated, possibly because it may exclude the foreign earnings of some major Canadian recording artists who receive revenue from foreign markets directly from recording companies outside Canada.

In addition to the royalty payments made by record companies, there are also royalty payments made by broadcasters and other users for the public performance of music. Most such performances are of recorded rather than live music. These payments flow directly to agencies which represent composers, authors and music publishers rather than to record producers or distributors. There are two such societies in Canada — the Performers Rights Organization of Canada (PROCAN) and the Composers, Authors and Publishers Association of Canada (CAPAC). PROCAN and CAPAC had combined revenues in 1980 of approximately $32 million. Roughly $2.5 million in revenue was earned from foreign sources. By comparison, CAPAC and PROCAN paid at least $15 million directly to affiliated foreign societies. In addition, a very substantial percentage of the money the societies paid to music publishers in Canada would have been passed on directly to foreign publishers. Most major music publishers in Canada are subsidiaries of foreign-controlled music publishing companies.

A reasonable estimate would be that Canada has a net deficit of $20 million in performing rights payments. However, it should be noted that there was a considerable improvement in this area over the 1970s. CAPAC, for example, reports that its revenue from foreign sources increased by 336 per cent, from $321,000 in 1970 to $1.4 million in 1979, while total revenues during the same period increased by 189 per cent.

If one includes in the balance of trade figures trade in finished records and tapes, mechanical royalties and licence fee payments and advances, and performing rights payments, then the deficit for the recording industry in 1980 was at least $90 million. This figure excludes dividend payments, management charges and other payments made by the subsidiaries to their parent firms.

As Table 4-16 indicates, the manufacturing of records and tapes in Canada accounted for $86.8 million in value added in 1979. Record manufacturers provided 2,713 man-years of employment, paying $35.2 million in wages and salaries. Of the 2,713 jobs, 1,816 were accounted for by production and related workers.

The survey of the recording industry, beginning in 1980, also provides employment data. However, there is probably some overlap between the recording industry and the record and tape manufacturing surveys, with six companies responding to both surveys. While the recording industry survey respondents report that they have 2,579 full-time employees and pay salaries and wages of $43.4 million, it can be estimated that approximately 1,000 are additional to those reported in the manufacturing survey. A conservative estimate would be that there are 3,700 full-time jobs in record manufacturing companies in Canada and in other companies included in the recording industry

TABLE 4-16
ECONOMIC DATA FOR RECORD/DISC MANUFACTURE IN CANADA, 1971-79

Year	Number of Employees	Salaries and Wages ($000's)	Value of Shipments ($000's)	Value Added ($000's)
1971	1,752	10,735	33,022	21,339
1972	1,921	12,548	40,265	27,023
1973	1,844	12,712	42,869	27,646
1974	2,033	16,980	57,545	37,020
1975	2,337	21,207	82,026	54,979
1976	2,447	26,225	90,197	62,460
1977	2,501	28,454	98,601	69,937
1978	2,653	33,566	119,158	78,365
1979	2,713	35,195	130,375	86,851

Source: Statistics Canada, *Miscellaneous Manufacturing Industries* (Cat. No. 47-205).

survey and that wages and salaries in 1980 were just over $50 million. Completely excluded from these figures are the Canadian composers, musicians, recording studio staff and other individuals not directly employed in the recording industry. As a result, the above figures understate employment related to the operation of the recording industry in Canada.

While some serious efforts have been made in the film industry to assess the number of man-years of employment and financial flows generated by the actual production process for films, no comparable analysis is available at present of the employment or financial impact of record production. To a considerable extent, this reflects the less expensive and less complicated process characteristic of record production. However, it also reflects the fact that relatively little investment is made in master production on an annual basis in Canada.

What is known is that in 1980 the sale of records and tapes made from Canadian-produced master tapes produced gross revenues of $24 million, of which a reported $18 million was related to recordings which included Canadian content. A rough estimate would be that every $1 million invested in the production of Canadian master tapes results in approximately $4 million in gross revenue returned to the independent labels from their distributors as a result of tape and pre-recorded disc sales which would have a retail value at list price of approximately $10 million. In the case of a recording which is

Canadian in its creative content, such sales result in the payment to Canadians of an estimated $960,000 in royalties for performers, $200,000 to music publishers, composers and authors, manufacturing expenditure of $900,000, as well as amortization of master production costs and other minor expense. Each $4 million in revenue from disc and tape sales returns $1,260,000 in average gross margin to the independent label which produces it,[11] out of which overhead, advertising and promotion and new record development must be financed, as well as any profit that may be earned. In the case of records produced from foreign masters, of course, the expenditure on master production has almost always been incurred outside Canada and all royalty payments are made to non-Canadians.

Marketing and Distribution

Once a master tape has been produced and a commitment has been made to produce discs and pre-recorded tapes for sale to the public, there are three separate channels through which exposure must be achieved before success can be realized. First, it is necessary to achieve as much exposure for the recording artist or musical group as possible — through touring activity, radio and television interviews and appearances, and so on. Second, as much radio broadcast exposure as possible of the record itself is needed. Third, the records and discs, ideally with point-of-purchase promotional material and media advertising support, must be made available in the record distribution system. The key point is that both artists and recordings need exposure.

Touring and Broadcast Appearances

Particularly for new artists, the cost of touring within Canada is beyond the resources of most of the companies that are actively involved in developing new Canadian recording talent. The exception to this general situation is the case of French-language recording artists in Quebec. However, while their primary home market is much smaller than the English-language market and is easily reached, the large French market for their records is very difficult and expensive to reach.

As a means of encouraging the booking of Canadian performers, a number of provinces provide an exemption from admission or entertainment taxes on live performances which feature Canadian performers. The result has been a significant incentive to providing exposure for Canadian performers.

While broadcast exposure is less expensive and reaches a wider audience, there are few regular programs on radio or television in Canada which provide opportunities for new Canadian musical performers. There are, for example, no national network programs on CBC's English television network or on CTV which regularly introduce and feature new Canadian recording artists.

Touring in the United States is potentially limited because U.S. immigration regulations provide that only established, successful foreign performers may perform in the United States. However, in practice these regulations have been used very little by U.S. immigration authorities.

In the case of classical music, a very substantial amount of federal and provincial direct government support is provided. In 1979-80, the Canada Council alone provided over $10 million in support for Canadian composers and individual musicians, live performances by orchestral, operatic, choral and chamber music companies in Canada, as well as for touring grants and a variety of related support programs. Grants from provincial and municipal governments would add very substantially to the level of total support for classical music by governments in Canada. In 1978, attendance at symphony concerts was 1.5 million, while attendance at operatic performances was 425,000. Despite the popularity of Canadian orchestras and other classical performing groups and companies, there has been, however, relatively little support available for the recording of Canadian classical compositions or performances. The exception has been the support provided by the CBC which will be looked at in more detail later in this chapter. In the case of non-classical music, there is no support available, either for touring or recording by Canadian performers.

Radio Broadcast Exposure
The only substantial federal government initiative that encourages Canadian recording activity is the CRTC requirement that 30 per cent of all musical selections presented daily on AM radio and a variable percentage of FM music should be Canadian. The CRTC also requires that at least 5 per cent of all musical selections must contain either lyrics or music written by a Canadian.

While there have been disagreements concerning the details of this CRTC policy, there is widespread agreement that it is an essential part of any approach that will effectively create opportunities for the development of Canadian music and musical performances of every kind, and for the development of Canadian recordings. Rather than being a restrictive measure, the Canadian-content requirement was a response to a situation in which the opportunities for Canadian expression in music were unreasonably limited. The goal of the policy was and is to achieve a measure of balance which purely commercial market factors would deny. Most of the proposals presented to the CRTC in connection with its current review of radio policy suggest changes that would make the Canadian-content policy more effective. The record industry has, for example, proposed that the content requirements apply equally to each period of the day and to FM as well as AM radio.

However, while there remains a widespread commitment to the Canadian-content policy, there is increasing recognition that by itself this regulatory measure is not sufficient to produce a balanced, varied selection of high quality Canadian sound recordings. For that goal to be met will require the development of a much stronger recording industry and a broad effort to encourage the development of new recording artists throughout Canada.

The Distribution Structure

As indicated earlier, the major record companies in Canada own their own distribution companies. Because the foreign-controlled companies distribute both their own records and those from many independent Canadian-controlled record labels, their dominance in the distribution sector is probably higher than the 84.4 per cent share for which they account through sales of their own discs and tapes. As CIRPA noted in its brief to the Federal Cultural Policy Review Committee, "The Canadian-owned distributors are generally quite small and under-capitalized, and none can offer the range of services of a major."[12]

The trend towards control over distribution by the major record companies was described as follows in a recent U.S. study:

> In the early 1970s, several major record companies stopped using independent distributors and set up their own distributing branches throughout the country. In order for branch distribution to be financially and administratively feasible, it is necessary for the distributors to handle a fairly large volume of business; consequently only the largest record companies can afford to own distributors.
>
> By eliminating the independent distributors as middlemen, the record companies often find they can better plan their production schedules and control distribution by more direct access to the final market. This has often led to increased sales and increased market shares for these companies.[13]

169

The extent to which concentration of control over distribution in the United States increased as a result of these changes was measured by the authors of this study. They found on the basis of an analysis of revenue information collected by *Billboard* magazine that the two largest firms increased their share of total best-selling album sales volume from 33.7 per cent in 1970 to 47.5 per cent in 1981. The six largest increased their share from 61.5 per cent in 1970 to 86.9 per cent in 1981; the ten largest from 79.5 per cent to 99.1 per cent over the same period.

Having established their own distribution companies to replace independent distributors, the majors then sought to increase the volume of sales handled by their distribution companies by establishing distribution arrangements with smaller record labels owned by independent firms. With so much more clout in the marketplace, the majors were able to attract the independent labels away from independent distributors, thereby further weakening the independent distribution structure.

Commenting on the results of the expansion of the major record companies into the distribution sector, a study carried out by the American consulting firm, Frost & Sullivan, noted that

> Some parent companies offer discounts, some offer long-term credit, free goods, almost anything to persuade retailers that the parent's records are and should be the first to go. The parent company and branch distributors are part of a whole network which collectively plans the most effective way to force consumers to like their records.[14]

The same study notes that as a result of eliminating the profit of the independent distributors who had functioned as middlemen, the majors "can sell record stores an album that lists at $7.98 for about $4.05, while the independents charge $4.25. The retailer can either discount the album or earn a higher profit margin." In addition, "The majors also spend more on in-store promotion posters and paraphernalia and take great pains to see that their songs get played on the in-store sound systems."[15] The Frost & Sullivan study observed that "Without that type of clout, the smaller independent labels have found themselves at a terrific disadvantage" and "have been deserting independent distributors in droves and *making deals with their competitors' distribution arms.*"[16]

The study goes on to note that there are problems that may result for the independents from the use of a branch of one of the major companies for distribution: "For the branch systems, marketing and policy decisions are made through corporate channels, so some labels in the system will take priority over others."[17] By comparison, the use of an independent distributor may give the independent label "a more realistic idea of the market and how to serve the market" and, as a consequence, "it may be more likely that a release from an independent label through an independent distributor would have a better chance of making it."[18]

While all the above analysis refers to the relative positions of the independent labels and the major integrated record companies in the United States market, the basic analysis and the issues raised are relevant to Canada. The major difference here is that the division in Canada is not merely between majors and independents, but at the same time is a division between foreign-controlled and Canadian-controlled companies. Most importantly, since the Canadian-controlled companies produce most Canadian records, the issue is how effectively the present structure of the recording industry in Canada functions in the financing, marketing and distribution of Canadian records.

As the information above indicates clearly, there are substantial differences in the performance of foreign- and Canadian-controlled companies. Despite the enormously greater market share and financial resources of the foreign-controlled firms, they produce far fewer Canadian recordings than the Canadian-controlled companies. The submission to the Federal Cultural Policy Review Committee by CIRPA, which represents the domestic industry, stated that the current structure of the Canadian record industry is a major reason for the relatively limited market share achieved by Canadian records.[19]

At the secondary level of distribution, by far the most important distribution channel is the rack jobber, accounting for an estimated 80 per cent of record sales.[20] Rack jobbers operate in a manner similar to that of the geographical wholesalers in the mass paperback book and periodical industry in that they normally own the inventory they place in each retail outlet and, therefore, control the decisions as to what records and tapes should be displayed. Emphasis is placed on the established hit records, particularly the "top 100" on the hit parade. In its brief to the Federal Cultural Policy Review Committee, CIRPA — the independent producers' organization — states that the rack jobbers "are the most conservative buyers in the distribution chain, and either refuse or are reluctant to stock records from independent labels or small distributors."[21] Many of the major foreign-controlled record companies — including CBS, WEA (a subsidiary of Warner Communications), Polygram and Capitol-EMI — maintain their own rack jobbing or retail operations, giving them a further edge in the Canadian marketplace.

The independents and Canadian recordings are much more likely to achieve exposure in "full-line" specialized record stores. Therefore, to the extent that the market share of the rack jobbers increases, it becomes more difficult to maintain a varied range of record production. Because Canadian recordings, and especially those by new artists, have smaller promotion budgets and involve higher retail risks, their potential for success has been adversely affected by the expansion of the rack jobbers' market share. There was a substantial increase in the rack jobbers' share of total sales in the 1970s.

In the United States, CBS Records indicated in its 1979 Annual Report that sales of "catalogue" or previously produced recordings had declined and it was more dependent now than in the past on the sale of new releases. More recently, with the sharp downturn in the fortunes of the record industry after 1979, a more cautious industry is placing greater emphasis on catalogue sales, which tend to provide a more stable component of corporate revenue from year to year.

Current Public Policy

At the present time the most important policy pursued by the federal government that provides an incentive for the recording of Canadian music or musical performances by Canadians, is the CRTC's Canadian-content policy. The CRTC policy has the effect of ensuring that a certain amount of air-time is devoted to Canadian musical performances and to music composed by Canadians.

Of considerable importance also is the present tariff policy. A 15 per cent tariff is levied on imported finished discs and tapes. Duty of $3.4 million was collected in 1981 on dutiable imports valued at $23.1 million. At the same time, while the same 15 per cent tariff is also levied on imported masters, it is assessed on the basis of their value as blank tape and is, therefore, negligible. The net effect of the present tariff policy is to encourage the manufacture in Canada rather than abroad of discs and tapes based on foreign masters. From an economic perspective, this may have the positive effect of producing more manufacturing jobs in disc and tape manufacturing than would otherwise exist. On the other hand, in the absence of other policy initiatives, it may exaggerate the inherent advantage in the Canadian market of recordings produced from foreign masters by comparison with recordings produced from Canadian masters. From an economic perspective, such a disincentive to Canadian production may result in larger net outflows of royalty and licence payments than would otherwise occur, accompanied by reduced opportunities for recording by Canadian recording artists and of musical compositions by Canadians.

There are, at present, no loan capital assistance programs, no significant cultural grants, and no tax incentives either for investment in Canadian-controlled recording companies or for investment in the development and production of Canadian-content recordings. The special export market assistance that was available was phased out in 1981. There is also no policy with respect to the ownership and control of the record production and distribution industry; nor is there any competition policy affecting the degree of industry concentration or the extent of vertical integration. Overwhelming foreign control and high levels of vertical integration are the present reality, along with declining investment, according to Statistics Canada data, in the development of Canadian masters.

In the case of classical recordings and other special-interest recordings, the CBC has been involved for many years in producing masters in Canada and either leasing those masters to companies in the record industry or releasing them itself. In the case of its own releases, however, the CBC was not until 1982 free to sell its own releases commercially. This situation has now changed and, as a result of an agreement with the American Federation of Musicians (AFM), CBC is now able to release its recordings commercially. A number of new releases have been issued under this arrangement, although the CBC will also continue to lease masters to private-sector record companies.

At the provincial level, the government of Quebec has provided loan capital and other direct assistance to domestic record production companies. The Ontario government has also assisted the industry on a one-time basis through its Half-Back Program, which stimulated the sale of Canadian-content recordings by allowing lottery tickets that did not win prizes to be used for a six-month period as coupons on the purchase of Canadian recordings.

Policy Issues and Proposals

For the recording industry as a whole, the period 1979 to 1982 has been very difficult. After a decade of phenomenal expansion, sales have declined. A variety of reasons are offered, including the economic recession, the sale of illegally produced recordings, home taping, unsound record industry structures and practices, and the rise of video product sales as a competitor to sound recordings.

However, the industry remains a substantial and important one and, if corrective measures are taken by government and industry in Canada and throughout the world, will continue to be for the foreseeable future, although possibly at a lower level of sales revenue. Whatever expanded future there may be for videodiscs and videocassettes — and rapid growth appears inevitable — sound recordings will no more disappear with the arrival of videodiscs and videocassettes than radio disappeared with the arrival of television. Instead there will be a division of functions in some respects comparable to that which exists between radio and television.

Government initiatives in Canada should address both the general problems of the recording industry as a whole and the specifically Canadian problems of changing the incentive structure of the industry to encourage the production of Canadian recordings and strengthening the structure of the domestic recording industry. The immediate focus should be on developing a strategy to strengthen the domestic recording industry and to stimulate Canadian record production.

Ownership and Control

While foreign ownership and control of the recording industry does not raise issues of principle comparable to those that arise in the publishing industries or in broadcasting, where the independence or sovereignty of editorial expression is a major policy concern in itself, there are obvious practical reasons for concern. With the present extraordinarily high level of foreign ownership, there is now a situation in Canada in which branch companies, with only very limited local decision-making authority, dominate the Canadian marketplace for records and discs and generate the vast majority of the capital which might be available for Canadian production.

At a minimum, the federal government should not, except in the most unusual circumstances, permit new foreign ownership in either the record production industry or any part of the distribution sector. Such a policy, if adopted by cabinet, would not only help prevent the further expansion of foreign control of the production industry, but would also help to curtail "downstream" purchases and increased vertical integration by foreign-controlled recording companies already operating in Canada.

While this may appear to some to be a negative approach to strengthening and expanding Canadian participation in the recording

174

industry, it must be remembered that the industry is organized around the production of discs and tapes from imported masters, with 90 per cent of industry revenue derived from that source. It is simply unrealistic to believe that there can be viable Canadian recording companies that are not involved in production from leased foreign masters as well as from Canadian masters. It should be noted that this will be even more the case in the developing video recording industry. In fact, most major sound recording companies are involved in both sound and video recording.

Some major Canadian communications companies have already established a degree of involvement in the recording industry — e.g., Selkirk Communications and Quebecor. However, there needs to be a very substantial expansion in the Canadian sector. There is considerable scope for joint ventures between major foreign and Canadian firms in sound and video recording ventures, given the appropriate public policies. In this connection, it was disappointing to note the June 1982 decision by the federal cabinet to permit the British firm, Thorn-EMI, to acquire full control of both Capitol Records-EMI of Canada Ltd. and of Kensington Distributors Ltd. Control by integrated foreign companies over the record distribution structure is particularly worrying in its implications for the development of a domestic industry and requires an explicit, publicly stated policy aimed at reducing the level of such control very substantially.

The basic point concerning the industry's structure was put bluntly in 1977 by Sam Sniderman, founder and president of the major Canadian retail chain, Sam the Record Man, and a member of the Federal Cultural Policy Review Committee: "There is no Canadian head office based record company that is nearly large enough or financially able to compete either within Canada or in the international marketplace."[22] In an extremely interesting analysis, Sinderman noted that the impetus provided by the CRTC Canadian-content regulations had never been capitalized on because the necessary domestic record production and distribution structures did not exist. Commenting on the consequences of the control of the industry in Canada by branches of foreign recording companies, he stated, "It is apparent with their almost total dominance . . . that the exposure of Canadian talent and the development of Canadian culture will be continually handicapped." While the companies all claim that they spend as much as is justified on Canadian talent, he noted that "You could hear this argued for days on end with many logical statements made that best suit the economic structure of companies that must show a profit to a foreign-based board of directors." He went on to make the important point that "given the potential artist, sufficient time and money for development, and proper promotion and distribution, you can create artists and recordings that will be wanted by the public and internationally competitive."[23]

At the present time, the Canadian-controlled firms lack the resources to carry out these functions as effectively as they wish and as is necessary, while, with some exceptions, the foreign-controlled firms generally commit only limited resources to Canadian talent. Any public policy that ignores the structural problems of the recording industry will almost certainly fail.

The CBC

With respect to classical music and other categories of music without mass appeal, the role of the CBC in producing masters both for lease to other companies and for release by the corporation itself is an extremely important one. To the extent that the federal government decides to embark on a strategy for strengthening the Canadian-controlled recording industry, the CBC should give strong preference to establishing lease arrangements with Canadian-controlled companies. The CBC should continue to expand its role in the sound recording industry, working in cooperation with Canadian-controlled private labels where that arrangement is mutually advantageous. There are many Canadian artists of high quality whose work will never be available on records unless at least the production of the master is carried out by the CBC.

Direct Financial Assistance

At the present time, the Canadian independent record production companies are not eligible for the support given manufacturing sector companies because they do not own their own record pressing or tape duplicating facilities and are, therefore, not defined as manufacturers. On the other hand, unlike book publishers, they are not eligible — except in Quebec — for special loan capital assistance, nor do they to any substantial degree benefit from direct assistance for recordings of particular cultural significance.

At a minimum, whether through expansion of the definition of manufacturing to include the record producers, or preferably through the expansion of the scope of special cultural industries development corporations, assistance in achieving access to loan capital should be provided by either federal or provincial governments in Canada. In addition, a decision should be made either greatly to expand the activities of CBC in master production, or to provide increased arts council support to private-sector producers. It must be recognized that certain kinds of culturally important recordings simply cannot be produced without such assistance.

Taxation

The present (1983) tax structure treats equally the production and sale of discs and tapes from imported masters and from domestic masters, although the investment and the risks involved in the latter activity are far higher. As noted in the previous chapter, a comparable situation exists in the book publishing industry. In neither industry is there any incentive for domestic production activity or ''new product innovation.''

A major tax incentive should be established for the Canadian recording industry. Specifically, a refundable investment tax credit should be provided to all companies which are 75 per cent owned and effectively controlled by Canadians. The tax credit should be set at least at 25 per cent and should be based on such companies' expenditure on the development in Canadian studios of new Canadian-content masters.[24] As the figures cited earlier in this chapter indicate, such an incentive would not involve major costs to the federal government. This approach would be far simpler than the capital cost allowance proposal explored in 1979 and would almost certainly result in a net financial, as well as cultural, benefit to Canada. Even if investments in master production by Canadian firms were to increase fivefold from the current level of $2 million, the cost to government would be limited — $2.5 million if the credit were set at 25 per cent. However, in addition to the matching $7.5 million the industry would invest in producing these master tapes in Canada, the industry would also spend $9 million on manufacturing costs, pay over $10 million in royalties to Canadians, and generate gross revenues of over $40 million.

There are precedents for investment tax credits set at high levels. An investment tax credit of 50 per cent was established in the 1980 federal budget to attract new capital investment in manufacturing plant and equipment in selected underdeveloped regions. In the case of the recording industry, there are both economic and cultural reasons for an incentive set at a high level, at least at 25 per cent and possibly as high as 50 per cent. There is also precedent for a refundable tax incentive in section 129 of the federal Income Tax Act. The refundable provision is essential in an industry not now earning reasonable profits on a regular basis. However, the result of such a policy would not be to direct public funds into companies which have committed no resources of their own. As already indicated, the companies themselves would still be providing a substantial majority of the financing.

Some industry representatives have argued that the 9 per cent federal sales tax on discs and pre-recorded tapes should be eliminated. However, the effects would be of benefit primarily to foreign recordings and foreign-controlled companies and would not likely have any significant effects at all beyond an increase in the profits of the dominant foreign-controlled corporations. In this connection, it should be noted that value added taxes — the European equivalent of the federal sales tax — are levied on sound recordings by virtually every country in Western Europe, including England, West Germany, France, Italy and Sweden. As a rule, the rates of value added tax in Western Europe are much higher than in Canada — 13 per cent in West Germany, 15 per cent in England, 33⅓ per cent in France, and 20.6 per cent in Sweden.

Tariff Policy

The tariff now levied on the importation of finished discs and tapes should be continued. There appears to be general agreement in the recording industry that this should be done. However, there is considerable controversy over the basis on which the customs duty on imported masters should be calculated. As noted already, masters are now valued for the purpose of calculating customs duty as though they were blank tapes. Their intrinsic value to the importer as the basis for the manufacture and sale of discs and tapes in Canada is not considered. As a result, the inherent attractiveness of production in Canada from imported masters is increased.

On the average, 2,500 masters for albums and 2,000 for singles are imported annually. Sales revenue from discs and tapes produced from imported masters is roughly $200 million per year. The related manufacturing expenditures are about $70 million. If these records were imported rather than produced here, they would incur tariff charges of roughly $15 million, which is a significant disincentive. Moreover, the costs of manufacturing in the United States are higher than in Canada and transportation costs are increasingly rapidly, which also makes the importation of finished records and tapes a relatively unattractive alternative.

If, for example, each of the masters for albums were valued at an average of $10,000 and singles at $2,000, the resulting increase in tariff charges on imported masters based on a 15 per cent tariff would be about $4.4 million. Statistics Canada data suggest that 97 per cent of any added customs duty charges would be borne by foreign-controlled companies, which in 1979 reported sales of $184.6 million for discs and tapes based on foreign masters by comparison with $5.8 million for Canadian-controlled companies. However, Canadian-controlled firms report an additional $12.1 million and foreign-controlled firms an additional $9.3 million in sales for which the origin of the master is not specified. As a result, revenue from disc and tape sales based on foreign masters might be as high as $17.9 million for Canadian-controlled firms and as high as $193.9 million for foreign-controlled firms. If this were the case, then 91.5 per cent of any additional customs duty would be paid by foreign-controlled firms, 8.5 per cent by Canadian. Assuming the above averages resulted from a revised system for valuing foreign masters, then as much as $375,000 in extra charges might fall on Canadian-controlled companies by comparison with just over $4 million for foreign-controlled firms.

These calculations are offered not as precise and definitive calculations, but as reasonable estimates. Their purpose is to indicate that, while a revised basis for customs evaluation of foreign masters appears both fair and in line with the public policy objective of stimulating production from Canadian masters, such a change could arguably have significant negative consequences for the Canadian-controlled sector of the industry, which would be unable to absorb such charges and might be less capable of passing them on than the major companies. It has also been argued that such a change would lead to an erosion of record manufacturing activity in Canada. While such a change should be made, it has not been possible in the course of preparing this study to carry out the careful examination necessary to evaluate the impact on the industry of making such a change at the present time. The change should not be made until such an investigation has been carried out.

Distribution
The proposal has already been made that the federal government ought to adopt a policy objective of reducing the vertical integration of foreign-controlled recording industry companies in Canada. The result would be immediate, since such a policy would be reflected in FIRA's deliberations, but limited, since there already is an excessive level of

179

integration. It is one thing for foreign record companies to make their products available to Canadians, but quite another for those companies to have achieved such a high degree of control over the distribution system that Canadian recordings can succeed only to the extent that directly competing foreign firms are willing to give them effective distribution.

While it is outside the scope of this particular study to evaluate in any detail whether and to what extent such vertical integration should be permitted, it does seem clear that a policy with respect to both concentration and vertical integration in this and other cultural industries must be developed. Such a policy ought to affect both foreign- and Canadian-controlled firms and ought to be implemented through effective review procedures.

Within the European Economic Community, particular attention has been given to the consequences of price-cutting on the structure of the retail distribution system. This is a problem that has affected both the recording and book publishing industries. There is a growing concern in Western Europe that unless retail price maintenance is permitted, the "full-line," "full-service" record and tape retailers, like the specialized bookstores, may continue to lose market share to the rack jobbers whose business is to sell vast quantities of relatively few "hit" recordings, with only the largest urban centres possessing full-service retail outlets. From the perspective of a cultural concern with variety, quality, the provision of opportunities for innovation, and the satisfying of minority needs and interests, the protection of a distribution structure that fosters such variety is important. This issue merits a place on the policy development agenda if it is agreed that cultural as well as industrial goals should be considered in formulating public policies affecting the recording industry.

A strategy for stimulating the Canadian recording industry should go beyond measures to strengthen the domestic market base. Of all forms of cultural expression and entertainment, none travels better than music. As a complement to the measures proposed above, support for the participation of companies involved in producing Canadian recordings in promotion and marketing outside Canada should be reinstated. This is particularly important for Quebec companies for whom the record market in France in particular can result in substantially enhanced total earnings.

It would also be valuable to provide the Canadian recording industry with support for management development and the kind of ongoing professional development activities which the Canadian-controlled companies in the industry cannot now afford to carry out. Comparable assistance to the book publishing industry appears to be producing positive results.

Broadcast Regulations
The general quota of 30 per cent for Canadian content on radio broadcasting should be maintained. It should apply to all AM radio services, whether broadcast, carried by cable, or transmitted in any other manner, and it should apply through all periods of the day. With the growing success of FM radio and the increased blurring of distinctions between musical styles and between AM and FM radio, the content levels for FM radio should be increased. Once a more varied recording industry output was achieved, it should be possible to increase the content requirement for almost all FM licensees to the 30 per cent requirement which must now be met only by AM radio stations.

Copyright Protection
The infringement of copyright through piracy, bootlegging and counterfeiting is a major factor in the problems now confronting the recording industry. However, as noted in CIRPA's brief to the Federal Cultural Policy Review Committee, the sanctions against the illegal duplication of records are very weak. In the revision of the Copyright Act which is now being carried out, provision should be made for effective remedies and sanctions against the duplication and sale of unauthorized copies of sound recordings.

While the piracy and counterfeiting problems can be addressed by the enforcement of strong provisions in a revised copyright act, there is no administratively feasible means of preventing home taping, regardless of whether it continues, as at present, to be defined as an infringement of copyright. The magnitude of the problem is suggested in a recent study carried out for Warner Communications in the United States. The study found that in 1980, 39 million people in the United States used $600 million worth of blank tape to copy music and other professional entertainment. An estimated 251 million record albums were taped and over 2 billion individual selections.[25] The study concluded that a conservative estimate of the value of this recorded music was $2.85 billion. For purposes of comparison, *Billboard* magazine reports that U.S. record and pre-recorded tape sales were $3.7 billion in 1980.[26]

In response to this problem a number of countries — for example,

Austria and Sweden — have established a tax on the sale of blank tape, with the proceeds from the tax dedicated to the development and support of the music industry. Comparable action should be taken in Canada as part of any strategy for the development of the Canadian recording industry and of music in Canada.

Radio

5

Introduction

Radio and television differ from the other sectors dealt with in this study in two essential respects. The first is that both radio and television are regulated industries. The second is that, in both radio and television, unlike the other sectors, a major role is played by the public sector. Licences to operate radio and television stations or services in Canada have been viewed, since the beginning of broadcasting in Canada, as public property. Any licensed station or network in Canada is, therefore, considered to be making use of public property and to be subject to the terms and conditions of its licence to which, in principle, it has claim only for the period of time the licence specifies.

Before describing radio broadcasting in Canada it is, therefore, important to provide a brief account of the development of the regulatory structure for radio and to provide background information on the structure and role of the public and private broadcasters as they have developed in Canada. Much of the following information applies both to radio and television.

The Regulation of Broadcasting in Canada

Regular radio broadcasting began in Canada, as it did in the United States, in 1919 when Station XWA in Montreal received a licence to broadcast. By 1923, sixty-two private commercial broadcasting licences had been issued. As early as 1925, many Canadians had begun to be concerned over the cultural effects of the predominant use that was being made of foreign entertainment programming on Canadian stations.

A royal commission, the first of many special inquiries into broadcasting, was established in 1928 under the chairmanship of Sir John Aird. In an excellent study published in 1979, David Ellis noted that the principal reason for the establishing of the Aird Commission was "the threat posed to Canadian sovereignty by the burgeoning radio empires of the United States." The American networks were a threat, both because they operated outside any effective legislative framework in the United States itself, and because there did not exist any fair agreement on a sharing of the air waves between Canada and the United States. The Aird Commission concluded in its report to the government that "the interests of the listening public and of the nation can be adequately served only by some form of public ownership, operation and control."[2] The commission recommended a radio broadcasting system owned and operated by a single publicly-owned company, which would owe much to the British model. While the primary purpose of the system would be to produce programs of high standard from Canadian sources, high quality programs should also be sought from foreign sources.

From the beginning, there was direct and heated conflict between the owners of private radio stations, many of which were earning substantial profits, and the supporters of a public system. While the private broadcasters opposed Aird's recommendations, the case for a public system was argued effectively by the Canadian Radio League,[3] which saw in a public system enormous potential for nation building. The league provided a focus for public support of such a system. At the same time, the Radio League saw in private radio the threat of overwhelming reliance on foreign — and mainly American — radio programming, which could be acquired less expensively and, therefore, provided a basis for greater commercial success.

There existed also from the very beginning, a conflict over whether the federal or provincial governments had jurisdiction over broadcasting. A request to the Supreme Court by Quebec, New Brunswick, Manitoba and Saskatchewan in 1931 led to a ruling that the federal government had jurisdiction. However, there were to be substantial conflicts related to broadcasting jurisdiction in the future.

On the basic issues of principle affecting radio broadcasting, the federal government's position was stated in May 1932 by Prime Minister R.B. Bennett:

> This country must be assured of complete control of broadcasting from Canadian sources, free from foreign interference or influence. Without such control, radio broadcasting can never become a great agency for communication of matters of national concern and for the diffusion of national thought and ideals, and without such control, it can never be the agency by which national consciousness may be fostered and sustained and national unity still further strengthened. . .;

184

Secondly, no other scheme than that of public ownership can ensure to the people of this country, without regard to class or place, equal enjoyment of the benefits of radio broadcasting. . .;

The use of the air . . . that lies over the soil or land of Canada is a natural resource over which we have complete jurisdiction . . . and I cannot think that any government would be warranted in leaving the air to private exploitation and not reserving it for development for the use of the people.[4]

Bennett's speech set out the three basic issues around which debate over broadcasting policy has been focused for the past fifty years. The first is that national sovereignty should be protected and, by implication, that incursions by U.S. broadcasters should not be permitted. The second is that Canadian broadcasting services should be available equally to Canadians in all parts of the country. The third is that the broadcasting system should not be left to private exploitation, but should be treated as a single publicly-owned system which exists for the use and benefit of the people of Canada.

While Bennett set out firm principles, the response of government has been characterized from the beginning by conflicting views of what action should follow from those principles and by repeated compromises. Even Bennett himself as David Ellis notes, "had a strong commitment to both the protection of vested private interests and the principles of public ownership." This built-in conflict between public and private interests has led to a mixed public and private system and a marked ambiguity in the commitment both to developing a public system and developing high quality Canadian programming. However, the basic principles set out by Bennett provide, as much now in an age of television, satellites, cable and fibre optics as in the early days of radio, a clear identification of the basic questions. Is there to be a separate Canadian system which can be regulated by the government of Canada in the public interest? Have all Canadians, regardless of the region in which they live, a legitimate and equal right to Canadian program services? What balance should be struck between private vested interests and both public regulation of the system as a whole and the operation of public broadcasting services?

The bipartisan nature of support for public broadcasting in the 1930s was evident after the defeat of Bennett's Conservative government. Action by the Liberal government in 1936 greatly strengthened the national radio broadcasting system, which had been established as a result of the 1932 Canadian Radio Broadcasting Act. The Canadian Broadcasting Act passed in 1936 brought into existence the Canadian Broadcasting Corporation. Under the 1936 legislation, the broadcasting system was conceived as a single system, reflecting in this respect the position articulated by the Aird Commission and by R.B. Bennett in 1932. Although the private stations were accepted as part of the system, the Board of the CBC was responsible for both the administration of the national public radio service and the overall direction of the radio system as a whole, including both its public and private components.

The regulatory structure established by the 1936 act would remain in effect until after the introduction of television in the 1950s. In the 1951 *Report* of the Massey-Lévesque Royal Commission, the commissioners wrote that the great majority of the 170 voluntary organizations which had discussed broadcasting in their submissions to the commission had expressed their support for the existing system. The commissioners themselves expressed their support for the CBC's success in keeping in mind "its three objectives for broadcasting in Canada," namely "an adequate coverage of the entire population, opportunities for Canadian talent, and for Canadian self-expression generally, and successful resistance to the absorption of Canada into the general cultural pattern of the United States."[5]

The Massey-Lévesque Commission also addressed the objections the private broadcasters had expressed to the commission over the continued operation of broadcasting in Canada as a single system in which the CBC, as the public agency, was dominant. The commission rejected the private broadcasters' claims, stating that the private broadcasters "have no civil right to broadcast or any property rights in broadcasting." Reiterating the basic view of broadcasting frequencies as a scarce and publicly-owned resource, the Massey-Lévesque Commission concluded that the proposals of the private broadcasters, which would establish separate private- and public-sector broadcasting systems under a single and separate regulator, would "either divide and destroy, or merely duplicate the present system of national control."[6] Amendments to the Canadian Broadcasting Act passed by the government shortly after publication of the Massey-Lévesque *Report* accepted its basic recommendations with respect to radio broadcasting, reaffirming the concept of a single broadcasting system with the CBC as operator and regulator.

However, despite this continued support for the principles of a single system with the dominant role played by the national public

186

network, serious financing problems had already compromised the development of the CBC's radio broadcasting service, as they would later its television service. The CBC had been unable to finance its own stations throughout Canada and had to rely instead on affiliated private-sector stations whose commercial interests often were in conflict with the objectives established for the CBC by Parliament. At the same time, the CBC also was heavily dependent on advertising revenue and had no predictable level of revenue on which it could depend in planning its development. The radio licence fee, which was to have provided a vitally important revenue source for the CBC, remained fixed at $2.50 from 1938 until the 1950s and was finally phased out in 1953; in addition, the government refused to establish a television licence fee to raise funds for the public system. At the same time, the government also refused the suggestions of most major inquiries that the level of support granted directly to the CBC by Parliament should be provided on a predictable, long-term basis in order to permit competent medium- and long-term planning.

Concern over the financing of the CBC was the primary reason for the establishing of the Royal Commission on Broadcasting in 1955, under the chairmanship of Robert Fowler. However, the broader issues related to the structure and regulation of radio were also addressed. Like the Massey-Lévesque Commission before it, the Fowler Commission argued that the private stations had been granted "a valuable public franchise" and not a property right, and should have to justify continuation of that grant, and that

> for the foreseeable future, we will continue to have a single broadcasting system in which all Canadian radio and television stations, public and private, present and future, will be integral parts, regulated and controlled by an agency representing the public interest and responsible to Parliament.[7]

On the subject of financing, the Fowler Commission argued strongly that the CBC must be given a firm basis for financing which would not leave it subject to the political or economic circumstances of the moment. Specifically, it recommended a fixed funding formula based on a designated percentage of the level of personal expenditure on consumer goods and services.

While twenty-five years after the Aird *Report,* Fowler was basically reaffirming the wisdom behind the basic structure of the broadcasting system, there was soon to be a major break with this tradition and a fundamental change in the balance of the broadcasting system. In

1958, a new Broadcasting Act was passed which brought to an end the "single system" concept and established a separate regulatory board with responsibility for both the public and private elements of the system. At the same time, the financing proposal for the CBC which Fowler had recommended, and which would have ensured that CBC financing kept pace with population and economic growth, was firmly rejected.

The entire issue of how to structure and regulate the Canadian broadcasting system was reopened by an Advisory Committee on Broadcasting in 1965. The fact that the issue was reappraised by the committee was not surprising, given that its chairman, Robert Fowler, had chaired the earlier 1955 Royal Commission on Broadcasting. The Fowler Committee placed the blame for the growing problems of the Canadian broadcasting system on a Parliament and a government that had neither clearly defined what it wanted the broadcasting system to achieve nor provided the means for the attainment of any goals which had been designated. Specifically, Fowler judged the dual system, set up in 1958 against the advice of every previous inquiry, to have been a failure. He proposed the re-establishing of a single Canadian Broadcasting Authority, repeating all of the arguments that had been made for such a structure over the previous thirty-five years. The Fowler Committee also reiterated the view that all broadcasting licences were public and not private property and that "no one has an automatic right to the 'renewal' of a licence." However, by the time the Fowler Committee *Report* appeared, private commercial broadcasting interests had come to dominate the system to such a degree that there were major political obstacles in the form of powerful vested interests to any real structural reform or any substantial assertion of the basic principles which R.B. Bennett had articulated in 1932 when broadcasting was just beginning in Canada.

In response to Fowler, the government produced a White Paper in 1966. The White Paper rejected the Fowler Committee's proposal for reinstituting a single authority over broadcasting. Instead, it proposed that there continue to be separate boards for the CBC and the regulatory agency, but that the CBC be placed clearly under the authority of the regulatory agency. While the White Paper proposed that the powers of the regulatory agency be greatly strengthened, it did not propose greater powers over the private sector and, despite the Fowler Committee's recommendations, set out no specific objectives for private broadcasting in Canada.

The White Paper expressed a more equivocal government attitude on the issue of Canadian sovereignty and control over broadcasting than had been the case in the past, asking "How can the people of Canada retain a degree of collective control over the new techniques of electronic communication that will be sufficient to preserve and strengthen the political, social, and economic fabric of Canada, which remains the most important objective of public policy?"[8]

With respect to the dominance of the public element of the system, the White Paper was unclear. The need for both public and private broadcasting was accepted and it was stated that "the place of the public element should predominate in policy areas where a choice between the two is involved." However, the precise meaning of this statement on priority was vague, and both before and after 1966, the federal government has rarely resolved any choice between the private and public sectors in favour of the latter, regardless of whether the public sector could better meet the fundamental goals of furthering Canadian cultural expression, developing a greater sense of national identity, ensuring an effective flow of economic, social and political information throughout Canada — or however Canada's national, social, political and cultural goals might be expressed.

The White Paper did, however, repeat the recommendation of all previous inquiries that the CBC be provided with long-term funding based on a fixed formula. Specifically, a statutory five-year grant was proposed, based on a formula related to the number of television households.

Two years later, the government passed new broadcasting legislation. The new act has provided the basis since 1968 for the operation of both radio and television broadcasting in Canada. Section 3 of the 1968 act sets out the following statement of basic broadcasting policy:

    a. Broadcasting undertakings in Canada make use of radio frequencies that are public property and such undertakings constitute a single system, herein referred to as the Canadian broadcasting system, comprising public and private elements;

    b. The Canadian broadcasting system should be effectively owned and controlled by Canadians so as to safeguard, enrich and strengthen the cultural, political, social and economic fabric of Canada;

    c. All persons have a responsibility for programs they broadcast, but the right to freedom of expression and the right of persons to receive programs, subject only to generally applicable statutes and regulations, is unquestioned;

    d. The programming provided by the Canadian broadcasting system should be varied and comprehensive and should provide reasonable, balanced opportunity for the expression of differing views on matters of public concern; and the programming provided by each broadcaster should be of high standard, using predominantly Canadian creative and other resources;

e. All Canadians are entitled to broadcasting service in English and French as public funds become available;

f. There should be provided through a corporation established by Parliament for the purpose, a national broadcasting service that is predominantly Canadian in content and character;

g. The national broadcasting service should —

 i. be a balanced service of information, enlightenment and entertainment, for people of differing ages, interests, and tastes, covering the whole range of programming in fair proportion,

 ii. be extended to all parts of Canada as funds become available,

 iii. be in English and French, serving the special needs of geographic regions, and actively contributing to the flow and exchange of cultural and regional information and entertainment, and

 iv. contribute to the development of national unity and provide for a continuing expression of Canadian identity;

h. Where any conflict arises between the objectives of the national broadcasting service and the interests of the private element of the Canadian broadcasting system, it shall be resolved in the public interest, but paramount consideration shall be given to the objectives of the national broadcasting service;

i. Facilities should be provided within the Canadian broadcasting system for educational broadcasting; and

j. The regulation and supervision of the Canadian broadcasting system should be flexible and readily adaptable to scientific and technical advances.

The act also states that the above objectives "can best be achieved by providing for the regulation and supervision of the Canadian broadcasting system by a single independent public authority." Since 1968, the regulatory authority has been the CRTC.

The above policy statement should be kept in mind in examining the functioning of radio and television broadcasting in Canada. Incorporated in the act is a basic contradiction that continues to be reflected in the debates and confusion that characterize broadcasting in Canada. While the legislation asserts the "single system" concept and repeats the statement that radio frequencies are public property, it, in fact, sets out completely different expectations for the private and public components of the system. Subsection 3(g) states a number of objectives that one might have expected to be applied to the system as a

190

whole, particularly in the light of the assertion in 3(a) that the system is a single system comprising broadcasting undertakings all of which are public property. Yet, while the public sector is to provide a balanced service of information, enlightenment and entertainment, serve special regional needs, contribute to the flow and exchange of cultural and regional information and entertainment, express Canadian identity, and so on, none of these objectives are applied to the private sector. Indeed, all that the policy statement says about private broadcasting is that the stations and networks should be Canadian-owned and -controlled and their programming should be "of high standard, using predominantly Canadian creative and other resources." Almost as a pious hope, subsection 3(b) seems to express an assumption that, if the system is Canadian-owned and -controlled, it will "safeguard, enrich and strengthen the cultural, political, social and economic fabric of Canada." While Canadian ownership may be a necessary condition for achieving those objectives, it has not proved sufficient. This relative silence on the objectives of the private sector has contributed substantially to the chaotic state of Canadian broadcasting policy.

Radio Broadcasting in Canada

With respect to radio broadcasting, the following analysis describes the system that ultimately emerged from the conflicts between the public and private radio services, giving particular attention to trends through the 1970s and the present role of radio among the other Canadian media and cultural industries.

The Canadian-content regulations which were established by the CRTC soon after its creation under the terms of the Broadcasting Act of 1968 were designed to provide greater exposure, on private as well as public stations, for Canadian programming, and particularly for recorded music. As noted in the previous chapter on the recording industry, this 1971 initiative has not yet been complemented by a strategy for stimulating the development of a wide variety of high quality Canadian recordings. A separate and comprehensive FM radio policy was implemented in 1975. The CRTC initiated a review of its policies for radio broadcasting in 1979.

While in the early days of radio air-time was filled with programming produced explicitly for radio broadcast, much of which was broadcast live, at least half of radio broadcast time is now filled with recorded music. AM stations program approximately half of the total broadcasting time with recorded music, while most FM stations fill considerably more than half of their air-time with recorded music.

191

This extensive use of records resulted in the present close interrelationship between radio and the recording industry which was described in the previous chapter.

The Canadian Market

The Audience for Radio
The continued popularity of radio is evident in the fact that 98 per cent of Canadian households have at least one radio with AM receiving capability, while 90 per cent now can also receive FM radio broadcasts. For FM radio, which had been available to only 56 per cent of Canadian households in 1970, the present figure reflects a rapid increase in household penetration over the past decade. In addition to having radios in their homes, 89 per cent of Canadians also report that they have car radios and, in 1980, 40 per cent had FM radios in their cars.

The Bureau of Broadcast Measurement (BBM) reports that 96 per cent of all Canadians are radio listeners.[9] Not only do a high percentage of Canadians listen to radio, but radio listeners report that they spend an average of 19.2 hours per week listening to radio. The peak listening period is 7:30 to 8:30 a.m. when over 30 per cent of Canadians listen to the radio.

As Table 5-1 indicates, there has been a significant increase in radio listening over the past few years. For all Canadians (aged 7 and over), the average number of hours spent listening to radio increased by 10.3 per cent — from 17.4 hours a week in 1977 to 19.2 hours in 1981. In absolute terms, the number of radio listeners increased substantially over the period 1970 to 1980. While total population increased by 12 per cent through the period, the number of Canadians 18 years and over increased by 26 per cent. Because the adult population is the

TABLE 5-1
AVERAGE HOURS OF RADIO LISTENING PER WEEK, SPRING SURVEYS, 1977, 1979, 1981

	1977	1979	1981
All (7+)	17.4	18.0	19.2
18+	19.6	20.1	21.3
Teens	13.2	13.8	14.0

Source: BBM, *Radio and Television Data, 1981.*

major audience for radio, there has been in absolute terms an increase of considerably more than 12 per cent in the total audience for radio.

While the percentage of Canadians who listen to radio did not change much between 1970 and 1980, there was a steady trend towards FM radio listening. As already noted, the percentage of households capable of receiving FM broadcasts increased to 90 per cent in 1980, while the percentage of automobiles with FM reception capacity increased to 40 per cent. However, the percentage of Canadians who actually listen to FM radio is considerably lower, in large measure because there are still many regions of Canada where there are either no FM stations or relatively few. While only 19 per cent of Canadians reported in 1975 that they ever listened to FM radio, the percentage had increased to 43 per cent by 1980. More recently, BBM has provided data on FM radio's share of total radio listening time. These figures indicate that FM's share of radio listening increased from 17 per cent in 1977 to 26 per cent in 1980.

Content

From the beginning, the programming content of radio and the degree to which radio services were available to Canadians were affected by the vast geographical area to be covered and the relatively small population of Canada by comparison with the United States. The early commercial radio stations were financially profitable only in the larger urban centres and their profitability was based largely on the use of recorded music, almost all of it foreign, and American programs in areas such as radio drama and variety, which could be purchased for far less than the cost of producing comparable Canadian programs.

As recently as 1968, it was estimated that while most of the ''talk'' on private radio stations in Canada was Canadian, Canadian musical selections accounted for between 4 and 7 per cent of all music played. This situation has changed markedly over the past decade, primarily as a result of Canadian-content requirements implemented by the CRTC after public hearings held in 1970.

For AM radio, as we saw in chapter 4, the regulations require that 30 per cent of all musical selections played must be Canadian. To qualify as Canadian, a musical selection must meet two of the following four criteria:

- the instrumentation or lyrics were principally performed by a Canadian;
- the music was composed by a Canadian;

193

- the lyrics were written by a Canadian; and
- the live performance was wholly recorded in Canada, or was wholly performed in Canada and broadcast live in Canada.

In addition, at least 5 per cent of all selections must be of music composed or lyrics written by a Canadian. The CRTC's *Special Report on Broadcasting in Canada* concluded that "As, overwhelmingly, the non-musical elements in the programming are Canadian and at least 30 per cent of the musical programming is Canadian, it can be concluded that the content of AM radio in Canada is predominantly Canadian."[10] However, as the definition above indicates, this may mean that the music played is a Canadian performance of foreign songs or compositions.

In the case of FM radio, the CRTC implemented a policy after 1975 which reflected a different approach to Canadian content. With respect to recorded music, the CRTC's policy reflected the relatively greater reliance of FM stations on recorded music and the fact that in certain musical categories (as noted in the previous chapter on the recording industry) there is a real scarcity of Canadian recordings. The general policy is that, while 30 per cent Canadian content is required for FM stations playing popular music, the level is as low as 10 per cent for stations playing primarily instrumental music.

The general goal of the CRTC's FM policy has been to encourage FM stations to provide service which complements that offered by AM radio, meeting the needs of minority audiences not well served by AM. A further objective was to encourage a more detailed and thoughtful treatment of news and public affairs than is provided on AM radio and to encourage programming innovation. At the present time, however, FM radio does not meet the policy requirement set out in section 3 of the Broadcasting Act. Private FM radio stations do not, in almost all cases, meet the requirement set out in subsection 3(d) that the programming provided by each broadcaster should use "predominantly Canadian creative and other resources." Unless an effort were made to expand the range of recording activity in certain categories, it is difficult to see how this standard could be met, except at the expense of the legislative goals of establishing a variety of programming. In the previous chapter, it was argued that the necessary initiatives to expand the quantity and variety of Canadian recordings produced should be taken.

The Radio Broadcasting Industry

Number of Public and Private Stations

As Table 5-2 indicates, there was a steady increase in the number of French- and English-language radio stations in Canada over the decade

TABLE 5-2
TOTAL NUMBER OF AM AND FM ORIGINATING RADIO STATIONS IN EACH PROVINCE AND IN ALL CANADA BY LANGUAGE OF BROADCAST, NOVEMBER 1967 AND NOVEMBER 1977

Province	Year	English-Language AM	FM	French-Language AM	FM	Multilingual AM	FM	Total AM	FM
Nfld	1967	14	0	0	0	0	0	14	0
	1977	25	6	1	0	0	0	26	6
PEI	1967	2	0	0	0	0	0	2	0
	1977	3	1	0	0	0	0	3	1
NS	1967	16	4	0	0	0	0	16	4
	1977	18	5	0	0	0	0	18	5
NB	1967	11	1	2	0	0	0	13	1
	1977	13	2	4	0	0	0	17	2
Ont	1967	77	30	7	0	1	0	85	30
	1977	84	45	9	1	1	1	94	47
Man	1967	13	5	1	0	0	0	14	5
	1977	16	6	1	0	1	0	18	6
Sask	1967	18	3	2	0	0	0	20	3
	1977	19	4	2	1	0	0	21	5
Alta	1967	19	5	1	0	0	0	20	5
	1977	30	8	1	0	0	0	31	8
BC	1967	42	7	0	0	0	0	42	7
	1977	64	10	0	1	1	0	65	11
Total excl. PQ	1967	212	55	13	0	1	0	226	55
	1977	272	87	18	3	3	1	292	91
PQ	1967	7	4	53	9	1	0	61	13
	1977	6	5	74	16	1	1	81	22
Canada	1967	219	59	66	9	2	0	287	68
	1977	278	92	92	19	4	2	373	113

Source: CRTC, *Special Report on Broadcasting, 1968-78.*

of 1967 to 1977. While the number of AM stations increased by 30 per cent over the decade, the number of FM stations increased by 66 per cent.

A 1978 CRTC study noted that "Although the growth of sound broadcasting in Canada has been found to be steady over the last 27 years, the present growth rate is exceeding the long-term rate."[11] Noting that the factors which were contributing to this growth would probably continue into the future, the CRTC observed that "In those areas where the demand is highest, the AM broadcast band is virtually

TABLE 5-3
NUMBER OF RADIO STATIONS IN CANADA
(as of March 31, 1979)

	Private Independent	Private CBC Affiliates	Private Total	CBC O&O	Total
AM	264	85	349	41	390
FM	144	—	144	24	168
Total	408	85	493	65	558

NUMBER OF RADIO STATIONS BY PROVINCE
(as of March 31, 1979)

	Private			CBC-O&O			Total Stations		
	AM	FM	Total	AM	FM	Total	AM	FM	Total
Nfld	19	3	22	5	1	6	24	4	28
PEI	4	—	4	—	—	—	4	—	4
NS	20	6	26	2	1	3	22	7	29
NB	14	3	17	4	1	5	18	4	22
PQ	73	27	100	8	5	13	81	32	113
Ont	93	71	164	7	3	10	100	74	174
Man	16	7	23	3	1	4	19	8	27
Sask	17	5	22	3	3	6	20	8	28
Alta	34	9	43	3	1	4	37	10	47
BC	54	10	64	2	3	5	56	13	69
NWT	1	0	1	1	—	1	2	—	2
Yukon	4	3	7	3	5	8	7	8	15
Total	349	144	493	41	24	65	390	168	558

Source: CRTC, *Annual Report, 1978-79.*

saturated'' and, therefore, FM stations would have to supply most of the future needs for radio broadcasting. More recently, the federal government has reached an agreement internationally that will provide additional AM frequencies, but this expansion will only relieve the problem in the very short term. In the longer term, expansion of the FM band is more likely to meet future frequency expansion requirements.

As noted in the background to this chapter, there are both public and private elements in radio broadcasting. Table 5-3 indicates the number of AM and FM public and private stations operating in each province.

Coverage

''Coverage'' is a term used to describe and define the extent to which Canadians have access to radio broadcasting. As early as 1967, virtually everyone in Canada could receive at least three Canadian radio broadcasting stations, while two-thirds of the population could receive nine or more. By 1977, over 80 per cent of Canadians could receive nine or more Canadian stations.

Off-air coverage by U.S. stations is relatively limited. Increased coverage of the Canadian market by U.S. radio services will depend both on the extent to which the CRTC permits their marketing by cable companies in competition with Canadian services, and on the degree to which the emerging framework of international and bilateral agreements may make them available directly off U.S. satellites. The issue of cable carriage will be examined briefly later in this chapter.

Within the province of Quebec, there were twelve English-language radio stations in 1977 and 86.2 per cent of the population had at least one English-language station available. Outside Quebec, the number of French-language stations increased from thirteen to twenty-one between 1967 and 1977. However, very few people outside Quebec had any choice of French-language stations in 1977 and coverage in Newfoundland, Manitoba, Alberta and British Columbia for Radio-Canada was relatively slight in 1977, although subsequently it has been increasing quickly through the establishing of additional relay transmitters. In addition, there were six radio stations operating multilingual services — two each in Toronto and Montreal, and one in both Winnipeg and Vancouver.

The CBC's English-language AM service reaches 97 per cent of all Canadians, including 99 per cent of English-speaking Canadians (as of October 1980). The English-language FM service reaches 69 per cent of all Canadians and 74 per cent of English-speaking Canadians. The

CBC's French-language AM service is available to 91 per cent of Canadians, the FM service to 25 per cent. However, the French-language AM service reaches 99 per cent of French-speaking Canadians, while the French-language FM reaches 67 per cent of French-speaking Canadians.

Audience Shares

The audience shares for English- and French-language stations did not change much over the decade 1967 to 1977. About 75 per cent of listening in Quebec is to French-language stations, while in the remainder of the country, 97 per cent is accounted for by English-language stations (see Table 5-4).

Most radio listening is to stations featuring a mix of "general popular," "rock" or "country" music. In Table 5-5, categories 1 through 7 are substantially dominated by various mixtures of these three types of music. Categories 5, 6 and 7 also include, as a minor component of musical programming, what the CRTC defines as "serious music." Table 4-7 in the preceding chapter provides a categorization of record releases in Canada, which can be looked at in relation to the use radio makes of various categories of music.

It is also interesting to look at the audience shares for CBC/Radio-Canada and for both Canadian and American private radio stations (see

TABLE 5-4
AUDIENCE SHARES FOR ENGLISH- AND FRENCH-LANGUAGE RADIO IN CANADA, 1967 AND 1977
(percentages)

		English-Language Stations		French-Language Stations	
		1967	1977	1967	1977
Quebec	AM	19.23	15.61	70.37	60.65
	FM	4.89	9.45	4.83	14.05
	AM & FM	24.12	25.06	75.20	74.70
All other	AM	93.59	81.56	1.76	1.23
provinces	FM	4.10	15.71	0.01	0.14
	AM & FM	97.69	97.27	1.77	1.37

Source: CRTC, *Special Report on Broadcasting, 1968-78*, vol. 1, p. 66.

TABLE 5-5

AUDIENCE SHARE FOR ENGLISH- AND FRENCH-LANGUAGE STATIONS BY PROGRAMMING FORMAT, 1967 AND 1977

(percentages)

	English-Language Stations				French-Language Stations			
	AM		FM		AM		FM	
	1967	1977	1967	1977	1967	1977	1967	1977
1. Contemporary middle-of-the-road (MOR)	15.48	27.49	19.00	12.53	37.39	57.85	—	35.34
2. Contemporary	13.34	13.86	27.96	—	1.21	10.80	—	—
3. Progressive album-oriented rock (AOR)	—	—	6.32	16.74	1.17	—	—	8.04
4. Country	2.42	7.06	1.54	12.94	—	—	—	—
5. Middle-of-the-road	45.27	31.04	15.02	4.55	14.77	14.15	0.79	22.24
6. Easy listening	5.67	2.20	11.69	33.73	18.21	0.04	—	25.11
7. Traditional middle-of-the-road	—	—	0.46	0.67	—	—	—	—
8. Information and talk	0.29	1.60	—	1.28	—	—	—	—
9. CBC[1]	4.80	8.44	6.05	11.19	8.29	9.99	4.76	6.91
10. Block[2]	11.71	7.13	8.71	1.59	9.04	2.26	22.50	0.12
11. Other	1.02	1.17	3.24	4.77	9.93	4.91	71.95	2.23

Notes: [1] Includes CBC owned and operated stations only.
[2] While most stations include a mix of programming interspersed with talk, the "block" category comprises "discrete blocks of specific programs generally consisting of only one category of material."

Source: Compiled from CRTC, *Special Report on Broadcasting, 1968-78,* vol. 2, Tables 5-10, 5-11 and 5-12.

199

TABLE 5-6
NUMBER OF STATIONS AND AUDIENCE SHARES[1] FOR CBC/RADIO-CANADA AND PRIVATE RADIO STATIONS

	English-Language Stations				French-Language Stations			
	1967		1977		1967		1977	
	# of Stations	% Share	# of Stations	% Share	# of Stations	% Share	# of Stations	% Share
EXCLUDING QUEBEC								
CBC/R.C.—AM	20	4.57	22	6.77	6	18.18	8	9.18
—FM	4	0.30	10	2.09	—	0.02	3	1.25
Total CBC/R.C.	24	4.87	32	8.86	6	18.20	11	10.43
CBC/R.C. affiliates	54	14.39	67	10.74	6	40.07	8	40.23
Total CBC/R.C. & network	78	19.26	99	19.60	12	58.27	19	50.66
Private, unaffiliated—AM	138	76.40	183	65.58	1	41.19	2	39.02
—FM	51	3.87	77	13.92	—	0.55	—	10.32
U.S. stations	—	0.47	—	0.90	—	—	—	—
Total private AM & FM and U.S.	189	80.74	260	80.40	1	41.74	2	49.34
QUEBEC								
CBC/R.C.—AM	1	3.93	1	7.55	3	7.76	5	8.11
—FM	1	0.71	2	1.46	1	0.31	3	1.30
Total CBC/R.C.	2	4.64	3	9.01	4	8.07	8	9.41
CBC/R.C. affiliates	1	3.96	1	3.16	22	18.24	31	14.98
Total CBC/R.C. & network	3	8.60	4	12.17	26	26.31	39	24.39
Private, unaffiliated—AM	4	71.83	4	51.58	29	67.57	38	58.10
—FM	3	19.56	4	36.24	8	6.12	13	17.51
U.S. stations	—	—	—	—	—	—	—	—
Total private AM & FM and U.S.	7	91.39	8	87.82	37	73.69	51	75.61

Note: [1] When interpreting audience shares of English-language stations in Quebec and French-language stations outside Quebec, it should be remembered that all English stations in Quebec have 25.06 per cent of audience in 1977, while French stations outside Quebec have 1.37 per cent.

Source: CRTC, *Special Report on Broadcasting, 1968-78*, vol. 1, pp. 70 and 71.

Table 5-6). First, the audience share for CBC-owned and -operated stations increased between 1967 and 1977 from 4.87 to 8.86 per cent for English-language stations outside Quebec, and from 8.07 to 9.41 per cent for French-language stations in Quebec. Including CBC's affiliated private stations, the network's audience share was fairly steady at just under 20 per cent for English-language stations outside Quebec and at about 25 per cent for French-language stations in Quebec. U.S. stations accounted for just 0.9 per cent of total listening in 1977, up from 0.47 per cent a decade earlier. The private unaffiliated stations have held a relatively steady 80 per cent of radio audiences for English-language radio and 75 per cent for French-language radio stations.

Industry Revenue Trends

The Public Sector

The CBC is supported primarily by public funds. In the case of the radio broadcasting services of the corporation, advertising time is no longer sold. The only commercial revenue the public radio system receives is the limited amount ($532,000 in 1980) that is derived from programs such as the broadcast of the Metropolitan Opera, which are only available to the corporation as sponsored broadcasts.

The cost of the CBC's radio broadcasting operations is not available separately from the overall costs of the corporation's total broadcasting services. The CRTC's *Special Report on Broadcasting, 1968-78*, noted that the total cost of the CBC's operations increased by 210 per cent over the period 1967 to 1977. During the same period, the total revenue of private television stations increased by 249 per cent, while the total revenue of private radio stations increased by 205 per cent. The GNP over this period increased by 216 per cent. The relatively more rapid growth of the private sector was more marked in the period 1972 to 1977, when the revenues of private television stations increased by 132 per cent and of private radio stations by 88 per cent, while CBC expenditure for radio and television combined increased by 101 per cent. More recently, as Table 5-7 indicates, public-sector broadcasting has been growing much more slowly than the private sector. The revenues of private radio and television broadcasters grew at a rate of 59 per cent between 1977 and 1980, while the net cost of CBC operations increased by just 32 per cent.

TABLE 5-7
GROWTH COMPARISON FOR PUBLIC AND PRIVATE-SECTOR
RADIO AND TELEVISION, 1977-80
($000's)

	1977	1978	1979	1980	% Increase
Canadian Broadcasting Corporation Net cost of operations [1]	410,832	482,630	539,887	542,852	32
Private Radio and Television Stations Total operating revenue	602,736	712,411	828,725	959,230	59

Note: [1] The available Statistics Canada data do not indicate the total revenues of the CBC. However, the corporation's total revenues are approximately 20 per cent higher than the net cost of operations, reflecting the fact that the CBC earns about 20 per cent of its revenue from television advertising. The net cost of operations data provide a sound basis for comparing the growth rates of the public and private sectors.

Source: Statistics Canada, *Radio and Television Broadcasting, 1979* and *1980* (Cat. No. 56-204).

Advertising Revenue

As Table 5-8 indicates, the advertising revenues of radio stations in Canada have maintained a remarkably steady 11 per cent of total media advertising expenditure since 1970. Virtually all of this revenue, as already noted, flows to private radio stations. Radio is primarily a local medium with local advertising accounting for 73 per cent of radio advertising revenue in 1980. By comparison, television stations earn 75 per cent of their advertising revenue from national, rather than local advertising.

There is a further extremely important difference between the advertising revenues of radio and television stations in Canada. While Canadian television stations receive on a per capita basis far less revenue than their American counterparts, there is no substantial difference between the per capita income of radio broadcasters in Canada and the United States. Radio advertising in Canada was 93 per cent of the U.S. per capita level in 1970, rose to 105 per cent in 1975, and declined to 90 per cent in 1980. By comparison, on a per capita basis, Canadian television broadcasters in 1980 earned only 47 per cent as much as their U.S. counterparts.

TABLE 5-8
NET RADIO ADVERTISING REVENUE, 1970-81

Year	Advertising Revenue ($000's)	As % of Total Media Advertising
1970	113,667	10.7
1971	124,688	10.9
1972	144,703	11.1
1973	160,300	10.8
1974	182,854	10.3
1975	207,679	10.7
1976	241,800	10.8
1977	269,080	11.0
1978	305,475	10.9
1979	352,010	10.9
1980	391,985	10.8
1981	440,000	10.8

Source: Maclean Hunter Research Bureau, *A Report on Advertising Revenues in Canada, 1981.*

Profitability

The radio broadcasting industry remained profitable over the decade 1970 to 1980. The industry earned an aggregate operating income in 1970 of $13.2 million, equal to 14.2 per cent of total revenue; by 1980, this had increased slightly to 15.5 per cent of total revenue, or $61.4 million. However, while the industry as a whole has remained profitable, there are many smaller stations that are not operating profitably. In its presentation to the CRTC's 1982 review of its radio broadcasting regulations, the Canadian Association of Broadcasters stated that 38 per cent of all commercial stations were losing money, most of them small stations.

In a study published in 1980 by the Institute for Research on Public Policy, the authors noted that the overall rate of return for radio in 1975, at 18 per cent, was significantly lower than that for television at 32.2 per cent.[12] However, the rate of return for both sectors of the broadcasting industry was well above the 13 per cent bench mark level for 1975 which the authors identified as necessary to attract investment capital. The authors of this study also noted that they found no evidence of above-average risk involved in investment in radio. In assessing the reasons for the lower profitability of radio than

203

television, the authors attributed this "both to the larger number of competitors in the radio sector and the higher cross elasticity of demand between radio and media other than television."[13]

Concentration

In Canada, as in the United States and most other countries, foreign ownership and control of broadcasting outlets is not permitted. As a result, all radio stations in Canada are at least 80 per cent Canadian-owned and are effectively controlled in Canada by Canadians. While no recent data are available on the level of concentration within the radio broadcasting industry or the extent of cross-ownership, the study noted above indicated that, in 1975, 81 per cent of all radio stations were group-owned, a significant increase from the 1968 level of 64 per cent.

In 1975, the ten largest groups of radio stations accounted for 44 per cent of industry revenues. The two largest groups, CHUM and Standard, accounted for 14 per cent of industry revenues. Both groups developed on the basis of their success in radio broadcasting, but are now involved in television and other industries as well. In fact, the four largest radio groups, which include CHUM, Standard, Western and Southam-Selkirk, were all among the ten largest television groups as well. From the perspective of cross-media ownership, the study noted that there were a significant number of cities in which there was common ownership of television stations, AM and FM radio stations, and newspapers.

Economic Impact

It is important to recognize that radio, like television, is both a producer of programming and a purchaser of programming from other sources. As has already been stated, the major source of programming for private-sector radio broadcasters is recorded music, which accounts for over 50 per cent of private AM stations' air-time and a higher percentage of FM time. As indicated in chapter 4, the broadcasters make royalty payments to the performing rights organizations, CAPAC and PROCAN, which accounted for a substantial proportion of these organizations' total revenues of $32 million in 1980. While most of this money flows outside Canada to foreign composers and performers, the Canadian-content regulations established by the CRTC have substantially increased the proportion of such payments that are made to Canadians.

For the recording industry, radio air-time exposure represents the major vehicle for the promotion of their products. To the extent that the content regulations provide exposure for Canadian recordings, they are a necessary element of any strategy for stimulating the production and sale of Canadian recordings. The potential economic impact of expanded sales of Canadian recordings was described in the preceding chapter.

Table 5-9 provides data on total radio programming expenditure for the CBC and the private sector. The breakdown between program production and program purchases is very different for radio and television. While program purchases account for a large percentage of television programming expenditure, only 5 per cent of total radio programming expenditure in 1977 was accounted for by the purchase of programs. However, over the preceding five-year period, purchases had grown by 227 per cent, while production expense had increased by just 106 per cent.[14]

While CBC radio accounted for an estimated 30 per cent of the Canadian radio broadcasting industry's total revenue, the corporation accounted for 45 per cent of radio programming expenditure. Music accounts for approximately 40 per cent of CBC's AM broadcasting time and between 65 and 70 per cent of FM time. Almost all of CBC's non-musical programming is Canadian-produced. The CBC employs 232 radio producers and is virtually the only employer of radio producers in Canada, especially for drama production. The CBC is a

TABLE 5-9
RADIO PROGRAMMING EXPENDITURE, SELECTED YEARS, 1971-80[1]

	1971	1974	1977	1980
CBC	26,177	40,085	56,507	96,998
Private radio stations	7,849[2]	50,021	79,983	119,103
Total	33,966	90,106	136,490	216,101

Notes: [1] Data for private radio stations are from Statistics Canada and cover the broadcast year, which runs from September 1 to August 31. Data for CBC are from the annual reports of the corporation for the year ending March 31.
[2] The definition of costs changed between 1971 and 1972. As a result, the 1971 figure for the private sector should be interpreted with caution.

Sources: CRTC, *Special Report on Broadcasting, 1968-78;* Statistics Canada, *Radio and Television Broadcasting, 1980* (Cat. No. 56-204).

major source of news, public affairs, background information, drama, classical and special interest musical programming, both at the national and the regional or local level.

While the CBC does not provide separate data for its radio and television operations, the corporation as a whole had 12,104 employees in 1980, down slightly from 12,233 in 1978. An estimated 3,300 are employed in CBC's radio broadcasting services. The CBC also made $78.2 million in freelance payments in 1980, thereby generating substantial additional employment. It is not possible to estimate accurately the proportion of these expenditures that are related to radio. They include payments to musicians, actors, writers and performers; royalties to authors, composers and musicians' associations; and other production fees and performing rights payments. For many performing arts organizations in Canada, the CBC is a major source of support. The CBC was a major source of revenue for the Atlantic Symphony Orchestra, for example, paying $225,000 to the symphony in 1980, although that revenue was not enough in combination with other revenue sources to ensure the symphony's survival.

The private-sector radio broadcasters had 9,547 employees in 1980, up significantly from 8,674 in 1978 (see Table 5-10). The assets of the private radio broadcasters in 1980 had a net value of $104.7 million. Broadcasting equipment, including tower and antenna systems, transmitter equipment, and studio and technical equipment, accounted for 55 per cent of total assets. CBC radio and the private radio stations represent an important market for such technical equipment.

Distribution

While the implications of satellite and cable distribution are widely recognized with respect to television, they receive far less attention with respect to radio. This is primarily the result of a general sense of satisfaction with the success of radio in Canada. Canadian stations account for 99 per cent of all radio listening in Canada, in large measure because Canadian radio broadcasters have not had to compete with wholesale importation of foreign broadcast signals as have Canadian television broadcasters. However, the combination of satellites and cable has the potential to change this situation significantly and indeed has begun to.

Just as the CRTC a decade ago allowed the cable companies to sell their subscribers U.S. television channels as part of their basic service, so the commission since 1979 has been allowing cable companies to

TABLE 5-10
REVENUE, EXPENSES AND EMPLOYEES, PRIVATELY-OWNED
RADIO BROADCASTING, 1980
($000's)

Reporting stations	381
Operating revenue	
Advertising sales—local	286,685
—national	103,941
—network	831
Total advertising	391,457
Production and other—syndication revenue	134
—production revenue	2,073
—other revenue	3,529
Total production and other	5,736
TOTAL OPERATING REVENUE	397,194
Departmental expenses	
Program	119,104
Technical	17,629
Sales & promotion	82,400
Administration & general	116,622
TOTAL DEPARTMENTAL EXPENSE	335,755
Depreciation	12,393
Interest	15,394
Other adjustments	11,827
NET PROFIT BEFORE INCOME TAXES	45,479
Provision for income taxes	21,621
NET PROFIT AFTER INCOME TAXES	23,858
Salaries and benefits included in expenses	181,007
Average number of employees	9,547

Source: Statistics Canada, *Radio and Television Broadcasting, 1980.*

include U.S. radio stations in the package of services they sell. In its brief to the CRTC's review of radio policy, the Canadian Recording Industry Association (CRIA) stated that

> The Commission has no control over programming originating in the U.S.A. and the Commission's opening of the floodgates for the

rediffusion of American FM stations is obviously in conflict with the objectives of the Broadcasting Act.[15]

The Broadcasting Act, of course, states that the programming of each broadcaster should be predominantly Canadian. However, as CRIA notes, in the case of these U.S. stations "The programming is not subject to Canadian-content regulation and the American stations themselves would be unable to get licences to broadcast in Canada."[16]

The result of this major policy change by the CRTC, as CRIA argues, is to establish practices which "constitute an erosion of the whole concept of Canadian content, and at the same time, allow certain licensees an unwarranted exemption from the Canadian-content regulations imposed on the broadcasting industry."[17] Just as such practices have eroded the legitimacy and fairness of the Canadian-content regulations for television, they will also make it difficult to insist on Canadian-content requirements in radio.

In establishing the current policy in 1979, the CRTC stated that it would not allow the importation of foreign FM stations unless such services were distinctly different from those available from local FM broadcasters. In a survey of its members, the Canadian Association of Broadcasters found that 74 per cent believed the cable companies were not abiding by the policy. However, even if this policy were followed, the inevitable effect of such a policy is that increasingly the Canadian radio stations will want to be relieved of CRTC regulation so that they can compete unhindered with the cable companies' importation of U.S. stations. There is an alternative to simply licensing the carriage of U.S. services. The CRTC should instead permit the development of additional Canadian radio services and/or the carriage by cable of distant Canadian services rather than U.S. services.

The deregulation of radio in the United States and the emergence of a growing number of powerful U.S. radio networks based on satellite distribution will create a considerable challenge to Canadian radio. As the CBC stated in its brief to the CRTC's radio policy review, "Most of these networks assume a continental market and have efficient salesmen in Canada." In this situation, it remains essential not just to reassert the need for Canadian sovereignty over radio broadcasting, but to ensure that satellites and cable are used aggressively to strengthen rather than erode the provision of radio broadcasting from Canadian sources that meets the criteria of high quality and diversity while also being predominantly Canadian.

Current Public Policy

The key elements of public policy at present are, of course, the provision of a national broadcasting service by the CBC and the regulation of the private sector to ensure Canadian control and to attempt to meet the requirements set out in the Broadcasting Act, including the requirement that the service provided by each broadcaster shall be of high standard and use predominantly Canadian creative and other resources and that the system as a whole should provide a varied and comprehensive range of programming.

As Table 5-5 suggests, while the number of radio stations available to the public has increased greatly, there is not a correspondingly large diversity of programming choices available to the public. A recent study developed and tested a model for predicting the program performance of a broadcasting industry comprised of private broadcasters financed by advertising revenue.[18] Advertisers constitute the primary market for private radio broadcasters. The private radio broadcasters are basically in the business of selling audiences for commercial messages. The model tested would lead to the following programming hypothesis:

> Diversity and choice in a market are expected to increase with the number of stations in a market, but if the stations are private broadcasters dependent on advertising revenue, it will increase only at a very slow rate. The balance and diversity of programming by networks and other groups are thought to depend on whether the network is private or public, with the former providing less balance and diversity because of their concentration on popular programming.[19]

While the authors of the study were not able to test this hypothesis fully with respect to radio broadcasting, they did conclude that there was a very substantial emphasis both on private AM and FM on similar kinds of light entertainment. However, they did find some evidence of real complementarity between the AM and FM radio services in Canada.

It is this tendency to give relatively little attention to minority interests that provides the basis for government support to public radio services. A second major factor is the heavy reliance of commercial stations on the use of recorded music, which provides a low-cost source of content. The real test of public broadcasting is its success both in satisfying minority interests and in programming the expensive, original Canadian programming that the private sector either cannot finance or has no motivation to finance.

The recent change of policy by the CRTC with respect to the carriage of U.S. radio stations by cable licensees has created serious new policy problems, problems parallel to those created by permitting cable carriage of U.S. television over a decade ago. As a result, cable companies are now allowed to sell their subscribers radio services without Canadian content, while Canadian commercial radio stations may only sell to their advertisers a radio service that meets the CRTC's content requirements.

While radio is primarily a federal concern, some of the provinces also help to finance educational radio services and services that meet special cultural interests.

Policy Issues and Proposals

All policy issues with respect to radio in Canada arise out of the CRTC objective of ensuring a radio broadcasting system that is diverse, of high quality, predominantly Canadian, provided by Canadian-controlled corporations, and that meets local as well as regional and national needs. To the extent that radio relies on the use of recorded music, these goals can only be met if a diverse range of high quality Canadian recordings is produced. Proposals for achieving this objective were set out in the preceding chapter.

Regulation alone is not sufficient, however, to ensure that the goal of diversity is met or that certain kinds of Canadian programming, especially non-musical programming, is available. The CBC provides a significant and unique contribution.

The decline in financial support for the CBC, while it first affects the corporation's television service, is having an increasingly adverse effect on CBC's radio services. One of the most disturbing consequences of curtailed financing is to shift the public service, which meets an obvious public need, into a defensive stance in which it cannot contemplate any expansion or strengthening of its service. With the changes that are occurring in the media, it would be tragic if the CBC were unable to take the necessary measures to position itself to continue to play a central role in radio. The corporation ought, for example, to be able to look at the special need for complementary cable-delivered services that are now being met by the importation of U.S. signals. While this is by no means an area that should necessarily be primarily within the CBC's purview, the corporation, along with the private sector, should be used to provide whatever expanded radio services need to be added to the Canadian system.

For the corporation to be able to plan its future radio and television services, it requires now, as it always has, a long-term financial commitment based on some appropriate objective indicator. CBC's recording activities need to be substantially expanded, through the production of Canadian masters and their lease to private Canadian-controlled record companies or release by the CBC itself, as a means of furnishing the supply of Canadian recordings in those specialized categories of music where Canadian production is now so limited that the provision of predominantly Canadian radio services is difficult to achieve.

With the steady shift of radio listeners to FM radio and the increasingly blurred distinction between AM and FM radio programming, the 30 per cent Canadian-content requirement for recorded music should be applied to FM as well as to AM stations.

In its submission to the CRTC's review of radio policy, the Canadian Recording Industry Association noted that "Certain broadcasters attempt to end-run the regulations by playing the majority of their Canadian-content recordings in low audience periods."[20] As recommended by both CRIA and CIRPA, the Canadian-content requirement should apply to the peak listening periods, as well as to the whole of the broadcast day. The recording industry has also argued that at least one-sixth of the Canadian recordings played, or one musical selection out of twenty, should be a new, uncharted Canadian selection. At least for popular music stations, this proposal should be implemented.

With the rise of television, "networking" in radio, which is the interconnection of stations for common and simultaneous distribution of programs and advertising, became of only limited importance. Radio became primarily a local medium, featuring hosted talk shows and recorded music. To the extent that radio networking is becoming more prominent again in the United States, a significant amount of non-musical, low-cost foreign programming is becoming available to Canadian radio broadcasters. While the CRTC's *Special Report on Broadcasting* was able to state that the non-musical elements in Canadian radio were "overwhelmingly Canadian," there may be a significant shift in this pattern in the future, at least for some kinds of stations. The growing importance of "information" programming on AM radio makes this a matter that deserves attention.

The overall objective of the CRTC should be to ensure that the programming of radio stations is predominantly Canadian. This may require growing attention from the CRTC, in terms of both its regulatory requirements and its willingness to support networking and other proposals from private broadcasters to the extent that they will be productive of high quality, non-musical Canadian content of all kinds.

Finally, the carriage of foreign radio signals by cable should either be phased out completely or far more carefully circumscribed. To the extent that the CRTC is convinced that additional radio services are required, the commission should define those services and invite proposals from public- and private-sector Canadian broadcasters to develop proposals for new licensed Canadian services. If the required services are to exclude advertisements, then consideration should be given to these services being provided as "pay-radio" services, either paid for by the cable system operators or offered, perhaps as a group of stations, as a discretionary extra purchase to cable subscribers. Given the far lower costs of radio programming by comparison with television, significant new radio services might be developed through such initiatives.

Part III

Moving Images

Moving Images

While the use of the terms "print" and "sound" to identify the subject matter of Parts I and II of this study raises few questions, it is important to clarify the scope of this section. The term "moving images" is used to encompass both film and videotape production. Film is simply a specific technology for the production of moving visual images. Videotape, a less expensive means of producing the same product, is improving significantly in quality and is, therefore, being used more frequently.

For most of the first fifty years of this century, very little use was made of the potential to distribute moving pictures electronically, although for a substantial part of this period, the technical ability to do so existed. Instead, from approximately 1900 to 1950, the standard practice was to distribute copies of film for use with a film projector, primarily but by no means exclusively, in motion picture theatres. However, since the early 1950s, the electronic distribution of moving visual images, initially by broadcasting and later through cable distribution, has become the dominant distribution technology. When this shift occurred, close links developed between the industry which had produced films for the theatres and the new television distribution system. Theatrical films became an important part of the content of television, while the theatrical production companies diversified into the production of programs explicitly for the television market. In the United States, which almost totally dominated the Canadian theatrical market, the major film production/distribution companies established extremely close links with the three major television networks that emerged. Independent U.S. producers and programming from foreign producers were almost totally excluded from the U.S. networks.

An interesting study, *Movies as Mass Communication,*[1] notes that, with the arrival of television, the new medium's situation comedies, police shows and made-for-television films assumed the role once filled by Hollywood's "B-movies." As a result, "Moviegoers are more selective in their attendance, they go to *a* movie rather than to *the* movies."

In Canada, no substantial private-sector film production and distribution companies existed when Canadian television arrived. As a result, the new stations and networks either produced their own programs or bought from foreign sources. The CBC, in particular, became a major program producer. The only major Canadian film company that existed prior to the arrival of television was the public-sector corporation, the National Film Board (NFB), which concentrated on the production of documentary, non-theatrical film. The arrival of television did not lead to a refocusing of the Film Board's activities on production explicitly for television, although the NFB has recently begun to devote greater attention to the television market for its programs. It is only since 1968 also that an independent private-sector film and television production industry has developed in Canada.

More recently, thirty years after the arrival of television, a third major technology for distributing moving images has begun to attract growing audiences. Videodiscs and videocassettes provide a direct parallel to sound recordings, in that they can be purchased or rented for playing on machines in the viewer's home.

The focus of Part III is on the first two elements of the system for exhibiting moving images — the theatrical film industry and television. The close links between these two elements of the system will also be explored.

Theatrical Film

6

Introduction

The movies have been described as "the most visible and prestigious of the current forms of mass communication."[1] That such a statement can be made long after the arrival of television testifies to the continuing fascination of the public with the movies.

The production of theatrical feature-length movies, with which this chapter is primarily concerned, is a complex process. The creative ingredients for a successful film include a well-written script, an experienced director, talented and, ideally, well-known actors and actresses, a director of photography, editor, music composer, and so on. The process also requires both expensive equipment and competent technical crews. The result is that the production of feature films is far more expensive than the production of other forms of entertainment or cultural expression.

The high costs and related risks involved in feature film production have made it a special challenge for smaller countries such as Canada to design public policies that permit production activity. The existence of two major language groups in Canada presents special challenges. However, virtually all countries, regardless of whether they have socialist or market economies, have considered it essential to provide for the production and exhibition of their own distinctive feature films, reflecting their own interests and imagination and their own history.

The sense of importance attached to feature production reflects an awareness of their influence on their audiences. A recent study notes that "Movies, like all the mass media, serve as a potent source of informal education, and thus their content, no matter how innocuous it may appear, is never entirely free of value judgments or even of ideological or political bias."[2] The same study also recognizes that "The export of a cultural (ideological) perspective is particularly exacerbated when it is accompanied by an equally pervasive form of

217

economic domination."[3] Thus, there has always been a concern with both the cultural and economic results of heavy dependence on foreign films.

The technology of film production was developed in the 1890s. While there were many ways in which the new medium might have been employed, it was clear in the United States, as early as 1910, that film was to be essentially a private-sector commodity. As a result, the dominant use of film since that time has been as a mass entertainment medium; and, as early as the 1920s, the relatively few companies involved in film production embarked on a vigorous effort to achieve vertical integration.

From the very beginnings of film production, the industry in the United States displayed a propensity towards concentration of ownership and control. As a study on media ownership notes, the industry "has been characterized by repeated attempts at domination by a small number of firms that customarily tried either to exclude others from the business or to deprive competitors of resources."[4] From a position of almost total dominance in their large home market, the U.S. film majors, by recouping the bulk of their costs in the home market, could provide relatively big budget movies to foreign markets at relatively low costs. Their control of their U.S. product in foreign markets provided them with the leverage to establish just as strong a position in foreign markets as at home, at least as long as foreign governments permitted them to function unimpeded. Since no action has ever been taken in Canada restricting in any way the direct control of the U.S. majors in the Canadian marketplace, the powerful distribution arms of the U.S. producers have dominated the Canadian marketplace. Until 1968, any efforts to develop a Canadian film industry were focused on non-commercial, non-competitive production.

Prior to the development of television in the early 1950s, the "movies" were by far the dominant influence in visual entertainment and cultural expression in Canada. And the films Canadians watched were overwhelmingly American. A 1976 study commissioned by the federal Department of the Secretary of State found that 93 per cent of all revenues from the rental of films to theatres in Canada was paid just to the seven major Hollywood studios.[5]

While the advent of television has reduced theatre attendance to a significantly lower level, the same major producer/distributors sell both their feature films and the television programs they produce to Canadian television networks and will be the major suppliers of feature films to the recently licensed Canadian pay-television services. In addition, without carefully planned public policy, the same companies will soon consolidate their developing position of overwhelming control over the distribution of videocassettes and videodiscs in Canada.

As the following analysis demonstrates, Canada has not yet established any solid industrial base for the production and distribution of feature films. Whereas in the United States the domestic producers control the distribution structure and are closely linked to the exhibition and retailing systems, the Canadian producers are isolated from and have little or no control over the Canadian distribution and exhibition systems. Any effort to develop a strong, healthy Canadian film industry will have to address and redress the historical tradition of a production sector divorced from its major home market.

One possible attitude towards the question of the need to establish a distinctive Canadian film industry is simply to say that films are just entertainment and it does not matter if only foreign films are available in Canada. The United States, however, has always known better. As Frank Shakespeare, a former CBS executive and later United States Information Agency head, has stated:

> The technology which is the essence of the communications revolution was created in this country. In the use of that technology for the dissemination of ideas and information and entertainment, we were the world's leaders. We dominated motion pictures and television for years; we still do.[6]

And a recent American study on the ownership and control of the media observed that:

> Although films overtly entertain, they covertly teach . . . Their propaganda value certainly was the reason why the industry and the government worked together to have them broadly distributed overseas in the years after World War II . . . Inasmuch as the social and cultural role of film has always been acknowledged, it is not surprising that many countries are now beginning to rebel against the cultural invasion by American media. Nor is it surprising that American media struggle to maintain their foreign markets.[7]

The Canadian Market

While there are connections between film and television that link the two very closely, the continuing strength of the theatrical market and the existence of other significant markets for feature film make it

219

useful to look at theatrical features separately. This chapter will focus on theatrical films and on the independent film production industry in Canada.

Sources of Distributor Revenue
As Table 6-1 indicates, the theatrical market remains the largest single market supplied by private-sector distribution companies in Canada. In 1979, the theatrical market accounted for 53 per cent of the total revenues of film and videotape distributors, followed by television at 35 per cent, and non-theatrical markets at 12 per cent.

Only $18.5 million or 9 per cent of the distributors' total revenues of $210.5 million in 1979 was derived from the sale of Canadian films and videotapes. In the major theatrical market, Canadian productions earned 1.8 per cent of total revenue, while in the television market, they did only somewhat better, earning 7.3 per cent or $5.4 million out of total revenues of $74.2 million. The only substantial market for Canadian productions was the relatively small non-theatrical market in which such productions earned 56 per cent of their total revenue. Foreign-controlled distribution companies accounted for 64 per cent of the total revenues of the distribution sector, including 73 per cent of total theatrical revenues.

The Theatrical Market
Table 6-2 charts the decline of theatrical attendance after the coming of television in the early 1950s. Theatre attendance reached a peak in 1952, when 14.4 million Canadians went to the movies an average of eighteen times each that year. By 1980, Canadians went to the movies an average of just over four times a year. However, going to the movies remains important to Canadians. In 1978, urban Canadian families spent an average of $38.90 a year on movie tickets — substantially more than the $21.50 spent on attendance at plays, concerts, operas and ballet, and more than twice as much as the $18.20 they spent on spectator sports.

The number of theatre admissions stopped declining in 1963 and actually rose by 10 per cent between 1970 and 1980. What the theatres may have accomplished is the kind of successful adaptation to television competition that has been achieved by the magazine industry and in radio broadcasting. However, in the case of the theatres, it must be remembered that the feature films they exhibit are also distributed through television stations and networks and are, to an increasing extent, available in videocassette or videodisc form for viewing at

TABLE 6-1
REVENUE OF PRIVATE-SECTOR CANADIAN- AND FOREIGN-CONTROLLED FILM AND VIDEOTAPE DISTRIBUTORS BY MARKET, 1979

	Canadian-Controlled Distributors ($000's)	Foreign-Controlled Distributors ($000's)	Total ($000's)	Total (% of market)
Theatrical Market				
Canadian productions	1,967	—[1]	1,967	1.8
Foreign productions	27,599	81,564	109,163	98.2
Total	29,566	81,564	111,130	100.0
Television Market				
Canadian productions	5,435	—[1]	5,435	7.3
Foreign productions	20,105	48,737	68,842	92.7
Total	25,540	48,737	74,277	100.0
Non-theatrical Market				
Canadian productions	10,345	—[1]	10,345	41.2
Foreign productions	10,252	4,488	14,740	58.8
Total	20,597	4,488	25,085	100.0
Total Market				
Canadian productions	17,747	703	18,450	8.8
Foreign productions	57,956	134,086	192,042	91.2
Total	75,703	134,789	210,492	100.0

Note: [1] Included with Canadian-controlled.

Source: Statistics Canada, *Film Industry, 1979* (Cat. No. 87-620).

TABLE 6-2
TRENDS IN THEATRE ATTENDANCE, PRICES AND ADMISSION REVENUE, 1950-80

Year	Number of Paid Admissions (millions)	Average Admission Rate	Revenue from Paid Admissions ($ millions)
1950	236	0.41	96.7
1960	118	0.66	78.2
1970	92	1.48	137.1
1980	101	3.24	311.4

Source: Statistics Canada, *Film Industry, 1978* and *1979* (Cat. No. 87-620) and *Canadian Film Digest, 1982 Yearbook.*

home. How these alternative distribution channels will affect the theatres in the future is impossible to predict, but it would appear foolish in 1982 to assume that the appeal of going out to a movie will vanish.

As Table 6-3 indicates, the motion picture theatres continue to function profitably, producing an operating profit of $76.5 million in 1979, which represented 22.6 per cent of the revenues of $351.1 million. The major element in their cost structure is the $99.2 million in film rentals that they paid.

While the purchase of the Odeon theatre chain by Canadians has greatly reduced the level of foreign ownership in the motion picture theatre industry, as Table 6-4 indicates, most of the largest theatres in Canada are still foreign-controlled, the bulk of them by Gulf and Western, which also owns the major production/distribution company, Paramount. Of the fifty theatres in Canada which earned over $1 million annually in 1979, thirty-two were foreign-controlled and they accounted for 71 per cent of the total revenues of theatres in this category. While only 18 per cent of all regular theatres in Canada are foreign-controlled, they account for 40 per cent of total revenue. These large theatres handle the first run of most major feature films.

Table 6-5 provides a clearer indication of the extent to which the theatrical market is the property of a relatively few U.S. production/distribution companies. The table also indicates why the U.S. majors feel that Canada is simply a part of their domestic market. The seven largest companies accounted for 89.1 per cent of total U.S. and Canadian revenues from films earning rentals of $1 million or more;

TABLE 6-3

REVENUE, EXPENSE AND OPERATING PROFIT OF THEATRES, 1979 ($000's)

Revenue				Expenditure					Operating Profit (as % of Revenue)
Admissions	Refreshment Sales	Other	Total Revenue	Staff Salaries	Film Rentals	Cost of Merchandise Sold	Other¹	Total	
276,951 (79%)	70,467 (20%)	3,632 (1%)	351,050 (100%)	65,662 (24%)	99,283 (36%)	28,192 (10%)	81,410 (30%)	274,547 (100%)	76,503 (22.6%)

Note: ¹ Includes maintenance, building rentals and utility fees.

Source: Statistics Canada, *Film Industry, 1979.*

TABLE 6-4

ADMISSION RECEIPTS FOR CANADIAN- AND FOREIGN-CONTROLLED THEATRES BY REVENUE GROUP, 1979 ($000's)

Revenue Group	Canadian-Controlled		Foreign-Controlled		Total	
	Number of Theatres	Admission Receipts	Number of Theatres	Admission Receipts	Number of Theatres	Admission Receipts
Regular theatres						
Less than $499,999	826	93,694	69	17,370	895	111,064
$500,000-$999,999	60	32,367	59	33,553	119	65,920
$1 million and over	18	17,875	32	44,099	50	61,975
	904	143,936	160	95,023	1,064	238,959
Drive-ins	272	34,456	19	3,537	291	37,992
Total	1,176	178,392	179	98,560	1,355	276,951

Source: Statistics Canada, *Film Industry, 1979.*

TABLE 6-5

MAJOR COMPANIES' SHARE OF U.S.-CANADIAN MARKET
RECEIPTS FOR FILMS EARNING RENTALS OF $1 MILLION OR
MORE, 1970-78
(percentages)

Companies	1970	1971	1972	1973	1974	1975	1976	1977	1978
Columbia	14.1	10.2	9.1	7.0	7.0	13.1	8.3	11.5	11.6
Metro-Goldwyn-Mayer[1]	3.4	9.3	6.0	4.6	—	—	—	—	—
Paramount	11.8	17.0	21.6	8.6	10.0	11.3	9.6	10.0	23.8
Twentieth Century Fox	19.4	11.5	9.1	18.8	10.9	14.0	13.4	19.5	13.4
United Artists	8.7	7.4	15.0	10.7	8.5	10.7	16.2	17.8	10.3
Universal	13.1	5.2	5.0	10.0	18.6	25.1	13.0	11.5	16.8
Warner Bros.	5.3	9.3	17.6	16.4	23.2	9.1	18.0	13.7	13.2
Total — 7 largest, 1978	75.8	69.9	83.4	76.1	78.2	83.3	78.5	84.0	89.1
Buena Vista	9.1	8.0	5.0	6.5	7.0	6.0	6.7	5.6	4.8
Amer. International	—	—	—	—	3.8	3.4	3.8	3.4	1.4
Total — 9 largest, 1978	84.9	77.9	88.4	82.6	89.0	92.7	89.0	93.0	95.3

Note: [1] Distributed by United Artists since 1974.

Source: Table reproduced from Benjamin M. Compaine, ed., *Who Owns the Media?*
(Knowledge Industry Publications, 1979), p. 223 (based on information from *Variety*).

the top nine companies accounted for 95.3 per cent. In Canada, the distribution arms of these U.S. companies distributed no Canadian feature films in 1978 or 1979, and just two in 1980.

What provides the major companies with much of their influence in the marketplace is, of course, the fact that they distribute the relatively limited number of ''block-busters'' that account for a large percentage of total theatrical box office. The top ten films in 1978 had gross box office receipts of $1.2 billion in the United States-Canadian market, while total box office revenue was approximately $3 billion. The six largest production/distribution companies in 1978 distributed twenty-five of the twenty-seven films which earned more than $10 million in North America rentals.[8]

If the U.S. majors vigorously defend their oligopoly control of the Canadian marketplace, it is because they recognize the extent to which direct market control can reduce the risks involved in producing big-budget feature films. There is an obviously circular character to this argument, since it is by producing block-busters that these companies solidify their domination both of their domestic market and of foreign markets. The Washington Task Force on the Motion Picture Industry argued in a 1978 report that "the major producer/distributors are effectively limiting competition by maintaining tight control over the distribution of films, both by their failure to produce more films and by their failure to distribute more films produced by others." The same study charged that the major companies "tacitly limit production among themselves and . . . create sufficient barriers to effectively squash new competition."[9]

Because the Canadian movie producers, unlike producers in Britain and, in fact, in almost all European countries, do not benefit from any substantial government initiatives to compensate for their relatively small and heavily foreign-dominated domestic theatrical market, they have had to function within an integrated continental market dominated by an oligopoly of major American producer/distributors. The latter companies have acted as the "gatekeepers" in the Canadian as well as American market, determining which movies can enter the system and on what terms. The U.S. majors are not at all interested in distributing films whose primary market will be in Canada. To the extent that they are interested in Canadian-produced films, they want films that are not recognizably Canadian and will be acceptable to mass American audiences.

The Television Market
Diagram 6-1 indicates the additional markets to which producers of theatrical films might look for revenue. The Canadian-content requirements established by the CRTC could give Canadian productions an advantage in selling to Canadian television broadcasters that they do not have in the theatrical market. However, the CRTC regulations do not specify that any minimum percentage of the feature films and other drama or variety programs shown by television licensees must be Canadian. The total revenue derived from a network television sale to the CBC would be $150,000 to $250,000 for showing in prime time, while CTV pays somewhat less. By comparison, a sale to a U.S. network can produce from $1.5 to $2.5 million on the average. Even for feature films in the lower budget category of $1.5 million to $2 million, the Canadian television market does not return a substantial proportion of total costs. In Canada, television syndication revenues account for only a few thousand dollars.

What has proved more useful to producers is the opportunity to co-produce features with the Canadian television networks.

DIAGRAM 6-1
DISTRIBUTION CHANNELS FOR THEATRICAL FILM

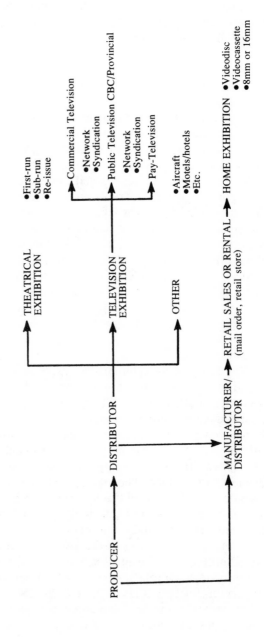

CBC/Radio-Canada has entered into co-production agreements for such films as *Les Plouffes*, and CTV has done so for a few Canadian films, including *Two Solitudes* and *Why Shoot the Teacher*?

Pay-Television

Pay-television services have existed in the United States since the mid-1970s. Growth has been rapid, with Home Box Office, which dominates the U.S. industry, increasing its subscriber base between 1975 and December 1980 from 250,000 to over six million. The second largest U.S. pay-television service, Showtime, had only 1.6 million subscribers in December 1980.

Pay-television has developed in the United States, as the name Home Box Office suggests, primarily on the basis of providing early access in subscribers' homes to recently released feature films made for theatrical exhibition. The return from this new market, while still not comparable to either the theatrical market or the U.S. network market, is assuming a rapidly expanding importance for feature film producers.

The introduction of pay-television in Canada was delayed for almost a decade after pressure first began to be applied by Canadian cable television companies for its introduction. For cable companies, pay-television represented a potentially important new source of revenue. A 1978 CRTC policy statement on pay-television found that there was little public interest in its introduction and little evidence that such services would do more than provide a new channel for importing U.S. films. More recently, in April 1981, the CRTC proceeded with a request for applications to provide Canadian pay-television services. In inviting applications, the commission stated that the ability of pay-television services to "make available high quality, Canadian programming" would be "a major criterion" in ·its assessment of applications. The commission also raised the question of the character of pay-television's Canadian programming, urging applicants to "respond to the particular social, cultural, linquistic and geographic characteristics of Canada."[10]

Canadian movie producers hoped that pay-television would help them to recoup a significantly higher proportion of their investment from the domestic market. The level of expenditure which applicants proposed to make on a per film basis varied from a high of $1 to $1.5 million for TeleCanada, a non-profit national service, to a much lower level for regional and special-interest services. The highest expenditure promised by a national commercial service was the $500,000 promised by First Choice Canadian Communications Ltd. However, First Choice's promise was conditional on being granted a monopoly in the provision of the first-run American feature films which will provide the basis for the marketing of such a service. If directly competing rather than complementary services were licensed, First Choice's average expenditure would fall to $190,000 per feature. If the company's higher projection of market penetration was not met, the expenditure per film would be significantly lower.

Subsequently, the CRTC decided to license competing commercial services and at least to delay the introduction of a non-commercial service. As a result, the Canadian pay-television market will not, in the near future, provide an important enough market to affect significantly the production of Canadian feature films. The American pay-television market, however, will be of steadily increasing importance to Canadian movie producers as a potential alternative to reliance on American theatrical distribution. These characteristics of the market will continue to affect the character of the films that can be produced in Canada.

The results of the CRTC decision will be particularly disappointing because of the extraordinarily loose definition the commission uses in identifying television programming as Canadian. The fact that the CRTC operates with no clearly articulated definition of Canadian programming leaves the Canadian pay-television licensees free to meet their Canadian-content requirement by functioning as minor investors in feature films and other television programs which are funded primarily by U.S. pay-television services and which will be designed explicitly for U.S. audiences. Canadian settings and Canadian themes will almost certainly be avoided in the vast majority of the "Canadian" programming that results.

The Film Production/Distribution Industry in Canada

The Public Sector
The National Film Board was created by the federal government in 1939. Under its revised mandate of 1950, the board has a responsibility to produce and distribute films "designed to interpret Canada to Canadians and to other nations." With the exception of the Canadian Broadcasting Corporation, the NFB is the largest single producer of Canadian film. The NFB has regional production offices in Halifax,

Toronto, Winnipeg, Edmonton, Vancouver and Moncton, and operates the largest Canadian-controlled film distribution organization. The total expenditure of the board, although in decline relative to inflation since 1978-79, was $57.8 million in 1980-81 (see Table 6-6).

Although the NFB has, with only occasional exceptions, confined its production activity to documentary and educational film for the non-theatrical markets, its relatively few feature films include some of the best Canadian features that have been produced. In the other fields in which the NFB has been particularly active, it has achieved major successes, including the winning of such major film awards as the Oscars in Hollywood. Despite its infrequent forays into feature film, it could be argued that the NFB has an unusually high success rate in producing high quality movies. In keeping with the mandate of the NFB, those features have contributed to the development of a distinctive Canadian film culture.

TABLE 6-6
REVENUE, EXPENDITURE AND NET COST OF OPERATIONS FOR THE NATIONAL FILM BOARD, 1976-81
(year ending March 31/$000's)

	1976	1977	1978	1979	1980	1981
Expenses						
Production[1]	21,254	21,524	26,709	30,103	28,967	34,213
Distribution	12,486	12,922	14,973	14,993	14,891	16,005
Administration	4,242	4,782	5,660	5,816	6,219	6,973
Research and development	642	490	525	573	584	620
Other	74	135	30	—	—	—
Total expenses	38,697	39,853	47,897	51,484	50,661	57,811
Revenues						
Production	5,858	4,867	7,149	7,703	7,824	9,928
Distribution[2]	5,029	4,974	5,471	5,049	5,441	6,189
Total revenues	10,888	9,841	12,151	12,752	13,265	16,117
Net Cost of Operations	27,809	30,011	35,276	38,731	37,395	41,694

Notes: [1] Note that films sponsored by government departments and agencies accounted for a significant share of total production ($6,586,630 in 1978 rising to $8,072,830 in 1981).

[2] From 1978 on, the annual reports of the NFB separate governmental and non-governmental revenue from distribution. Distribution revenue from non-governmental sources was $3,148,380 in 1978 and $2,733,427 in 1979.

Source: NFB Annual Reports.

Private-Sector Distribution

While in the United States the production and distribution functions are combined in the major companies, thereby reducing the risk of investments in production, in Canada the two sectors tend to be separate, with distribution controlled by the subsidiaries of the major U.S. companies and production almost entirely done by Canadian companies. Data for the two sectors are, therefore, examined separately.

Table 6-7 provides basic operating data for all private-sector distributors of film and videotape in Canada. The ninety-two companies included, as indicated in Table 6-1, operate in the television and non-theatrical as well as the theatrical market.

Royalty payments accounted for 72 per cent of the distributors' operating expenditures in 1979. Of the total revenues of $212.4 million earned by the distributors, 62 per cent or $132 million was paid out in royalties to producers. The extent to which the markets served by the distributors were served by foreign films in 1979 is evident in the fact that 96 per cent of all royalties paid, or $126.8 million, went to foreign copyright holders, with only $5.2 million going to Canadian copyright holders (see Table 6-8). This ratio would have shifted somewhat in 1980 and 1981 to reflect the recent boom in film investment stimulated by the accelerated capital cost allowance provisions in the federal Income Tax Act. However, the change has not been a major one, and the major decline in investment in 1981 and 1982 suggests that it may not be permanent.[11] The tax incentive and its effects will be looked at later in this chapter.

In addition to making royalty payments of $132 million, almost entirely to foreign copyright holders, the film distributors earned operating profits in 1979 of $28.5 million, which represented 13.4 per cent of revenue. The nine companies reporting sales of $5 million and over, which included the U.S. majors, reported operating profits equal to 15.6 per cent of revenue.

Private-Sector Production

The most recent year for which detailed Statistics Canada data on the private-sector film production industry are available is 1979. As Table 6-9 indicates, the industry showed an aggregate operating loss of $1 million in 1979 on total revenues of $104.5 million. Total revenue from the sale and rental of productions accounted for $92.3 million.

Tables 6-10 and 6-11 indicate the nature of the productions that were being produced and the markets to which they were being sold. As

230

TABLE 6-7

REVENUE, EXPENSE AND AVERAGE PROFIT OF DISTRIBUTORS BY REVENUE GROUP, 1979
($000's)

Revenue Group	Number of Companies	Operating Revenue	Operating Expenses Salaries & Wages	Operating Expenses Royalties	Operating Expenses Other	Total Operating Expense	Pre-Tax Profit Total	Pre-Tax Profit As % of Revenue
Less than $1 million	64	18,434	3,193	7,701	5,356	16,251	2,183	11.8
$1 million-$4,999,999	19	44,444	4,244	29,929	7,236	41,408	3,036	6.8
$5 million and over	9	149,509	5,672	94,425	26,106	126,203	23,306	15.6
Total	92	212,387	13,110	132,055	38,698	183,862	28,525	13.4

Source: Statistics Canada, *Film Industry, 1979.*

TABLE 6-8

ROYALTIES, RENTALS AND COMMISSIONS PAID BY CANADIAN- AND FOREIGN-CONTROLLED DISTRIBUTORS TO PRODUCERS, BY OWNERSHIP OF COPYRIGHT OF THE PRODUCTION, 1979 ($000's)

Ownership of Copyright in Production	Distributors Canadian-Controlled	Distributors Foreign-Controlled	Distributors Total
Canadian	5,250	—[1]	5,250
Foreign	40,815	85,990	126,805
Total	46,065	85,990	132,055

Note: [1] Included with Canadian-controlled.   Source: Statistics Canada, *Film Industry, 1979.*

TABLE 6-9

REVENUE, EXPENSE AND AVERAGE PROFIT OF PRIVATE-SECTOR FILM AND TELEVISION PRODUCTION COMPANIES, 1979 ($000's)

Revenue Group	Number of Companies	Revenue			Expenditure				Operating Profit	
		Production	Other	Total	Wages & Benefits	Freelance Fees	Other	Total	Total	As % of Revenue
Less than $100,000	129	4,114	556	4,670	2,613	3,873	7,873	14,359	(9,689)	(207.5)
$100,000-$999,999	114	28,921	3,098	32,019	6,917	5,543	15,910	28,369	3,650	11.4
Over $1 million	25	59,274	8,554	67,828	12,122	8,797	40,844	61,764	5,358	7.9
Total	268	92,309	12,208	104,517	21,652	18,213	64,627	104,492	(681)	(0.7)

Source: Statistics Canada, *Film Industry, 1979*.

TABLE 6-10

REVENUE OF PRIVATE-SECTOR PRODUCTION COMPANIES BY MARKET AND REVENUE GROUP FROM SALE AND RENTAL OF PRODUCTIONS, 1979 ($000's)

Revenue Group	Number of Companies	Theatrical			Television			Non-Theatrical	Total
		Features	Shorts	Total	Programs	Commercials	Total		
Less than $100,000	129	420	235	655	721	541	1,262	2,198	4,115
$100,000-$999,999	114	1,629	1,690	3,319	6,816	10,208	17,024	8,578	28,921
Over $1 million	25	764	271	1,035	17,550	28,668	46,218	12,020	59,273
Total	268	2,813	2,196	5,009	25,087	39,417	64,504	22,795	92,309
Percentage of revenue		3.0	2.4	5.4	27.2	42.7	69.9	24.7	100.0

Source: Statistics Canada, *Film Industry, 1979*.

TABLE 6-11
REVENUE OF PRIVATE-SECTOR PRODUCTION COMPANIES BY
CUSTOMER CATEGORY, 1979

Customer Category	Revenue ($000's)	Percentage of Total Revenue
Television broadcasters	18,300	17.5
Advertising agencies	22,100	21.1
Distributors	6,400	6.2
Educational institutions	11,200	10.7
Governments	15,700	15.0
Industries	22,700	21.7
Other	8,100	7.8
Total	104,500	100.0

Source: Statistics Canada, *Film Industry, 1979*.

recently as 1979, 67.4 per cent of industry revenue was derived from the production of television commercials and from the non-theatrical market, which includes the educational, industrial and government markets. Theatrical productions accounted for just 5.4 per cent of total revenue and theatrical features for just 3.0 per cent, down from the 6.4 per cent of revenue earned from theatrical films in 1978.

While the production industry as a whole was not profitable in 1979, the losses were accounted for mainly by small companies whose expenses were far in excess of revenue. These figures for small companies reflected the influx of investment capital into feature films produced in that period.

Measures to Stimulate Feature Film Production

The Canadian Film Development Corporation
Beginning in 1968, the federal government adopted measures designed to stimulate private-sector production of feature films. The Canadian Film Development Corporation (CFDC) was created in 1968 with a mandate "to foster and promote the development of a feature film industry in Canada," and specifically, to provide financial and other assistance to the private-sector producers of films which "have a significant Canadian creative, artistic and technical content."

In 1968, only ten Canadian feature films were produced, with an average budget of $250,000. Over the next decade, the CFDC injected $26 million in financing, primarily in the form of equity financing, into the production of feature films. It is worth noting that this ten-year figure is less than the annual level of funding to the NFB. The total budgets of the films CFDC invested in was $66 million. Through most of this period, the average budget of Canadian films remained relatively low. In 1976, forty features were produced with an average budget of $500,000 (see Table 6-12).

During this period, Canadian films were generally unsuccessful in getting significant theatrical distribution or promotion in Canada or abroad, a reflection of both American control over the theatrical distribution and exhibition systems in Canada and the limited resources of the Canadian producers and distributors. In addition, in the increasingly important television market, these films also received very limited distribution in Canada. Even the English-language service of the CBC, which has a special mandate to reflect Canada to Canadians, did not act as though it saw Canadian film producers as allies in achieving a common cultural purpose. When the CBC did occasionally purchase such films, it paid very little for them, a small fraction of what it would have cost to fill the same time slot with its own dramatic programming, and far less than CBC was paying for foreign films.

While between 1968 and 1977 the CFDC succeeded in increasing the number of Canadian films produced and the annual level of investment, it was not successful in building a strong domestic production and distribution industry. Although many Canadian films were produced during this period, the CFDC earned back only $5 million of its investments.

During this decade, the average ratio of English to French productions was six to four. However, the average budgets of English-language films were usually three or four times as large as those for French-language films.

The general comments above concerning the lack of interest by domestic television networks in Canadian features did not apply to French-language productions. Both Radio-Canada and Radio-Quebec helped finance French-language productions, providing essential pre-production financial commitments. While only 20 per cent of the English-language features produced between 1968 and 1977 were purchased by television networks and fewer were ever aired, most French-language features were purchased and shown on television. French-language productions also received more effective theatrical

FEATURE FILM INDUSTRY OUTPUT, 1960-80 (dollar figures in millions)

Year	Number of Feature Films			Total Production Costs[1]	CFDC Films[2]			100% CCA Films		100% CCA/CFDC Films	
	Total	English	French		Number	Total Production Costs	Total Invested by CFDC	Number	Total Production Costs	Number	Total Production Costs
1960	3	2	1								
1961	7	6	1	Average							
1962	2	1	1	total							
1963	1	0	1	costs							
1964	6	3	3	per year							
1965	4	1	3	$0.75m							
1966	6	3	3								
1967	7	6	1								
1968	10	7	3	2.5	} 17[3]	} 4.2[3]	} 1.7[3]				
1969	19	12	7	4.5							
1970	32	18	14	10.6	26	7.3	2.5				
1971	20	8	12	8.2	24	6.3	2.5				
1972	35	18	17	16.8	33	10.4	3.9				
1973	22	12	10	9.9	19	7.6	2.9				
1974	27	11	16	6.2	26	7.5	3.3	2	1.4	2	1.4
1975	37	26	11	17.5	18	5.4	3.0	20	7.6	11	3.9
1976	40	24	16	20.0	16	12.0	2.9	28	18.1	9	7.6
1977	43	34	9	39.0	20	5.6	1.6	37	29.3	6	4.6
1978	54	27	27	52.0	27	49.9	5.6	31	36.7	12	22.9
1979	87	60	27	107.0	34	107.0	10.0	55	150.0	23	68.5
1980	77	53	24	140.0	28	85.6	5.9	50	130.0	—	—

Notes: [1] Estimated from available data.
[2] Data here are based on CFDC fiscal years (April 1 to March 31); since other data in the table are based on calendar years, data are only approximately comparable.
[3] Includes both 1968 and 1969 productions.

Source: R. M. Bird, M. W. Bucovsky and A. Yatchew, *Tax Incentives for the Canadian Film Industry* (Institute for Policy Analysis, 1981).

235

distribution in the mid-1970s, accounting for more than 40 per cent of the total theatrical earnings of all Canadian films. Their theatrical success may well reflect the greater degree of control by Quebec producers over film distribution and exhibition.

The Capital Cost Allowance

In 1974, the federal government amended the Income Tax Act to offer a 100 per cent capital cost allowance in the first year on investments in "certified feature films." In order to be certified, films had to satisfy a requirement that they be made by a Canadian producer and that Canadians perform a specified number of the creative functions. This important government initiative created a new tax incentive for investors and made it possible to atttract private investment into films which met the requirements for certification. The tax incentive was extended in 1976 to certified short films and videotape as well as feature films, and, at the same time, the capital cost allowance for non-certified films was reduced from 60 per cent to 30 per cent.

Subsequently, in 1978, the CFDC shifted its own focus from the provision of equity financing for lower budget Canadian films to the provision of interim and bridge financing for films that were intended to be financed by private investors under the provisions of the capital cost allowance. The combination of the tax incentive and the altered role of the CFDC resulted in a sudden and dramatic increase in the average budget of English-language Canadian films. In the French-language sector, the capital cost allowance did not have the same effect and there was not the same shift in the focus of CFDC activity.

It should be noted that there are some discrepancies in the available information on the number of features produced under the capital cost allowance and their average budgets. The figures from the Canadian Film Certification Office (CFCO) shown in Table 6-13 deal only with certified films and probably represent the most reliable source. The CFCO figures indicate that the average budget of certified films increased from $829,000 in 1977 to $1.3 million in 1978. The following year saw a sharp increase to $2.7 million and a phenomenal increase from $47.1 million to $180 million in total investment. Because of the lack of commercial success of films produced in 1978 and 1979, producers began to encounter difficulty in late 1980 in attracting investment to new features. As the CFCO figures indicate, the result was a precipitous decline in investment in 1981, with total investment at about one-third of the 1979 level and just thirty-seven features certified.

TABLE 6-13
NUMBER AND VALUE OF PRODUCTION OF CERTIFIED
FEATURE FILMS, 1975-81

	1975	1976	1977	1978	1979	1980	1981
Number of certified features	18	34	42	35	67	59	37
Value of certified feature production	$6.3m	$19.5m	$34.8m	$47.1m	$180m	$156.5m	$64.7m

Source: Canadian Film Certification Office.

There is now widespread agreement that changes in film policy are essential if both the cultural and industrial objectives of policy are to be met. As a recent study prepared by the Institute for Policy Analysis for the Federal Cultural Policy Review Committee observed "by 1980, the apparently recurrent malaise of the Canadian film industry was once again apparent."[12] Not only were there problems resulting from a lack of economic success, there were serious concerns over the lack of success from a cultural perspective. The Institute for Policy Analysis noted that

> it could well be argued that one result of the expanded investment in Canadian film production resulting from the film tax incentive has been a reduction in "truly Canadian" films. Some evidence of this may perhaps be seen in the marked decline of French-language film production in the last few years, in part because some money that might have gone to these films has been channelled instead to big budget English-language productions aimed at the U.S. market.[13]

Out of total investment since 1978 of over $360 million, only 3 per cent, or less than $10 million, went into French-language films. The average budget of those French-language films remained below $500,000, while the average budget for English-language films increased to over $3 million.

A recent Ontario Economic Council (OEC) study goes somewhat further, concluding that "present policies have not been primarily motivated by the positive cultural externalities argument."[14] The OEC study argues that policies affecting the film industry have up to the present time been focused primarily on serving economic rather than cultural goals. As a result, the authors of the study conclude that "private interests seem to have benefitted vastly more from current policies than has any perceived general 'public interest' in promoting a stronger Canadian cultural identity — either by showing Canadians to themselves or by showing the rest of the world what Canadians can accomplish.''[15]

In the absence of any major expansion of the domestic markets, the rapidly escalating budgets made it imperative that the resulting English-language films succeed in the American market. Because they recognized this, the Canadian film producers featured U.S. stars in their films and generally avoided Canadian themes and recognizably Canadian settings. While the distribution of these relatively de-nationalized films improved significantly, both in Canada and in the United States, the rate of return has in most cases not been sufficient to satisfy investors. Most Canadian producers recognize the need to strengthen their own distribution facilities and to achieve for most of the films they produce a much higher return from their domestic market.

Economic Impact

Table 6-14 provides partial data on employment generated by film production and distribution companies in the private sector in 1979. Of the total 1,930 full-time jobs in film production and distribution, 1,201 were in the production sector. While this imbalance, to some extent, simply reflects the difference in the nature of the production and distribution activities, it may also reflect the degree to which the distribution companies are simply branch offices of companies based in the United States. The production industry made freelance payments of $18.2 million, in addition to the total of $20.6 million paid in salaries and wages. The production and distribution sectors combined

TABLE 6-14
NUMBER OF EMPLOYEES, WAGES AND SALARIES, AND FREELANCE FEES PAID BY PRIVATE-SECTOR PRODUCTION AND DISTRIBUTION COMPANIES, 1979

	Part-time Employees	Full-time employees	Total Salaries and Wages ($000's)	Freelance Fees
Distribution companies	57	729	13,110	—
Production companies	268	1,201	20,575	18,213
Total	325	1,930	33,685	18,213

Source: Statistics Canada, *Film Industry, 1979*.

paid total wages and salaries of $33.7 million in 1979. There was a further substantial increase in freelance payments by private producers in 1980, to $24.7 million. The general pattern of employment in the industry is to rely on freelance workers. While Statistics Canada data for the period since 1980 are not yet available, there is clear evidence of a rapid decline in payments by private-sector independent producers to freelance workers.

In the case of writers and performers, figures provided by their union, ACTRA, indicate that after increasing sharply from $2.9 million in 1978 to $11.2 million in 1980, the earnings of writers and performers from independent producers dropped 32 per cent to $7.6 million in 1981. For the period January to July 1982, there was a drop of a further 39 per cent from the comparable period in 1981. While revenue from independent producers accounted for 22 per cent of the total earnings of Canadian film and television writers and performers in 1980, up from 8.5 per cent in 1978, it will probably account for less than 10 per cent again in 1982. The largest percentage of the revenue of ACTRA's members continues to come from the Canadian Broadcasting Corporation which accounted for 38 per cent of their total earnings in 1981.

Industry and government estimates indicate that a total of 10,000 Canadians work freelance on film and television productions for all public and private production companies, as writers, editors, directors, cameramen, technicians and performers. To a large extent, as a result of the increased investment stimulated from 1978 through 1980 by the capital cost allowance, industry sources now suggest that Canada has at least twenty-five experienced feature film production crews and could generate in excess of 200 feature films per year. The laboratories and processing equipment now exist to handle a high volume of film production in Canada. There are also thirteen production studios of high quality.

In a speech in 1978, the then secretary of state, John Roberts, drew attention to the fact that the vast majority of theatrical rentals in 1975 of $60 million left the country, with just 1 per cent of the total being paid to Canadian film copyright holders. As noted above, the distribution industry in 1979 paid $126.8 million to foreign copyright holders, of which $19 million would have been payable in federal withholding taxes, with the remaining $108 million leaving Canada. Canadian productions, by comparison, have earned only sporadic and relatively limited royalties from foreign markets. The deficit in such payments in 1983 would certainly exceed $100 million.

There has been considerable debate as to the costs and benefits associated with the capital cost allowance for films. With respect to the actual tax expenditure involved in the capital cost allowance incentive, the most recent and detailed study concludes that the actual cost in forgone revenue to both federal and provincial governments in 1979 was $14.5 million on films budgeted at $150 million.[16] The federal cost was $8.5 million. The authors note that this is far less than the cost of the MURB or drilling fund incentives and far less than is commonly assumed.

It is sometimes argued that the economic benefits in additional employment generated compensate for the costs of this tax incentive, and that the activities the incentive stimulates return compensating tax revenues to government. However, the public and private funds which have gone into film production as a result of the incentive would have gone into other activities in the absence of the incentive. Those alternative activities would also have stimulated employment and resulted in tax revenues to government. Whether the funds might have generated more or less employment, or more or less tax revenue, if invested in other industries, is a matter of conjecture. From an economic perspective, perhaps no more can be said than that film production is employment intensive.

The key point is that the introduction of the tax incentive, which has induced substantially increased film investment, was based on the argument that, in its absence, there would have been too little investment in films in a cultural and social sense. The important question is whether these social and cultural benefits have been achieved, a question that cultural groups such as the Canadian Conference of the Arts had raised in their presentations to the Federal Cultural Policy Review Committee. On this issue, there seems to be little disagreement that the benefits of the tax incentive policy have not been satisfactory.

Policy Issues and Proposals

The Capital Cost Allowance

The federal budget of November 12, 1981 reduced the capital cost allowance for certified Canadian film from 100 per cent to 50 per cent, as well as introducing a reduction in the maximum rate of taxation for individuals from 68 per cent to 50 per cent and eliminating the deduction of interest charges on loans made to finance such investments. These changes were announced in the climate of investment uncertainty that had developed already in the film industry and were met by remarkably unified opposition from the industry unions and from production, distribution and exhibition organizations. In objecting to this unexpected change, the industry expressed its dismay at "an apparent contradiction of the government's clearly stated cultural objectives for the Canadian film industry." The industry statement went on as follows:

> This film industry was deliberately created by a clearly defined government policy of incentives, including the capital cost allowance system. This had the intention and effect of building a permanent base to give expression to and provide the manifestation of a cultural and national Canadian identity. It was designed to foster the development and growth of production entities, producing on a continuous basis, Canadian films directed by Canadians, written by Canadians, starring Canadians, made with Canadian technicians in Canadian labs.[17]

What is remarkable about this statement, in the light of the kinds of films that had actually been made over the previous two or three years, is its focus on cultural objectives and Canadian creative participation. To a significant degree, the statement reflects both an acknowledgement by the industry that the tax incentive had been supported initially primarily as a social and cultural development measure, and an awareness that the industry itself needed, for industrial as well as cultural reasons, to focus more of its attention on the domestic market.

In response to this industry pressure, the finance minister agreed to delay the changes in the budget for twelve months. What would appear desirable during this period is for the communications minister and the industry to reach an agreement on further changes to the tax incentive which would provide more investment in films that meet a higher Canadian-content standard. The statement quoted above suggests that the industry would agree to such changes.

A sound approach to achieving that goal would be to establish two categories for capital cost allowance purposes in the future. With perhaps some minor amendments, the current criteria would continue to apply to films eligible for the existing capital cost allowance incentive. However, in recognition of the higher risks involved in producing films which are entirely Canadian, a 150 per cent capital cost allowance would be provided. A comparable level of incentive is provided by the Australian government to encourage the production of Australian films. Such an incentive in Canada would affect most French-language production, as well as those fully Canadian productions in English which have had so little success in raising funding through the existing program.

241

An additional change that should be made is to require that any certified film should be produced by a Canadian-owned and -controlled production company. The criteria used to define Canadian ownership and control might be the same as those already applied to television broadcasting stations licensed by the CRTC.

It is also desirable and reasonable to expect that films produced under the capital cost allowance be distributed in the Canadian market by Canadian-owned and -controlled distribution companies. However, there are at least two problems with such a proposal. The first is that distribution arrangements are often not in place at the time certification is granted. While that problem might be overcome, it is a potential administrative complication. The more serious immediate problem is the fact that the Canadian-controlled sector of the distribution industry is so weak that such a requirement would limit the attractiveness of the tax incentive. As a result, such a restriction should not be added to the criteria of the capital cost allowance until a more comprehensive strategy has been implemented that would strengthen the Canadian-controlled component of the distribution industry very substantially.

However, adjustments to the capital cost allowance will never be sufficient to achieve the cultural objectives on the basis of which film policy initiatives have been justified. The tax incentive must be viewed simply as one among an array of instruments through which the production and distribution of Canadian films is stimulated.

Taxation of Distributor/Exhibitor Revenues

At the present time, some provincial governments levy amusement taxes on the box office receipts of the theatres. In 1980, these taxes totalled $10 million. In Europe, such taxes are usually federal and the tax collected is normally a levy that is put back into domestic film production, either in the form of an automatic increment to box office returns for domestic films or other direct support to production.

Since the provinces have jurisdiction to collect such taxes, they have the potential to use such revenues to support the production of films that further their cultural and industrial development objectives. A 10 per cent admissions tax nationally would generate over $30 million for the provincial governments to use in stimulating film production. The fact that this has not been done reflects the past weakness of the film industry in Canada and the fact that the provincial governments, like the federal government, have only recently begun to articulate cultural policies and particularly policies affecting the cultural industries.

A 10 per cent tax on theatre admissions was recommended recently in Quebec by the Fournier Commission, which was set up in 1981 to make film policy recommendations to the government of Quebec. This recommendation was accompanied by a recommendation that a 10 per cent tax also be levied on the cable television industry's revenues. In Ontario also, by freezing at $3.50 the level at which theatre admissions are exempt from tax, the Ontario government has begun to collect a 10 per cent tax on most theatre admissions. However, while the tax proposal in Quebec calls for the funds collected to be used to support film production, Ontario's box office tax was implemented outside the framework of provincial film policy concerns.

If the provincial governments were to implement such initiatives, it would be desirable to provide, through the use of part of the resulting revenues, an incentive for the exhibition of Canadian films as well as support for their production. The exhibition incentive might take the form of a partial rebate to the theatres of the admissions tax or levy collected based on rental payments for Canadian films. The remainder of the fund would be used to provide an automatic increase to the theatrical rentals for Canadian films and/or to provide financial support for the production of Canadian films and the strengthening of the Canadian industry.

While the theatres come within the jurisdiction of the provinces, the federal government has the authority to levy taxes on the distribution industry. As stated earlier, the industry paid royalties to foreign copyright holders of $126.8 million in 1979 on which the federal government now collects a withholding tax of 15 per cent. Federal ministers responsible for cultural policy have expressed concern frequently over the fact that little of this money is ever invested in Canadian films. In 1978, Secretary of State John Roberts stated that "the present imbalance of rentals and the returns of investment for Canadian productions cannot endure." Specific initiatives have been presented to the federal government going back at least to 1947. Over the following thirty-five years, nothing significant has been done and the outflow of rental income has continued to increase. The most effective approach would be to levy increased withholding taxes on the export of distribution revenues and to permit a reduction or rebate in such taxes on the basis of each distributor's rental payments from foreign markets to producers of Canadian film.

Public-Sector Involvement
Because of the difficult economics of producing either French-language films or English-language Canadian films that are innovative

or unlikely to find mass audiences outside Canada, the role of public agencies must continue to be extensive. As the executive director of the Canadian Film Development Corporation has stated, "You could develop — with the CCA and only the CCA — a very good American film industry in Canada."[18] At the present time, the CRTC, the CBC, the NFB, the CFDC and the Canada Council are all involved with one or more of the following: the training of filmmakers, film production, the financing of production, film exhibition, the regulation of film exhibitors (the broadcasters), and programs of support to filmmakers. Yet there has been little cooperation among these agencies and they have frequently operated at cross-purposes. For example, the CFDC's efforts between 1968 and 1977 to develop Canadian feature films received little support from the English-language service of the CBC and none from the CRTC with respect to television exhibition of Canadian features. More recently, the CRTC decision on pay-television rejected the advice of the CFDC, which has responsibility for the development of the independent film and television production industry, as well as the advice of the NFB and the CBC.

While it is important that these agencies of government all function at arm's length from government in their day-to-day decision-making, it is equally important, since they all spend public funds and work within a framework of authority derived from Parliament, that they function within a coherent policy framework. The responsibility for formulating that framework rests with the minister of communications, whose responsibility it should be to provide the comprehensive and public stated objectives and strategy within which the agencies operate. In the absence of such coordination, little can be achieved and the scarce resources available are not used to best advantage.

Vertical Integration
By far the most important company in the Canadian film industry is Gulf and Western. Gulf and Western's film exhibition subsidiary, Famous Players Ltd., had 1979-80 revenues of $152 million and ranked 285th in the *Financial Post*'s 1981 list of the 500 largest industrial companies. Gulf and Western also owns the major production/distribution company, Paramount Pictures, which accounted for 23.8 per cent of total distributors' rentals in 1978 in the U.S.-Canadian market.

Integration of production/distribution companies with theatre chains in the United States is not permitted. The majors were required by the Justice Department to divest their holdings in the exhibition system after a Supreme Court decision in 1948. A recent U.S. study notes that after the separation of distribution from exhibition:

> Columbia, Universal, United Artists, and some smaller companies were able to obtain larger shares of the market. Theatre owners gained greater control over their business, especially in the selection of films, while independent producers and foreign filmmakers had better opportunities to have their films exhibited.[19]

Comparable action should be taken in Canada to separate Famous Players from Paramount. It is ironic that Canada continues to allow foreign-controlled companies a degree of market control through vertical integration that was terminated as unacceptable by their home government decades ago.

Foreign Control of Distribution

There were ten distribution companies in Canada in 1980 with revenues of $5 million or more. These companies accounted for 74 per cent of the distribution industry's total revenues. Of these ten major companies, seven were foreign-controlled. However, these seven companies accounted for 84 per cent of the revenues of the large firms.

The only large Canadian-controlled distribution company is Astral-Bellevue Pathé, which acts as the distributor in Canada for Columbia Pictures and, as of 1980, for Twentieth Century Fox. Recently, there have been a number of changes in the ownership of the U.S. majors. Metro-Goldwyn-Mayer purchased United Artists in 1981 for $350 million; Marvin Davis, through TCF Holdings, purchased Twentieth Century Fox in partnership with a subsidiary of the commodities trading firm, March Rich & Company, for $722 million; while more recently, Coca-Cola agreed to buy Columbia Pictures for $855 million.

The Astral-Bellevue model is a preferable one for the importing and distribution of foreign films in Canada. It is worth remembering that for a country like Canada, which is overwhelmingly dependent on the importation of Hollywood films, the way in which those films enter the Canadian market is the key determinant of industry structure. If they enter through directly controlled subsidiaries, then those subsidiaries will control the Canadian marketplace. Unless there are compelling reasons to the contrary, it should at the minimum be the policy of the federal government, enforced through FIRA, that there should be no new foreign ownership in the film industry and that the Canadian-controlled sector should be substantially expanded. A comparable policy has begun to provide benefits in the book publishing industry by creating opportunities for the purchase of subsidiary companies when there is a change in control of the parent firm.

If the Canadian-controlled distribution industry can be strengthened, then a reasonable share of the profit made from distributing foreign films in the Canadian market will be in Canadian hands. The foreign-controlled distributors invested less than 1 per cent of their $80 million Canadian earnings in Canadian films in 1980. In addition, there will be a greatly enhanced potential for Canadian films to achieve better distribution in the Canadian market. However, this does not mean that Canadian films will necessarily benefit greatly from such a change unless it is part of a broader strategy. What is essential is to reduce the level of direct control of the Canadian marketplace by foreign-controlled distribution companies which are integrated with the major U.S. film production companies. The record of those companies over many decades indicates that their dominance of film distribution in Canada is not compatible with the development of a strong Canadian film production industry.

The 1982 licensing of pay-television services in Canada also provided an important opportunity to strengthen the Canadian-controlled distribution companies. The CRTC has stated that it will require the general-interest pay-television licensees to spend 60 per cent of their programming funds on Canadian feature films and television programs. If the licensees are able to meet their market projections, they will spend between $300 million and $350 million on acquiring or investing in Canadian programs and a further $200 million on foreign programming. Had the CRTC required that the licensees purchase either just their Canadian programs or both Canadian and foreign programs through Canadian-controlled production or distribution companies, the result could have been a substantial strengthening of the Canadian distribution companies.

In the absence of such a requirement, the development of pay-television services in Canada will do very little to strengthen the structure of the domestic industry. Producers will continue to be vulnerable to demands by U.S. theatrical producer/distributors and, more importantly, pay-television companies to give them Canadian as well as U.S. rights. It is ironic that the Canadian pay-television rights for most of the Canadian movies made under the provisions of the capital cost allowance are now held by Home Box Office, a subsidiary of Time Inc.

Foreign control over film distribution in Canada appears to be increasing. Between 1979 and 1980, the market share of foreign-controlled companies increased from 64 per cent to 65 per cent. More importantly, in the rapidly growing television market their share increased from 66 per cent to 69 per cent. The largest companies, which include the dominant U.S. firms, are accounting for an increased share of industry profit. While the nine companies with revenues of over $5 million in 1979 accounted for 82 per cent of industry profit, the ten firms in this revenue category in 1980 accounted for 97 per cent of the distribution industry's profit.

Since 1980, several Canadian-controlled distribution companies have gone bankrupt, despite the fact that the market for the distribution industry is expanding rapidly. The simple fact is that the economic survival of Canadian-controlled distributors depends on their access to foreign as well as Canadian films for distribution in Canada.

The growing dominance of foreign-controlled distributors in Canada is not being achieved through their distribution of Canadian films. In 1980, less than $1 million of the total revenues of foreign-controlled distributors of $160 million was earned from the distribution of Canadian films. While Canadian-controlled distributors account for a minor share of total industry revenue, they account for almost all of the revenue earned from the distribution of Canadian films.

In 1982, two new U.S.-controlled distribution companies began operating in Canada, concentrating their attention on the distribution of "classic" films to the "art-house" theatre circuit. Because of the foreign corporate links of these companies, they will have access to the lion's share of foreign films and have the potential to achieve the same control of the art-house market that foreign distributors now have over the commercial theatres. In the past, the art-house market has been an essential market for the Canadian-controlled distributors.

The major lever the federal government has to effect a Canadianization of the distribution industry is its regulatory control over television broadcasting. With the advent of pay-television in 1983, the television market for film will become the largest single market. The CRTC could make it a condition of licence at a prescribed date in the future that all licensees purchase both their foreign and Canadian programming from a Canadian-controlled distribution company. Such a requirement would be consistent with the current requirements concerning Canadian control of television stations themselves. If the effective date for such a requirement were set a number of years in the future, an orderly patriation of this vitally important component of the film industry could be achieved.

Alternatively or perhaps as an intermediate measure, action could be taken to restrict the foreign-controlled distribution arms of U.S. producers to distributing only those films they themselves had produced. Such action might be taken through Customs and Excise regulations. While the effects of any such initiative would have to be examined carefully, it would be very desirable to lessen immediately the concentration of distribution control in the hands of the major U.S. companies and such an initiative might contribute significantly to achieving this result.

A 1979 Council of Europe study began with the recognition that "distribution . . . is the key sector of the economy of the film industry."[20] Recent statements by Communications Minister Francis Fox indicate quite clearly that he recognizes the urgent need to establish a strong Canadian-controlled film distribution industry.[21] Such measures need to be part of any realistic strategy for the development of the film industry.

In Quebec, the 1982 report of the Fournier Commission on the film industry has also focused attention on the need for domestic control over film distribution in Canada, recommending that all film distribution companies operating in Quebec be 80 per cent owned and effectively controlled by Canadians. The Quebec government is expected to be generally responsive to the recommendations of this commission, particularly because recent moves by the foreign majors to establish control over art-house films constitute a major threat to the survival of existing French-language Canadian film distributors.

A recent article documenting the decline of the Canadian distribution companies, as their access to screen time in the theatres steadily eroded, concluded that "Over the last three years, the majors have consolidated and strengthened their positions over the independents (in the United States, as well as Canada)."[22] Unless that decline can be reversed, it will not be possible to make progress towards the development of a strong, stable Canadian film industry.

Theatrical Exhibition

The article noted above states that "The illusion of a free market is an albatross around the neck of every independent film distributor in Canada."[23] In fact, as is evident already, the industry is an extraordinarily tightly controlled oligopoly. With respect to theatrical distribution, the article notes that the half-dozen majors have been expanding both their own production and their purchase of independent U.S. productions. As noted already, they distributed no Canadian features in 1978 or 1979. The pattern that exists for the two dominant Canadian theatrical chains is that:

> A regular and constant flow of films from Paramount, United Artists, and Warner Bros. will always end up on a Famous screen and Odeon can count on the faithfulness of Columbia Pictures and Universal to fill its screens. Twentieth Century Fox splits between the two circuits.[24]

In these circumstances, continued support for Canadian film production, without firm action to ensure the availability of screen time, is irresponsible and futile. It has not worked up to now and will not work in the future.

A quota should be established by the provincial governments to ensure the exhibition of both Canadian theatrical features and short films. The proposed quota should be introduced at the same time as an incentive is initiated to encourage theatres to give favourable exhibition time to Canadian films. A 1980 opinion survey indicated that 60 per cent of Canadians would favour a requirement that 10 per cent of screen time be devoted to Canadian films.[25] It is worth remembering that a comparable initiative related to the use of Canadian recordings by radio stations has proved an effective means of stimulating the development of Canadian talent and has also generated significant economic benefits.

Such a quota is a controversial issue in the film industry, although a number of provinces have made provision for its implementation. In 1975, for example, the Ontario government amended the Ontario Theatres Act to provide for quotas on the exhibition of Canadian films. The 1973 Bassett Report had recommended that a quota be implemented.[26] Although this legislation has not yet been used, the Ontario Ministry of Citizenship and Culture has recently been examining the possibility of a quota on short films.

On balance there seems to be a very strong case for the need for theatrical quotas in Canada, parallel to those which are in effect in almost all Western European countries. However, many Canadian producers are concerned that quotas would not likely help them to get the favourable screen time they need and are concerned that the U.S. distributors might retaliate by blocking their access to U.S. screens. It is interesting, however, that the same producers, without exception, supported a strong quota on pay-television service, the electronic outlet for their films. While these concerns of Canadian producers must be addressed, they do not seem strong enough to offset the benefits of developing a stronger domestic market base in the theatres as well as in pay-television for Canadian films, especially if such an initiative is combined with proposed provisions affecting the withholding tax on royalty payments to foreign copyright holders.

Television

A comparable quota with respect to the exhibition of Canadian movies on both the CBC and private television stations should also be implemented by the CRTC. Such a requirement also seems to have significant public support, with 65 per cent of the respondents to the survey noted above stating that they would favour a 10 per cent quota.

However, of considerably greater importance, especially in the future, will be the use of Canadian films by pay-television. As noted already, the CRTC decision to license too many competing movie channels will mean that the revenue per film of Canadian film producers from this market will be relatively slight. However, the CRTC has indicated that it may proceed with a new cable industry-financed channel as part of basic cable service. This proposed television service, referred to as a "universal" service or a cable entertainment network, could provide an extremely important source of revenue to Canadian movie producers and is dealt with at greater length in the next chapter.

In the United States market, film producers now have a substantial market for "made-for-television" feature films. The budgets of such films are usually in the $1.5 to $2.5 million range. The U.S. networks for which such films are made normally pay most of the production costs, in return for which they acquire rights to at least the initial two television showings. At the present time, no Canadian television network provides comparable opportunities to Canadian producers, primarily because it is far cheaper for them, unlike their U.S. counterparts, to buy existing theatrical films for exhibition than to pay most of the cost of made-for-television features. The only possible way in which such films will be made for Canadian television is if the CBC/Radio-Canada is given the necessary financing and/or if a new cable industry-financed entertainment network is licensed. In the absence of such a development, the only made-for-television movies made by Canadian producers will be those that are designed for American pay-television services.

Television

7

Introduction

If the feature film industry can be accurately described as the most visible and prestigious of the current forms of mass communication, television is the medium people spend most of their time with on a day-to-day basis. Few parents do not wonder about the effects of excessive television watching on their children. In fact, a 1981 Gallup poll[1] indicated that 45 per cent of Canadians think that television is not a good influence on family life. Dissatisfaction with the effects of television had increased from 27 per cent in 1966. In 1981, only 36 per cent thought television had a good influence, down from 48 per cent in 1966 and 66 per cent in 1956.

Concerns regarding television tend to have focused on its lowest common denominator programming and to link such programming to dependence on advertising. However, recognition has also been given to the potential ability of television to expand public access to high quality entertainment and art forms, as well as documentaries and educational programming. A paper produced in 1980 for a Council of Europe conference on the role of the state vis-à-vis the cultural industries noted that "93 per cent of the U.S. population had watched a play on television. . ., but only 16 per cent had been to see a performance in a professional theatre. Similarly, while 4 per cent had seen a live ballet, 22 per cent had watched one on television."[2] Moreover, many more people now watch films on television than ever get to the cinema. If there is frustration with the current realty of television, it is largely a result of an awareness of tremendous unfulfilled potential.

Television content is, of course, not simply comprised of the carriage of earlier existing entertainment and artistic forms. The medium has developed its own forms, while at the same time transmuting the earlier forms when it does carry them. In addition,

251

television has always been an important source of news and information programming and an important medium for the analysis and discussion of public policy issues, both domestic and foreign.

The recent development of cable distribution systems and satellite transmission of television programming has turned television into simply one of several subcategories of the services and content provided by larger industries which are completely separate from television. Now that Canadian television broadcasters and networks no longer deliver their programming directly off-air to most of their audience, there is a tremendous and explosive potential for direct conflicts of interest between the Canadian television stations and networks and their carriers, both satellite and cable. Given these conflicts, the relative ranking by Canadian governments, and particularly the federal government, of their cultural, economic and technological objectives will dictate the future of Canadian television production and programming. This is the case simply because the television stations and networks themselves, as well as both cable and satellite distribution systems, fall within the direct regulatory control of government. Information on the development of public- and private-sector broadcasting services and the existing legal and regulatory framework within which the industry functions has already been provided in chapter 6.

All recent indications suggest that the preoccupations of both the CRTC and the Department of Communications are economic and technological. A 1980 study published by the C.D. Howe Institute noted that:

> The Department of Communications remains the lead agency for communications policy-making within the Federal Government, but its basic character seems to be changing. The Department is coming to be perceived more as a science-based unit promoting an increasingly important aspect of Canada's overall industrial strategy and less as a culture-oriented unit responsible for managing the instruments whereby Canadian identity is shaped.[3]

The study argued that the department must, in the future, perform *both* roles and that the cultural role required reinforcement.

In 1981, the Canadian Conference of the Arts (CCA) made similar observations concerning the Department of Communications:

> The Department seems to be developing an approach to the [television] industry in which purely economic factors dominate over the concern

252

policy as root of problem?

with self-expression through the broadcasting system and the development of Canadian programs which are Canadian in character, rather than simply produced in Canada. All of the lessons of fifty years of broadcasting experience and analysis in Canada seem to be either outside the knowledge and understanding of many of the individuals involved in policy development or unrelated to what they consider to be their basic mandate.[4]

Trudeau

The CCA drew attention to the fact that when, in late 1980, the Arts and Culture Branch of the Department of the Secretary of State was moved to the Communications Department, the communications minister, Francis Fox, offered the following explanation:

> This change should help to ensure that communications policy is conducted with the highest concern for the cultural content and the cultural implications of communications technology. . . .It is the Prime Minister's view that such progress should serve more and more to strengthen our culture and identity.[5]

Despite these expressions of concern on the one hand, and intent to respond on the other, there has been no change whatever in the way that the CRTC and the Department of Communications operate.

The tensions that exist between competing interests and objectives in the television industry are without equal in the cultural industries in their complexity and in the vehemence with which they are pursued. The following analysis draws together in as concise a form as possible a description of the industry and an analysis of its problems primarily from the perspective of Canadian cultural policy. In addition, some specific suggestions are put forward for a program of substantial, but realistic, changes that might reverse the trends now evident in the industry.

Background

The first Canadian television station, CBFT in Montreal, went on the air on September 6, 1952, thirty-three years after the initiation of radio broadcasting. The technology had, in fact, already existed for a long time, having been demonstrated in England twenty-five years earlier and tested experimentally in Canada in the 1930s.[6]

Canadians' first exposure to television was through trans-border reception of American broadcasting services, which began to operate earlier than Canadian television stations. The initial plans for television in Canada provided for a national, publicly-owned service to be

253

provided by the CBC. From the beginning, the CBC provided both Canadian and foreign, largely American, programming, attempting both to repatriate audiences in the areas close to the border and provide a balance of Canadian and foreign programming to the many Canadians not able to receive U.S. programming directly. Within two years the CBC, although having to rely to a substantial degree on affiliated private-sector stations, reached 60 per cent of the population.

A coast-to-coast microwave system for television, 4000 miles long, was completed in 1958. Construction of this system reflected a conviction that with television, as with radio broadcasting, the railway and the airlines, a national communications system linking east and west was essential. The content CBC delivered over the system was 60 per cent Canadian on the English-language service and 75 per cent in French.

As mentioned in chapter 6, new broadcasting legislation was passed in 1958. Additional private-sector stations were licensed subsequently and in 1961 a private-sector national network, CTV, was licensed. From the beginning, the private network relied primarily on American programming for its entertainment content, while producing Canadian news and public affairs programming.

The 1958 Broadcasting Act set out for the regulatory body, the Board of Broadcast Governors, the following objectives:

> The Board shall, for the purpose of ensuring the continued existence and efficient operation of a national broadcasting system and the provision of *a varied and comprehensive broadcasting service of a high standard that is basically Canadian in content and character*, regulate the establishment and operation of networks of broadcasting stations, the activities of public and private broadcasting stations in Canada and the relationship between them. . .[7] (emphasis added).

While, as argued in chapter 5, the structure established by the 1958 act created serious problems, the objectives established for the Canadian broadcasting system were particularly significant. It is worth noting that the objective of a Canadian broadcasting system that is "Canadian in content and character" was narrowed to apply only to the CBC in the new legislation passed subsequently in 1968.

As a major element in the fulfilment of its mandate to ensure the Canadian character of broadcasting, the Board of Broadcast Governors announced in 1959 that it would require that all television broadcasters show a minimum of 45 per cent Canadian content, with the level rising to 55 per cent in 1962. The Canadian Association of Broadcasters and

254

the Association of Canadian Advertisers both fought the decision. The private broadcasters' interest was in being able to make maximum use of U.S. programs dumped into Canada at low rates, thereby permitting the station owners to continue to earn exceptionally high profits. The advertisers, many of the major ones subsidiaries of U.S. firms, were concerned that because Canadian programs cost the broadcasters more, they would push advertising rates up. Under pressure from broadcasters and advertisers, the board softened its standards, defining Canadian content to include, for example, the World Series. The board was never able to fulfil its mandate of ensuring that the broadcasting system as a whole was Canadian in content and character, because of its failure to regulate the private sector successfully. In the 1968 act, the federal government abandoned any efforts to have the regulatory agency attempt to get private broadcasters to provide programming that was Canadian in character, but did not at the same time make any renewed commitment to public broadcasting as the only effective means of generating such content.

While private-sector television broadcasting has grown rapidly over the past twenty-five years, the CBC's television services grew much more slowly than had been intended. Of forty-four television stations licensed by 1958, only eight of them were owned by the CBC. The corporation received inadequate funding and received it on a year-to-year basis, never being able to plan effectively for the future. As a result, the CBC has depended heavily on private-sector affiliates to reach its audiences.

The general pattern from the beginning of television in 1953 until the present has been one of a rapidly expanding private television broadcasting system, and an under-financed public system. The pattern of CBC development has been conditioned by reliance on private-sector affiliates to reach its audience and a continuing dependence on advertising revenue. These two factors, combined with insecure and inadequate financing, have resulted in CBC schedules that continue to include a substantial amount of foreign content and reflect the corporation's confusion as to its identity and purpose as a programmer. By contrast, however, neither the Board of Broadcast Governors nor its successor, the CRTC, has yet been able to use its regulatory powers to get the private sector to produce a significant amount of Canadian programming except in the fields of news, current affairs, sports and low-cost entertainment such as game shows.

Much more recently, of course, the rapid expansion of cable television through the 1970s and the rapidly expanded use of satellite distribution technology have added tremendous pressures to a Canadian television system that Canada as a nation had never previously been able to structure and regulate satisfactorily in order to pursue its own objectives. After a decade of steady erosion, it is now widely recognized that the system requires urgent and bold action if it is ever to provide a reasonable balance of Canadian and foreign programming.

The Canadian Market

The Audience for Television
Ownership of a television set is now as common as ownership of a radio. Ninety-eight per cent of Canadians have at least one television set in their homes and, in 1979, 35.5 per cent had more than one set.

The number of hours spent watching television has changed only slightly over the past decade. The Spring 1981 survey by the Bureau of Broadcast Measurement indicated that the average Canadian watched television 24 hours per week, an increase from 22.1 hours in Spring 1971 (see Table 7-1). Whatever the average, of course, the number of hours individuals spend watching television varies greatly. For example, the 20 per cent of viewers who watch television least account for just 5 per cent of all viewing and watch an average of just 6.5 hours per week. By comparison, the 20 per cent who watch television most on the average devote over seven times as much of their average week (48.7 hours) to watching television and account for 41 per cent of all viewing.

Content
As Table 7-2 (page 258) indicates, while television includes a variety of different kinds of programming, it is watched primarily as an entertainment medium. Included in the entertainment category are variety programs, game shows, situation comedies, drama series, feature films and so on. If one also includes sports programming in the entertainment category—to which it really belongs—over 80 per cent of all television watching is of entertainment programs. The remainder of viewing time is devoted to news, current affairs and information programs. While, for French-language viewing, the percentage of viewing time devoted to non-entertainment programs was relatively steady over this period, there was a significant increase—from 14.02 per cent to 17.84 per cent—in the amount of time spent watching English-language news, current affairs and information programs.

TABLE 7-1
WEEKLY HOURS OF TELEVISION VIEWING
PER CAPITA, 1970-81

	1970-71	1971-72	1972-73	1973-74	1975-76
Fall survey	23.6	22.8	22.7	23.4	23.9
Spring survey	22.1	22.2	22.8	23.6	22.3
	1976-77	1977-78	1978-79	1979-80	1980-81
Fall survey	23.7	23.0	22.9	23.7	24.5
Spring survey	22.2	22.0	22.8	23.0	24.0

TELEVISION VIEWING BY QUINTILE, 1980

Viewers	Percentage of Total Viewing	Hours of Viewing per Week
20	5	6.5
20	12	14.3
20	17	21.0
20	25	29.5
20	41	48.7

Source: BBM, *Television and Radio Data, 1981.*

The CRTC now requires that both private and public Canadian television stations and networks have 60 per cent Canadian content between 6:00 a.m. and midnight, calculated on an annual basis. CBC stations are also required, on an annual basis, to meet the 60 per cent requirement between 6:00 p.m. and midnight, while privately-owned stations are required to meet a 50 per cent Canadian-content requirement in this time period. What constitutes Canadian content continues, as in the 1960s, to be very loosely defined. Co-productions, for example, qualify regardless of the financial or production involvement of other countries. In addition, foreign programs dubbed into English or French are assigned a 25 per cent Canadian-content level. The practice of accepting dubbed programs as partially Canadian is reflected particularly in the "Canadian" viewing levels for French-language broadcasters who make extensive use of dubbed foreign programming.

TABLE 7-2
PERCENTAGE DISTRIBUTION OF VIEWING TIME

Program Category	1967 Canadian	1967 Foreign	1967 Total	1972 Canadian	1972 Foreign	1972 Total	1976 Canadian	1976 Foreign	1976 Total	1978 Canadian	1978 Foreign	1978 Total
ALL ENGLISH TV STATIONS												
News	7.57	1.18	8.75	11.30	1.39	12.69	11.20	1.30	12.50	13.16	1.09	14.25
Current affairs	4.88	0.32	5.20	3.41	0.03	3.44	4.30	0.20	4.50	1.93	0.49	2.43
Information	0.07	0.00	0.07	0.25	0.00	0.25	1.28	0.00	1.28	1.05	0.11	1.16
Sports	6.47	0.20	6.68	5.17	0.86	6.03	4.30	1.50	5.80	5.47	1.14	6.61
Entertainment	9.60	68.78	78.38	14.22	63.11	77.33	7.70	68.20	75.90	8.72	66.18	74.90
Other	0.48	0.44	0.92	0.06	0.20	0.26	0.10	0.00	0.10	0.20	0.46	0.66
Total	29.07	70.93	100.00	34.41	65.59	100.00	28.90	71.10	100.00	30.53	69.47	100.00
ALL FRENCH TV STATIONS												
News	10.70	0.00	10.70	13.39	0.00	13.39	10.06	0.00	10.06	14.31	0.00	14.31
Current affairs	7.68	0.00	7.68	4.20	0.00	4.20	5.21	0.16	5.37	4.04	0.00	4.04
Information	0.53	0.00	0.53	0.00	0.00	0.00	1.66	0.00	1.66	0.78	0.00	0.78
Sports	6.70	0.00	6.70	6.29	0.00	6.29	15.18	0.00	15.18	4.70	0.00	4.70
Entertainment	32.21	39.05	71.26	41.46	33.65	76.11	32.67	35.06	67.72	30.28	45.72	75.99
Other	0.86	2.27	3.12	0.00	0.00	0.00	0.00	0.00	0.00	0.09	0.08	0.17
Total	58.29	41.31	100.00	66.35	33.65	100.00	64.78	35.22	100.00	54.20	45.80	100.00

Sources: CRTC, *Special Report on Broadcasting, 1968-78*, and CRTC Research Directorate, *Television Viewing Patterns During Prime Time, 1978.*

As Table 7-2 demonstrates, despite the content regulations of the CRTC, the level of viewing time devoted to Canadian content as defined by the CRTC was just 30.53 per cent for English-language programming in 1978, down from 34.41 per cent in 1972. For French-language programming the percentage of viewing time devoted to Canadian programs also fell between 1972 and 1978 from 66.35 per cent to 54.20 per cent. The 1972 figures provide the earliest available measure of Canadian-content viewing after the establishment of the CRTC.

While 90.5 per cent of all viewing of English-language news, current affairs and information programs in 1978 was of Canadian programs, 88.4 per cent of entertainment viewing was of foreign programs. In the case of the viewing of Canadian news programs, it should be noted that, as in the case of Canadian newspapers, domestic television newscasts can and do make extensive use of news clips from foreign broadcasters to provide coverage of foreign news. A more extensive examination would, therefore, be required before concluding that Canadians are actually seeing on domestic newscasts either primarily Canadian news coverage or a reasonable balance of foreign and Canadian coverage of non-Canadian stories and events.

One could conclude from the low percentage of English-language viewing of Canadian entertainment that English Canadians just do not like or are not attracted to Canadian drama or other kinds of domestic entertainment. Before doing so, however, two points need to be recognized. First, the private Canadian broadcasters can meet the bulk of their 50 per cent Canadian-content requirement between 6:00 p.m. and midnight with news and sports programming. What the private broadcasters need over a seven-day week is twenty-one hours of Canadian programming between 6:00 p.m. and midnight. If a station runs an hour of news between 6:00 and 7:00 p.m. and a half hour at 11:00 p.m., that alone accounts for half of the Canadian-content requirement each week. Second, if the broadcaster covers two or three sports events a week, he can add five to eight hours of Canadian content, with the remainder of the Canadian-content requirement being met through co-productions with foreign broadcasters or producers, through a public affairs show, the showing of a Canadian movie, or other odds and ends tucked unobtrusively into the schedule.

This problem of the availability and scheduling of Canadian entertainment programming was recognized in the CRTC's *Special Report on Broadcasting*, which contained the following conclusion:

> While the rules [concerning Canadian content] have, on the whole, been

observed, they have not been effective in achieving the scheduling of Canadian programming in peak viewing hours. . . .between 8:00 p.m. and 10:30 p.m., which is peak viewing time for television, most private Canadian networks and stations schedule programming which is not Canadian.[8]

More recently, some doubts have been raised about the degree of compliance by private broadcasters with the promises of performance made by individual licensees with respect to Canadian content. The auditor-general of Canada, Kenneth Dye, has criticized the CRTC for having no effective system for checking on whether stations meet their promises of performance to the commission. Auditor-General Dye complained that the system was so lax that licences were rarely cancelled and that complaints from the public had taken the place of any systematic monitoring of licensees.[9]

For French-language television viewers, 100 per cent of news, current affairs and information programs watched were Canadian in 1978, while 39.8 per cent of entertainment programming viewed was Canadian.

Table 7-3 provides a useful complement to Table 7-2, since it focuses on the extent of Canadian content available in the 8:00 p.m. to

TABLE 7-3
CANADIAN CONTENT IN PEAK VIEWING TIME
(8:00 p.m. to 10:30 p.m.)

Network or Station	Percentage of Canadian Content		
	1967-68	*1977-78*	*1978-79*
CBC English	45.7	71.4	68.5
Radio-Canada	67.1	74.2	71.4
CTV	22.8	11.4	5.7
TVA (CFTM)	38.5	34.2	28.5
Global (CKGN)	—	51.4	22.8
CHCH Hamilton	20.0	17.1	22.8
CITY Toronto	—	28.5	40.0
CKND Winnipeg	—	28.5	28.5
CFAC Calgary	—	22.8	22.8
CITV Edmonton	—	17.1	22.8
CKVU Vancouver	—	31.4	25.7

Sources: CRTC, *Special Report on Broadcasting, 1968-78*, vol. 1, and CRTC Research Directorate, *Television Viewing Patterns During Prime Time, 1978*.

10:30 p.m. period on Canadian television services. Only the public-sector television networks were providing programs that were predominantly Canadian in the period of the day when most Canadians watch television. By comparison, the percentage of Canadian programming on the private stations and networks—and it should be remembered that Canadian content is both loosely defined and includes sports coverage—was quite low.

The CTV network and its member stations' twenty-year history of progressively more blatant defiance of the intent of Parliament, as expressed in the Broadcasting Act, and of the CRTC, as expressed in its regulations, has done particularly serious damage to the achieving of the objectives of Canadian television broadcasting. The steady decline to 5.7 per cent Canadian content in peak viewing time over the period 1967-68 to 1978-79 marks a new low point in Canada's history of failure in regulating private-sector television. Moreover, as a 1979 publication stated:

> Many of the shows which CTV applauds as home-grown are as Canadian as the New York Yankees. "The Julie Show" was a prime example. The host, Julie Amato, was Canadian. But of the fifty-two guests who appeared on her show, thirty-five were Americans and only seventeen Canadians. "Canadian" dramas such as "Search and Rescue" are often co-productions, and the financial backing is American. They lack Canadian flavour and could just as easily be broadcast in Houston as in Halifax.[10]

The Television Industry in Canada

Number of Public and Private Canadian Stations

As Table 7-4 indicates, there were 111 originating television stations in Canada in 1980. Thirty-one stations are owned by the CBC, while a further thirty-one are private-sector affiliates of the CBC. Twenty-six stations are part of the CTV network, while six are part of its French-language private-sector counterpart, TVA. Of the total of 111 licensed originating stations, 85 per cent or ninety-four stations, are a part of either the CBC or CTV/TVA networks. The Global network is made up of just a single originating station and five rebroadcasting stations. The thirteen independent stations are, as one would expect, confined to the large urban centres. There are an additional 989 rebroadcasting stations, three-quarters of which are owned by or affiliated to the CBC. Most of the remainder are part of the CTV network.

261

TABLE 7-4
TELEVISION STATIONS BY PROVINCE AND NETWORK AFFILIATION, 1980

Network	Nfld	PEI	NS	NB	PQ	Ont	Man	Sask	Alta	BC	Yukon	NWT	Total
ORIGINATING STATIONS													
CBCO[1]	3	1	2	1	6	5	2	2	4	4	1	—	31
CBCA[2]	—	—	—	1	7	11	1	3	3	5	—	—	31
Ind[3]	—	—	—	—	1	8	1	—	2	1	—	—	13
TVA	—	—	—	—	6	—	—	—	—	—	—	—	6
CTV	3	—	2	1	1	9	1	2	4	3	—	—	26
TVO	—	—	—	—	—	1	—	—	—	—	—	—	1
ORTQ[4]	—	—	—	—	2	—	—	—	—	—	—	—	2
Global	—	—	—	—	—	1	—	—	—	—	—	—	1
Total	6	1	4	3	23	35	5	7	13	13	1	—	111
REBROADCASTING STATIONS													
CBCO[1]	78	1	31	4	77	58	36	43	51	85	6	23	493
CBCA[2]	5	—	1	9	47	10	10	18	15	126	12	5	258
Ind[3]	—	—	—	—	—	—	—	—	7	4	—	—	11
TVA	—	—	—	1	6	—	—	—	—	—	—	—	7
CTV	30	1	9	9	1	15	7	16	26	90	—	—	204
TVO	—	—	—	—	—	8	—	—	—	—	—	—	8
ORTQ[4]	—	—	—	—	3	—	—	—	—	—	—	—	3
Global	—	—	—	—	—	5	—	—	—	—	—	—	5
Total	113	2	41	23	134	96	53	77	99	305	18	28	989

Notes: [1] CBCO — CBC owned and operated. [3] Ind — Independent.
[2] CBCA — CBC affiliate. [4] ORTQ — Office de radio-télédiffusion du Québec (Radio-Québec).

Source: CRTC, *Annual Report, 1979-80*.

These originating and rebroadcasting stations provide the basis for reaching the Canadian population with off-air broadcast services. The construction of the CTV and CBC networks has been an extremely expensive undertaking and one that has been going on since the first station began operation in 1952. Canadian geography has made the construction of a national system of transmitter facilities for the major private and public national systems extraordinarily expensive by comparison with any other country in the world and has restricted expenditure on Canadian programming.

One study of the Canadian television system noted by way of comparison that the British Broadcasting Corporation can reach all of the 55 million people in Britain with 113 transmitters. By comparison, the CBC and its affiliates utilized 813 transmitters in 1980 to reach 98 per cent of the Canadian population of 24 million.

While as recently as 1968, off-air reception of broadcast television services provided 85 per cent of Canadian households with television reception, by 1980, the percentage of Canadians who relied on off-air reception had dropped to 45 per cent. This change was a direct result of the rapid expansion of cable television distribution over the previous fifteen years. In 1967, just 13.2 per cent of Canadian households both had access to and chose to pay for cable reception. By 1980, the figure had increased to 55 per cent (see Table 7-5 on page 264).

Number of Channels Available
The shift from channel scarcity to channel abundance in the years since 1967 is at the heart of the transformation now occurring in the Canadian television production and distribution system. The appropriate response to this change in channel availability is the major public policy issue concerning the future of television in Canada. In 1967, 64 per cent of all Canadians could receive three or more television channels, while only 2 per cent could receive seven channels or more. A decade later, 91 per cent of Canadians could receive three or more channels, while 61 per cent could receive seven or more.

Coverage
As Table 7-6 (page 265) indicates, only CBC and CTV stations reached more than half of all Canadians in 1967. By 1977, there were nine different categories of station that reached more than half of all Canadians. The coverage of Radio-Canada had been greatly expanded, while educational television stations and networks operated by the provincial governments had also expanded to cover 54 per cent of the

TABLE 7-5
CABLE TELEVISION, 1970-80[1]

Year	Number of Households (000's)			Number of		Subscribers (000's)	Total Operating Revenue ($000's)
	Total Canada	In Cable TV Licensed Areas	In Areas Served by Cable TV	Operating Systems	Employees		
1970	5,646	2,986	2,392	314	1,992	1,164	54,940
1971	5,799	3,096	2,681	326	2,180	1,398	66,620
1972	6,108	3,712	3,313	344	2,598	1,689	82,464
1973	6,266	4,079	3,715	362	3,098	2,116	106,973
1974	6,493	4,366	4,045	375	3,691	2,561	133,433
1975	6,703	4,500	4,233	388	4,084	2,861	162,273
1976	6,918	4,985	4,706	403	4,640	3,143	199,215
1977	7,022	5,304	5,051	427	4,946	3,417	232,958
1978	7,320	5,866	5,536	463	5,293	3,776	273,223
1979	7,558	6,211	5,942	482	5,569	4,084	313,747
1980	7,807	6,378	6,111	505	5,396	4,339	352,172

Note: [1] In 1980, 55 per cent of total households had cable TV compared to 52 per cent in 1979, 50 per cent in 1978, and 46 per cent in 1977.

Source: Statistics Canada, *Cable Television* (Cat. No. 56-205).

TABLE 7-6
POPULATION COVERAGE AND VIEWING AUDIENCE SHARE
FOR CANADIAN AND U.S. TELEVISION STATIONS, 1967 AND 1977

	Population Coverage		Audience Share	
	1967	1977	1967	1977
English-language				
CBC	90.46	94.88	34.14	18.93
CTV	68.37	92.28	18.93	24.95
Canadian independent	19.92	53.07	2.53	10.33
Canadian educational	0.00	54.05	0.00	0.74
CBS	40.99	63.66	7.20	7.27
NBC	28.87	62.27	3.78	6.41
ABC	36.55	62.30	4.94	7.25
Multi-affiliate	10.70	2.29	1.65	0.35
U.S. independent	1.47	14.82	0.17	1.34
PBS	0.00	57.05	0.00	0.83
French-language				
Radio-Canada	39.88	79.61	14.43	10.48
TVA	27.62	28.15	12.32	11.12

Source: CRTC, *Special Report on Broadcasting, 1968-78*, vol. 2.

national audience. In addition, the CRTC had licensed a substantial number of independent Canadian stations, particularly in the Ontario market. A total of five different categories of Canadian stations were available to over half the national market, of which three were public-sector (although the CBC/RC networks are also advertiser-supported), while two categories of private-sector Canadian services reached more than half of all Canadians.

However, the most significant change that occurred over the decade was that, because the CRTC permitted cable companies to sell to their subscribers the three advertiser-supported U.S. television networks, the percentage of the Canadian market covered by CBS, NBC and ABC was increased by 55 per cent, 116 per cent and 70 per cent respectively. The CRTC decision to permit the marketing of the U.S. networks by cable began a process that would, if carried to completion, turn the three U.S. networks into U.S.-Canadian networks, with implications for the future of Canadian industry as a whole, and advertiser-supported private Canadian television stations and networks

265

in particular, that will be examined later in this chapter. Permitting Canadian companies in the cable industry to sell foreign programming services that are not required to make any contribution to Canadian programming or to meet any Canadian-content criteria has substantially eroded the legitimacy of the content requirements imposed on those private Canadian companies running television stations and networks, stiffening their already strong resistance to such requirements.

In addition to the expanded coverage of the Canadian market by the three U.S. commercial networks, the non-profit American network, PBS, also has expanded through cable carriage to reach 57 per cent of Canadians.

Audience Shares by Station/Network Category
As Table 7-6 indicates, there was a significant decline in the share of total Canadian television audiences taken by French-language television services between 1967 and 1977. While 26.7 per cent of all viewing had been of French-language television stations in 1967, the comparable figure for 1977 was 21.6 per cent. More recent data from

TABLE 7-7
TRENDS IN AUDIENCE SHARE FOR CANADIAN AND U.S. STATION GROUPS, 1970-80
(percentages)

| Year | English | | | | French | |
	CBC English	CTV	Independent Canadian	U.S. Stations	Radio-Canada	TVA
1970	32.8	20.0	2.8	18.4	14.2	11.8
1971	29.7	23.5	3.2	19.1	14.0	10.5
1972	28.8	23.1	3.6	19.2	14.4	10.9
1973	27.3	24.1	3.0	21.0	14.2	10.4
1974	24.8	24.0	5.5	21.0	13.6	11.1
1976	20.1	24.8	9.3	22.0	11.8	11.2
1977	19.8	25.1	9.8	22.1	11.0	11.6
1978	20.7	24.8	10.1	22.6	10.3	11.2
1979	19.8	25.6	10.0	22.6	9.6	11.5
1980	17.5	23.7	11.6	24.5	8.3	13.3
% change 1970-1980	−46.6	+18.5	+314.3	+33.2	−41.5	+12.7

Source: BBM, *Television and Radio Data, 1981.*

266

the Bureau of Broadcast Measurement (BBM) indicate no further change in 1980 and suggest that this level may have stabilized (see Table 7-7). There was also a slight decline in the share of national television audiences accounted for by English-language Canadian television services between 1967 and 1977, from 55.6 to 54.9 per cent. The BBM data indicate a further decline to 52.8 per cent in 1980.

The most significant change that has occurred in the period 1967 to 1980 is the 38 per cent increase in the share of Canadian television viewing accounted for by U.S. stations. In 1967, American stations attracted 17.7 per cent of the national audience; by 1980, the audience share for U.S. stations had increased to 24.5 per cent. If one looks at English-language viewing only, then 32 per cent of the time that Canadians watch English-language television is spent looking at U.S. television stations.

The Department of Communications has already completed a full-scale study of the feasibility of distributing the three commercial American networks by Canadian satellite to all parts of Canada. The result, of course, would be to further increase the penetration of the Canadian market by CBS, NBC and ABC and to erode the advertising base of Canadian television broadcasters. The same effect would also result if the U.S. networks were to distribute their signals across Canada off American satellites, although there are international and bilateral agreements that provide a basis for efforts to minimize such spillover. This satellite distribution issue will be examined more carefully later in this chapter.

The Components of the Television Industry
Historically, the television industry has had two principal sources of revenue in Canada: television services received their revenue either from government or from advertisers. In the case of the CBC, of course, revenue has in the past come from both sources. More recently, with the development of cable television, subscriber revenue has become increasingly important.

While there has been a tendency to think of both publicly-funded and advertiser-supported television as "free," all broadcasting services have to be paid for. The most accurate distinction that can be drawn is between television services that are paid for indirectly—through taxation or through advertising expenditures which are included as a expenditure item in the cost of producing goods and services—and television services that are paid for directly—as in the case of cable television or other pay-television services.

Publicly-supported Television Services

While CBC radio no longer relies on advertising revenue, CBC television continues to receive a significant percentage of its total revenues from advertising. As Table 7-8 indicates, the corporation earned $100 million from television advertising in 1980, which represented 16.4 per cent of all Canadian television advertising revenues, including 39 per cent of all network advertising.

As noted in chapter 5, the CBC does not provide separate financial data for its radio and television operations. However, it is known that CBC revenues have been growing much more slowly than those of private television stations. While the revenues of private television stations increased by 132 per cent between 1972 and 1977, CBC's net cost of operations grew by just 101 per cent.

What makes this continuing shift in the balance between private- and public-sector broadcasting significant are the figures on ''peak'' time programming noted in Table 7-3 above. These figures make it obvious that, especially in English-language broadcasting, it is only the public sector that produces a significant amount of Canadian entertainment programming and exhibits it in peak viewing time. The fifteen-year trend towards reduced support and a diminished position for the public sector has, therefore, both damaged the quality and quantity of CBC's own programming and reduced dramatically the proportion of Canadian programming available in peak viewing time. This trend in public broadcasting, if combined with continued lack of success in regulating the private sector, represents a phase-out strategy for Canadian entertainment programming.

TABLE 7-8
DISTRIBUTION OF TELEVISION ADVERTISING, 1980

	CBC/Radio-Canada		Private Television		
	$000's	% of Total	$000's	% of Total	Total ($000's)
Local advertising	10,485	6.9	140,924	93.1	151,409
National advertising	39,530	12.0	290,161	88.0	329,691
Network advertising	50,360	39.0	78,874	61.0	129,234
	100,375	16.4	509,959	83.6	610,334

Source: Statistics Canada, *Radio and Television Broadcasting, 1981* (Cat. No. 56-204).

The addition to the system of provincially-funded educational services has also provided audiences in those provinces that have established such services with an additional, specialized public broadcasting service. The difficulty at the present time is that some provinces, in large measure for financial reasons, have not been able to allocate the resources required to offer an educational channel.

Private, Advertiser-supported Television
While there has been a substantial relative decline in the position of public-sector Canadian television, there are also considerable difficulties in Canada in the development of advertiser-supported television services. While television advertising revenue has been increasing rapidly and assuming a larger share of total advertising revenue (see Table 7-9), the advertising revenues of Canadian television stations have, on a per capita basis, always been relatively low. The following figures indicate the magnitude of the difference between per capita television advertising expenditures in Canada, the United States and Australia:

	1977	1980
Australia	$45.00	n.a.
United States	46.00	58.40
Canada	18.60	27.20

There have been two major factors influencing the level of Canadian per capita television advertising expenditures. First, many Canadian businesses have simply purchased advertising time on U.S. stations in

TABLE 7-9
PERCENTAGE SHARE OF ADVERTISING REVENUE BY SECTOR, 1965-81

	1965	1970	1975	1980	1981
Radio	10	11	11	11	11
Television	12	13	14	17	17
Daily newspapers	29	28	29	25	24
Non-daily newspapers	4	5	5	6	6
General magazines	3	3	4	4	5
Business publications	4	3	3	3	3
Directories	5	5	6	7	7

Sources: Maclean Hunter Research Bureau, *A Report on Advertising Revenues in Canada, 1981,*
for 1980 and 1981; Statistics Canada data for 1965, 1970 and 1975.

neighbouring markets that spilled into the major Canadian markets advertisers wished to reach. The decision to amend the federal Income Tax Act in 1976 to disallow as a business expense the purchase of time by Canadian advertisers on the U.S. border stations has helped to ameliorate this particular problem. As the per capita figures above suggest, the level of Canadian expenditure relative to U.S. expenditure improved from 40 per cent to 47 per cent between 1977 and 1980. The same impact is suggested in Table 7-9, which shows an increase from 12 to 14 per cent in the percentage of media advertising going to television in the decade between 1965 and 1975, followed by an increase of 3 percentage points over the next five years. As a percentage of GNP, television advertising, after declining slightly between 1965 and 1975, increased from 0.16 per cent to 0.21 per cent between 1975 and 1980.

The second major factor affecting the amount of television advertising is the increasing coverage of the Canadian market by the major commercial U.S. networks. What happened as the availability of the U.S. services increased was that, as Table 7-6 indicated, they added to their share of the total television audience. In an analysis of the effects of adding U.S. channels to cable systems in areas where they had not been available, the CRTC found that where two commercial U.S. channels were added to an existing two Canadian channels, they typically took 40 per cent of the television audience. Where the three U.S. networks were added to the two major Canadian networks, they took 53.3 per cent of the audience.[11] The effect of such changes on Canadian television are complex, but the major effects are two. First, to the extent that major multinational companies can reach Canadian consumers by placing their ads on U.S. networks, they are not likely to bother as much or even at all with television advertising on Canadian networks. Second, to the extent that the percentage of the Canadian television audience reached by Canadian stations and networks is reduced, their attractiveness as an advertising vehicle is reduced.

While the relatively lower level of Canadian advertising expenditures affects mainly television, it is also a major factor for magazines. Table 7-10 indicates the overall difference between total advertising expenditure levels as a percentage of Gross National Product in the United States and in Canada. From a level of 68.8 per cent of the U.S. level in 1962, Canadian advertising expenditure dropped to 62.6 per cent in 1978, increasing slightly to 64 per cent in 1981. These lower levels of advertising revenue are at the least a significant factor in

270

TABLE 7-10
PERCENTAGE GROWTH RATE OF ADVERTISING
EXPENDITURE AND RELATIONSHIP TO GROSS NATIONAL
PRODUCT, U.S. AND CANADA, 1962-81

Year	Ad Expenditure % Increase over Previous Year		Ad Expenditure % of GNP	
	U.S.	Canada	U.S.	Canada
1962	4.5	5.7	2.21	1.52
1964	8.0	7.4	2.23	1.45
1966	7.3	9.3	2.22	1.42
1968	7.3	4.4	2.09	1.38
1970	0.7	4.7	2.00	1.33
1972	12.3	13.3	1.99	1.32
1974	6.4	15.9	1.90	1.24
1976	19.6	16.1	1.97	1.25
1978	15.6	13.6	2.06	1.29
1979	13.0	15.5	2.05	1.31
1980[p]	10.3	12.2	2.08	1.33
1981[e]	12.9	12.5	2.06	1.32

[p]—preliminary
[e]—estimated

Source: Maclean Hunter Research Bureau, *Report on Advertising Revenues in Canada, 1981.*

creating the demand for greater direct support of Canada's media by governments.

The implications of domestic advertising expenditure levels for directly related employment are evident in Table 7-11. Maclean Hunter estimates that there were 100,000 jobs in Canada in 1980 directly related to advertising, a substantial majority of such employment being provided in the media the advertisers use to reach their audiences. As a result, the level of Canadian advertising expenditure has significant economic as well as cultural implications. If the level of advertising relative to GNP in Canada were at the U.S. level, there would be 56,000 more jobs in Canada; if it were even at 75 per cent of the U.S. level, there would be an additional 17,000 jobs. While there are no simple solutions to this problem, the implications of relatively limited advertising expenditure levels for the media in Canada are serious and the importance of adopting measures that would result in an improvement is evident.

TABLE 7-11
DIRECT EMPLOYMENT RESULTING FROM ADVERTISING
EXPENDITURE, 1970-80

	1970	1975	1980
Newspaper & periodical publishing	38,882	42,998	47,500
Radio & television	19,541	23,499	28,336
Signs & displays manufacturing	5,694	6,519	7,000
Advertising agencies	4,850	4,721	5,800
Total	68,967	77,737	88,636[1]

Note: [1] Maclean Hunter estimates that if freelance employment and internal advertising departments are included, total employment related to advertising in 1980 was about 100,000.

Source: Maclean Hunter Research Bureau, *Report on Advertising Revenues in Canada, 1981.*

In the case of the television industry specifically, the extent of the difference in advertiser support for Canadian television services, by comparison with the U.S. services, is enormous. If Canadian television stations received the same per capita levels of advertising as U.S. stations, they would have had revenues of $1.3 billion in 1980 instead of $610 million, and $1.5 billion in 1981 instead of $695 million. If advertising support for Canadian television was only at 75 per cent of the U.S. level, the result would have been an additional $365 million in revenue in 1980 and an additional $430 million in 1981. Or, to look at the matter somewhat differently, if Canadian television broadcasters—like Canadian radio broadcasters—had earned advertising revenues on a per capita basis at 90 per cent of the U.S. level in 1980, they would had revenues of $1,170 million instead of $610 million.

The result of lower levels of advertising support in Canada has not been that private-sector television is unprofitable—in fact, profits in the industry are exceptionally high. Instead, the major results appear to be that the availability of national advertising time is relatively limited; rates on a cost per thousand basis, especially for national network ads, are relatively high; and the potential of advertiser-supported Canadian television to generate high quality Canadian programming is relatively limited. However, since at the present time the industry invests far less than it could afford to in Canadian programming, there would not necessarily be any corresponding increase in Canadian programming expenditure if greater advertising revenues were generated by Canadian television.[12] Whether or not increased Canadian programming expenditure would result would depend upon the regulatory environment; but the potential for such investment would be very greatly increased.

Television advertising rates and the availability of advertising time has an important effect on any business in Canada that is selling goods or services. The existence of a national market for goods and services simply assumes that the national media exist through which such goods and services can be effectively marketed. In this respect, the importance and the specific impact of media advertising rate structures, and the strength of local, regional and national media, have been studied very little in Canada. By contrast, careful attention has been paid to such issues in the United States.

As Table 1-6 demonstrated, the cost of television advertising rates rose significantly more rapidly than the cost of other media through the 1970s. During the five years between 1975 and 1980, as Table 7-12 indicates, the cost of television advertising was rising almost twice as quickly as the cost of consumer magazine or daily newspaper advertising and 50 per cent faster than the cost of radio advertising. Since television is the most important medium for national advertising, the implications are important. These comparisons are, of course, comparisons of the costs in each medium of reaching 1,000 readers/viewers, and not comparisons of the number of dollars it costs to advertise in each medium. If, for example, the average cost of a 30-second ad on CTV is increased 15 per cent, but the audience reached increased by 20 per cent, the network's revenue would increase, but the advertiser would be paying less to reach potential consumers. Or to put the point in reverse, to the extent that the audience reach of local Canadian stations and Canadian networks contracts, the cost per thousand of television advertising tends to escalate.

The CRTC has not, at least in the past, ignored the growing problem created by spillover U.S. television advertising. Over the past decade, the commission has explored the following alternative measures:

- selective or total deletion of the commercials on cable-transmitted U.S. channels;
- substitution of a Canadian station's or network's signal into the schedule of a U.S. station or network carried on cable, either when

TABLE 7-12
TRENDS IN MEDIA COSTS, 1975-80
(1975=100)

Medium	1976			1978			1980		
	Rate	Aud.	CPM[1]	Rate	Aud.	CPM	Rate	Aud.	CPM
Consumer magazines (1 page, 4 colours)	109	101	108	122	103	119	138	101	137
Daily newspapers (1,000 lines, black and white)	112	99	113	133	106	125	149	114	135
Outdoor (3 to 5 months showing)	122	102	120	155	104	149	180	104	176
Radio (60 seconds)	111	113	98	144	112	129	166	122	144
Roto (newspaper) supplements (1 page, 4 colours)	109	100	109	122	105	116	130	104	126
Television (30 seconds, prime time)	110	99	111	135	93	147	164	97	167
Transit (interior, full showing, 3 to 5 months)	110	104	108	142	112	125	167	112	155
All-item consumer price	110	—	—	132	—	—	151	—	—

Note: [1] CPM = Cost per Thousand.

Source: The Canadian Media Directors' Council, *Media Digest, 1980-81*.

both the Canadian and U.S. station or network are showing a particular program at the same time, or regardless of whether the Canadian and U.S. stations are exhibiting the program simultaneously (usually referred to as simultaneous and non-simultaneous program substitution); or

• control or elimination of carriage of U.S. signals by cable companies.

At the present time, the CRTC requires cable companies to substitute the Canadian station's signal when a foreign program purchased by the Canadian station or network is being shown at the same time on a U.S. station. The present CRTC regulations regarding simultaneous program substitution were adopted in 1976.

The rationale for any policies designed to protect the advertising revenues of Canadian television stations and networks that have acquired the right to broadcast foreign programming is that

- the revenue base of the Canadian broadcasters must be protected so that they can perform their functions under the Broadcasting Act, particularly with respect to the financing of Canadian programming;
- the U.S. stations carried on cable are not licensed to serve Canadian audiences or to sell advertisers access to the Canadian market, and
- the Canadian broadcasters have purchased the right to use the foreign programs they broadcast and, therefore, have legitimate financial and legal rights that merit protection.

With the passage of revised copyright legislation in the United States, cable companies in the U.S. are now required to make copyright payments to broadcasters for the carriage of television programs. While no such legal requirement exists in Canada, the fact that such payments are made in the United States puts the question of the continued carriage and marketing of U.S. signals by Canadian cable companies without permission from or payment to the U.S. stations into a somewhat different light. The U.S. owners of the border stations are now saying that they should be compensated for the programs they provide, which Canadians want to see and hear and which help to enrich Canadian cable companies.[13]

The revision of the Canadian Copyright Act, which is expected in 1983, is not expected to create comparable legal requirements to those now in effect in the United States because most of the payments resulting from such a provision would flow out of Canada to foreign program suppliers. However, since the original foreign producers of such programs receive no payment from Canada when their programs are carried by cable as part of the schedule of a U.S. station, but are paid by Canadian television stations when the programs are acquired by Canadian stations, the latter arrangement is clearly both more desirable and more legitimate. Measures to increase the proportion of foreign programming legitimately purchased for Canada might, therefore, be seen to be attractive to foreign producers and easier to justify within the framework of Canada-United States relations, while at the same time improving the advertising revenues of the Canadian system.

The existing CRTC policy of simultaneous program substitution has been an important factor in the increase in Canadian television advertising that occurred between 1976 and 1980. Combined with the

Income Tax Act changes already described, these measures have had a significant effect. However, in the long run, the major factor in determining advertising revenues in Canada is the penetration of the Canadian market by U.S. stations and networks, which is increasing.

The extent to which the present policy of simultaneous program substitution can be effective depends on the proportion of U.S. programming that is purchased and the willingness of Canadian purchasers to schedule those programs at exactly the same time as U.S. networks or stations. While the percentages vary from market to market, a CRTC study indicated that in the Toronto market, in the 7:00 p.m. to 11:00 p.m. time period, 29 per cent of the programs on the U.S. stations could have been replaced by simultaneous Canadian broadcasts and another 30 per cent were duplicated in other time periods, while 41 per cent of programming in that period was not duplicated. In 1981, a submission to the CRTC by CFTO-TV indicated that, in the 8:00 p.m. to 11:00 p.m. period in Toronto, 34.9 per cent of the schedules of the three Buffalo stations carried on cable were subject to the simultaneous program substitution regulations, 38.9 per cent of schedules were made up of programs not purchased by Canadian broadcasters, while 26.2 per cent of U.S. station schedules included programs purchased by Canadian broadcasters, but not scheduled at the same time on Canadian and U.S. stations.

Because the benefits of the current policy are available only if Canadian stations schedule their U.S. programs at the same time as the U.S. networks, a major result of the policy has been to help drive Canadian programs out of the prime-time schedule, thereby ensuring that relatively little will be spent on them and that they will not earn a high level of advertising revenues. A growing percentage of the viewing of Canadian stations is now accounted for by the viewing of substituted programs carried in U.S. station schedules. The implications of this shift are alarming if one considers the fact that the Canadian channel and the Canadian programmer are becoming less and less necessary. At the point at which Canadian audiences are reached effectively without a sale to a Canadian broadcaster, the sale may simply not be possible because the cost to the Canadian broadcaster will be too high, given the limited advertiser interest.

If the products advertisers sell are available in both the Canadian and U.S. markets, then exactly the same ad can be used in Canada and the United States. As Table 7-13 indicates, the extent to which the products advertised on U.S. stations are widely available in Canada is very high. About half of all commercials, including 80 per cent of U.S.

TABLE 7-13
NUMBER OF COMMERCIALS BY TYPE AND INTENDED
AUDIENCE ON AMERICAN BORDER STATIONS,[1] 1977 AND 1978

Type of Commercial Broadcast	Intended Audience							
	American		Canadian		Both		Total	
	1977	1978	1977	1978	1977	1978	1977	1978
American network	397	378	—	—	1,588	1,511	1,985	1,889
American spot	435	663	—	—	806	776	1,241	1,439
American local	537	565	—	—	—	—	537	565
Canadian spot	—	—	507	617	—	—	507	617
Canadian local	—	—	137	153	33	34	170	187
Total	1,369	1,606	644	770	2,427	2,321	4,440	4,697

Note: [1] KVOS, KOMO, WKBW, WGR, WIVB, WPTZ, WCAX.

Source: Broadcast Monitoring Services Ltd., Monitoring Reports, May 24 to 30, 1977 and 1978.

network advertising, is for the products of multinationals which are available both in Canada and the United States. To the extent that those multinationals can reach Canadian audiences just as effectively through ads placed on CBS, NBC and ABC, rather than CBC, CTV, TVA, Global or independent Canadian stations, they are not likely to place television ads in Canada. This lack of interest in advertising in Canada is, to some extent, reinforced by a tight supply of television advertising time in Canada, particularly for national network advertising.

Recognizing the severity of this problem, the CRTC has kept open the additional options noted earlier. What we now know is that Canadian stations are continuing to lose market share and that advertising revenues remain far lower than in such countries as Australia or the United States, despite the implementation of simultaneous program substitution in 1976. The question then is whether there are real alternatives that should now be implemented.

The first and perhaps obvious point is that simply having cable companies delete the commercials from the U.S. networks is not an acceptable option. While such a policy was always open to accusations of piracy, these accusations have acquired added legitimacy now that U.S. broadcasters receive copyright payments from cable systems in their own market.

A second alternative would be to expand the program substitution policy to permit non-simultaneous substitution. Such action would end the forced duplication of U.S. network schedules by Canadian broadcasters and would result in a much higher proportion of the schedule being duplicated, thereby substantially reducing the spillover effect of U.S. commercial channels on cable. Although there appear to be some significant practical problems and costs involved in implementing such a policy, it remains a defensible and effective option.

A significant variation on this proposal was put forward in CFTO-TV Ltd.'s December 1981 submission to the Canadian-content review being carried out by the CRTC. CFTO asked that CRTC have cable operators "delete programs appearing on foreign television channels carried on cable systems where such programs have been licensed to Canadian broadcasters, provided the broadcasters make available a *Canadian program* for substitution by the cable operators."[14] Such a policy would have the advantage of increasing the exposure of Canadian programs and, as a result, increasing their ability to earn advertising revenue. In addition, it would increase the audience share that Canadian broadcasters get for the foreign programs they acquire.

If the figures in the CFTO submission are accurate — as they presumably are — then the magnitude of the audience and advertising revenue loss that results from cable carriage of foreign programs acquired by Canadian broadcasters on the U.S. as well as the Canadian station is staggering. In the Toronto market, the Canadian stations reach only 48 per cent of the total audience for foreign programs that are not run simultaneously with their exhibition on a U.S. station. However, if the programs are carried simultaneously and the Canadian signal is substituted into the U.S. station's schedule, then the Canadian broadcaster gets 72 per cent of the total audience.

While the CFTO proposal would have some strange effects — for example, leaving CFTO's peak-time schedule essentially foreign, while putting Canadian programs into prime time on U.S. schedules — the problems it addresses must be dealt with. One interesting effect of any decision to establish non-simultaneous program substitution would be that it would result in over 60 per cent of the schedules of the U.S. stations being replaced. At that point, surely one might begin to question why the U.S. channels should continue to be carried by cable companies as part of their twelve-channel basic service.

With respect to the remaining U.S. network programs which are not now required by Canadian stations, it would appear preferable if they also were acquired legitimately for broadcast in Canada with proper payment made to the foreign program producer and with advertising time sold to Canadian advertisers. On this issue, the 1980 Report of the CRTC's Therrien Committee stated that

> The Committee believes . . . that the demand for more choice of entertainment tends to be mistakenly equated with the viewing of U.S. stations in their entirety, whereas in fact much of their programming other than entertainment is of no interest to Canadian viewers. If this view is correct, Canadian satellite services carrying the best of American entertainment may prove as attractive as the broadcasts of U.S. stations whether the latter are carried by satellite or by cable systems.[15]

This issue will be looked at further later in this chapter.

Subscriber-supported or Pay-Television Services
As noted earlier, consumers ultimately pay for all television services. However, the way in which television services are paid for now includes both indirectly and directly supported services. At the present time, the balance is shifting towards a greater emphasis on direct subscriber-supported television.

The first and most important subscriber-supported or pay-television service developed in Canada was that provided by the cable television companies. This fact was recognized by the 1980 Report of the Therrien Committee, which stated that "more than half the television households in Canada were indulging in a form of pay-TV, in that they pay for cable service."[16] As Table 7-14 indicates, the subscriber revenues of cable television have grown far more rapidly than those of any other component of the television system, increasing almost fifteenfold over the period 1967 to 1980. During that time, there has been a marked shift in the relative importance of publicly-funded television, private advertiser-supported television and subscriber-supported television. While the revenues of the system as a whole have increased more rapidly than the rate of growth in GNP (450 per cent by comparison with 336 per cent), public broadcasting's share of total revenue has declined significantly, while private broadcaster revenues have grown much more slowly than those of cable.

The shifting importance of the three basic revenue sources led to escalating concern throughout the 1970s over the need to devise policies that would result in the production of more Canadian drama and variety programming by the advertiser-supported private broadcasters. The performance of the commercial broadcasters has already been

279

TABLE 7-14
BROADCASTING AND CABLE: TOTAL REVENUES 1967 AND 1980

Components	1967		1980		
	$000's	% of Total	$000's	% of Total	% Growth[1]
Private television	95,178	26.7	562,036	28.7	491
Private radio	88,761	24.9	397,194	20.3	347
Total private broadcasting	183,939	51.6	959,230	49.0	421
CBC/Radio-Canada	150,097[2]	42.1	647,004	33.0	331
Cable	22,115	6.2	352,172	18.0	1,492
Total	356,151	100.0	1,958,406	100.0	450

Notes: [1] GNP grew by 336 per cent between 1967 and 1980.

[2] CBC/Radio-Canada figures include both radio and television.

Sources: CRTC, *Special Report on Broadcasting, 1968-78*, vol. 2, Table 9A, and Statistics Canada, *Radio and Television Broadcasting, 1980*.

examined. The same concerns have also been expressed, however, about the need to structure a combination of subscriber-supported services that will direct adequate revenues into Canadian program production.

At the present time, only a small percentage of the revenues of the cable companies goes into program production. Cable companies make no payments for the carriage of the Canadian programs produced by the public and private broadcasters whose signals they market and they invest relatively little in programming they themselves produce. Most of the program expenditure of the cable companies goes into programming the community channel which they are required by the CRTC to provide as a component of basic cable service.

The monthly fee charged by cable companies to their subscribers represents a single basic service rate. Although most cable companies provide additional services on a "channel converter," which allows subscribers to receive extra channels in addition to the basic twelve-channel service, they are not permitted, apart from installation fees plus the sale or rental price of the converter, to levy any additional monthly charges for this augmented basic service.

Concern has been expressed by the CRTC itself, in many public reports, including those of the Clyne Committee and the Therrien Committee, and by ministers and deputy ministers of communication, over the need to tie a much more substantial percentage of the cable industry's existing revenues into the financing of Canadian television programming. Proposals for increasing cable's contribution to Canadian programming have included the following:

- increased funding of the community channel;
- a levy on cable revenue which would be dedicated to financing Canadian programming;
- payments for rediffusion of Canadian programs produced by broadcasters;
- new television services provided by the cable industry;
- establishing a new, national, cable industry-financed entertainment service which, like the existing community channel, would be provided as part of basic cable service.

While some of these proposals involve expanding cable's own role as a program originator and scheduler, most involve the contribution by cable of an increased share of its rapidly growing revenues towards the cost of Canadian programs produced independently of the cable industry. Given the widely-held concern that expanded direct cable involvement with programming services would create conflicts of interest that are unacceptable, it appears certain that only suggestions in the second category are likely to receive serious consideration by government.

The revenue sources of cable companies will increase very substantially in the near future as a result of the probable addition of at least a second tier of television services for which a relatively small additional monthly fee will be charged, and the certain addition of individual, relatively high-cost, pay-television channels featuring first-run feature films, big-budget specials, and so on. The total revenue from pay-television subscribers will be split between the pay-television licensees and the cable companies, with the latter receiving between 40 and 50 per cent of total revenue for exhibiting and retailing the service.

The suggestion that cable companies be allowed to offer tiered services has often been associated with the removal of the American channels from basic cable service, permitting a restructuring of basic service to include only Canadian channels. It has often been assumed that the advertiser-supported U.S. channels would then be sold to subscribers as part of a second tier. However, if this were done without a continuation of the CRTC's program substitution policy, the result would be a greatly accelerated erosion of the advertiser support base of Canadian television. It would be preferable to provide more of the entertainment programs used by the U.S. networks through the purchase of those programs by Canadian broadcasters. The U.S. channels, subject to a strong program substitution policy, might continue to be available as part of augmented basic service available on the channel converter without additional charge.

Clear guidelines need to be developed before additional tiers of service are established. The CRTC held a public hearing in December 1982 to consider what these guidelines should be. The major requirement that should be adopted is that the services offered on the second or additional tiers should be complementary to the basic service. No television service offered as part of an additional tier should be such as to threaten in any substantial way the basic Canadian channels provided on the basic service. Channels offered as part of additional tiers should be programmed in Canada and, where they are in part advertiser-supported, should carry Canadian advertising. If these services are genuinely complementary, they will provide a valuable advertising vehicle for certain categories of Canadian business. As high a percentage as possible of special-interest, supplementary kinds of Canadian programming should be carried on each channel, although Canadian-content levels may vary from channel to channel. Where appropriate, the CBC should be used to provide some of these services. Payment would be made for the carriage of channels on the additional tiers from the revenues of the cable companies carrying such services.

While no date has been set for the initiation of a second or additional tiers of channels, the CRTC has already licensed seven individual pay-television channels: two at the national level and five on a national or provincial basis. Applications for additional pay licences to serve Manitoba, Saskatchewan and British Columbia have also been invited. Six of the licensed services are expected to begin operation in February 1983.

In calling for applications for separate pay channels in April 1981, the CRTC had reversed its earlier position[17] on the need to avoid direct competition among Canadian pay-television services, at least during the initial years of its operation in Canada. That earlier position had been based on more than five years of research and extensive public hearings. Instead, in 1981, the commission indicated that it intended to license directly competing services. In the face of the advice of virtually all applicants and intervenors, and despite analysis carried out by its own staff and the evidence presented at the hearing, the CRTC proceeded to do precisely what it had said it would do. Rather than licensing a number of complementary services, which most applicants and intervenors had favoured, the commission licensed directly competing commercial services based on Hollywood feature films.

The response of the vast majority of the cultural community and the production industry was predictable. The decision was appealed to cabinet by a wide range of production industry organizations — including major unions and guilds, the French-language television production industry, and the feature film production industry — as well as by the Canadian Conference of the Arts and one of the unsuccessful applicants. All argued against the decision on much the same grounds: basically that it was not compatible with either Canada's cultural interests or its industrial interests. In its appeal of the decision, the Canadian Conference of the Arts stated that

> By licensing too many competing services, the Commission has unnecessarily weakened the financial viability of those services it has licensed with the result that inadequate provision has been made for air-time for Canadian programs; there will be insufficient funds to permit the production of high quality Canadian programs, and there will be no effective cross subsidization of either French or regional program production.[18]

In a puzzling and unprecedented rationale for this decision, the CRTC chairman acknowledged implicitly that the result of the decision would indeed be that it was not possible for the licensees to produce high quality programming directed explicitly to Canadian audiences. Somewhat euphemistically the chairman stated that "the scenario is based on the evolution of a system congenial to Canadians because it will reflect their North American tastes."[19] He added that the original system might be supplemented later by a service which "would be heavily Canadian, and would respond to quite different economic, social and cultural stimuli." What seems to be meant is that the additional service which might or might not be set up later would respond to Canadian stimuli, while the original package will result in programming designed primarily for the much larger American audience. Not only will the existing licensees rely on their purchases of big-budget U.S. programs, but even the "Canadian" programs they carry will be designed for U.S. audiences.

How such a decision is to be reconciled with the views expressed by Communications Minister Francis Fox, and the statement attributed to the prime minister that communications policy "should serve more and more to strengthen our culture and identity," is not clear. How the decision can be related to the federal government's efforts to persuade French-speaking Quebecers that the federal government can and will protect their cultural interests, it is difficult to see.

What seems to have happened in this decision is that the pro-competitive, anti-regulatory thinking that has affected telecommunications policy decisions over the past few years has spilled over into regulatory decisions affecting television. Since 1976, of course, the CRTC has been responsible for telecommunications as well as radio and television. The difficulty is that the CRTC examined the results of a pro-competitive decision on pay-television entirely from an economic and perhaps, to some extent, an ideological perspective. Competition was viewed a priori as a good thing. What was neglected was the effect that a pro-competitive decision would have on the character of the resulting programming and the balance between French- and English-language programming. The pay-television system licensed will not be able to generate any reasonable level of high quality production without almost complete reliance on programming co-produced with foreign companies, who will provide the bulk of the necessary financing and retain control over the character of the programs.

The implications of the CRTC decision are clearest if one looks at its effect on the level of expenditure per hour on Canadian programming. The national licensee, First Choice Communications, had indicated to the commission that, while its performance would not be affected by the licensing of complementary pay services, its average expenditure on a per hour basis would drop from $330,000 to $120,000 if a directly competing service were licensed. Similarly, payments by First Choice for Canadian feature films would drop from an average of $500,000 to $190,000 in the first year. The regional licensees will have even less to spend on a per hour basis. Since it is generally accepted that a minimum of $350,000 must be spent to produce an hour of drama programming of acceptable quality, the impact of the decision on Canadian program production is obvious and dramatic. For feature film producers, the $190,000 per feature will not be of any significant help in financing Canadian feature films. The Canadian program producers will be forced into a pattern of minority partnership in co-production with dominant foreign and primarily American partners; or else they will produce relatively low budget programs.

Despite these fundamental flaws in the pay-television decision, there

284

are important elements in the decision that could, in the future, be beneficial to Canadian program production. First, the CRTC has made it a condition of licence that a fixed percentage of each licensee's programming expenditure and gross revenue go into Canadian programs. Second, in order to encourage the production of dramatic programming, the licensees are required to put a fixed percentage of Canadian program funds into drama. These are important innovations and, if the commission persists in enforcing compliance and uses a comparable approach in dealing with existing commercial television broadcasters, the effects on the television system as a whole might prove beneficial. However, in relation to pay-television, the competitive structure established — in combination with a very loose definition of Canadian content — will not lead to the desired results from these regulatory innovations. The commission itself seems to have recognized that this will be the case.

Fairness dictates that the commission not be judged too early on the pay-television decision. While the CRTC's history does not justify much optimism, the commission has insisted it will not amend the conditions of licence and, by implication, that it is prepared to see some licensees fail financially if they cannot comply with the terms of their licence. If predictions of financial fragility are accurate, there may, therefore, be significant changes in the initial structure which would permit it to function more successfully in meeting Canadian programming objectives.

Further, it must be recognized that the CRTC itself has stated clearly in its pay-television decision that additions will be made to the system in the future. The major addition contemplated is the establishing of a new non-profit television service which would, like the community channel, be operated as a part of basic cable television service, thereby achieving the objectives of directing a greater share of the cable industry's existing revenues into Canadian programming. The new service might be operated by a public-sector corporation, possibly the CBC, or by a non-profit private-sector corporation.

While the CRTC decision on pay-television recognized the potential value of such a service as a source of very substantial funds for the production of high quality Canadian programs, it is not clear when the CRTC might make a final decision on whether to proceed. A hearing to explore the matter further was held in December 1982. If such a service does go ahead, it will add a further $150 million annually to the revenues available to Canadian film and television producers from the domestic market. As already noted, such a service could pay between

$1 and $2 million per feature film exhibited and would be able to offer a high level of funding on a per hour basis for Canadian drama.

The relative importance of the pay-television services licensed in 1982 can be judged by looking at their anticipated revenues. It is anticipated that the licensed pay-television services will have revenues from subscribers of between $150 and $200 million by 1984, rising to between $300 and $400 million in 1987. However, these subscriber revenues will be split between the pay-television licensees and the cable television industry, probably on a 55/45 basis. As a result, the revenues of the cable industry will rise substantially, while the pay-television services will have revenues of $80 to $110 million in 1984, rising to $160 to $220 million in 1987.

The Profitability of the Components of the Television Industry

Private, Advertiser-supported Stations
As Table 7-15 indicates, the operating profits of the private television industry have been remarkably high and surprisingly consistent over the period 1968 to 1981, rising from 17.6 per cent in 1968 to 19.8 per cent in 1981. A study published by the Institute for Research on Public Policy (IRPP) in 1980 calculated that the average *weighted* rate of return for the television industry in 1975 was 32.2 per cent.[20] By comparison, private radio broadcasting earned a rate of return of 18.1 per cent in 1975. The same study noted that a competitive bench mark rate of return for 1975 was 13 per cent, commenting that "Overall returns on capital investments in excess of this rate would be indicative of super normal profits attributable to positions of market power." In the case of television, which is a regulated industry, it should be added that such a high rate of return measures not just the market power of the companies involved, but the lack of success of the regulator in ensuring that the companies use that power to achieve the public policy objectives on which the existence of regulation is predicated.

While the profits of the private television industry are extraordinarily high, they vary greatly according to company size. The highest rate of return in 1975, 39.6 per cent, was earned by the corporations with the largest broadcasting asset base. The smallest earned 19 per cent, while the intermediate-sized companies had rates of return that averaged from 10 to 13 per cent.

TABLE 7-15
PRIVATE TELEVISION STATIONS: SELECTED ECONOMIC
STATISTICS, SELECTED YEARS, 1968-81
($000's)

	1968	1971	1974	1977	1980	1981
Total revenue	99,178	115,789	194,233	331,697	562,036	652,385
Operating profit	17,484	13,420	32,966	81,369	100,439	128,859
Pre-tax profit	—	—	22,771	68,905	102,965	127,729
Total program expenses	—	27,862[1]	88,195	137,848	255,187	283,260
program production	—	9,338	51,805	82,449	—	—
program purchase	—	18,524	32,514	49,108	—	—
Gross fixed assets	—	111,941	157,493	220,280	322,012	352,041
Net fixed assets	—	47,739	71,797	110,649	163,592	171,883

Note: [1] The definition of costs used on the annual returns changed between 1971 and 1972; thus caution in the interpretation of changes in costs and profits over this period is advised.

Sources: CRTC, *Special Report on Broadcasting, 1968-78;* Statistics Canada, *Radio and Television Broadcasting*.

Cable Television

The operating profit of the cable industry, like that of private television broadcasting, has changed very little over the past decade, falling slightly from 45.1 per cent in 1970 to 42.5 per cent in 1980. The cable companies, however, have a substantially higher level of investment in fixed assets. The net value of the fixed assets of the industry in 1980 was $389.1 million.

The IRPP study noted above concluded that cable companies had a high average level of profitability, although not as high as television broadcasters. The unweighted average rate of return for the cable industry in 1975 was 24 per cent.[21] In commenting on the average level of profitability in the cable industry, the authors of the study noted that "cable firms are licensed by the CRTC and this licence represents an entry barrier which creates a monopoly in a given area. As a result, the firm is able to earn above-normal profits, all or part of which is rent attributable to the artificial barrier."[22] The CRTC does not regulate the cable industry on a rate of return basis, although it does approve the monthly rates charged to subscribers by cable licensees.

287

The Television Production Industry

By comparison with the television broadcasters and the cable companies, the private-sector program production companies in Canada are relatively small and do not earn profits that would attract additional investment capital if it were not for the capital cost allowance provisions in the federal Income Tax Act. As is now evident, even this incentive measure cannot sustain a reasonable level of investment unless a more secure market develops for the Canadian films and television programs produced as a result of this tax incentive.

As Table 6-10 indicated, the private-sector production companies derived 69.9 per cent of their total revenue, or $64.5 million, from the television market in 1979. Of this revenue, $39.4 million was derived from the production of commercials, $25.1 million from the sale of films or television programs to the television market. With the exception of the production companies which are owned by companies in the television broadcasting industry, any independent production company has had to rely on the CBC as its only significant market for programs produced for television. CTV and the other private network have made use almost exclusively of the production companies they themselves control.

In 1979, the Canadian production industry had an aggregate operating loss of 1 per cent of gross revenues. The twenty-five companies with revenues in excess of $1 million — many of whom depend on the production of television commercials — had an average operating profit of 8.9 per cent of revenues. Not only is the profitability of Canadian television program production low by comparison with television broadcasting, but the risks are infinitely higher.

The major cause of the production industry's difficulties is the lack of market outlets in Canada prepared to cover a reasonable proportion of the cost of productions. In a paper prepared for the CRTC hearings on pay-television,[23] Richard Nielson and Pat Ferns of the production company Primedia, compared the situation of independent Canadian producers to that of producers in other countries. In the United States, producers generally receive 75 per cent of their programming costs from the U.S. networks for the first run of their productions, with the networks advancing the funds. The remainder of their revenue comes from the sale of reruns and from foreign sales and syndication. In France, production companies usually recover 90 per cent of their costs from pre-production commitments by the television networks. In Germany, independent producers usually recover 90 per cent of their costs from domestic sales, while in the U.K., producers usually recover all of their costs in the domestic market. The exception to this pattern is international co-productions, i.e., programs jointly produced by companies in different countries. In such cases, each partner usually attempts to recover his share of the cost in his domestic market.

By comparison, independent Canadian producers are rarely able to get back 30 per cent of their production costs in Canada.[24] There is simply no way that a stable independent production industry can develop in Canada, if companies have to earn back at least 70 per cent of their money from foreign markets. Even if it could, the resulting dependence on foreign sales would dictate that all independently produced programs be tailored to foreign markets, with the result that they would contribute little or nothing to the development of programs that reflected Canadian realities.

Unless some way can be found substantially to increase the return independent producers derive from their domestic market, the industry will not develop and will be unable to make any real cultural contribution. While it had been hoped that pay-television would bring about a turnaround in the industry, the system that has been licensed will not bring about any improvement in the situation of the independent production industry. The total flow of funds, while substantial by comparison with present levels, will not provide an adequate base for the industry's development. In particular, the level of financing available from Canadian pay-television on a per hour basis will not permit Canadian producers to recover even half of the costs of a competitive drama program, except on an irregular or occasional basis.

The notion that a Canadian film and television production industry can be developed on the basis of export sales is a dangerous yet seemingly pervasive fantasy among policy-makers. The lessons that should have been learned from the experience of the collapse of the feature film production industry were not reflected in the CRTC's decision on pay-television. Until the Canadian industry has a domestic market for a steady and dependable volume of production, with co-production and "block-busters" added on as a high-risk bonus, the industry will be forced to treat mere survival as success.

The reality of the existing export market for Canadian production is that Canadian television programs earned $8 million from foreign markets in 1980, of which just $2 million came from the U.S. market. Even the powerful U.S. program production industry earns only an estimated 10 per cent of its total revenues from foreign markets. The industry can and should aim for a substantial increase in export revenues, but it is imperative to be realistic about the proportion of total revenues which, on average, can be expected to flow from foreign markets. One must also be realistic about the character of most export-dependent programming.

Concentration

In television as in radio, all Canadian stations and networks, as well as all cable television systems, are required under the terms of the Broadcasting Act to be Canadian owned and controlled. In 1975, the four leading ownership groups in the television broadcasting industry — Baton, Tele-Metropole, Southam-Selkirk, and Western Broadcasting — accounted for 40 per cent of industry revenue. This represents a significantly higher level of concentration than exists in radio broadcasting where the ten largest firms earn 44 per cent of industry revenue. In 1975, 56 per cent of all television stations were group-owned, up from 38 per cent in 1965. The top ten television groups accounted for 65 per cent of industry revenue in 1975.

A second aspect of concentration that must also be recognized is the network affiliation structure. As noted already, 85 per cent of all stations in Canada are part of one of the major networks. If it were not for the existence of the network structures in Canada, the television system would not be able to generate any reasonable amount of high quality Canadian programming in any program category. However, the nature of the CTV network is not one which is conducive to its making the contribution to Canadian programming of which a Canadian network structure is financially capable. The most serious structural obstacle to any improvement in the functioning of CTV is the fact that it is owned by the major stations which are part of the network. As a result, as a separate entity with its own motivation and distinct interests of its own in developing its programming role, CTV does not really exist. Instead, it is a creature of its member stations, whose priorities appear to include giving the network no more revenue than is absolutely necessary to provide certain essential categories of programs required to meet CRTC regulatory requirements at the lowest possible cost.

Ownership of CTV by its major member stations makes private-sector television in Canada far more concentrated in control than is immediately obvious. It would appear desirable for the CRTC to consider divestiture by the member stations in CTV and, if a second private English-language network were to be developed, whether or not it is based on Global, to avoid such a concentration of power and such inherent conflicts of interest.

There is also very significant cross-media ownership at the local level, both with respect to cross-ownership of radio and television stations, and of broadcasting stations and newspapers. Local media cross-ownership exists, for example, within the Southam-Selkirk group, Western Broadcasting, and the CHUM group. These issues of local concentration of media control were looked at in more detail in chapter 1.

The extent of corporate concentration in the cable television industry has also been increasing rapidly. While in 1975 the largest group, which was then Premier Cablesystems, accounted for 13 per cent of industry revenue, the largest group in 1982, Rogers Cablesystems, accounted for approximately 25 per cent of total industry revenue. In 1975, the four largest groups accounted for 41 per cent of industry revenue; the ten largest for 64 per cent.

Economic Impact

Import/Export Data

With the licensing of the Global Television network and a variety of independent stations in major Canadian markets, competition for the purchase of foreign programs has increased greatly. According to the latest figures in *Variety*, Canada's English-language networks, CBC and CTV, both pay more for a half-hour episode of U.S. programming than the United Kingdom ($10-$15,000 by comparison with $9-$10,000). If one takes into account the fact that Canada's English-language population is approximately 18 million while Britain's is over 55 million — not to mention the fact that one-third of Canadian English-language television viewing is of American stations anyway — the extent of Canada's overpayment for foreign programs is readily appreciated. The main reason for the difference is the fact that Canada buys foreign programs on a competitive basis, while almost all European countries do not.

Total expenditure on foreign programs has been escalating rapidly. According to the Canadian Association of Broadcasters, expenditure by private-sector television on foreign programs increased from $30.2 million in 1977 to $55.2 million in 1979. In constant dollars, the magnitude of the increase was 47.4 per cent and the rate of increase has probably continued. One effect of these increases was to slow expenditure on Canadian programs, which rose by just 17.1 per cent in real terms between 1977 and 1979.

While no precise data are available for CBC expenditure on foreign programs, a reasonable estimate would be that CBC spent between $20 and $25 million on foreign programs in 1979, bringing total expenditure by Canadian television on foreign programs to $75-$80 million. Beginning in 1983, Canadian pay-television services will also be acquiring foreign programs and are expected to spend a minimum of $25-$35 million on foreign programs in their first year of operation. The total revenue of U.S. television exporters from all foreign markets in 1982 is expected to be $475 million (U.S. currency). Despite its relatively small population and the limited market served by its domestic commercial television services, Canada will provide the United States with over 20 per cent of its total foreign earnings from television sales in 1982 — with pay-television resulting in a significant increase the following year.

Canadian revenue from foreign television sales was $5 million in 1978 and rose to $8 million in 1980, more slowly than the rate of increase in imports. As a result, Canada's trade imbalance in television programming in 1979 was approximately $70 million and appears certain to increase sharply, at least over the next few years.

Employment

The CBC had 12,104 employees in 1980, of whom an estimated 8,800 were employed in television broadcasting. The CBC also made $78.2 million in freelance payments in 1980, including payments to musicians, actors, writers and performers; royalties to authors, composers and musicians' associations; and other production fees and performing rights payments. An additional 6,685 employees worked in private television broadcasting in 1980, receiving $146.7 million in salaries and benefits. The cable television industry reported that it had 5,480 employees in 1980 and paid salaries and other benefits of $92.8 million.

While no comprehensive figures are readily available on freelance payments made by private-sector broadcasters, an estimate can be made on the basis, for example, of the relative level of CBC and private-sector payments to screenwriters and performers who are members of the English-language union which represents them. Payments to ACTRA members by CBC were $20 million in 1981. By comparison, payments by CTV and its affiliates were $4.6 million, while payments by Global and independent stations combined were $2.2 million.

As Table 7-16 indicates, the cost of producing various categories of television programming varies widely, as does the possibility of covering production costs from advertising revenue in Canada. These figures explain the reluctance of commercial, profit-motivated broadcasters to produce drama and variety programming. While costs vary greatly for different categories of programs, so too does the level of employment generated. The production of drama and variety

TABLE 7-16

AVERAGE COST AND REVENUE OF CANADIAN PROGRAMMING BY PROGRAM CATEGORY, 1978

	No. of Programs	Costs[1]	Revenues[2]	Audience[3] Actual	Break-even
English-Language Market					
Drama					
serials	4	$114,750	$59,536	921,500	1,776,300
short films	1	137,160	78,166	1,210,000	2,123,200
teledramas	2	112,830	46,318	717,000	1,746,000
Variety	2	115,620	74,452	1,152,500	1,789,800
Game shows	2	18,900	57,882	896,000	292,600
News	6	36,887	68,301	1,057,300	571,000
Documentaries	1	20,768	26,098	404,000	321,400
French-Language Market					
Drama					
soap operas	3	25,860	51,390	1,380,600	440,800
Variety	2	38,925	44,448	794,900	716,200
Game shows	2	21,090	42,620	708,500	193,400
News & information	2	29,730	36,025	687,500	567,400

Notes: [1] Costs are the average cost of a 30-minute program for a sample of programs in each category.

[2] The average revenue was obtained in the following manner: The minimum 30-second rate during prime time viewing for a network which had broadcast the program was multiplied by twenty time periods. This gave the revenue for a half-hour of programming for which the 15 per cent agency commission was subtracted. This income was divided by the average audience of the network during prime time, which gave the income per viewer. The average income by category of program was then obtained by multiplying the audience of each program by the revenue per viewer. The data are for rates and audiences in Fall, 1978.

[3] The actual audience is the audience observed for each sample program. The break-even audience is the one necessary to cover production costs.

Source: A Lapointe and J. LeGoff, *Television Programs and Their Production in Canada* (Department of Communications, May 1980), Tables 1.25 and 1.26.

293

TABLE 7-17
NUMBER OF EMPLOYEES FOR EACH 13 HOURS OF BROADCAST
TIME BY PROGRAM TYPE

Type of Program	Full-time, Man-years of Employment
Full-length feature films (90 min.)	881
Drama series (60 min.)	188
Full-length features made for TV (90 min.)	92
Variety (90 min.)	92
Short features (60 min.)	64
Variety (45-60-120 min.)	54
Drama series (30 min.)	48
Documentary (30 min.)	37
Short features (30 min.)	32
Public affairs (30-60 min.)	30
Documentary (60 min.)	28
News (national) (30 min.)	12
Game shows (30 min.)	10
Sports events (180 min.)	2
Talk show—soft information	1

Source: Lapointe and LeGoff, *Television Programs and Their Production in Canada*.

programming generates much higher levels of employment than other program categories (see Table 7-17).

Expenditure on Broadcasting Equipment
Private television broadcasters reported by 1980 an investment of $205.4 million in broadcasting equipment, including tower and antenna systems, transmitter equipment, studio and technical equipment and mobile equipment. The net value of this technical equipment was $83.6 million, which represented 51 per cent of the industry's net assets of $163.6 million. CBC reported an investment of $357.8 million in technical equipment, but did not provide separate information concerning its radio and television broadcasting facilities. Cable television companies had invested a total of $640.2 million in technical equipment by 1980, which represented 91 per cent of their total investment of fixed assets. In 1980, these equipment assets were carried at a net value of $320.1 million.

The broadcast and cable industries represent a significant market for technical equipment. The next major investment to be made will be in an upgrading of the facilities of cable television in connection with the offering of both tiered services and coding and decoding equipment for premium pay-television services. A variety of non-programming services now being developed and implemented will also necessitate substantial capital expenditures. The Therrien Committee recognized the potential value of the implementation of pay-television to the Canadian electronics manufacturing industry, and recommended in its 1980 report that the equipment for delivering pay-television be "wholly or largely of Canadian manufacture."[25] Such a condition was not set, however, in the CRTC's pay-television licensing decision, although the commission may intend to address this issue further in establishing exhibition arrangements for the licensed pay-television services.

Television as Advertising Vehicle

The availability and cost of television advertising and the size of the audiences that can be reached also have a powerful direct effect on the economy as a whole and on any business in Canada that is selling goods and services. The existence of a national market for goods and services simply assumes that the national media exist through which such goods and services can be marketed.

Both at the federal and provincial levels many millions of dollars have been spent on advertising campaigns designed to encourage Canadians to buy Canadian-made products. However, governments cannot expect to compensate for inherent weakness in the Canadian media system through special "Buy Canadian" advertising campaigns. Spillover advertising from the United States for U.S. goods and services helps to strengthen the market for the sale of U.S. goods in Canada, while relatively high costs and limited audience reach for Canadian media adversely affect the sale of the products of Canadian industry.

Satellite Distribution

The changes that the development of cable television has brought about in the distribution system for television signals have already been examined. More recently, satellite distribution has come to be used extensively as a means of distributing television signals in Canada. Late in 1981, the Federal Communications Commission (FCC) in the United States authorized a number of U.S. common carriers to deliver

U.S. television services into Canadian territory using U.S. and Canadian satellites. While FCC approval is conditional on agreement by the international agency, Intelsat, and by the Canadian government, there is considerable pressure on the Canadian government to consent.

While the complex issue of international satellite agreements and policy cannot be dealt with in any detail in this study, the issue is so important that it requires attention. As the 1979 Clyne Committee Report stated, ''satellite communications have greater significance for Canadian sovereignty than for that of any other country in the world.''[26] Satellites can be used to deliver programs conveniently to broadcasters and local cable systems for retransmission or rediffusion. Moreover, in the future, they will also be able to deliver a signal that can be received directly by individuals on a relatively inexpensive receiving dish.

Evidence of the damage that has already been done to the advertising base of Canadian television as a result of carriage of U.S. signals on cable has been examined previously. The critically important question in the future is whether Canadian television services will suffer a further major setback in the 1980s as a result of greatly expanded coverage of Canada by U.S. television services beamed directly into Canada by satellite and operating completely outside the framework of the regulatory power of the CRTC. Public policy initiatives in Canada and the United States will be the key factor affecting such developments.

It is essential to the success of any strategy for the development of Canadian television that the federal government take a strong position in response to this FCC decision. As the CRTC's *Report of the Committee on Extension of Service* noted, it is possible for the United States to develop its satellites using spot-beams which would greatly reduce the spillover of their signals onto Canadian territory. Canada must insist that this be done.

However, Canada's response to the technology of satellite distribution cannot simply be negative. If there is to be a viable private-sector component in the Canadian television industry, then it must be able to meet the principal needs for and interests of Canadians *in all parts of the country* in both foreign and Canadian programs. The satellite technology which has been to a significant degree pioneered in Canada provides an opportunity for the Canadian television system far more effectively to meet those needs.

New Canadian satellite-delivered domestic programming services could provide an alternative approach to the satellite issue — one that protected Canada's sovereignty, provided Canadian advertisers with more effective advertising vehicles, and had the potential to contribute to meeting Canada's own objectives for television. The central issue, in fact, is whether or to what extent there will be in the future a separate Canadian structure for the production and delivery of television services — a structure which reflects priorities Canadians themselves have established and which is responsive to their own cultural, social and economic needs.

If, in the future, a pattern of continental rather than national satellite delivery of television services develops, then the further decline of private-sector Canadian television is inevitable. To the extent that any private, commercial broadcasters in Canada survived, which is highly unlikely, it would be at the expense of reorienting their programming to meet the needs of the 90 per cent of their potential audience that was south of the border. For French-language Canada, the results would clearly be quite disastrous, with advertising revenues drained away from French-language television services and an inundation of foreign, English-language signals blanketing the province of Quebec.

In 1979, the Department of Communications financed a study[27] which gave serious and detailed consideration to a plan for transmitting the four U.S. networks by Canadian satellite to all parts of Canada. Canadian Satellite Communications Inc. (Cancom), the company licensed to supply expanded television services to the North by satellite, requested approval in 1982 to supply the estimated 600,000 households it serves with the four U.S. networks. No action to implement either of these plans should be taken. The effect of both would be to weaken further the Canadian television system.

The best of international television programming can and should be provided by Canadian stations, networks and other programming services; and, as a matter of national policy, increasing use should be made of Canadian satellites to carry such programming services. There is simply no way to avoid the fact that, if foreign television systems are allowed to extend their share of the Canadian market, Canada's own television system will be further weakened. Canada can and should instead be involved in developing and implementing realistic plans to strengthen all components of its own system so that it can more effectively satisfy the demands of Canadians for both foreign and Canadian programming.

Television Programming in Canada

Multiple Channels and Program Diversity

In an important study prepared for the Institute for Research on Public Policy in 1980,[28] an empirical analysis was carried out to measure the degree of balance, diversity and choice provided by the television broadcasting system in Canada. Based on an analysis of program data provided by the CRTC and the CBC, the authors of the study found that

- The CBC-owned French and English stations provided the most balanced program schedules, including balanced proportions of information, light entertainment and serious entertainment.
- The CBC-owned French and English stations also provided the widest diversity of kinds of programs, followed by the CBC's French and English affiliated stations. The least diversity was provided by Global's programming.
- The average number of viewing options available in a local market did not increase proportionally with the number of stations. In fact, *"the more stations there are in a market, the less likely that any one of them is offering, in any half-hour period, a program type different from all the others"* and *"the more stations there are in a market, the lower the proportion of options"* [29] (emphasis added).
- While the addition of U.S. commercial channels did increase the range of option to some degree, it did so at a decreasing rate as new channels were added.
- The addition of PBS to the system added more to viewer choice than four commercial U.S. stations.
- Diversity was lowest in those markets without a CBC-owned station.

The authors of the study concluded that the structure of the broadcasting industry was directly related to the system's programming. If, as the Broadcasting Act requires, the programming provided by the broadcasting system is to be "varied and comprehensive," then the role of the public sector is extremely important.

Expenditures on Television Programming in Canada

As indicated in Table 7-14, the revenues of private-sector television and cable have been increasing much more rapidly than those of the CBC. In the case of private television, revenues increased by 491 per

TABLE 7-18
ESTIMATES OF CANADIAN AND FOREIGN PROGRAM
EXPENDITURE,* 1980
($000's)

CBC/Radio-Canada	
Total expense[1]	498,000
Canadian program expense[2]	300,375
Foreign program expense[2]	27,506
Total program expense[3]	327,881
Private Television	
Total revenue[4]	562,036
Canadian program expense[5]	187,700
Foreign program expense[5]	67,500
Total program expense	255,200
Cable Television	
Total revenue[4]	352,172
Canadian program expense[4]	22,113
Combined	
Total CBC/RC expense plus	
private-sector revenue	1,412,208
Total Canadian program expense	510,188
Total foreign program expense	95,006
Total program expense	605,194

Note: * Excludes expenditure by provincial government television services.

Sources: [1] Estimates based on Lapointe and LeGoff, *Television Programs and Their Production in Canada*, Table 1.16.

[2] CBC, *Annual Report, 1980* indicates that the CBC spent at least $300,375,000 on Canadian programming. It is assumed that the remaining $27,506,000 was spent on foreign programs.

[3] CBC, *Annual Report, 1980*.

[4] Statistics Canada, *Radio and Television Broadcasting, 1980* and *Cable Television, 1980*.

[5] Estimate based on precise figures for 1977 to 1979 in Canadian Association of Broadcasters, "A Broadcasting Strategy for the Future" (March 1980).

cent between 1967 and 1980, from $95.2 million to $562 million. By comparison, the CBC's revenues increased by 331 per cent and those of the cable industry by 1,492 per cent. These trends in revenue share for the various components of the television system are significant, both because of the relative contribution each component of the system makes to program expenditure, and because of the typical programming characteristics of each component of the system.

As Table 7-18 (page 299) indicates, the CBC in 1980 put 65.8 per cent of its total revenues into programming expenditure and at least 60 per cent into Canadian programming. Despite the fact that its gross revenues were 11 per cent lower than those of private-sector television broadcasters, CBC invested 59 per cent more in Canadian programming. By comparison with the CBC, private television broadcasters invested 45.4 per cent of their total revenues in programming expenditure and 33.3 per cent in Canadian programming, while the cable television industry invested 6.3 per cent of its gross revenues in television programming, almost all of which was invested in local Canadian programming produced for the community channel.

Beginning in 1983, pay-television will add, to some extent, to the aggregate level of expenditure on Canadian programming. Table 7-19

TABLE 7-19
ESTIMATED CANADIAN PROGRAMMING EXPENDITURES[1] OF PAY-TELEVISION LICENSEES, 1983-87
($ millions)

	1983	1984	1985	1986	1987	Total
First Choice Communications	20-25	30-35	35-40	35-40	35-40	155-180
Regional General Interest Licensees[3]	15-20	20-25	25-30	25-30	25-30	110-135
Lively Arts (C-Channel)	4	7	8	9	10	38
	39-49	57-67	68-78	69-79	70-80	303-353

Notes: [1] Estimates are based on applications filed with CRTC as modified to reflect the CRTC decision regarding Canadian programming expenditure. The projections assume the applicants will all be able to meet their market projections and will operate profitably while meeting the conditions of licence with respect to Canadian programming.

[2] Figures are in 1980 dollars.

[3] Assumes additional regional services in Quebec and British Columbia will be licensed.

is based on the applications of successful pay-television licensees as modified to reflect the possible licensing of Quebec and British Columbia services and the conditions of licence established by the CRTC. Assuming that the pay licensees are all able to meet their market projections, they will provide an additional $40 to $50 million in financing for Canadian television programming in 1983, rising to $70 to $80 million in 1987. While there has been a great deal of legitimate scepticism expressed as to the likelihood that the licensees will meet these expectations, it is evident that, even if they do, they will not be providing a level of funding that will go far towards resolving the problem of generating the level of additional high quality Canadian television programming that is needed. As noted already, the effects of this additional funding will be vitiated by the relatively low expenditure level on a per hour basis that will be possible for each licensee.

The Economics of Producing Canadian Television Programs
As Table 7-16 indicated, the cost of producing television programs varies greatly depending on the kind of program that is being produced. Typically, Canadian drama and variety programming in English cost from three to six times as much per half hour as news, game shows or documentaries. The higher production costs for English-language entertainment reflect the need for English-language Canadian programs to compete directly with high-budget U.S. programming. While the production of news, documentaries and game shows can earn back substantially more than the cost of the production, this is not the case in English-language drama and variety programming.

While there would inevitably be an incentive for profit-motivated television broadcasters in Canada to import foreign and primarily U.S. programs rather than produce Canadian programs simply as a result of the cost differences, that incentive becomes something closer to an inevitability in a situation in which Canadian entertainment programs regularly lose money. The CRTC has actually been forced to go to the Supreme Court of Canada in order to get support for a requirement that the CTV network produce an average of a half-hour a week of Canadian drama programming after a decade of futile efforts at persuasion.

The notion enshrined in the Broadcasting Act that a broadcasting system owned and controlled by Canadians would "safeguard, enrich and strengthen the cultural, political, social and economic fabric of Canada'' has proved extraordinarily misguided. Based on the industry's performance to date, it would be more realistic to view private broadcasting, as most studies over the past fifty years have done, as a threat to Canadian nationhood because of its propensity to import American programs.

One profoundly misguided myth for which little or no evidence has ever been advanced is the claim that Canadians are not interested in Canadian programs. In the IRPP study referred to earlier in this chapter, the authors reported that "no statistical relationship was found between the volume of prime time Canadian programming and television station revenues." The real problem is that "Even if Canadian programming is able to attract advertisers, its production cost disadvantage provides an unambiguous market incentive for station owners to reduce their Canadian programming to the legally constrained minimum."[30]

Current Public Policy

There are a variety of specific measures in place affecting the television industry. The 1968 Broadcasting Act sets out some objectives for the broadcasting system and for individual broadcasters, although for the private sector those objectives are extremely vague. While the act provides for regulation by the CRTC, the commission's current regulatory framework cannot be considered successful. Part of the difficulty at least lies in the absence of any clear legislated objectives for the private sector which might serve as a basis for CRTC regulation.

The public-sector CBC now provides a substantial majority of all financing for Canadian programming. The services provided by the CBC remain the major national instrument for preserving Canada's social and cultural sovereignty. Only the public broadcasting service can and will take the risks involved in developing new talent, testing new concepts, and providing, on a continuing basis, access to a wide public for excellent Canadian entertainment and creative talent.

At present, there are two tax policy initiatives in place which affect television broadcasting, although neither was designed originally for that purpose. First, the capital cost allowance provisions developed originally for the film industry also apply to television production. However, since the major problem for independent producers is that there is no demand for the Canadian television programs they produce, this measure, unless complemented by measures to increase demand, will not result in any substantial increase in the production of independently-produced Canadian programs. As a 1980 study carried out for the Department of Communications concluded, "It is not advisable to contemplate such new measures as subsidies or tax credits before the demand is modified."[31]

The television industry is also affected by the provisions of section 19 of the Income Tax Act which permit the deduction of Canadian advertising expenditures only if the ads were placed on Canadian stations or networks. Originally, this measure was developed to strengthen the Canadian magazine publishing industry, as described in chapter 2. While the point is not often made, the effects of section 19 on the television industry are quite different from their effect on magazines. The magazine provisions are related to ads placed in Canadian-owned magazines whose content is not substantially the same as that of any foreign magazine. In this way, the high cost of initiating new editorial content for Canadian publications, by comparison with simply importing existing editorial content already published elsewhere, is recognized and to some extent compensated for. However, in the case of television, the legislation permits the deduction of television advertising costs regardless of whether the ads are linked to Canadian or foreign programs, as long as the television broadcaster is Canadian-controlled. And, in fact, most Canadian television advertising is related to foreign entertainment programs.

To make this point is not to argue against the way section 19 is drafted, but rather to identify both what this legislation does and what it does not do. It strengthens Canadian television stations, but does not necessarily strengthen Canadian programming because it does nothing to favour the placing of ads on Canadian programs.

Finally, under the terms of a 1972 agreement between Canada and the United States, the two nations agreed that neither would beam any satellite signals across the border without the prior consent of the other government, except on an incidental and peripheral basis. In 1981, however, the Federal Communications Commission in the United States issued licences to American common carriers to beam U.S. television signals into Canada. The United States has now asked Canada to agree. Consent would involve abandoning any commitment to maintaining an independent and sovereign Canadian nation and would result in the FCC regulating the major television services available to Canadians.

Policy Issues and Proposals

While it is beyond the scope of this study to put forward comprehensive and detailed recommendations for the future of Canadian television, there are some general proposals that follow clearly from the foregoing analysis. In addition, there are changes to basic television service in Canada that would significantly improve the performance of the television industry.

Canadian Sovereignty

The request by the United States to beam its television signals into Canadian territory should be denied except insofar as a minimal spillover is technically unavoidable. Whatever arrangements may be made to permit business communication or private communications of various kinds between the two countries, no such approval should be given in relation to the transmission into Canada, by Canadian or U.S. satellite, of any U.S. television programming service. Similarly, approval should not be given for U.S. television signals imported by microwave to be transmitted by satellite in Canada, either by the cable television industry or by Cancom, unless such transmissions are subject to existing or strengthened program substitution policies. However, if such policies are to be applied, then it probably makes more sense to transmit by satellite Canada's own expanded range of television signals. Any other policy will threaten the private-sector, advertiser-supported component of the Canadian television industry, which is important both as a potential source of expanded Canadian programming, and as a major advertising vehicle — particularly at the national level — for Canadian goods and services.

One fact that emerges clearly from this study is that the strength of the domestic cultural industries in Canada is directly dependent on whether they provide their readers, listeners and viewers with access to foreign as well as Canadian products and content. In every sector in which foreign content is either supplied directly to Canadian consumers primarily from foreign sources or supplied through Canadian subsidiaries of foreign companies, the domestically-controlled sector of the industry is financially weak and occupies a marginal position in the Canadian market.

One key issue for the 1980s will be what pattern will emerge for the supplying of foreign television programs to Canadians. If most foreign programming begins to be supplied directly from foreign programming sources, whether off satellites or by microwave import, then Canadian television services will become increasingly peripheral, with conse-

304

quences for advertisers as well as for the financing, distribution and viewing of Canadian programs. Canada must develop a Canadian system that can effectively meet the demands of Canadians for foreign programming, as well as providing a variety of Canadian programs. The need to maintain a separate Canadian system which can be regulated in Canada in the interests of Canadians was recognized fifty years ago and should not now be abandoned.

Objectives for the Private Sector
The present broadcasting legislation does not set out any clear objectives for the private sector of the television industry. The failure of Parliament to provide objectives for the system as a whole had been recognized by the Fowler Committee in 1965, which said that Parliament had

> . . . not stated the goals and purposes for the Canadian broadcasting system with sufficient clarity and precision, and this has been more responsible than anything else for the confusion in the system and the continuing dissatisfaction which has led to an endless series of investigations of it.[32]

The 1968 Broadcasting Act remedied this deficiency with respect to the public broadcasting service but, as already noted, rendered the objectives for the private sector even more vague than they had been in the 1958 act.

A 1980 broadcasting study, *Conflict Over Communications Policy*, noted the importance of not leaving the responsibility for the expression of Canadian identity to the CBC, commenting that "The CBC has been making a serious effort to meet its mandate in this regard, but the same cannot be said of the private broadcasters and the cable industry."[33] Similar observations on the inadequate contribution of the private sector were made by Robert Babe in a 1979 study. Babe concluded that "The schizophrenia of Canadian broadcasting today is the outstanding characteristic of the system, with the financial, market-oriented side rapidly increasing in dominance over the cultural."[34]

The (Clyne) Report of the Consultative Committee on the Implications of Telecommunications for Canadian Sovereignty recommended that the private broadcasters be required to provide for a continuing expression of Canadian identity and to contribute actively to the flow and exchange of cultural and regional information and entertainment.[35] Such provisions should be included in the new telecommunications legislation.

The Structure of Basic Cable Television Service

Instead of offering a lengthy list of proposals concerning various aspects of the television industry, it seems more useful to conclude by putting forward an alternative model for twelve-channel basic cable television service in Canada. At least the public-sector and advertiser-supported elements of the proposed system might also become available subsequently through direct broadcast satellite transmission in all parts of Canada.

The underlying assumptions of the proposed alternative structure are the following:

- As the report of the Therrien Committee stated "the real cost of establishing competitive Canadian programming must be measured not in tens of millions of dollars, but in hundreds of millions of dollars."[36]
- The broadcasting services of the CBC are the most important means of achieving Canada's social and cultural objectives and should be strengthened.
- Advertiser-supported Canadian television is and will continue to be the largest single programming component of the system, of major importance to advertisers of Canadian goods and services as well as a potential source of additional Canadian programming.
- There are measures that can be taken to strengthen advertiser-supported private-sector television and they should be taken.
- With 55 per cent of Canadians receiving television through cable reception, additional Canadian satellite-to-cable television services should be developed.
- The revenues of the cable television industry can and should make a greater contribution to the financing of Canadian programming.
- Instead of concentrating attention on the development of high-cost, premium television services, which many Canadians will not be able to afford, serious attention should also be given to providing a balanced, varied basic cable service at a reasonable monthly price.
- Only changes that can be made on a step-by-step basis without revolutionary disruption are realistic.

The intent in presenting this alternative model is to demonstrate what might be done if there were a willingness to act with a sense of urgency and to take bold, positive initiatives instead of either striking a defensive posture or retreating a step at a time before some supposedly inexorable technologically-determined tide.

In Table 7-20, the typical content of basic cable service is listed on the left. In addition to the ten channels included, most viewers also receive two additional private Canadian stations, often from neighbouring communities. The alternative structure proposed would involve the initiation of three new Canadian television services, which would be carried as part of basic cable service. Two of the three additional services have actually been proposed to the CRTC already, although they would not necessarily be licensed in the precise form in which they were proposed.

A principal feature of the alternative structure is that the U.S. channels would be removed from the twelve-channel basic cable service. However, the provision of additional foreign content through Canadian services would be effected through the development of a second national English-language commercial network and the establishing of a special advertiser-supported cable channel. These new commercial Canadian services could only be established on the basis of a decommercialization of CBC's services, the removal of the advertiser-financed U.S. channels from the twelve-channel basic cable service, and implementation of a strengthened program substitution policy.

Table 7-21 indicates the effect of the revised structure could have on the level of financing available for Canadian programs. The comments that follow are intended to explain the basic features of what is proposed in the case of each service and to suggest the way in which the various changes are interrelated. It should perhaps be noted again that this is not presented as a blueprint, but simply as an indication, based almost completely on real proposals that have been fully developed and proposed separately to the CRTC on other occasions, of what could be done if the will existed. The point will be adequately made if the proposed changes appear realistic without being definitive.

CBC/Radio-Canada

With respect to the CBC, what is proposed is that the major national services of the CBC—in French and English—be decommercialized. This would have to be done gradually, with advertising perhaps being phased out over a three- to five-year period. The elimination of advertising from the CBC might also be accompanied by a phasing out of CBC's affiliation agreements. However, the basic notion put forward here is that, in combination with independent stations in the

307

TABLE 7-20
RESTRUCTURED MODEL FOR BASIC CABLE TELEVISION SERVICE[1]

Components	Present Structure	Proposed Alternative
Public-sector broadcast services	1. CBC 2. Radio-Canada 3. Provincial educational	1. CBC I } decommercialized 2. Radio-Canada I } popular services 3. Provincial Educational
Private Canadian broadcast services	4. CTV or TVA 5. Global (Southern Ontario only) 6. Independent (major urban centres)	4. CTV/TVA 5. Second private *national* English-language channel (based on CBC's private affiliates, Global and independent stations) 6. Independent
Cable-only channels and satellite-to-cable channels	7. Community channel	7. Community channel } financed 8. National cable channel } from cable industry revenue 9. Foreign-program service (non-profit, advertiser-supported; revenues to support Canadian production) 10. CBC II/Radio-Canada II ("cultural" channels)
Private American broadcast services	8. CBS } With Canadian signals 9. NBC } substituted for programs acquired by Canadian broadcasters and aired at the same 10. ABC } time as on U.S. networks	U.S. channels would be moved to augmented basic service on converter with non-simultaneous program substitution policy adopted

Note: [1] In most cable systems, basic service includes two additional channels which might be taken up by multilingual stations or other non-local private Canadian services. As a result, there would be four public channels, five private, advertiser-supported broadcast channels, one cable-only, advertiser-supported channel, and two cable-financed services, one local and one national.

TABLE 7-21
FINANCING FOR CANADIAN PROGRAMMING UNDER CURRENT AND ALTERNATIVE MODELS[1]
($ millions)

Current Structure		Alternative Structure	
Service	*Funding in 1980 for Canadian Programs*	*Service*	*Target 1987 Funding for Canadian Programs (in 1980 Dollars)*
1. CBC 2. Radio-Canada	300	1. CBC I 2. Radio-Canada I	400
3. Provincial educational	30	3. Provincial educational	40
4. CTV/TVA 5. Global	190	4. CTV/TVA 5. Second English-language national network	275
6. Independent		6. Independent	
7. Community channel	22	7. Community channel	35
8. CBS		8. National cable channel	160
9. NBC	—	9. Foreign program service	50
10. ABC	—	10. CBC II/Radio-Canada II	30
Total	542		990

Note: [1] Assumptions are detailed in the text.

major markets and perhaps with Global, the CBC affiliates provide a basis for developing a second private, national English-language network. Only through networking arrangements can the ability of private-sector stations to generate higher cost categories of Canadian programs be developed.

While the CBC has been the most successful part of the television system in meeting Canadian objectives for broadcasting, its constant need to balance the pursuit of its special mandate against the interests of private-sector affiliates and reliance on advertising revenues has reduced its ability to perform its functions effectively. The CBC does not do enough to reflect English- and French-speaking Canadians to each other and to produce programming out of all the regions of Canada, for broadcast both regionally and nationally. These are tasks that will never be performed adequately by private television. This argument was made very effectively in a review of television policy carried out for the CRTC in 1980:

> A basic Canadian presence on the broadcasting system has to be guaranteed by public support before one can confidently move on to address the nature of the supplementary contribution that the private sector can provide. To approach this issue in any other way is to delude oneself that profit-making motives can easily be reconciled with social and cultural objectives. This is not to suggest that the private sector should not contribute to Canadian social and cultural objectives but that, in measuring or assessing what that contribution should be, the determinants of the commercial marketplace, such as profits and competition, must be faced.[37]

Obviously, this proposed change would involve committing additional funds to the CBC and making a commitment, as has been advocated by every study of broadcasting over the past fifty years, to make financial commitments over a five-year period. To make such a commitment would simply involve reversing the trend since 1967. CBC revenues have not been keeping pace with population increase and the expansion of the television industry. On a per capita basis, the Annan Report in Britain found that the CBC received less funding than other public broadcasting systems in Europe, despite its much higher distribution costs and the need to produce programming in two languages.

The CBC's president has stated that it now costs every Canadian about $1.60 a month to keep public broadcasting going in this country. While the precise costs of decommercialization and deaffiliation of the CBC cannot be provided in this study, a reasonable estimate is that if

310

CBC funding were increased in real dollars by 8 per cent a year over a five-year period, the change could be financed and CBC's Canadian programming budget strengthened. This is a commitment that should now be made.

Such an increase would also allow the CBC to initiate cable-only channels in both French and English, along the lines proposed in its original CBC II-Tele II proposal. The distribution costs for services delivered only by satellite to cable systems are very low—in the order of $7 to $10 million—and, therefore, a second service of this nature could be financed at a relatively low cost, adding not more than 5 per cent to CBC's total expenditures. The proposed cultural channels could provide a cultural service in some respects analogous to CBC's FM radio service.

The decision to finance such a transition in the public service is the critical element in the restructuring model suggested here. It permits all the other changes, especially the expansion of the private-sector commercial television system.

Private Canadian Broadcast Services
The major change proposed in the structure of the off-air broadcast services carried on cable is the organization of a second English-language national network. As Table 7-22 suggests, the CBC affiliates, Global and the independent stations have a sufficient share of the national English-language audience that through a combination of stations included in those categories, a strong, second national commercial network could be developed.

Cable Channels
In addition to the off-air CBC and private-sector services, basic cable service would include three new "satellite-to-cable" television services, as well as the existing locally-programmed community channel. The programming expenditure for the community channel in 1987 assumes that by that date the cable industry will have increased its funding of this service by over 50 per cent in real terms from the 1980 level.

The new national satellite-to-cable services would include government-funded, advertiser-supported and cable industry-financed services. The proposed publicly-funded second services for CBC/Radio-Canada were described above.

In the revised structure of basic cable service, the cable industry would finance the cost of a new satellite-to-cable national entertain-

TABLE 7-22
DETAIL OF AUDIENCE SHARE FOR CANADIAN AND U.S. TELEVISION GROUPS, 1980
(percentages)

ENGLISH-LANGUAGE STATIONS

Canadian

CBC owned and operated	10.3
CBC affiliates	7.2
CTV	23.7
Global	3.2
Other Canadian	8.4
Total	52.8

United States

All stations	24.5

FRENCH-LANGUAGE STATIONS

Canadian

Radio-Canada	8.3
TVA	13.3
Other	0.6
Total	22.2

Source: BBM, *Radio and Television Data, 1981*.

ment network. The proposed cable entertainment network would provide French- and English-language channels featuring films and television programs produced by independent Canadian film and television producers. The service would be programmed by a non-profit corporation licensed by the CRTC for that purpose. The budgeted level of $160 million in Canadian programming expenditure (see Table 7-21) assumes the cable companies will have a minimum of 5,670,000 subscribers in 1987 and will pay $2.50 per subscriber in 1980 dollars to buy the service.

The type of cable entertainment network proposed has sometimes been conceived of as a universal pay-television service. However, that concept assumed that individual subscribers would pay an extra charge in addition to the cost of basic cable service to receive the new network. What is suggested here is a network that would be a part of basic cable service and would be paid for by cable television companies.

The CRTC considered a proposal for such a service at the 1981 hearings on pay-television and "found persuasive the arguments presented at the hearing that a desirable way of ensuring the evolution of a distinctively Canadian pay television system may well be through the adoption of a universal pay television service."[38] The particular importance of such a service to Canadian film production was argued by the Canadian Film Development Corporation, which recognized that only such a service would ever have adequate funds to finance Canadian made-for-television movies and to provide theatrical features with a substantial additional Canadian market, able to pay a reasonable share of production costs. Programming for such a service, as originally proposed, would be carried out by independent production companies, providing a solid base for a major expansion of that industry. The service would, as the CRTC has already decided, have to be offered on a non-profit basis. Table 7-21 assumes that by 1987, the CRTC will have licensed such a service and that the service will, on the basis of the revenue figures provided above, provide $160 million for Canadian programming.

The cost to the cable industry of the strengthened community channel and the new national cable channels in French and English would be approximately $3.00 per month per subscriber. The cable industry has earned very substantial profits, despite the fact that as Table 7-23 shows, the cost of cable service rose very little between 1971 and 1981. The cost of basic cable television service is now between $7 and $10. While there would be no need for the cable industry to pass on all of the cost of the additional service proposed, even if all of the increase were passed on in some systems, the result would still be to leave the cost of basic cable service lower than if it had simply kept pace with increases in the Consumer Price Index. Cable would remain a bargain, but would make a reasonable contribution to financing Canadian program production.

TABLE 7-23
UTILITIES, CONSUMER PRICE INDEX AND CABLE TV: TOTAL
AVERAGE INCREASE BETWEEN 1971 AND 1981

Gas	Electricity	Consumer Price Index	Telephone	Cable TV
140.1%	124.1%	110.6%	59.5%	38.8%

Source: Statistics Canada data.

313

The Canadian cable television industry is expected to have revenues of approximately $1 billion in 1987. Pay-television, in addition to the implementation of non-programming services and the possible marketing of a second tier of service, will be responsible for this major increase in cable industry revenues.

Foreign Program Channel
Basic cable service now includes three U.S. channels which carry 100 per cent foreign content and primarily American advertising, and which spur complaints from U.S. stations along the Canadian border that Canadian cable companies are carrying their programming without authorization and without payment to them.

At present, as noted earlier, about two-thirds of the programming carried on the three U.S. commercial networks is purchased by Canadian stations. About one-third of the programming is shown at the same time on U.S. and Canadian channels and, as a result, is subject to the CRTC policy of simultaneous program substitution. That one-third of the programming on the U.S. channels is, therefore, not shown on cable television in Canada. Two changes are proposed here. The first is that a new Canadian English-language, non-profit cable channel be established. The corporation set up to deliver this service might be made responsible for acquiring all foreign programming that is purchased for use in the Canadian broadcasting system. As a result, the escalation in payments for foreign programming, which are clearly far in excess of what any other country is paying on a per capita basis, could be ended. The corporation would handle within Canada the selling of those programs to Canadian broadcasters.

However, the central purpose of the new corporation, which might be operated as a non-profit joint venture by the CBC and the private broadcasters, would be to select the best foreign programs not otherwise purchased by Canadian television services and schedule those programs on its service. The channel would consist entirely of foreign programs, but it would be one channel instead of the present three and the programming would have been legitimately purchased for exhibition in Canada. In addition, the channel would carry Canadian advertising, sold at cost per thousand rates comparable to those charged by the commercial networks and stations.

The surplus revenues of the channel would be used to support Canadian program production. One reasonable allocation of such funds would be that half should go to the public sector — divided between federal and provincial services in proportion to the government subsidy

314

they receive—with the remainder used to augment the advertising revenues earned by private stations on peak-time Canadian drama and variety programs. Such a practice might stimulate the scheduling of Canadian entertainment in peak time.

The closest parallel to this proposed service is the LaSette channel in Quebec, which packages and schedules in prime time a selection of the best programs from three networks in France. This French-language foreign programming channel, in fact, provides a precedent and to some extent a model for the English-language foreign programming channel that is proposed.

The second aspect of this change—and without it the maximum benefits would not be achieved—is that, if the U.S. channels were moved to converter channels, which would certainly be politically realistic, a policy of non-simultaneous program substitution would be adopted. This policy would affect almost all of the entertainment programming carried on such channels, with that programming now being legitimately bought and paid for by Canadian broadcasters rather than simply picked out of the air and carried without authorization or payment by cable companies.

The changes that are proposed would have a major effect on the amount of financing available for Canadian television programming, resulting in more than an 80 per cent increase in expenditure in constant dollars between 1980 and 1987. Of the total increase of over $400 million, the model assumes that only $120 million will come from the public sector. The model does assume, however, that the cable industry ought to spend between 20 and 25 per cent of its gross revenue on Canadian programming services. That does not appear to be an unreasonable expectation. It would give subscribers a number of new services; it would make use of Canada's technological capacity; and it is consistent with what the CRTC expects from other companies providing pay-television services, as well as from broadcast licensees. It could be done without unfair reductions in cable industry profitability and, by creating new programming services available only on cable, might increase market penetration for cable service.

These changes would require a coordinated and sustained effort between 1982 and 1987. However, unless some such strategy is adopted, the process of erosion will continue, with results that are not compatible with the survival of an independent Canadian nation.

Conclusions

A Growing Market

Expenditures on cultural products and programs in Canada are made by advertisers, by public and private consumers, and also through direct government support of production, particularly in the field of film and television. Total expenditure from these three sources in 1980 for newspapers, magazines, books, sound recordings, films, radio and television was $5.4 billion (see Table 8-1). These products are sold both in the advertising market and to the public. Revenue from sales of these products and programs to consumers accounted for the largest share of total expenditure, 47 per cent in 1980, while revenue earned from the advertising market accounted for 42 per cent. A further 11 per cent of revenue came directly from the federal government through its support to the National Film Board and the Canadian Broadcasting Corporation.

Advertising expenditure on daily newspapers, periodicals, radio and television increased from $621 million in 1970 to $2,266.5 million in 1980. This increase of 265 per cent was significantly greater than the 238.2 per cent increase in the Gross National Product over the same period. The advertising revenues of television increased most rapidly, going up by 338 per cent, followed by periodicals at 314 per cent, radio at 245 per cent, and daily newspapers at 228 per cent. However, in the case of both television and magazines, the increases occurred from a very low base in 1970 and revenues remain low by comparison with those in other countries.

A major factor in the low level of advertising revenues of the media system in Canada is the reliance of multinational advertisers on overflow magazines and television commercials from the United States. Many Canadian subsidiaries rely on the spillover of advertisements placed by their parent companies in U.S. magazines and on U.S. television to reach Canadian consumers. In a speech in June 1982, Donald Campbell, chairman of the Maclean Hunter Board of Directors, noted that "If Canadians spent the same amount on

316

TABLE 8-1
PUBLISHING, RECORDING, FILM AND BROADCASTING:
ESTIMATED CANADIAN MARKET,[1] 1980
($ millions)

Daily newspapers	advertising	$ 987.3
	circulation	266.1
		1,253.4
Periodicals	advertising	276.3
	circulation[2]	400.0
		676.3
Books		931.7
Records/tapes		265.1
Film	NFB (net cost of operations)	37.4
	private distributors	
	a. theatrical	115.3
	b. television	103.7
	c. non-theatrical	26.9
		283.3
Radio (private)	advertising	392.0
	production and other	5.7
		397.7
Television (private)	advertising	510.0
	production and other	52.1
		562.1
CBC	advertising	100.9
(radio and television)	net cost of operations	542.9
	production and other	3.7
		647.0
Cable television		352.2
Sub-totals by source	advertising	2,266.5
	consumption, production and other	2,522.0
	government subsidy (film & TV only)	580.3
Total expenditure		$5,368.8

Notes: [1] Estimates are of total spent by Canadian advertisers by medium plus *wholesale* revenue by medium from total sales in the Canadian market, plus government expenditure for broadcasting and NFB.

[2] Periodical circulation revenue is difficult to estimate (see Table 2-6). The estimate of $400 million is a cautious estimate based on reported revenue for Canadian periodicals of $121 million and imports valued for customs purposes at $277 million.

advertising as Americans on a per capita basis, there would be an infusion in our marketplace of $2.9 billion . . . in advertising expenditures.''[1] Canadian television stations and Canadian periodicals alone would have had an additional $860 million in revenue in 1980, if advertising expenditure in Canada had matched the per capital levels reached in the United States.

Consumer expenditure on cultural products has also been increasing rapidly. The wholesale revenue of Canadian record distributors increased by 304 per cent over the decade, from $65.7 million in 1970 to 265.1 million in 1980. While reliable figures for book sales in Canada are available only for the period 1975 to 1980, they indicate an expenditure increase of 95.4 per cent (from $476.7 million to $931.7 million). By comparison, the GNP increased by 75.3 per cent over the same period. The box office revenue of Canadian movie theatres showed a small increase in real terms over the decade, rising by 127 per cent from $137.1 million in 1970 to $311.4 million in 1980. The Consumer Price Index increased by 116.7 per cent over the same period. Finally, consumer expenditure on cable television service increased from just $54.9 million in 1970 to $352.2 million in 1980, almost a sevenfold increase.

As indicated in the chapters on radio and television, federal government expenditures in support of the CBC have not kept pace with the growth of the private sector in broadcasting. While the revenues of private radio stations increased by 247 per cent between 1970 and 1980, those of private television by 406 per cent, and those of cable by 541 per cent, government support for the CBC increased by 233 per cent.

A decision by the federal cabinet in 1975-76 to increase the CBC's budget steadily over the next five years was not acted upon. If it had been, the CBC's revenues would have been $850 million in 1980-81 rather than $680 million. Because neither the revenues of private television nor those of the cable system support significantly the production of Canadian entertainment programming, the reduced role of government expenditure on broadcasting has had the effect of substantially reducing the quantity and quality of Canadian entertainment programming available to Canadians.

In general terms the market for all of these cultural products and programs is expanding more rapidly than the economy as a whole. However, what this rapid growth has done through the 1970s is to focus increasing attention on the magnitude of the problems that now exist in all of these industries.

The Cultural Dimensions of the Problem

As Table 8-2 indicates, while the markets for all of these cultural products are increasing in Canada, only a very limited percentage of

TABLE 8-2
DOMESTIC MARKET SHARE BY ORIGIN OF CONTENT[1]
(percentages)

	Original Canadian Material	*Adapted Foreign Material*	*Foreign Material*
Newspapers			
Domestic coverage	close to 100		
Foreign coverage	0-5		95-100
Magazines	29	25	46
Books	16.1	4.4	79.5
Records	6.8		93.2
Radio[2]			
AM — music	30		70
talk	95-100		0-5
FM — music	10-30		70-90
talk	95-100		0-5
Film[3]			
Theatrical market	1.8		98.2
Television market	7.3		92.7
Non-theatrical	41.2		58.8
Television (English)[4]			
News, information, current affairs	90.5		9.5
All entertainment	11.6		88.4
Dramatic entertainment	4		96
All viewing	30.5		69.5
Television (French)[4]			
News, information, current affairs	100		0
All entertainment	39.8		60.2
All viewing	54.2		45.8

Notes: [1] Figures for newspapers and radio are estimates based on general industry studies. For derivation of other figures, see Tables 2-2, 3-4, 4-7, 6-1 and 7-2.
 [2] Based on percentages of air-time.
 [3] Based on distributors' royalties, rentals and commissions.
 [4] Based on audience viewing, 1978.

Sources: Statistics Canada for books, records and film; CRTC for radio and television; Audit Bureau of Circulations for magazines (consumer only); and the Davey and Kent Commissions for newspapers.

319

the content is of Canadian origin. As a general rule, the extent to which Canadian material is available and is being read, listened to, or watched is directly related to the nature of the content. In the case of domestic news, current affairs, sports and talk shows (on radio and television), the extent of Canadian involvement is quite substantial. By comparison, Canadian books, records, feature films and television entertainment programs have only a very limited share of the domestic market. In the chapters above, it has been demonstrated that this reflects the relatively limited presence of Canadian products in the marketplace and the relatively limited level of investment being made in producing Canadian material for these markets. Whether one looks at the limited range of Canadian books available from most book clubs, the limited variety of Canadian recordings distributed by most rack jobbers in the record industry, the relatively rare screenings of Canadian films in the theatres, or the paucity of Canadian television drama available in prime time, it is obvious that the major problem is not that properly financed Canadian cultural materials are being offered to the Canadian public and rejected, but that as a general rule, they are in limited supply, have limited financing available, and receive inadequate distribution or exhibition.

The Key Policy Issues

The objectives to be pursued in developing policies affecting these industries are complex. As stated in the Introduction, the goal is not simply to have more production activity in Canada and better distribution of that material. While increases in domestic production and sales are a legitimate goal in most other industries, in the case of the cultural industries expanded production is primarily a means to an end, not an end in itself. Thus, both the volume and the character of Canadian production activity are important. So too is the question of control over decisions as to what will be published, produced or broadcast.

In their details, the policy issues and proposals put forward in this study in relation to each sector vary considerably. In some sectors, for example the newspaper industry, the degree of corporate concentration of control over production is a major issue, as are the direct conflicts of corporate interests of press owners. In other sectors — book publishing and film distribution are good examples — the level of foreign ownership is excessively high and issues related to cultural sovereignty and the low performance level of foreign owners are important. In both

320

film and television, a key issue is the character of the "Canadian" production activity that is occurring.

Two general underlying problems emerge in relation to all of the sectors dealt with. The first is the fact that the structure of the domestic production and distribution industries in every case is organized around the supply of imported content to Canadians and will certainly continue to be so. The degree to which this is true varies from sector to sector and is lower for those media such as newspapers and radio which are to a large extent local media. However, it is true in all cases, and, therefore, issues related to the way in which foreign content enters the Canadian market are of critical importance.

Whether one looks at newspaper publishing, book publishing, periodical and mass market paperback distribution, book clubs, record production and distribution, film distribution, radio and television broadcasting, cable television, or satellite broadcasting packages, it is obvious that Canadian companies in all of these sectors must, if they are to be successful, satisfy Canadian demand for foreign as well as Canadian content. To the extent that foreign-based production and distribution companies or their subsidiaries in Canada satisfy Canadian demand for their products or programs directly, that direct supply pattern undercuts the potential for the development of Canadian production and distribution companies. As a result, the *potential* of the Canadian domestic production and distribution system to finance and effectively market Canadian products and programs is reduced.

The second underlying and common theme is that the incentive structure is loaded heavily against the origination of Canadian products or programming. In every sector, it is far cheaper and far less risky to import foreign material than to produce Canadian material, even though in the domestic market there is solid evidence that Canadian products and programs are far more popular than comparable foreign products or programs. To be more specific, foreign wire service copy can be acquired far more cheaply than sending Canadians out to look at and report on world events. Foreign books, foreign masters for record production, foreign editorial content for magazines, foreign films and television programs for distribution and exhibition, all can be acquired with little risk and at a small fraction of the cost of generating comparable Canadian content.

Easy and inexpensive access to foreign content is not in itself a bad thing. Problems arise only to the extent that the dominance of foreign content in the domestic market and the commercial incentive to import crowd out the Canadian alternatives that should be available to

321

Canadians and prevent individual Canadians from developing their talent and ability in all of these important activities which ought to be as open to them as to individuals in other countries. The degree to which that has occurred was reflected in the observations of the Pepin-Robarts Commission in their 1979 report:

> Sometimes the country seemed to us to be composed of a multiplicity of solitudes, islands of self-contained activity and discourse disconnected from their neighbours and tragically unaware of the whole which contained them.

The same report went on to ask, ''Why we have not learned better to employ this century's communications technology to talk together across the empty spaces?''[2]

General Policy Objectives

The proposals put forward in this study are designed to accomplish two general purposes. First, they are designed to bring about a strengthening of the domestic production and distribution structures in each of these industries through addressing issues related to the channels through which foreign content reaches Canadians.

Second, the proposals are designed to alter and to compensate for the current incentive structure. The ultimate goal of these measures is to encourage increased investment in the production of Canadian products and programs and to make provision for Canadians of both major language groups and in every region to have greater opportunities to express their perceptions, ideas and creative talent through these culturally important forms. The proposals reflect the assumption that unless there is a substantial and diverse volume of production occurring on a continuing basis, then the popular or critical successes are unlikely to occur. As in all other nations, Canadians will produce both good and bad work, both successes and failures. Creating opportunities for success necessitates also the provision of chances for failure. There is no magic formula for just producing the good, big-budget projects and forgetting the rest, unless Canadians are willing to build all their initiatives around creative talent developed in other countries.

Major Policy Proposals

Financing New Initiatives

While some of the proposals put forward in this study require no expenditure by governments, others do require financing. In preparing this study, it has been assumed that to the greatest extent possible any proposals put forward should involve a reallocation of government expenditure rather than the allocation of new funds.

The proposals put forward in this study would result in a substantial reduction in federal expenditure in two major areas. First, it is proposed that the exemption from the federal sales tax now provided for newspapers, magazines and books should be ended. The value of that tax expenditure in 1980 is estimated at over $150 million. In the case of both magazines and books, the expenditures are primarily of benefit to imported publications. Over $60 million of this expenditure in 1980 would have benefited imported foreign publications. In addition, the effect of this policy measure on publications produced in Canada is precisely the same regardless of the extent to which they are involved in financing Canadian editorial content. The expenditure benefits *Time* magazine, which invests nothing in Canadian editorial content, to exactly the same extent as it benefits *Saturday Night*, which pays the full cost of its content. Similarly, it benefits the newspaper publisher who puts less than 10 per cent of his revenues into editorial expenditure to the same extent as it benefits the publisher who puts over 20 per cent of revenue into editorial expenditures.

If one includes both the tax expenditure related to imported publications and that related to the production in Canada of Canadian printings of foreign publications or adaptations of foreign publications, then close to half of this total tax expenditure in 1980 benefited foreign content. Since the level of imports is rising quickly — going up, for example, from $680 million in 1980 to $769 million in 1981 — the expenditure seems increasingly inappropriate. Comparable exemptions are not provided in other jurisdictions. Value added taxes are levied on publications in most European countries, while in the United States, even at the retail level, publications are subject to tax in an increasing number of states.

The second area in which policy changes are proposed which would lead to reduced expenditure is that of postal rate subsidy to foreign-controlled magazines and to foreign direct mail publishers, book clubs and book wholesalers. While no precise estimate can be made of the total saving involved, the amount would have been at least $40 million and probably more than $50 million in fiscal 1980-81. With respect to foreign magazines which are mailed in Canada, reductions in the level of Canadian government subsidy have already begun. However, for foreign-controlled magazines printed and mailed in Canada, and for foreign book clubs, book wholesalers and direct mail publishers, very substantial subsidies continue to be provided. For reasons outlined in chapter 2, there is no reason to continue these subsidies. Postal rate subsidies should be restricted to Canadian newspapers and magazines, as provided for in the postal legislation passed by Parliament, and to book publishers and distributors which are part of the Canadian book publishing and distribution system.

The Estimates of the federal Department of Communications for 1982-83 indicate that the budget of the Arts and Culture Program of the department provides for the payment of $220 million to Canada Post Corporation to subsidize mailing costs. This represents a 50 per cent increase from the $146.3 million allocation two years earlier. Excluding the CBC, this is the largest expenditure item in the budget of the department. While no precise information is available, it is beyond question that a substantial part of that spending constitutes a subsidy of postal rates for foreign-controlled magazines and foreign book distributors. The categories of mailers eligible for subsidy through the cultural budget of the Department of Communications should be revised to eliminate such subsidies and to focus support on Canadian publications and the development of Canadian distribution structures.

The savings from the two initiatives proposed above would provide more than enough funds to pay the cost of all of the measures proposed in this study except that of increased funding to the CBC. In the case of the CBC, the position taken is that the gradual reduction in support for public broadcasting has been a serious policy error. What is proposed in this study is that, as a percentage of total government expenditure, the corporation's financing should be increased over a five-year period to approximately 1.5 per cent of total federal spending, which the corporation was receiving in the past and would be receiving now if the 1975-76 cabinet decision had been acted on. In 1982-83, the corporation will receive combined operating and capital grants equal to 0.99 per cent of total federal expenditure.

Imports and the Structure of Canadian Cultural Industries
There are three alternative channels through which foreign cultural products and programs can reach Canadians:

1. They can be supplied directly across the border (examples: foreign magazines, most foreign book clubs and mail order publishers, or foreign television services carried by cable or delivered directly by satellite).
2. They can be supplied through branch operations in Canada of

foreign companies (examples: foreign-controlled book publishers and foreign-controlled film distribution subsidiaries).

3. They can be supplied by Canadian-owned and -controlled corporations with head offices in Canada (examples: carriage of foreign wire service copy by Canadian newspapers, sale of foreign books by Canadian publishers under exclusive agency arrangements with foreign firms, production by Canadian-controlled record companies of discs and tapes made from leased foreign masters, distribution of foreign films by Canadian-controlled film distributors, use of foreign recordings by Canadian radio stations, and acquisition of rights for foreign television programs by Canadian television stations/networks).

To the extent that foreign content reaches Canadians directly from abroad, the potential for the development of Canadian production and distribution structures is reduced. In the case of advertiser-supported media, as noted earlier, the result is to reduce substantially the level of advertising revenue available to Canadian media. In the case of both magazine publishing and television, this is already a major problem, with per capita expenditure on magazine and television advertising at half the U.S. level.

With respect to the advertising spillover effect, two measures are proposed. First, the federal government should phase out postal rate subsidies for the distribution of foreign magazines in Canada, including both foreign magazines mailed in Canada and foreign-controlled magazines, such as *Time* and *Reader's Digest*, which are both printed and mailed in Canada. Second, Canadian television stations/networks should buy virtually all U.S. network television entertainment programs for exhibition in Canada, preferably through a common purchasing agency established for this purpose, rather than relying on the spillover of U.S. television signals, carrying U.S. advertising, to provide that programming to Canadians. At the same time, a policy of non-simultaneous program substitution should be adopted by the CRTC, which would have cable licensees substitute the Canadian showing of foreign programs and the related Canadian commercials on the U.S. networks carried by cable companies. The latter recommendation was also made in the 1979 Report of the Clyne Committee.[3]

In the case of the direct supply of foreign books to Canada by foreign book clubs and the direct provision of U.S. television signals by satellite, the following measures are proposed. First, the current postal rate subsidies now available to foreign book clubs and book wholesalers, which make the bulk of their purchases from foreign-based book publishers, should be eliminated. Support should be restricted to companies which are part of the publishing and distribution structure in Canada. Second, public institutions in Canada should be encouraged to buy from Canadian suppliers.

In the case of foreign satellite broadcast signals, the revised letters of agreement between Canada and the United States should require that the United States limit the border spillover of its broadcast signals to the greatest extent that is technically feasible and that it receive prior consent from Canada for satellite transmissions which will result in the spillover of U.S. programming services into Canada. In addition, new satellite-delivered Canadian television services should be established, carrying an expanded range of both foreign and Canadian programs.

The second situation is that in which foreign content is supplied to the Canadian market by subsidiary companies in Canada. The situation is typical of the book publishing industry where foreign-controlled branch companies handle over 75 per cent of all imported books. It is also typical of the record industry, where roughly 90 per cent of all sales of records and tapes made from foreign masters are accounted for by subsidiaries, and of the film distribution industry, where the releases of most of the U.S. "majors" are handled by distribution subsidiaries in Canada. The same situation does not arise in relation to Canadian newspapers, radio and television stations/networks, and arises to a limited extent only in the magazine industry (*Time, Reader's Digest*). The legislative provisions in the Income Tax Act affecting the deduction of advertising expenditures now preclude or restrict this pattern in newspaper and magazine publishing, while the requirements of the federal Broadcasting Act of 1968 preclude it in radio, television and cable.

Because imported books, films and records made from foreign masters account for a very substantial majority of total sales of books and records in Canada, and of total rental revenue for films, the companies that distribute those imported products dominate the Canadian marketplace. As we saw in chapters 3, 4 and 6, foreign-controlled firms account for most of the revenues and most of the profit in each of these industries, with Canadian-controlled firms having a relatively marginal position.

It is now the policy objective of the federal government that in the book publisher/agent industry the Canadian-controlled sectors of both the French- and English-language industry should be expanded so that they can play a dominant role in the French- and English-language markets in Canada. A comparable Canadianization objective should also be adopted in relation to film distribution in Canada and, at the minimum, the government should adopt the goal of expanding significantly the Canadian-controlled sector of the record production and distribution industry.

In the case of film distribution, the CRTC should notify television licensees, who will by 1983 represent the largest single market served by the distributors, that by a designated date in the future they will be required to make all program purchases through Canadian-controlled distribution companies. The same objective should become a major factor in the review of foreign takeovers and new foreign investment in the film distribution industry as, for example, in the case of the takeover of Columbia Pictures by Coca-Cola, which is now before the Foreign Investment Review Agency.

A policy decision should be made by the federal cabinet establishing that in both production and distribution activities in these and related industries (e.g., videodiscs and videocassettes), Canadian ownership and control is of special importance. The goal of substantially increased Canadian control should be adopted and pursued by the cabinet, providing a clear basis for decisions by investors and by the Foreign Investment Review Agency.

As a matter of procedural practice, all applications from new foreign investors in these industries should receive a full appraisal by FIRA rather than benefiting from the "small business" procedure, which provides for only limited scrutiny. The recent decision in the case of Random House indicates that there is reason for concern over the degree to which the federal government has backed off even on its existing commitment to increased Canadian control in the book publishing industry. That policy should be applied in future cases and the Canadianization goal broadened both to include other cultural industries and to cover the distribution, as well as the production, sector of those industries.

No plan to strengthen the Canadian-controlled sector of these industries can succeed unless direct foreign control over the distribution of foreign cultural products in Canada is significantly reduced.

The Incentive Structure
The Publishing and Sound Recording Industries
It has already been proposed that the current exemption of newspapers,

magazines and books from the federal sales tax should be ended. That exemption should be replaced by a refundable investment tax credit based on expenditure on Canadian-originated editorial content by Canadian-owned and -controlled magazine and newspaper publishers and on all pre-publication costs incurred by Canadian-owned and -controlled book publishers in the origination of new Canadian-authored books. A refundable tax credit should also be provided to Canadian-controlled recording companies based on their production of new Canadian masters.

In the case of the Canadian-controlled publishing industry, the incentive should be set at a high enough level that it will at least compensate for the loss of the sales tax exemption. The important result of this change would be a tax policy which benefited both publishers and record companies in proportion to their investment in providing Canadians with increased opportunities for cultural expression of all kinds. Such a policy change is essential given the heavy current disincentive to invest in Canadian content.

Table 8-3 provides information from the best available sources on current levels of investment in content by companies in Canada. In the case of the book publishing and recording industries, these figures include expenditures by both Canadian- and foreign-controlled companies.

At the present time, section 127 of the federal Income Tax Act contains provisions designed to stimulate an expansion in manufacturing capacity through increased capital expenditure, and to stimulate the development of new products and processes in Canada through increased current and capital expenditures for scientific research. No comparable measure exists that would stimulate the development of new Canadian cultural materials and reward companies in proportion to their investment in generating such content.

What is proposed, then, is that investment in new Canadian editorial content for magazines and newspapers, and in new Canadian books and recordings, be treated through tax policy in a way parallel to the current treatment of R&D expenditure by other industries. Not only would such an initiative result in substantial cultural benefit, it would also, at less cost than the current tax expenditure affecting the publishing industries, lead to expansion in the employment-intensive creative aspect of each of these industries.

As indicated earlier in this study, Canada has developed a significant number of major communications companies. Recently, the growth of these firms has been occurring through investments outside Canada

TABLE 8-3
ESTIMATED EDITORIAL/PROGRAM CONTENT EXPENDITURE,
1980
($ millions)

Daily newspapers	$ 184.5
Periodicals	Not available
Book publishing — editorial/design	15.7
''plant'' costs	16.8
	32.5
Sound recordings (master production)	5.6[1]
Radio — CBC	97.0
private stations	119.1
	216.1
Film and videotape investment — NFB	29.0
feature films	156.5[2]
short productions	57.9[2]
	243.4
Television program expenditure (acquisition plus production)	
CBC — Canadian programs	300.4
foreign programs	27.5
	327.9
Private stations/networks — Canadian programs	187.7
foreign programs	67.5
	255.2
Cable systems — Canadian programs	22.1
Total — Canadian programs	510.2
foreign programs	95.0
all programs	605.2
Total	$1,287.3

Notes: [1] In the case of the record industry, expenditure on master production may be understated significantly.

[2] In 1981, these investment levels plummeted to $64.7 million for features and $45 million for short production; they have continued to decline in 1982.

Sources: Kent Commission for daily newspaper expenditure; Statistics Canada for book publishing, sound recordings and radio; Canadian Film Certification Office for value of production of certified feature films and short productions. See Table 7-18 for television expenditure on programming.

and through investments within Canada in distribution rather than production activities (e.g., Southam's purchase of Coles bookstore chain or Maclean Hunter's rapid expansion in the cable television industry). There have, in fact, been examples of investments in Canadian production activities from which these firms have withdrawn. One effect of what is proposed here would be to encourage a change in the current development pattern for the large firms, as well as for smaller companies.

In the case of the recording industry, it should be noted that this incentive is complemented by current and proposed measures affecting demand — specifically, by the Canadian-content requirements for music broadcast on radio stations in Canada. In the absence of this measure and steps to strengthen the structure of the domestic recording companies, the proposed incentive would not likely prove effective.

The Film and Television Industries
In film and television, unlike the publishing industries, there is a mix at present of both public and private production activity. Moreover all of the private-sector production of Canadian feature films and television entertainment that occurs is already a result of significant tax incentive measures and the regulatory policies of the CRTC.

At the present time, public-sector television production activity is generally underfinanced, while in the private sector, despite a boom in 1979 and 1980, investment fell sharply in both 1981 and 1982. Moreover, in the case of both private feature film production and privately-produced television entertainment, the bulk of the programming produced has been "look-alike" U.S.-style programming with the stars, the themes and the setting chosen to satisfy U.S. viewers. In the case of features, a high percentage of the films rooted in Canada's culture — for example, *Mon Oncle Antoine* or *Les Plouffes* — have had major financing from the National Film Board or the CBC, as well as private investment. As of mid 1982, an attempt to film Mordecai Richler's *Joshua Then and Now* is stalled because the CBC's English Service Division, now undergoing extensive budget cuts, has not come up with the financing required to permit the project to proceed.

The cost of producing feature films and of television entertainment programs is so high that it is rarely possible at present for such programs to earn back their costs in the Canadian market. As a result, the policy measures necessary to ensure that Canadian production occurs at all and that the productions financed include a reasonable

330

balance of distinctive Canadian films and television entertainment are complex.

In the film and television chapters of this study, it was proposed that the capital cost allowance provisions of the Income Tax Act, which are designed to encourage private investment in Canadian features and television programs, should be continued. However, it was also argued that, in the absence of measures designed to increase the potential return that such programs could achieve in the domestic market, this tax incentive would not be successful. In addition, it is clear from the analysis in the preceding chapters that a way has not yet been found to permit private program producers to meet Canadian cultural needs. As many studies have argued, it is not easy to reconcile profit-making objectives in this sector with social and cultural objectives. The cases in which they have been able to do so are primarily those in which substantial funding has come from either the CBC or the NFB.

In order to ensure that domestic cultural needs are met, it is, therefore, not sufficient simply to ensure that a certain volume of financing is available. As pay-television will demonstrate, if this level of Canadian funding on a per film or a per hour basis is insufficient to trigger production activity, it will remain necessary for private producers to sell programs outside Canada first and to get most of their funds from foreign sources.

What is required is that the aggregate level of financing to Canadian films and television programs be increased; that at least some of that funding be focused so that all or most of the necessary financing for individual productions can be found in Canada; and that there be a strong public-sector element in the system to ensure that programs that reflect Canadian life and that come from both major language groups and all regions of Canada can be produced. Specifically, this study proposes a strengthening of the television services of the CBC and the establishment of a national cable television entertainment service to help achieve this purpose. In addition, measures are proposed which would increase theatrical earnings for Canadian production and which would both increase the advertising revenues of private broadcasters and strengthen the network structures that are necessary to maximize the private broadcasters' contribution to Canadian program production.

The CBC

In the case of the CBC, the recommendations of this study reflect a conviction that, whatever the problems of the corporation, those problems should be addressed directly. The incentive structure in television broadcasting is such that only public broadcasting can provide the core of Canadian programming that is Canadian in both content and character.

The Clyne Committee in 1979 made the recommendation that a task force be established to investigate and make recommendations on the management, programming and funding policies of the CBC, with reference to the following:

- quality and diversity of programming;
- "make or buy" policy for program production;
- the reflection to each other of the two principal linguistic communities in Canada, and the promotion of exchanges between the English-language and French-language networks;
- the proportion of the operational budget being devoted to program production;
- the decreasing audience share of the CBC network, in particular the English-language network;
- responsiveness to the public;
- the financial resources necessary to carry out the CBC's responsibilities under the Broadcasting Act;
- additional channels (off-air or on cable) to be used for CBC programming.

One might add to the above list the structure and responsibilities of the CBC Board of Directors, CBC's role in relation to sound recording and the new technologies (videotex, videodiscs and videocassettes), as well as the effects of reliance on advertising revenues. Moreover, the proposed task force seems a more important initiative now than at the time that the recommendation was made. An open and fair-minded inquiry into the CBC's structure and operations and its role in the future broadcasting system could help either to clear away some of the myths about the CBC's ineffectiveness or to give real problems an airing and develop proposals for addressing them.

What is required is not more CBC bashing, but a renewed effort to change the structure, financing and operation of the CBC in ways that will make public broadcasting in Canada more effective. Many of the major goals set out in the Broadcasting Act will either be met by public broadcasting in Canada or they will not be met at all. And because the role of the broadcasting system is so central to any strategy for cultural development in Canada or for the expansion of the cultural identity of Canadians, a successful broadcasting policy focused on clearly-stated cultural goals is of primary importance to Canadian cultural policy.

332

Notes

Notes

Introduction

[1] Canadian Institute for Economic Policy, Submission to the Federal Cultural Policy Review Committee, March 9, 1981, p. 4.

[2] Anthony Smith, *The Geopolitics of Information: How Western Culture Dominates the World* (London: Faber and Faber, 1980), p. 37.

[3] Ibid, p. 52.

[4] Ibid, p. 53.

[5] Ibid, p. 54.

[6] The Honourable J. Hugh Faulkner, "Notes for an Address to the Canadian Institute for International Affairs," Winnipeg, May 12, 1976, p. 11.

[7] The Honourable John Roberts, transcript of an Address to the Audit Bureau of Circulations, New York, November 9, 1977, p. 8.

[8] de Montigny Marchand, "The Impact of Information Technology on International Relations," *Intermedia*, November 1981, pp. 13, 14.

[9] For a more detailed report of these findings, see Howard Aster, "Who's Afraid of Canadian Culture? Not the Public!" September 1980 (unpublished paper).

[10] Gallup Report, July 26, 1980.

[11] Gallup Report, June 11, 1975.

[12] Market Facts of Canada, March 1977.

[13] The Honourable Francis Fox, "Notes for an Address to the Canadian Conference of the Arts," May 7, 1981, p. 7.

[14] Robert A. Russell, "Corporate Opportunities in the Cultural Marketplace," Discussion Paper, Delta Series, May 15, 1980, p. 2.

[15] Desmond Smith, "Culture and the Canadian Entrepreneur," *In Search*, vol. VIII, no. 3, p. 30.

Part I: Print

[1] Donald Campbell, "The survival of our best traditions will be firmly linked with print," *Financial Post*, January 16, 1982, p. 46.

Chapter 1: Daily Newspaper Publishing

[1] Special Senate Committee on Mass Media, *Report*, vol. 1, *The Uncertain Mirror* (Ottawa: Queen's Printer, 1970), p. vii.

[2] Royal Commission on Publications, *Report* (Ottawa: Queen's Printer, 1961), p. 3.

[3] Special Senate Committee on Mass Media, *The Uncertain Mirror*, p. 141.

[4] Royal Commission on Newspapers, Research Studies, vol. 1, *Newspapers and Their Readers* (Ottawa: Supply and Services Canada, 1981), p. 55.

[5] Ibid, p. 71.

[6] Royal Commission on Publications, *Report*, p. 4.

[7] Ibid.

[8] Ibid.

[9] Anthony Smith, *Subsidies and the Press in Europe* (London: Political and Economic Planning, 1977), p. 106.

[10] R.G.L. Fairweather, "Press Freedom: More Than A Platitude," Notes for an Address to the Gerstein Conference on Mass Communication and Canadian Nationhood, April 10, 1981.

[11] Government of Quebec, White Paper on Cultural Development (English-language text), vol. 2, p. 242.

[12] Ibid.

[13] Royal Commission on Newspapers, Research Studies, vol. 1, p. 95.

[14] Royal Commission on Newspapers, Research Studies, vol. 4, *The Newspaper as a Business* (Ottawa: Supply and Services Canada, 1981), p. 12.

[15] Ibid, p. 57. The commission quotes from Kesterton's contribution to the *Canada Year Book of 1959*.

[16] Special Senate Committee on Mass Media, *The Uncertain Mirror,* p. 19.

[17] Royal Commission on Newspapers, *Report* (Ottawa: Supply and Services Canada, 1981), p. 8.

[18] William T. Stanbury in the column "Business Forum," *Canadian Business*, April 20, 1980.

[19] Quoted in the *Globe and Mail*, August 15, 1980, p. B4.

[20] Newspaper Research Centre, *Competitive Circulation Performance, 1969-79*, January 1980, p. 3.

[21] Special Senate Committee on Mass Media, *The Uncertain Mirror*, p. 43.

[22] Stanbury in "Business Forum."

[23] For a description of the measures that have been adopted in Western Europe, see Anthony Smith, *Subsidies and the Press in Europe*.

[24] See, for example, Benjamin M. Compaine, ed., *Who Owns the Media?* (White Plains, N.Y.: Knowledge Industries Publications, 1979), p. 46. See also Compaine's *The Newspaper Industry in the 1980s: An Assessment of Economics and Technology* (White Plains, N.Y.: Knowledge Industries Publications, 1980) for an excellent discussion of the influence of new technologies on newspaper production.

[25] Thomson Newspapers Ltd., "The Daily Newspaper in a Competitive Media Environment," Submission to the Royal Commission on Newspapers, April 1981, p. 4.

[26] Ibid.

[27] Ibid.

[28] Southam Inc., *1979 Annual Report*, p. 14.

[29] Southam Inc., Submission to the Royal Commission on Newspapers, April 1981, p. 30.

[30] *Report of the Royal Commission on Corporate Concentration* (Ottawa: Supply and Services Canada, 1978) p. 411.

[31] Ibid, p. 410.

[32] W.F.W. Neville, Brief submitted to the Royal Commission on Newspapers, December 1980, pp. 5-6.

[33] See for example, Russell Hunt and Robert Campbell, *K.C. Irving: The Art of the*

336

Industrialist (Toronto: McClelland and Stewart, 1973), particularly chapter 5, "The Voice of New Brunswick."

[34] Southam Inc., *1979 Annual Report*, p. 14.
[35] See *Content*, no. 65, June 1976, p. 26.
[36] Southam Inc., Submission to the Royal Commission on Newspapers, p. 48.
[37] Ibid, p. 49.
[38] Ibid, p. 6.
[39] Royal Commission on Newspapers, Research Studies, vol. 1, "National Readership Study," pp. 9-89.
[40] Special Senate Committee on Mass Media, *Report*, vol. 2, *Words, Music and Dollars* (Ottawa: Queen's Printer, 1970), p. 242.
[41] Royal Commission on Newspapers, *Report*, p. 164.
[42] Ibid, p. 91.
[43] Ibid.
[44] Ibid, p. 80.
[45] Compaine, *The Newspaper Industry in the 1980s*, p. 21.
[46] Royal Commission on Newspapers, *Report*, p. 164.
[47] Special Senate Committee on Mass Media, *The Uncertain Mirror*, p. 153.
[48] Quoted in the Canadian Press, Submission to the Royal Commission on Newspapers, April 1981, p. 30.
[49] Ibid.
[50] From a CP memorandum from the managing editor regarding patterns for growth, December 17, 1980.
[51] Royal Commission on Newspapers, *Report*, p. 122.
[52] David Ablett, "The Inwardness of Canada's Press," *Options*, June/July 1980, p. 51.
[53] Special Senate Committee on Mass Media, *The Uncertain Mirror*, p. 233.
[54] Ibid, p. 233.
[55] Ibid, p. 64.
[56] Royal Commission on Newspapers, *Report*, p. 55.
[57] Ibid, p. 206.
[58] Ibid, quoted on p. 234.
[59] Ibid, p. 238.
[60] Ibid, quoted on p. 99.
[61] Ibid, p. 221.
[62] Ibid, p. 136.
[63] Ibid, p. 220.
[64] Ibid, p. 238.
[65] Senator D. Keith Davey, "How Misreading Jolted the Press," *Globe and Mail*, September 16, 1981, p. 7.

Chapter 2: Periodical Publishing

[1] Royal Commission on Newspapers, Research Studies, vol. 1, *Newspapers and Their Readers* (Ottawa: Supply and Services Canada, 1981), p. 15.
[2] These figures are from volume 1 of *Interim Profile of the Periodical Publishing Industry in Canada*, a study prepared for the federal Department of the Secretary of State by the federal government's Bureau of Management Consulting (BMC) and published in April 1981. While this study represents in many respects a useful first

attempt at a comprehensive analysis of the industry, it has the major disadvantage of not drawing distinctions between Canadian-originated magazines and other magazines produced in Canada, or between commercial magazines and non-profit or association publications produced as part of a larger activity. The "industry" is not defined in a way that permits real comparisons between comparable products of the Canadian periodical industry and those of foreign periodical industries. As the study itself notes (p. 137), some officials of the department felt that the approach taken by BMC greatly inflated the circulation of Canadian periodicals as compared to foreign periodicals. The study is used in this chapter on certain issues where no other data are available, but with the reservation that it tends to suggest a far stronger Canadian periodical industry than actually exists. In fairness to the authors of the study, one of the recommendations of its authors is that the department attempt to arrive at some consensus with the industry on the definition of the industry and the use of various terms.

[3] Ibid, p. 74.

[4] Based on tables compiled by Statistics Canada from U.S. sources and used by Yvon Ferland in a presentation to the Canadian magazine publishers in 1980.

[5] Statistics Canada, Imports by Commodity, classification #891-29.

[6] *Interim Profile of the Periodical Industry*, vol. 1, pp. 57, 74.

[7] I.A. Litvak and C.J. Maule, *The Publication of Canadian Editions of Non-Canadian Magazines: Public Policy Alternatives* (Department of the Secretary of State, October 1978), p. 47.

[8] Ibid, p. 49. Comparable data for the subsidiaries of other large U.S. subsidiaries in Canada are also noted on p. 50 of this study.

[9] See, for example, *Advertising and the Advertising Industry: Interim Report of the Select Committee on Economic and Cultural Nationalism* (Toronto: Queen's Printer, 1974).

[10] Special Senate Committee on Mass Media, *Report*, vol. 1, *The Uncertain Mirror* (Ottawa: Queen's Printer, 1970), p. 246.

[11] Royal Commission on Publications, *Report* (Ottawa: Queen's Printer, 1961), p. 41.

[12] Based on advertising revenues of $311 million (Table 2-3) and an assumption that an additional $93 million (30 per cent of $311 million) would be earned from single copy and subscription sales.

[13] Special Senate Committee on Mass Media, *The Uncertain Mirror*, pp. 154-55.

[14] The legislation defines Canadian magazines essentially as publications that are edited, printed and published in Canada by Canadian-owned companies, and specifies that not more than 20 per cent of the content should be the same as that of any foreign publication.

[15] *Interim Profile of the Periodical Industry*, vol. 1, pp. 94, 96, 98.

[16] Special Senate Committee on Mass Media, *The Uncertain Mirror*, pp. 153-68.

[17] For further detail, see Marianne Ackerman, "Happily Ever After," *Saturday Night*, August 1982.

[18] See *Interim Profile of the Periodical Industry*, vol. 1, p. 117 on this point.

[19] Royal Commission on Publications, *Report*, p. 37.

[20] Ibid, Appendix K, Table 6.

[21] Royal Commission on Book Publishing, *Canadian Publishers and Canadian Publishing* (Toronto: Queen's Printer, 1973), p. 358.

[22] *Interim Profile of the Periodical Industry*, vol. 1, p. 51.

[23] Royal Commission on Book Publishing, *Canadian Publishers and Canadian Publishing*, p. 307.

[24] I.A. Litvak and C.J. Maule, *Developments in the Distribution Systems for Canadian Periodical, Book and Newspaper Publishers* (Department of the Secretary of State, 1980).

[25] Ibid, p. 56.

[26] Ibid, pp. 78-79.

[27] As reported in *Extracts from the Report "La Distribution des Journaux et des Périodiques au Québec,"* a translation of parts of a study prepared in 1978 by Sorécom for the Quebec Department of Communications, p. 27.

[28] Ibid, p. 39.

[29] Special Senate Committee on Mass Media, *The Uncertain Mirror*, p. 99.

[30] *Extracts from the Report "La Distribution des Journaux et des Périodiques au Québec,"* pp. 40-44.

[31] Ibid, p. 48.

[32] Based on the assumption that imports were valued at approximately $300 million and that Canadian magazine publishers would have spent between $100 to $500 million on the manufacture of their magazines. These are rough estimates only, but they appear reasonable and are not likely to misrepresent substantially the real cost of the exemption.

[33] Royal Commission on Publications, *Report*, p. 88.

[34] Litvak and Maule, *The Publication of Canadian Editions of Non-Canadian Magazines: Public Policy Alternatives*, p. 62.

[35] Royal Commission on Publications, *Report*, p. 76.

[36] Ibid, p. 77.

[37] Letter to the Canadian Conference of the Arts, February 15, 1982.

Chapter 3: Book Publishing

[1] "Notes for a Statement by the Secretary of State, John Roberts, on the Canadian Book Publishing Development Program," Toronto, March 7, 1979, p. 1.

[2] Royal Commission on Newspapers, Research Studies, vol. 1, "National Readership Study" (Ottawa: Supply and Services Canada, 1981), p. 13.

[3] Dr. Horst Benzing, "Expansion or Stagnation? Recent Economic Developments and Future Perspectives on the Book Industry" (March 28, 1980), Paper presented to a Council of Europe conference on The State's Role vis-à-vis the Culture Industries, Strasbourg, April 1980.

[4] Benjamin M. Compaine, *The Book Industry in Transition: An Economic Study of Book Distribution and Marketing* (White Plains, N.Y.: Knowledge Industries Publications, 1978), p. 23.

[5] *The Canadian Book Industry* (Department of Industry, Trade and Commerce, 1970), p. 53.

[6] Royal Commission on Newspapers, Research Studies, vol. 1, p. 14.

[7] It should be noted that the vast majority of foreign sales of Canadian-published books appear to be accounted for by books that are printed outside Canada. In the case of Harlequin, the company which accounts for a substantial majority of sales in foreign markets, the books sold outside Canada are printed almost entirely outside Canada.

[8] Statistics Canada, *Culture Statistics: Book Publishing: A Financial Analysis, 1975-77* (June 1980), p. 35.

[9] Department of the Secretary of State, *The Publishing Industry in Canada*, a report

prepared by the Bureau of Management Consulting (Ottawa: Supply and Services Canada, 1977), pp. 258-59.

[10] Quoted in Federal Cultural Policy Review Committee, *Summary of Briefs and Hearings* (Department of Communications, 1982), p. 152.

[11] There are relatively slight discrepancies between the results of the two surveys, but not sufficient to suggest that these estimates are unreliable.

[12] Compaine, *The Book Industry in Transition*, p. 38.

[13] Federal Cultural Policy Review Committee, *Summary of Briefs and Hearings*, p. 162.

[14] J.P. Wilkinson, *Canadian Juvenile Fiction and the Library Market* (Canadian Library Association, 1976), p. 75.

[15] Federal Cultural Policy Review Committee, *Summary of Briefs and Hearings*, p. 163.

[16] These estimates are based on detailed Statistics Canada data for newly published textbooks. They are based on the assumption that the ratio of sales by authorship for previously published titles is the same as for those published in 1979.

[17] Royal Commission on Book Publishing, *Canadian Publishers and Canadian Publishing* (Toronto: Queen's Printer, 1973), p. 76.

[18] Reported in Julia Juner, "Need national policy, educators say. . .," *Globe and Mail,* September 16, 1980, p. 11.

[19] T.H.B. Symons, *To Know Ourselves*, The Report of the Commission on Canadian Studies (Ottawa: Association of Universities and Colleges of Canada, 1975). See, for example, vol. 2, p. 158.

[20] Royal Commission on Publications, *Report* (Ottawa: Queen's Printer, 1961), p. 8.

[21] Government of Quebec, White Paper on Cultural Development (English translation), p. 357.

[22] Royal Commission on Book Publishing, *Canadian Publishers and Canadian Publishing*, p. 66.

[23] Ibid, p. 69.

[24] Ibid, p. 63.

[25] Ibid, p. 72.

[26] Ibid, p. 68.

[27] Department of the Secretary of State, *The Publishing Industry in Canada*.

[28] Royal Commission on Book Publishing, *Canadian Publishers and Canadian Publishing*, p. 69.

[29] Statistics Canada, *Direct Selling in Canada, 1980* (Cat. No. 63-218).

[30] See, for example, Benzing, "Expansion or Stagnation? Recent Economic Developments and Further Perspectives on the Book Industry."

Chapter 4: The Recording Industry

[1] Data for EEC countries are available in Gillian Davies' study, *Piracy of Phonograms*, produced in 1980 for the Commission of the European Communities.

[2] Statistics Canada, *Culture Statistics: Recording Industry, 1978* (December 1980), p. 19.

[3] Industry revenue figures are from Alexander Belinfante and Richard L. Johnson, "An Economic Analysis of the U.S. Recorded Music Industry," Paper prepared for the Second International Conference on Cultural Economics and Planning, Maastrich, Netherlands, May 1982.

[4] As reported in J.P. Vignolle, "Recent Developments of National and International Systems of Record Distribution," Paper prepared for a Council of Europe conference on The State's Role vis-à-vis the Culture Industries, Strasbourg, April 1980.

[5] "The Availability of French-language Recordings in Quebec" (CRTC, September 1981), p. 14.

[6] See Vignolle, "Recent Developments," pp. 3, 4.

[7] As reported in Service Bulletin 87-001, vol. I, no. 2, *Recording Industry, 1980* (Statistics Canada, February 1982).

[8] Canadian Independent Record Production Association (CIRPA), "A Brief to the Federal Cultural Policy Review Committee," March 6, 1981, p. 4.

[9] Ibid, p. 6.

[10] "The Availability of French-language Recordings in Quebec," pp. 6, 10.

[11] Based on industry expenditure averages as estimated by the Canadian Independent Record Production Association (see their "Brief to the Federal Cultural Policy Review Committee," p. 6) and the information on annual levels of master production expenditure and wholesale revenues from the sale of discs and tapes produced from Canadian masters provided by the Statistics Canada survey.

[12] CIRPA, "Brief to the Federal Cultural Policy Review Committee," p. 5.

[13] Belinfante and Johnson, "Economic Analysis," pp. 16, 17.

[14] Frost & Sullivan Inc., *Recorded Music Market* (January 1981), p. 138.

[15] Ibid, p. 33.

[16] Ibid, emphasis added.

[17] Ibid, p. 139.

[18] Ibid, p. 140.

[19] CIRPA, "Brief to the Federal Cultural Policy Review Committee," pp. 1, 3-7.

[20] Ibid, p. 6.

[21] Ibid.

[22] Document submitted to the secretary of state, John Roberts, March 21, 1977.

[23] Ibid.

[24] For a useful example of a simple definition of a "Canadian sound recording," see CIRPA's October 1979 proposal, "A Tax Incentive for the Canadian Recording Industry."

[25] Warner Communications Inc., *A Consumer Survey: Home Taping* (1981), p. 41.

[26] *Billboard, 1981-82 International Buyer's Guide*, p. 8.

Chapter 5: Radio

[1] David Ellis, *Evolution of the Canadian Broadcasting System: Objectives and Realities, 1928-1968* (Department of Communications, 1979), p. 1.

[2] Ibid, p. 3.

[3] Now the Canadian Broadcasting League.

[4] House of Commons Debates, May 18, 1932, quoted in Ellis, *Evolution of the Canadian Broadcasting System*, pp. 8-9.

[5] As quoted in ibid, p. 30.

[6] As quoted in ibid, p. 32.

[7] As quoted in ibid, p. 37.

[8] As quoted in ibid, p. 63.

[9] Radio listeners are defined by BBM as individuals who listen to radio at least fifteen minutes during the week. The 96 per cent figure is for Fall 1980.

[10] Canadian Radio-television and Telecommunications Commission, *Special Report on Broadcasting, 1968-78*, vol. 1, p. 74.

[11] CRTC, *Sound Broadcasting Requirements for Canada: A Long Range Forecast*, (1978), p. 1.

[12] Stuart McFadyen, Colin Hoskins and David Gillen, *Canadian Broadcasting: Market Structure and Economic Performance* (Institute for Research on Public Policy, 1980).

[13] Ibid, p. 14.

[14] CRTC, *Special Report on Broadcasting, 1968-78*, vol. 1, p. 89.

[15] Canadian Recording Industry Association, "Radio Broadcasting and the Recording Industry: A Submission to the Canadian Radio-television and Telecommunications Commission," p. 17.

[16] Ibid, p. 5.

[17] Ibid, p. 7.

[18] McFadyen, Hoskins and Gillen, *Canadian Broadcasting*.

[19] Ibid, p. 108.

[20] Canadian Recording Industry Association, "Radio Broadcasting and the Recording Industry," p. 4.

Part III: Moving Images

[1] Garth Jowett and James Linton, *Movies as Mass Communication* (London: Sage Publications, 1980).

Chapter 6: Theatrical Film

[1] Garth Jowett and James Linton, *Movies as Mass Communication* (London: Sage Publications, 1980), p. 85.

[2] Ibid, p. 109.

[3] Ibid, p. 109.

[4] Benjamin M. Compaine, ed., *Who Owns the Media?* (White Plains, N.Y.: Knowledge Industry Publications, 1979), p. 179.

[5] Bureau of Management Consulting, *Film Study* (Ottawa: Supply and Services Canada, 1976).

[6] Quoted in Richard Barnet and Ronald E. Muller, *Global Reach* (New York: Simon and Schuster, 1974), p. 145.

[7] Compaine, ed., *Who Owns the Media?*, p. 191.

[8] Ibid, p. 219.

[9] Quoted in Compaine, ed., *Who Owns the Media?*, p. 186.

[10] Canadian Radio-television and Telecommunications Commission, Public Notice 1981-35, *Call for Applications for Pay Television* April 21, 1981.

[11] Based on April 8, 1982 Canadian Film Development Corporation briefing document prepared for the corporation's appearance before the House of Commons Committee on Culture and Communications.

[12] R.M. Bird, M.W. Bucovsky and A. Yatchew, *Tax Incentives for the Canadian Film Industry* (Institute for Policy Analysis, 1981), p. 70.

[13] Ibid, p. 89.

[14] S. Daniel Lyon and Michael J. Trebilcock, *Public Strategy and Motion Pictures: The Choice of Instruments to Promote the Development of the Canadian Film Production Industry* (Ontario Economic Council, 1982), p. 125.

[15] Ibid, p. 125.

[16] Bird, Bucovsky and Yatchew, *Tax Incentives for the Canadian Film Industry*, p. 64.

[17] Telex to the prime minister, the finance minister, and the minister of communications dated November 25, 1981, as reprinted in *Film and TV World*, December 15, 1981-January 15, 1982, p. 1.

[18] Interview in *Maclean's* magazine, May 4, 1981.

[19] Compaine, ed., *Who Owns the Media?*, p. 183.

[20] *Cinema and the State* (Strasbourg: Council of Europe, 1979), p. xi.

[21] See for example the minister's letter to the editor in the *Globe and Mail*, September 15, 1982, p. 7.

[22] Virginia Kelly, "Lament for an Industry," *Cinema Canada*, February 1982.

[23] Ibid.

[24] Ibid.

[25] CROP Report 80-5 reported in National Film Board brief to the Federal Cultural Policy Review Committee, March 1981.

[26] J. Bassett, *The Film Industry in Ontario* (Ontario Ministry of Industry and Tourism, 1973).

Chapter 7: Television

[1] Gallup Poll, November 28, 1981 (published in the *Toronto Star*).

[2] Graham Murdock, "The Role of Radio and Television in Shaping the Form and Contents of Audience Cultures — Broadcasting and Cultural Diversity," Paper prepared for a Council of Europe conference on The State's Role vis-à-vis the Culture Industries, Strasbourg, April 1980.

[3] R. Brian Woodrow, Kenneth Woodside, Henry Wiseman and John B. Black, *Conflict Over Communications Policy* (Montreal: C.D. Howe Institute, 1980), p. 65.

[4] Canadian Conference of the Arts, *More Strategy for Culture* (1981), p. 89.

[5] Quoted in ibid, p. 3.

[6] For a more detailed history of the development of television in Canada, see *CBC: A Brief History and Background* (CBC Information Services, 1972).

[7] Quoted in David Ellis, *Evolution of the Canadian Broadcasting System: Objectives and Realities, 1928-1968* (Department of Communications, 1979), p. 49.

[8] CRTC, *Special Report on Broadcasting, 1968-78*, vol. 1, p. 47.

[9] Reported in Bob Hepburn, "TV-radio watchdog is all bark, no bite," *Toronto Star*, December 9, 1981, p. A20.

[10] Maggie Siggins, *Bassett* (Toronto: James Lorimer & Co., 1979), p. 220.

[11] CRTC, *Special Report on Broadcasting*, vol. 2, pp. 4-2, 4-3.

[12] Information on the profitability of private television stations in Canada is provided later in this chapter (pp. 286-87).

[13] See for example, "Canada-U.S. TV Dispute Lingers," *Globe and Mail*, May 15, 1982, p. 14.

[14] CFTO-TV Ltd., Submission to the Canadian-content Review of the CRTC, December 1981.

[15] (Therrien) Committee on Extension of Service to Northern and Remote Communities, *The 1980s: A Decade of Diversity: Broadcasting, Satellites and Pay TV* (CRTC, 1980), p. 17.

[16] Ibid, p. 56.

[17] Articulated in the CRTC's 1978 Report on Pay-Television.

[18] Canadian Conference of the Arts, "An Appeal to the Governor-in-Council," April 26, 1982.

[19] Statement by Chairman John Meisel on CRTC Decision 82-240, March 18, 1982, p. 2.

[20] Stuart MacFadyen, Colin Hoskins and David Gillen, *Canadian Broadcasting: Market Structure and Economic Performance* (Institute for Research on Public Policy, 1980), p. 128. (Note: Rate of return was calculated on the basis of long-term debt plus shareholder's equity.)

[21] Ibid, p. 242.

[22] Ibid.

[23] Richard Nielson and Pat Ferns, "The Opportunity of Pay Television," September 1981.

[24] See Canadian Film and Television Association, Submission to the Federal Cultural Policy Review Committee, May 1981.

[25] Therrien Committee, *The 1980s: A Decade of Diversity*, p. 77.

[26] (Clyne) Consultative Committee on the Implications of Telecommunications for Canadian Sovereignty, *Telecommunications and Canada* (Ottawa: Supply and Services Canada, 1979), p. 54.

[27] Tamec Inc. and DGB Consultants Inc., *Feasibility Study for a Canadian Satellite Program Package* (March 1980), prepared for the Department of Communications.

[28] MacFadyen, Hoskins and Gillen, *Canadian Broadcasting: Market Structure and Performance*.

[29] Ibid, p. 209.

[30] Ibid, p. 257.

[31] Alain Lapointe and Jean-Pierre LeGoff, *Television Programs and Their Production in Canada* (Department of Communications, 1980), p. 207.

[32] Quoted in Ellis, *Evolution of the Canadian Broadcasting System*.

[33] Woodrow et al., *Conflict Over Communications Policy*, p. 71.

[34] Robert E. Babe, *Canadian Television Broadcasting: Structure, Performance and Regulation* (Economic Council of Canada, 1979), p. 236.

[35] Clyne Committee, *Telecommunications and Canada*, p. 34.

[36] Therrien Committee, *The 1980s: A Decade of Diversity*, p. 63.

[37] *Canadian Broadcasting and Telecommunications: Past Experience, Future Options*, Report prepared for the CRTC (Supply and Services Canada, 1980), p. 34.

[38] Canadian Radio-television and Telecommunications Commission, Decision 82-240, *Pay Television*, March 18, 1982, p. 14.

Chapter 8: Conclusion

[1] Donald G. Campbell, "How You Can Increase Your Billings 72%," Address to the Institute of Canadian Advertising, June 21, 1982, p. 2.

[2] Task Force on Canadian Unity, *A Future Together: Observations and Recommendations* (January 1979), p. 6.

[3] (Clyne) Consultative Committee on the Implications of Telecommunications for Canadian Sovereignty, *Telecommunications and Canada* (Supply and Services Canada, 1979), p. 81.

The Canadian Institute for Economic Policy Series

The Monetarist Counter-Revolution: A Critique of Canadian Monetary Policy 1975-1979
Arthur W. Donner and Douglas D. Peters

Canada's Crippled Dollar: An Analysis of International Trade and Our Troubled Balance of Payments
H. Lukin Robinson

Unemployment and Inflation: The Canadian Experience
Clarence L. Barber and John C.P. McCallum

How Ottawa Decides: Planning and Industrial Policy-Making 1968-1980
Richard D. French

Energy and Industry: The Potential of Energy Development Projects for Canadian Industry in the Eighties
Barry Beale

The Energy Squeeze: Canadian Policies for Survival
Bruce F. Willson

The Post-Keynesian Debate: A Review of Three Recent Canadian Contributions
Myron J. Gordon

Water: The Emerging Crisis in Canada
Harold D. Foster and W.R. Derrick Sewell

The Working Poor: Wage Earners and the Failure of Income Security Policies
David P. Ross

Beyond the Monetarists: Post-Keynesian Alternatives to Rampant Inflation, Low Growth and High Unemployment
Edited by David Crane

The Splintered Market: Barriers to Interprovincial Trade in Canadian Agriculture
R.E. Haack, D.R. Hughes and R.G. Shapiro

The Drug Industry: A Case Study of the Effects of Foreign Control on the Canadian Economy
Myron J. Gordon and David J. Fowler

The New Protectionism: Non-Tariff Barriers and Their Effects on Canada
Fred Lazar

Industrial Development and the Atlantic Fishery: Opportunities for Manufacturing and Skilled Workers in the 1980s
Donald J. Patton

Canada's Population Outlook: Demographic Futures and Economic Challenges
David K. Foot

Financing the Future: Canada's Capital Markets in the Eighties
Arthur W. Donner

Controlling Inflation: Learning from Experience in Canada, Europe and Japan
Clarence L. Barber and John C.P. McCallum

Canada and the Reagan Challenge: Crisis in the Canadian-American Relationship
Stephen Clarkson

The Future of Canada's Auto Industry: The Big Three and the Japanese Challenge
Ross Perry

Canadian Manufacturing: A Study of Productivity and Technological Change
Volume I: Sector Performance and Industrial Strategy
Volume II: Industry Studies 1946-1977
Uri Zohar

Canada's Video Revolution: Pay-TV, Home Video and Beyond
Peter Lyman

The above titles are available from:

James Lorimer & Company, Publishers
Egerton Ryerson Memorial Building
35 Britain Street
Toronto, Ontario M5A 1R7